English Grammar

For Competitive Examination

Neharika Jayani

Published By

Invincible Publishers

Published by
Invincible Publishers
201A, SAS Tower, Sector 38, Gurugram – 122003
Phone. +91-124-4034247, +91 9355675555
www.i-publish.in

First edition – 2020

ISBN. 978-81-945481-2-6

Author's email. neharika.jayani@gmail.com

Printed at Replika Press Pvt. Ltd.

Acknowledgements

I am forever grateful to my Grand-parents Shri Deviram Jayani & Smt. Savitri Jayani, and Ch. Ranbir Singh Siag whose foresight and values paved the path for a privileged education for me. Great thanks to my Parents Mr. Raamesh Kumar Jayani & Mrs. Laalita Jayani, who gently offered counsel and unconditional support at each and every turn of my life. I would like to thank my In-Law, Mr. Joginder Singh and Mrs. Kanta Devi who never treated me as daughter-in-law but as their daughter and supported me everytime.

Heartily thanks to my Husband Mr. Saurabh Singh, who never accepted less than my best efforts to complete this book and supported me throughout the entire journey of my life and to my sweet little one who throughout accompanied me in this journey.

I would also like to express my gratitude to my friends, well wishers and many other people who are always there for me. Special Thanks to all my students as my success is because of them and Mr. Sagar and Invincible Publication because of whom this book is available to all.

Content

ANSWER

SECTION–A
English Grammar Rules for SSC

NOUNS

RULE 01. Common Nouns like Doctor, teacher, student, servant, engineer, driver etc. are followed by Masculine Gender.

Error. A student should not blindly accept everything it finds in a book.

Correct. A student should not blindly accept everything he finds in a book.

RULE 02. Add 'S' to the main word in compound noun to make it plural.

Sister-in-Law, the plural form is Sisters-in-Law, not Sister-in-Laws, Brother-in-Law, the plural form is Brothers-in-law, not Brothers-in- Laws.

RULE 03. "It, Its" are used as pronouns for collective nouns.

It is used for the noun, Its is used to show possession.

Example. Its members.

Error. The team has declared that they will win the match.

Correct. The team has declared that it will win the match.

RULE 04. People are often confused or they commit mistakes in the use of certain nouns.

(A) Lecturership is wrong. lectureship is correct.

(B) Freeship is wrong; free – studentship is correct.

(C) Boarding is wrong; boarding house is correct.

(D) Family members is wrong; members of the family is correct.

(E) English teacher is wrong; the teacher of English is correct.

(F) Cousin – brother or sister is wrong; only cousin is correct.

(G) Wages means punishments when used in the singular.

Ex- The wages of sin is death.

(H) It also means charges for the labour when used in the plural sense.

Ex- The wages of daily workers have been raised

RULE 05. Feminine Gender is used for the following words.

Moon, Earth, Spring, Hope, Virtue, Humidity, Charity, Mercy, faith, peace, ship, river, nation, liberty, fame etc.

Error. Spring has its own charms and delights.

Correct. Spring has her own charms and delights.

RULE 06. Masculine Gender is used for the following words.

The sun, time, death, winter, wind, summer, thunder, ocean, love, war, wine etc.

Error. The sun shot its bright rays.

Correct. The sun shot his bright rays.

RULE 07. The possessive case of a

compound noun is formed by adding 'S' to the last word.

Father-in-Law, Father-in-Law's property.

Sister-in-Law, Sister-in-Law's property.

RULE 08. An "Apostrophe" and 'S' should be used with living beings only to show possession.

The table's legs were broken. ×

(This is wrong, because the table is a non living thing)

We can say "The legs of the table were broken" ✔

But, nouns that denote time, distance or weight, An "Apostrophe" and 'S' is used.

Ex- a stone's throw, in a year's time, the earth's surface.

RULE 09. "it, its" is used for Child/ Infants / Baby if gender is not specified.

Error. The Child has broken his right leg.

Correct. The Child has broken its right leg.

RULE 10. With Collective Noun, we generally use singular verb and substitute it with singular pronoun.

But when member of group acting as individual, we use plural verb and substitute it with plural pronoun.

Error. The team are strong.

Correct. The team is strong. (Team is acting as a singular unit here.)

RULE 11. If a word is acting as an adjective, it should not be used in plural form.

"A five rupees note", " A two miles walk" is Wrong

"A five rupee note", " A two mile walk" is Correct

RULE 12. With Material Noun, generally we do not use any article (a, an, the) before Material Noun.

Error. This is a Silver, not a Gold.

Correct. This is Silver, not Gold.

RULE 13. (Noun 01 + preposition + Noun 01)

In such format, noun remains singular.

Example.

Town after town, Row upon row, Door to door etc.

Error. Ships after ship is arriving.

Correct. Ship after ship is arriving.

RULE 14. When two nouns are connected by "and", and are closely related, add an apostrophe and 'S' to the last noun.

Kareena's and Saif's house ×

(if you think they are wife and husband then this sentence is wrong)

Kareena and Saif's house (as they live in a SINGLE house) ✔

But you can say "India's and Pakistan's population" ✔

RULE 15. Nouns like Million, Hundred, Thousand, Pair, Dozen, Score, gross and couple that are plural in meaning take the same form in singular and plural only when they are used after definite numerals.

Error. He bought two pair of sleepers.

Correct. No error.

Exception. When indefinite numeral is used they take plural form.

Example – Ravi lost dozens of bananas.

Many pairs of shoes, hundreds of people, dozens of women.

RULE 16. Titles of books and other works of art are always considered singular even if the title sounds plural.

Error. "A Thousand Splendid Suns" are an incredible chronicle of thirty years of Afghan history.

Correct. "A Thousand Splendid Suns" is an incredible chronicle of thirty years of Afghan history.

RULE 17. Some nouns like gentry, poultry, cattle, people, infantry, cavalry, children, police etc. looks singular but always used as plural. And it is unwise to put "s" after them to make plural.

Error. The childrens are playing in the field.

Correct. The children are playing in the field.

RULE 18. Some nouns like deer, sheep, series fish, crew, family, team, jury, aircraft, counsel etc. take the same form both in singular and plural.

Example.

One fish is there in the pond.

There are many fish in the pond.

RULE 19. If two adjectives are joined by 'and' and 'The' is used before the first adjectives, A plural noun is used after the second Adjective.

The + Adjective + and + Adjective + Plural Noun

Error. Laalita likes literature of the 16th and 17th century.

Correct. Laalita likes literature of the 16th and 17th centuries.

RULE 20. If two adjectives are joined by 'and' and 'The' used before both Adjectives or each Adjective, A singular noun is used after the second Adjectives.

The + Adjective + and + the + Adjective + Singular Noun

Error. The fifth and the seventh chapters of this book are interesting.

Correct. The fifth and the seventh chapter of this book are interesting.

RULE 21. Proper Nouns are sometimes used as common Nouns. In such case, "The" article is used with Proper noun.

Example –

Wrong. Rahul is Gandhiji of our Class

Correct. Rahul is the Gandhiji of our Class.

Here, Gandhiji doesn't mean Mahatma Gandhi. The word here stands for the possessor of the qualities that Gandhiji is most known for. Thus, Gandhiji is used as a metaphorical common noun.

RULE 22. Meaning of some Nouns in plural form is very different from the meaning in singular form.

Example.

1. Advice – counsel
   Advises – information
2. Respect – regard
   Respects – compliments
3. Compass – extent
   Compasses- instrument or range
4. Custom- habit
   Customs – duties levied on
5. Ground – earth
   Grounds – reasons
6. Iron – Metal
   Irons – fetters made of iron
7. Mean – average
   Means – way or method
8. Physic – medicine
   Physics – natural science

RULE 23. Some noun words have two plurals with different Meanings.

1. Brother & Brethren
   Ex – I have two brothers. (sons of the same parents)
   Ex – We must support our weaker brethren.
2. Clothes & Cloths
   Ex – I took off my shoes and clothes (meaning things that people wear)
   Ex – Cotton, nylon, silk are different kinds of cloths (meaning kinds or pieces of cloth).

RULE 24. The unit of measurement (such as - hour, pound, kilo, mile...etc.) is always used in the singular form in the structure –

'Half + a/an + unit of measurement'; as, 'Half a kilo', 'Half an hour'.

Note. The unit of measurement (such as – hour, pound, kilo, mile...etc.) is also used in the singular form in the structure –

'A + half + unit of measurement'; as, 'A half kilo', 'A half hour'.

Example. Only Half an hour left to finish this work.

RULE 25. A plural noun is used after 'one and a half'; as 'One and a half kilos'

While 'A/An + singular noun + and + a half' is used in English Language; as,

'A kilo and a half kilos',

'An hour and a half'.

RULE 26. The structure – 'Numeral Adjectives + plural noun + and + a half'

or

Numeral Adjectives + and + a half + plural noun is used in the English Language.

Numeral Adjectives. One, two, three, four…..etc. some, all, many, few…..etc. are called Numeral Adjectives.

Example -

'Two kilos and a half' 'Five hours and a half' 'Two and a half kilos'.

RULE 27. Generally, the plural of a proper noun is not possible. But the plural of a proper noun can be formed (=made) by adding 's' according to need.

Example

There are two Mohans in my class.

(Here, it represents two boys with same name Mohan)

RULE 28. A plural noun or a plural pronoun is used after these phrases – one of, each of, either of, neither of, any one of, a few of, very few of, half of, a lot of, a large number of etc.

Example

One of the boys was innocent.

(These words are used for selection, thus plural noun should be used after them.)

RULE 29. Some nouns always remain in plural form. They take plural verb. These nouns have no singular form. These are -

Assets, alms, amends, annals, archives, ashes, arrears, athletics, auspices, species, scissors, trousers, pants. clippers, bellows, gallows, fangs, measles, eyeglasses, goggles, belongings, breeches. Bowels , braces ,binoculars, dregs, earnings, entrails, embers, fetters, fireworks, longings, lees, odds ,outskirts, particulars, proceeds, proceedings, riches, remains, shambles, shears, spectacles, surroundings, tidings ,tactics ,tongs ,vegetables, valuables, wages etc.

Examples

(a) My means were reduced substantially.

(b) Every means is good if the end is good.

RULE 30. Some nouns look plural in form but have singular meaning. Such nouns take singular verb. These are. news, innings, politics, summons, physics, economics, ethics. mechanics, mathematics, measles, mumps, rickets, billiards, draughts, etc.

RULE 31. Some nouns look singular but have plural meaning. Such nouns take plural verbs. These are. cattle, clergy, cavalry, infantry, poultry,peasantry, children, gentry, police etc.

RULE 32. Some nouns are always used in singular. These are uncountable nouns. We should not use article A/An with such nouns. These are -

Scenery, poetry, furniture, advice, information, hair, language. business, mischief, bread, stationery, crockery, luggage, baggage, postage, knowledge, wastage, money, jewellery, breakage etc,

We can not pluralise such nouns by adding `S' or 'es'.

Example It is incorrect to write sceneries, informations, furnitures, hairs.

If hair is used as countable it can be pluralised. e.g., one hair, two hairs.

Example I need three hairs of a black horse.

RULE 33. Some nouns have plural meaning. If a definite numeral adjective is used before them they are not pluralised. e.g., pair, score. Gross , stone ,hundred, dozen, thousand. million. billion. etc.

Otherwise these nouns can well be pluralised.

Dozens of women, Hundreds of people, Millions of dollars, Scores of shops. Many pairs of shoes, thousands millions etc.

CROWN – 01

(Collection of Result Oriented Worksheet by Neharika)

Correct the following sentences.

1. Error. Cities after cities were destroyed by the army.
2. Error. Hours after hours were passed, but she didn't turn up.
3. Error. I gave her three and a half apples.
4. Error. His salary is two times and a half to that of mine.
5. Error. I have two and a half rupees only.
6. Error. Rows upon rows of pink marble are soothing to the eyes.
7. Error. Have you deposited the proceed in the bank or not?
8. Error. You can buy the scissors that is sharp.
9. Error. A farmer was leading oxes to his field for ploughing early in the morning.
10. Error. What is the criteria of selection in the examination?

CROWN – 02

(Collection of Result Oriented Worksheet by Neharika)

Correct the following sentences.

1. There are three childrens in the park
2. He gave me many informations.
3. Ram bought his furnitures by goods train.
4. Every candidate should write their names neatly.
5. Your's faithfully, P.K. Sharma
6. I want to purchase ten knifes.
7. Three young mans and two young womans were present in the hall.
8. How many MP's were present in the meeting.
9. This is a girl's hostel.
10. My son's-in-law sister is coming tomorrow.

SOLUTIONS - CROWN – 01

(Collection of Result Oriented Worksheet by Neharika)

1. City after city was destroyed by the army.
2. Hour after hour was passed, but she didn't turn up.
3. I gave her three apples and a half.
4. His salary is two times and a half to that of mine.
5. I have two rupees and a half only.
6. Row upon row of pink marble is soothing to the eyes.
7. Have you deposited the proceeds in the bank or not?
8. You can buy the scissors that are sharp.
9. A farmer was leading oxen to his field for ploughing early in the morning.
10. What is the criterion of selection in the examination?

SOLUTIONS - CROWN – 02

(Collection of Result Oriented Worksheet by Neharika)

1. There are three children in the park
2. He gave me many information.
3. Ram bought his furniture by goods train.
4. Every candidate should write his names neatly.
5. Yours faithfully, P.K. Sharma
6. I want to purchase ten knives.
7. Three young men and two young women were present in the hall.
8. How many MPs were present in the meeting.
9. This is a girls' hostel.
10. My son-in-law's sister is coming tomorrow.

PRONOUN

A word used in place of a Noun. This replaced noun is called an antecedent. The pronoun should be placed fairly close to its antecedent and agree in gender and number.

TYPES.

- PERSONAL PRONOUNS. I, me, we, us, you, he, him, she, it, her, they, them.
- POSSESIVE PRONOUNS. mine, ours, yours, his, hers, theirs.
- DEMONSTRATIVE PRONOUNS. this, that, these, those.
- REFLEXIVE PRONOUN. myself, ourselves, yourself, yourselves, himself, herself, itself, themselves, oneself.
- EMPHATIC PRONOUN. myself, ourselves, yourself, yourselves, himself, herself, itself, themselves, oneself.
- RECIPROCAL PRONOUN. each other, one another.
- DISTRIBUTIVE PRONOUN. each, either, neither, every, none.
- INDEFINITE PRONOUNS. everybody, somebody, nobody, anybody, someone, everyone, no one, anyone, everything, something, nothing, anything, all, some, any, both, another, much, few, little.
- INTERROGATIVE PRONOUNS. who, whom, whose, which etc.
- First person. person speaking.
- Second Person. person or thing spoken to.
- Third Person. Standing for a person or thing spoken of.
- **RULE 34**. Pronoun used before Verb should be in Nominative Case(Subjective case)

Pronoun used after Verb should be in Objective Case.

Error. I teach he.

Correct. I teach him.

RULE 35. After noun, Possessive pronoun should be used.

Before Noun, Possessive Adjective should be used.

Example. This is my pen.

This pen is mine.

RULE 36. If more than one pronoun is used in a pleasant (good sense) form, we use (231) form.

Example. You, he and I are partners.

You and I can do this work.

RULE 37. If more than one plural pronoun is used or pronouns in bad sense is used, we use (123) form.

Example. We, you and they can purchase that complex.

We, you and they should now get down to work.

NOMINATIVE CASE	OBJECTIVE CASE	POSSESIVE CASE (adj.)	POSSESIVE CASE (pro.)
I	Me	My	Mine
She	Her	Her	Hers
They	Them	Their	Theirs
We	Us	Our	Ours
He	Him	His	His
It	It	Its	
You	You	Your	Yours

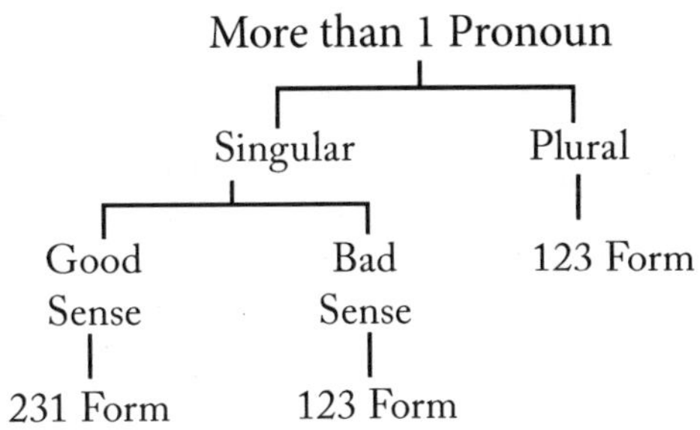

RULE 38. With "Each , Either , Neither", Singular pronoun is used.

Error. Each of the students is ready to do their duty.

Correct. Each of the students is ready to do his duty.

RULE 39. "Either , Neither" are used for two persons or things.

"Any/ No one / None" are used for More than two.

Error. The road was straight, with fields on any side.

Correct. The road was straight, with fields on either side.

RULE 40. "Each other" is used for two persons or things.

"One another" is used for More than two.

Error. The twins dislike one another.

Correct. The twins dislike each other.

RULE 41. Two singular nouns preceded by "each or every" and connected by "and" - singular pronoun is used in such case

Error. Every solider and every sailor was in their place.

Correct. Every solider and every sailor was in his place.

RULE 42. When two or more Singular nouns are joined with "and " and before each noun article is used, - Plural pronoun is used.

Error. The secretary and the treasurer did not do his work himself.

Correct. The secretary and the treasurer did not do their work themselves.

(In this case, secretary and treasurer are two different persons)

RULE 43. When two or more Singular nouns are joined with "and" and only before first noun article is used, - Singular pronoun is used.

Error. The secretary and treasurer did not do their work themselves.

Correct. The secretary and treasurer did not do his work himself.

(In this case, secretary and treasurer represents one person)

RULE 44. When two or more Singular nouns are used with "or" , "either ....or" , "neither...... nor" , verb should be according to the nearest subject.

Error. Shyam or Ram should deposit their dues.

Correct. Shyam or Ram should deposit his dues.

(Here, his is used because Ram is singular)

Error. Either the principal or the teachers failed in his duty.

Correct. Either the principal or the teachers failed in their duty.

(Here, their is used because 'teachers' is plural)

RULE 45. After Let, Verbs, like, between, but, except, prepositions - Objective Case is used.

After Let , prepositions – Possessive Case can also be used.

Example. Let **me** do this work.

He laughed at **me.**

I prefer your help to **hers.**

RULE 46. Comparison between two Subjects using "as/than" – Nominative Case is used.

Comparison between two Objects using "as/

than" – Objective Case is used.

Error. I run faster than him.

Correct. I run faster than he.

RULE 47. Possessive case is not used with "separation, leave, excuse, mention, report, pardon, sight, favour"

Error. I need your favour.

Correct. I need favour from you.

RULE 48. Reflexive pronoun is used with words like. Acquit, resign, avail, adapt, pride, absent, enjoy, adjust, exert, avenge, reconcile, amuse, apply.

Error. The students exert a lot at the time of examination.

Correct. The students exert themselves a lot at the time of examination.

RULE 49. Reflexive pronoun is not used with the words like. keep, turn, qualify, move, rest, hide, stop.

Error. You should keep yourself away from bad people.

Correct. You should keep away from bad people.

RULE 50. If "All" is used for any object/thing, "that" is used, not "who, which, whom".

Error. All which glitters is not gold.

Correct. All that glitters is not gold.

RULE 51. "All + uncountable noun + that" structure is used.

Error. All the money which I gave her has been spent.

Correct. All the money that I gave her has been spent.

RULE 52. If "All" is used for any person , "who/that" is used, not " which, whom".

Error. All which are interested to do this work can start now.

Correct. All who/that are interested to do this work can start now.

RULE 53. Person + and + animal/thing – "that" is used.

Error. The man and the dog which I saw yesterday, is missing.

Correct. The man and the dog that I saw yesterday, is missing.

RULE 54. Everything, nothing, the only, everyone, all, none, the few, the little, much, little, nobody, none, the same – "that" is used.

Error. My parents have given me everything what I needed.

Correct. My parents have given me everything that I needed.

RULE 55. If one is to be selected from two or more than two – "which" is used.

Error. Who is your sister in the crowd?

Correct. Which is your sister in the crowd?

RULE 56. "whose" is not used for non-living things.

Error. This is the shop whose inauguration was done by Salman Khan.

Correct. This is the shop the inauguration of which was done by Salman Khan.

RULE 57. If "one" is used as subject

Nominative case – One

Objective Pronoun – Oneself

Example. One should do one's duty oneself.

RULE 58. "Both" is used for two people/thing.

Error. All of the two students are innocent.

Correct. Both of the two students are innocent.

RULE 59. "Both" is not used in negative sentences, "neither" is used in that case.

Error. Both of them are not well.

Correct. Neither of them is well.

RULE 60. When "who" refers to a personal pronoun (I, you, he, she, we, they), it takes the verb that agrees with that pronoun.

Incorrect. It is I who is sorry.

Correct. It is I who am sorry. (I am)

Incorrect. It is you who's mistaken.

Correct. It is you who are mistaken. (you are)

Rule 61. The possessive pronouns yours, his, hers, its, ours, theirs, and whose never need apostrophes. Avoid mistakes like her's and your's.

CROWN – 03

(Collection of Result Oriented Worksheet by Neharika)

Correct the following sentences.

1. You and he could not complete his work.
2. One should obey his elders.
3. The cow has hurt her legs.
4. Only those employees should be promoted whom are sincere.
5. Which house do you live ?
6. You, he and I have done their job.
7. None of the two girls could complete the job.
8. Please take the buffalo to her shed.
9. Who is she ? Who can abuse me like this ?
10. What place are you going ?

CROWN – 04

(Collection of Result Oriented Worksheet by Neharika)

1. I could not avail of the opportunity I got last year.
2. Those whose live in glass houses should not throw stones at others.
3. This was he who arrived first in the meeting.
4. One should take care not to make himself obnoxious to others.
5. I, you and he were present in the function.
6. My house is bigger than their.
7. The leaders which do not love their country are not respected.
8. This is easy to get her agreed.
9. One should respect not only his own parents but also others.
10. He and I have fastened his belts.

SOLUTIONS - CROWN – 03

(Collection of Result Oriented Worksheet by Neharika)

1. You and he could not complete your work.
2. One should obey one's elders.
3. The cow has hurt its legs.
4. Only those employees should be promoted who are sincere.
5. Which house do you live in ?
6. You, he and I have done our job.
7. Neither of the two girls could complete the job.
8. Please take the buffalo to its shed.
9. Who is she that can abuse me like this ?
10. What place are you going to ?

SOLUTIONS - CROWN – 04

(Collection of Result Oriented Worksheet by Neharika)

1. I could not avail myself of the opportunity I got last year.
2. Those who live in glass houses should not throw stones at others.
3. It was he who arrived first in the meeting.

4. One should take care not to make oneself obnoxious to others.
5. You, he and I were present in the function.
6. My house is bigger than theirs.
7. The leaders who do not love their country are not respected.
8. It is easy to get her agree.
9. One should respect not only his own parents but also other's.
10. He and I have fastened our belts.

ADJECTIVES

An adjective is a noun to qualify a noun or a pronoun.

TYPES.

- PROPER ADJECTIVE. from proper noun. Indian, African , American etc.
- ADJECTIVE OF QUALITY. specify the quality. Large, honest, small, beautiful, ugly etc.
- ADJECTIVE OF QUANTITY. specify the quantity. Whole, some, enough, little, entire etc.
- ADJECTIVE OF NUMBER. specify the number.

Cardinal Number. One, two, five etc.

Ordinal Number. first, second, third etc.

- DEFINITE NUMBER ADJECTIVES. one, two, second, third etc.
- INDEFINITE NUMBER ADJECTIVES. some, little, many, certain etc.
- DISTRIBUTIVE ADJECTIVES. Either, neither, each, every etc.
- DEMONSTRATIVE ADJECTIVE. Points out person, thing. This, that, such, these etc.
- INTERROGATIVE ADJECTIVE. What, whose, which, where etc.
- EMPHASISING ADJECTIVE. Own, very, quite etc.
- EXCLAMATORY ADJECTIVE. What a beautiful girl! , What an idea!
- POSSESSIVE ADJECTIVE. my, his, her, your, their etc.

Comparison of Adjectives

POSITIVE DEGREE	COMPARATIVE DEGREE	SUPERLATIVE DEGREE
GOOD	BETTER	BEST
STRONG	STRONGER	STRONGEST
WISE	WISER	WISEST
THIN	THINNER	THINNEST
HEAVY	HEAVIER	HEAVIEST
BEAUTIFUL	MORE BEAUTIFUL	MOST BEAUTIFUL
LITTLE	LESS/LESSER	LEAST

RULE 62. Use of two comparative adjectives together is wrong.

Error. I didn't find more costlier gift.

Correct. I didn't find more costly gift.

RULE 63. Use of two Superlative degree adjectives together is wrong.

Error. He is the most strongest of all.

Correct. He is the strongest of all.

RULE 64. In some sentences "a most" is used in place of 'very'.

Example. This is a most interesting book.
(in the library)

She is a most beautiful girl.
(in the school)

- As in case of superlative, here in such cases 'in the library' or 'in the school' should not be used.

RULE 65. preposition "to" is used with adjectives like senior, junior, posterior, superior, inferior, anterior etc.

Also used with elder, prefer, preferable.

Example. He is superior to me.

Sita is junior to me.

Note. Major, minor, exterior, interior, ulterior, lower, upper, former, inner etc. look comparative degree adjectives but they are not.

RULE 66. When qualities of one person is compared, Comparative adjectives ending with "er" should not be used, "more" should be used.

Error. Ram is stronger than intelligent.

Correct. Ram is more strong than intelligent.

RULE 67. "the" should be used before superlative adjective.

- If possessive pronoun is used before superlative adjective, "the" should not be used.

Error. She is best student in our college.

Correct. She is the best student in our college.

Error. This is his the best dress.

Correct. This is his best dress.

RULE 68. Sometimes "best" and "most" can be used with 'like'. But in such cases, "the" is not used before superlative.

Error. Which of the story do you like the most ?

Correct. Which of the story do you like most?

RULE 69. While comparing two things, comparison of same type of things should be clear in the sentence.

Error. The climate of Delhi is hotter than Jaipur.

Correct. The climate of Delhi is hotter than that of Jaipur.

Error. My shirt is better than you.

Correct. My shirt is better than yours.

My shirt is better than your shirt.

RULE 70. Superlative degree is not used for two things.

Error. Which is the cheapest ; Silver or Gold ?

Correct. Which is cheaper ; Silver or Gold ?

Which is the cheapest ; Silver, Gold or Bronze ?

RULE 71. When two adjectives are joined with "and " , degree of each should be same.

Error. Raju is wise and stronger than Ram.

Correct. Raju is wiser and stronger than Ram.

RULE 72. 'Kind' and 'sort' are singular number, "this" and "that" is used with them not "these" or "those".

Error. I don't like these kinds of dresses.

Correct. I don't like this kind of dresses.

RULE 73. Some adjectives are used only in positive or superlative degree, not in comparative degree.

Positive degree	Superlative degree
Top	Topmost
Northern	Northernmost
Southern	Southernmost
Eastern	Easternmost
Western	Westernmost

RULE 74. "the" is used before some adjectives to make them 'adjective plural common noun'. Ins such cases, plural verb is used.

Rich, poor, needy, aged, blind, dead, meek, wicked etc.

Example. The rich (rich people) usually exploit the poor (poor people).

RULE 75. After verbs of sensation (seem, look, appear, feel, taste, sound and smell), adjective is used not adverb.

Example. The soup smells delicious. (not deliciously)

Error. He feels badly.

Correct. He feels bad.

RULE 76. Adjectives are used after. be, become, turn, get, grow, keep, make, prove.

Example. When he heard the news, he became sad (adj.).

RULE 77. Some nouns are part of hyphenated

or compound adjectives. These can not be used in plural form.

Error. I delivered a two-hours lecture.

Correct. I delivered a two-hour lecture.

RULE 78. If a noun works as an adjective, it cannot be plural.

Error. Lasers are indispensable tools for delicate eyes surgery.

Correct. Lasers are indispensable tools for delicate eye surgery.

RULE 79. If "times" is used, comparative degree cannot be used.

Error. My Car is three times bigger than yours.

Correct. My Car is three times as big as yours.

RULE 80. If more than one type of adjectives are used, then their order should be as follows.

Opinion Size
Age Shape Color
Origin Material Purpose

Opinion. beautiful, ugly, pretty etc.

Size. big, small, tiny, minute etc.

Age. old, new, recent etc.

Shape. round, oval, heart-shaped etc.

Color. blue, red, pink etc.

Origin. Indian, German etc.

Material. wooden, leather etc.

Purpose. wedding, dining, sleeping etc.

EXAMPLE. I bought a beautiful, tiny, heart-shaped, red, american, diamond, wedding ring.

RULE 81. To emphasize Comparative degree, Much, far, by far, far and away, still can be used.

Example. Ram is much wiser than shyam.

This magazine is far better than that.

The book is better by far.

This magazine is still better.

- "All the" can also be used to emphasize Comparative.

  Example. It is all the better.

- "Rather" can be used before Comparative but not "fairly"

  Example. She is rather better today.

RULE 82. Adjectives like – Supreme, universal, extreme, complete, entire, excellent, absolute, impossible, perfect, unique, ideal, chief, eternal etc don't have comparative or superlative degree. These adjectives denote absolute position.

Error. This is the most perfect example.

Correct. This is a perfect example.

('the most' should not be used with 'perfect' as the word 'perfect' represents superlative degree.)

RULE 83. "Little" is used for quantity (Little, less, least)

Used in negative sense (Hardly any)

"A little" means not much (some)

Used in positive sense.

Error. Little common sense can bring success to you.

Correct – A little common sense can bring success to you.

(As the above sentence is used in positive sense)

'The little' means not much but all.

RULE 84. Later – Refers to time (is the opposite of earlier)

Latter – Refers to position (is the opposite of former)

Error – She came latter than I.

Correct – She came later than I.

RULE 85. Ordinal is placed before Cardinal.

Example – The first two chapter

The last three classes.

RULE 86. An adjective after noun is placed when the noun is followed by preposition.

For example –

Error – The subject is a worthy matter of note.

Correct – The subject is a matter worthy of note.

RULE 87. When two adjectives require different prepositions, appropriate prepositions should be used with both adjectives.

Example – He is senior and older than I.

Correct – He is senior to and older than I.

RULE 88. Adjectives like – Ready, unable, alike, sorry, well, alone, ill, sure, afraid, asleep, due, worth etc. cannot be used before nouns.

Ex- The man is ill.

This book is worth reading.

Seema alone is responsible for my problems.

RULE 89. Adjective "Older/oldest" is used for persons (not blood relation) and things. It refers to both age and time.

Elder/Eldest is used for persons only in case of blood relations. It refers to age only.

CROWN – 05

(Collection of Result Oriented Worksheet by Neharika)

Correct the following sentences.

1. He is the richest of all man in the city.
2. He is my the best friend.
3. He is braver than stronger.
4. The quality of this shirt is superior than yours.
5. The Ghee of Haryana is better than Rajasthan.
6. This is mine bed, which is your?
7. It is as difficult to swim as driving.
8. It smells badly.
9. Your problem is comparatively easier than that of mine.
10. This is all the more better.

SOLUTIONS - CROWN – 05

(Collection of Result Oriented Worksheet by Neharika)

1. He is the richest of all men in the city.
2. He is my best friend.
3. He is more brave than strong.
4. The quality of this shirt is superior to yours.
5. The Ghee of Haryana is better than that of Rajasthan.
6. This is my bed, which is yours?
7. It is as difficult to swim as drive.
8. It smells bad.
9. Your problem is comparatively easy than that of mine.
10. This is all the better.

CROWN – 06

(Collection of Result Oriented Worksheet by Neharika)

Complete the following sentences using Later/last/latest/latter

1. Ram came ____ than Shyam.
2. The _____ half of the Century saw many revolutions
3. Ram was promoted as officer at a ____ date.
4. At ____ the president gave thanks to the audience.
5. This is the _____ technology.
6. I have _________influence in the potential field now.
7. There is __________ hope of his recovery, he is very serious.
8. She had donated ______ property, she had.
9. He slept ________ and felt better.
10. _____ knowledge is a dangerous thing.

SOLUTIONS - CROWN – 06

(Collection of Result Oriented Worksheet by Neharika)

1. later
2. latter
3. later
4. last
5. latest
6. little
7. little
8. the little
9. a little
10. a little

VERB

Verbs indicate thoughts and actions. Verbs indicates; when the action happened, how many things were acting, and can describe the action.

Classification
- Main Verbs
  - Transitive
  - Intransitive
- Auxiliary Verbs
  - Primary
  - Modal

- TRANSITIVE VERBS. take objects. These verbs carry the action of a subject and apply it to an object.
- INTRANSITIVE VERBS. do not take an object

NOTE. Some verbs can function both transitively and intransitively. So it is not reasonable to classify a verb as transitive or intransitive, instead we should say that the verb is used transitively or intransitively.

Verbs used transitively	Verbs used intransitively
He speaks the truth.	Sita speaks slowly.
He flies kites.	A bird flies.

RULE 90. A verb when preceded by a preposition must be the gerund.

Error. They were warned for come late.

Correct. They were warned for coming late.

RULE 91. Two auxiliaries can be used with one principal verb, only when the form of the principal verb is appropriate to both the auxiliaries.

Error. The MD never has and never will take such partial decision.

Correct. The MD never has taken and never will take such partial decision.

RULE 92. Modal auxiliaries are not used together. But two auxiliaries can be connected by a conjunction.

Error. He should must do it.

Correct. He should and must do it.

RULE 93. If there are two subjects in a sentence with different numbers, then both subjects should have their separate auxiliaries.

Error. In the accident, three injured and one were killed.

Correct. In the accident, three were injured and one was killed.

RULE 94. For two subjects one verb should be used, only if the form of the verb is same for both the subjects. Otherwise separate verbs should be used for each subject.

Error. I am going to school and my sister home.

Correct. I am going to school and my sister is going to home.

RULE 95. In Imperative sentences starting with Let us/ let's, "shall" as a question tag is used.

Error. Let us dance together, can we?

Correct. Let us dance together, shall we?

RULE 96. When there are two principal verbs, auxiliary should be associated correctly with both.

Error. Two hundred aspirants have cleared the mains only one failed.

Correct. Two hundred aspirants have cleared the mains only one has failed.

RULE 97. The auxiliary verb 'should' be used, when the subordinate clause comes after 'lest' irrespective of the verb tense in the main clause.

Error. Walk fast lest you shall miss the train.

Correct. Walk fast lest you should miss the train.

RULE 98. "should" is used with "lest" to show negative purpose.

Example. He ran fast lest he should miss the train.

Note. instead of "should + V1" , "V1" can be used with "lest". Here, V1 form should be used without s/es.

Example. Help him lest he fail.

RULE 99. If 'dare' and 'need' is used in positive sentences, "to + V1" is used after that.

Example. He needs to work hard.

RULE 100. If 'dare' and 'need' is used in negative sentences, "to " is not used after that.

Example. I need not come tomorrow.

RULE 101. When need or dare is followed by 'not' , "needs/dares" cannot be used.

Error. Ram needs not come here.

Correct. Ram need not come here.

RULE 102. "will and shall" are not used in following sentences.

1. sentences starting with past tense.
2. two continuous future work. work 1 ... work 2 ; and work 2 is dependent on work 1, then

Work 1 – Simple present tense

Work 2 - Simple future tense

Error. If I will come, I will meet you.

Correct. If I come, I will meet you.

Note. Simple present tense is used after words like.

If/as soon as / in case / provided / unless / until / before / after / when.

RULE 103. Infinitive 'to+V1' is used with "ought" and "used".

Example. We ought to respect our country.

RULE 104. 'able to' is not used with can/could.

Error. He cannot be able to do this work.

Correct. He cannot do this work.

RULE 105. In imaginary sentences, "were" is used.

Error. I wish, I was a bird.

Correct. I wish, I were a bird.

RULE 106. "V1 + ing" is used after 'Verb + used to' , to show habitual action.

Note. After some verbs/adjective/phrase, "to + V1 + ing " is used.

Be used to , accustomed to , with a view to, addicted to , devoted to, in addition to, to look forward to, object to, owing to, given to, taken to, prone to, to averse to.

Example. He is addicted to smoking.

RULE 107. 'use to' or 'uses to' cannot be used for present routine action. Simple present tense is used to represent 'present routine work'.

Error. He uses to study till 9 p.m.

Correct. He studies till 9 p.m.

RULE 108. To modify a verb, an adjective or another adverb , we use an adverb.

Error. She speaks very intelligent.

Correct. She speaks very intelligently.

CROWN – 07

(Collection of Result Oriented Worksheet by Neharika)

Correct the following sentences.

1 (a) He ordered (b) as if he (c) was my minister (d) no error

2 (a) God saves (b) the queen (c) Victoria (d) no error

3 (a) If it was so (b) poetry (c) would cease to matter (d) no error

4 (a) The merit (b) of these books (c) are known to everyone (d) no error

5 (a) The condition of (b) people living in (c) rural area (d) are very bad

6 (a) The smell (b) of these rose (c) flowers are (d) very sweet

7 (a) Economic cooperation (b) between the two countries (c) have increased substantially (d) no error

8 (a) A band of musicians (b) have been

engaged
(c) for the inaugural function
(d) no error

9 (a) The number interested (b) of persons
(c) in psychology are small. (d) generally

10 (a) A part of (b) the mango
(c) are rotten (d) no error

SOLUTIONS - CROWN – 07

(Collection of Result Oriented Worksheet by Neharika)

1. c were
2. a save
3. a were
4. c is
5. d is
6. c is
7. c has
8. b has been
9. c is
10. c is

CROWN – 08

(Collection of Result Oriented Worksheet by Neharika)

Correct the following sentences.

1. (a) A part of (b) the mangoes
   (c) are rotten (d) no error
2. (a) The governing body at
   (b) its first meeting
   (c) have decided
   (d) to conduct the test again
3. (a) The banker's association
   (b) has submitted a memorandum
   (c) for the fulfilment of
   (d) their demands
4. (a) Five quintals of wooden coal
   (b) are
   (c) his annual requirement
   (d) for the unit
5. (a) Dickens have criticised
   (b) the philosophy
   (c) in 'Hard Times'
   (d) no error
6. (a) The manager's comments
   (b) on the preperation of the test matches
   (c) for this tour
   (d) has been generally praised
7. (a) The details
   (b) of the incident
   (c) was not known
   (d) to me
8. (a) The majority of
   (b) writers never
   (c) passes this stage (d) no error
9. (a) All his money (b) is spent
   (c) and all his
   (d) hopes ruined
10. (a) This rule may
    (b) and ought to be
    (c) disregarded for the time being
    (d) no error

SOLUTIONS - CROWN – 08

(Collection of Result Oriented Worksheet by Neharika)

1. d no error
2. c has
3. d its
4. b is
5. a has
6. d have been
7. c were
8. c pass
9. d hopes are
10. a may be

Subject Verb Agreement

RULE 109. When two subjects are joined by 'AND' the verb is plural

Error. My friend and his father is in India

Correct. My friend and his father are in India

RULE 110. When two singular nouns joined by AND refer to the same person or thing, the verb is singular.

Error. The secretary and treasurer have been arrested.

Correct. The secretary and treasurer has been arrested.

Error. The district magistrate and collector are on leave today

Correct. The district magistrate and collector is on leave today

RULE 111. Article 'THE' is used only once when the two nouns refer to the same person or thing. If the two nouns refer to different persons or things, article 'THE' is used before each noun. In such cases, the verb will be in the plural form.

Error. The secretary and the president has been given warm welcome.

Correct. The secretary and the president have been given warm welcome.

RULE 112. If two different singular nouns express one idea, the verb should be in the singular form.

Error. Bread and milk are good for Breakfast.

Correct. Bread and milk is good for Breakfast.

Error. Rice and curry are my favorite dish.

Correct. Rice and curry is my favorite dish.

RULE 113. When two singular subjects are practically synonymous the verb should be in the singular form.

Error. The law and order situation in the state are under control

Correct. The law and order situation in the state is under control

Error. His power and influence are on the decline.

Correct. His power and influence is on the decline.

RULE 114. If two singular subjects combined by AND are preceded by each or every, the verb should be in the singular.

Error. Every boy and girl were present in the class Yesterday.

Correct. Every boy and girl was present in the class Yesterday.

Error. Every man and every woman have the right to express his or her view.

Correct. Every man and every woman has the right to express his or her view.

RULE 115. When the subjects joined by (Either-or), (Neither-nor) are of different persons, the verb will agree in person and number with the noun nearest to it.

Error. Either Radha or Rani have done this mischief.

Correct. Either Radha or Rani has done this mischief.

Error. Neither you nor he are to take up this task.

Correct. Neither you nor he is to take up this task.

Error. Either the CM or the Cabinet Ministers is responsible for this problem.

Correct. Either the CM or the Cabinet Ministers are responsible for this problem.

RULE 116. If connectives like with, together with, 'as well as' accompanied by etc. are used to combine two subjects the verb agrees with the subject mentioned first.

Error. The president of India together with his personal secretaries are invited to this function.

Correct. The president of India together with his personal secretaries is invited to this function.

Error. The actress, along with her manager and some friend, are attending the function.

Correct. The actress, along with her manager and some friend, is attending the function.

RULE 117. When (Not only-but also) is used to combine two subjects, the verb agrees with the subject close to it

Error. Not only Hari, but also his brothers was arrested.

Correct. Not only Hari, but also his brothers were arrested.

RULE 118. Use of None/No.

None can take either a singular or a plural verb depending on the noun which follows it.

None + of the + (non-count noun) + singular verb

None + of the + (plural count. noun) + plural verb

Error. None of the counterfeit money have been found

Correct. None of the counterfeit money has been found

Error. None of the students has finished the exam yet.

Correct. None of the students have finished the exam yet.

RULE 119. No can take either a singular or plural verb depending on the noun which follows it.

Structure. [No + Singular Noun + Singular Verb]

Structure. [No + plural Noun + plural Verb]

Error. No employee have received the salary.

Correct. No employee has received the salary.

RULE 120. Majority can be singular or plural. If it is alone it is usually singular, if it is followed by a plural noun, it is usually plural.

Important Note. Majority by itself is singular but when majority refers to a set of people it is plural.

Error. A majority are always right.

Correct. A majority is always right.

Error. A majority of students is right.

Correct. A majority of students are right.

RULE 121. Many words indicating a number of people or animals are singular.

The following nouns are usually singular.

(If the individual members are acting separately, they are plural and take plural verb.)

[Congress, Family, Group, Committee, Class, Organisation, Team, Army, Club, Crowd, Government, Jury, Minority, Public]

Error. The family were happy at the news

Correct. The family was happy at the news

Error. The family was fighting over inheritance.

Correct. The family were fighting over inheritance.

RULE 122. The number/A number

The number is singular.

Correct. The number of acres destroyed by wildfires has increased dramatically over the past several years.

A number is plural.

Correct. A number of students are standing outside the office.

RULE 123. Collective nouns indicating time, money and measurements used as a whole are Singular and take a singular verb.

Error. Twenty five rupees are not such a big amount for him

Correct. Twenty five rupees is not such a big amount for him

Error. Two miles are too much for this man to run.

Correct. Two miles is too much for this man to run.

RULE 124. when a lot of, a great deal of, plenty of, most of and some of refer to number, a plural verb is used.

Error. A lot of people was present in the party.

Correct. A lot of people were present in the

party.

But, if these expressions refers to an amount, the verb is in the singular number.

Error. A lot of work have to be completed before we go.

Correct. A lot of work has to be completed before we go.

RULE 125. When the percentage or a part of something is mentioned with plural meaning the plural verb is used.

Error. 30 % of Indian women is literate.

Correct. 30 % of Indian women are literate.

Error. Three-quarters of the food have been eaten.

Correct. Three-quarters of the food has been eaten.

RULE 126. Barracks, Headquarters, Whereabouts, Alms etc. take a singular verb, as well as plural verb.

Error. The headquarters of the UNO is/are New York

Correct. The headquarters of the UNO is/are New York.

RULE 127. In sports, while referring to the players, the name of the country is followed by plural verb.

Error. England has won the World Cup.

Correct. England have won the World Cup.

RULE 128. When the word ENEMY is used in the sense 'Armed forces' of a nation with which one's country is at war, we have to use the plural verb.

Error. The enemy was forced to Retreat.

Correct. The enemy were forced to Retreat.

RULE 129. When sentences start with "there" or "here," the subject will always be placed after the verb, so care needs to be taken to identify it correctly.

Error. There is four hurdles to jump.

Correct. There are four hurdles to jump.

Error. Here is the papers you requested.

Correct. Here are the papers you requested.

RULE 130. When gerunds are used as the subject of a sentence, they take the singular verb form of the verb; but, when they are linked by and, they take the plural form.

Error. Standing in the water were a bad idea.

Correct. Standing in the water was a bad idea.

Error. Swimming in the ocean and playing drums is my hobbies.

Correct. Swimming in the ocean and playing drums are my hobbies.

RULE 131. If two infinitives are separated by and they take the plural form of the verb.

Error. To walk and to chew gum requires great skill.

Correct. To walk and to chew gum require great skill.

RULE 132. Don't get confused by the words that come between the subject and verb; they do not affect agreement.

Error. The dog, who is chewing on my jeans, are usually very good.

Correct. The dog, who is chewing on my jeans, is usually very good.

RULE 133. Remember, only the subject affects the verb!

CROWN – 09

(Collection of Result Oriented Worksheet by Neharika)

Correct the following sentences.

1. (a) Neither he/ (b) nor his friends/
   (c) is going out/
   (d) for the shooting of documentary./
   (e) NO ERROR
2. (a) Most of the girls/
   (b) has bought the apparatus home/
   (c) in order to perform the/

(d) experiment of chemistry./

(e) NO ERROR

3. (a) Indian politics currently/

(b) seem to be a battle between/

(c) a juggernaut and a footnote./

(d) NO ERROR

4. (a) Electoral politics with its wide repertoire of tactics/

(b) teach you that you can indeed make a/

(c) silk purse out of sow's ear./

(d) NO ERROR

5. (a) He is one of/

(b) the soldiers who has/

(c) gone to kargil/

(d) during the time of war./

(e) NO ERROR

6. (a) The new tagline/

(b) for the television sets/

(c) are attracting more and more/

(d) customers day by day./

(e) NO ERROR

7. (a) A lot of/

(b) singers encourages the crowd/

(c) to dance and to enjoy/

(d) the moment up to the fullest./

(e) NO ERROR

8. (a) The doctor with/

(b) his two daughters/

(c) were unable to find/

(c) the reason behind his son's sudden demise./

(e) NO ERROR

9. The Department

(1) / assured us that

(2) / a series of seminars

(3) / were to be arranged

(4) / No Error (5)

10. A great many

(1) / students has

(2) / been declared

(3) / successful

(4) / No Error (5)

SOLUTIONS - CROWN – 09

(Collection of Result Oriented Worksheet by Neharika)

1. (c) Neither and nor will take verb according to the nearest subject
2. (b) Have will come in place of has.
3. (b) Seems will come as Indian politics is a singular subject.
4. (b) Teaches will come as electoral politics is a singular subject.
5. (b) Have will be used in place of has as who is a relative pronoun here and its antecedent is soldiers.
6. (c) Is will come in place of are as tagline is singular subject
7. (b) A lot of + plural countable noun + plural verb
8. (c) Was will come in place of were as 'with' will take verb according to the first subject.
9. (d) The Department assured us that *a series* of seminars was to be arranged.
10. (b) A great many students have been declared successful.

CROWN – 10

(Collection of Result Oriented Worksheet by Neharika)

Correct the following sentences.

This news were (1) / broadcast (2) / all over the world (3) / from ABC Radio. (4) / No Error (5)

The United States (1) / of America (2) / are the richest (3) / country of the world. (4) / No Error (5)

More than one (1) / student have (2) / taken the interview (3) / for this company. (4) / No

Error (5)

Everybody (1) / among (2) / your friends (3) / like playing. (4) / No Error (5)

Three-fourths of (1) / the land (2) / have been (3) / ploughed. (4) / No Error (5)

(a) Neither of them/ (b) are going to attend/ (c) the party on 10th October./ (d) No error

(a) He walked five miles which are really a great distance/ (b) for a man like him who is not only old but also ill./ (d) No error

(a) Either my colleague/ (b) or a peon are coming home/ (c) with the material today./(d) No error

(a) The rise and fall/ (b) of the tide are due/ (c) to lunar influence./ (d) No error

(a) Many a man/ (b) have succumbed/ (c) to this temptation./ (d) No error

SOLUTIONS - CROWN – 10

(Collection of Result Oriented Worksheet by Neharika)

This news **was** broadcast all over the world from ABC Radio.

The United States of America **is** the richest country of the world.

More than one *student* **has** taken the interview for this company.

Everybody among your friends **likes** playing.

Three-fourths of the land **has** been ploughed.

(b) is

(a) is

(b) is

(b) is

(b) has

ARTICLES

RULE 134. a/an is used before the name of profession.

Sita is a nurse.

I am a teacher.

RULE 135. a/an is used with certain numbers.

a hundred, a million, a dozen

RULE 136. a/an is used with many/rather/ quite/such

Many a woman would welcome such a chance.

It was quite an impossible task.

He is rather a lazy boy

RULE 137. a/an is used in expressions of price, speed, ratio etc.

She can run twelve kilometers an hour.

The price of apple is ₹ 100 a kg.

Every customer will be given extra sugar on purchasing a litre oil.

RULE 138. a/an is used in exclamations, before singular, countable nouns.

What a dog!

What a beauty!

What an idea !

RULE 139. a/an is used when a verb is used as a noun

He goes for a walk daily.

He has gone for a ride.

RULE 140. the is used while using a particular person or thing or one already referred to.

She found a purse. The purse contained a golden chain.

RULE 141. the is used when a singular noun is meant to represent a whole category/class.

The masses suffered.

The poor

The rich

The young

RULE 142. the is used before superlatives.

she is the most beautiful girl in our college.

RULE 143. the is used with the names of building, gulf, river, ocean, sea etc.

The Ganga

The Pacific Ocean

The Gulf of Kutch

The Caspian sea

The Taj Mahal

RULE 144. the is placed only before the plural sounding names of islands and the mountain ranges, chains of mountains, plural sounding names of countries.

The Neitherlands, the Himalayas, the Alps, The Phillipines

Mount Everest is the highest peak of the Himalayas.

RULE 145. the is not generally used before the name of countries but if the name of countries contain words like. states, kingdom, republic etc., we used 'the' before that.

The USA, The USSR, The UK

He went to Mexico.

RULE 146. the is used before the names of directions.

The East/ The West/ The North

RULE 147. the is used before the names of persons (family) in plural

The Raymonds, The Ambanis, The Birlas.

RULE 148. the is used before the names of important, renowned books.

The Ramayana, The Mahabharata

RULE 149. terms referring Nationality or Community. Ex. The Indians, The French.

RULE 150. a proper noun , only when it is qualified by an adjective. Ex. The brave Napolean.

RULE 151. Ordinals. Ex. The first man, the sixth chapter.

RULE 152. Names of Musical Instruments and of Inventions.

RULE 153. Names of newspapers, community, political party, historical event, train, ship, aeroplane etc.

The Hindu , The Brahmins, The BJP, The Jaliyavala bagh incident, The Bullet train, The Titanic, The Indian Airlines

RULE 154. Comparative degree being used for selection or comparison. Ex.

He is the stronger of the two.

RULE 155. A person being referred by his designation. Ex. The director, The Chairman

RULE 156. Names of committee, club, foundation and trust. Ex. The Lions Club, The Rotary Club, The United Nations, The WHO, The Rajiv Gandhi Trust etc.

RULE 157. Article is Omitted.

- Before a proper noun. If it is used before proper noun it becomes common noun.
- Before names of regular meals. Ex. Breakfast, Lunch, Dinner
- But if the meal becomes particular, article is used.
- The dinner hosted by the queen was superb.
- Before names of languages or colors.
- Before the names of public institutions (Church, School, University, Prison, Hospital, Court etc.)
- Before the names of games, sports
- Before names of seasons.

CROWN – 11

(Collection of Result Oriented Worksheet by Neharika)

Complete the following Passage with articles A/AN/THE. Write NA if no article required.

Number…….1…….. Hundred and two …….2…….. House next door to us, is for sale. Its quite………3………. Nice house with ………..4………… Big rooms ………5………… Back windows look out on …………6………… Park. I don't know what………..7…….. Price ………8………. owners are asking. You could give them ……….9……. and make them …………10……… Offer.

CROWN – 12

(Collection of Result Oriented Worksheet by Neharika)

Complete the following Passage with articles A/AN/THE. Write NA if no article required.

………1…….. Tallest gentlemen is ………2……………. Teacher, ………3………. man who has ……4…… Stick in his hand is……5……… teacher's uncle. He lives in Chennai. He has come here to attend……6……… Wedding. I don't know who ……7……. Third man is. I know ………8……… person sitting beside …………9……… Teacher.

SOLUTIONS - CROWN – 11

(Collection of Result Oriented Worksheet by Neharika)

1	2	3	4	5
-	The	A	-	The

6	7	8	9	10
The/A	-	The	A	An

SOLUTIONS - CROWN – 12

(Collection of Result Oriented Worksheet by Neharika)

1	2	3	4	5	6	7	8	9
The	A	The	A	The	A	The	The	The
C	A	C	A	C	A	C	C	C

ADVERB

An Adverb a word which modifies a verb or an adjectives or another adverb.

TYPES.

- ADVERBS OF MANNER. tell us the manner or the way in which something happens. They answer the Question 'How?'
- ADVERBS OF PLACE. tell us the place where something happens. They answer the question 'where?'
- ADVERBS OF TIME. tell us something about the time that something happens. They answer the question 'when?'
- ADVERBS OF DEGREE. tell us the degree or extent to which something happens. They answer the question 'how much?' or 'to what degree?'
- ADVERBS OF FREQUENCY. tell us how many times the action occurs or occurred or will occur. Examples. Rarely, daily, sometimes, often, seldom, usually, frequently, always, ever, generally, monthly, yearly.

Comparison of Adverbs

POSITIVE DEGREE	COMPARATIVE DEGREE	SUPERLATIVE DEGREE
Early	Earlier	Earliest
Fast	Faster	Fastest
Hard	Harder	hardest
High	Higher	Highest
Heavily	More heavily	Most heavily
Loudly	More loudly	Most loudly
Quietly	More quietly	Most quietly

RULE 158. After the words - taste, feel, seem, appear, look, smell, remain, adjective should be used, not adverb.

Error. Honey tastes sweetly.

Correct. Honey tastes sweet.

RULE 159. 'Very' should be used before Positive degree and 'much' should be used before Comparative degree.

Example. He is much better than you.

He spoke very loudly.

RULE 160. 'Quite all' cannot be used together.

Either 'quite right' or 'all right' should be used.

Example. He said it was quite right to reject the offer.

- 'Quite' denotes 'perfectly, completely'. It cannot be used to replace 'very'.

Example. She is very lovely.

Error. He is quite handsome.

Correct. He is very handsome.

RULE 161. 'Lately' is an adverb that denotes 'recently'.

'Late' denotes 'after the fixed, right or usual time'.

Example. Has he come lately? (Recently)

Did he come late? (After the fixed time)

Error. She was heavily fined last month for coming lately. Correct. She was heavily fined last month for coming late.

RULE 162. 'Too' denotes 'more than required'. It is generally used with unpleasant adjectives. e.g. too ugly, too bad, too wicked etc.

Note. Too happy, too healthy, too pleased etc should not be used with 'too' as you don't really mean "more than required happy" or "healthy - more than required".

Error. I am too glad to meet you.

Correct. I am very glad to meet you.

Error. I am too glad to receive the offer letter of this company.

Correct. I am very glad to receive the offer letter of this company.

RULE 163. 'Too...to' can be used with pleasant adjectives.

Error. He is too intelligent be cheated.

Correct. He is too intelligent to be cheated.

RULE 164. 'Much too' is followed by 'adjective'; whereas 'too much' is followed by 'noun'.

Error. Her failure is too much painful for our family.

Correct. Her failure is much too painful for our family.

- much too + unpleasant adjectives
  e.g. much too careless, much too reckless, much too painful
- too much + noun

e.g. too much carelessness, too much recklessness, too much pain

RULE 165. Fairly' is used with pleasant adjectives e.g. fairly good, fairly wise etc.

'Rather' is used with unpleasant adjectives e.g. rather dull, rather difficult etc.

Error. The amount which the Company has paid to the dependents of the dead worker is fairly unjustified."

Correct. The amount which the Company has paid to the dependents of the dead worker is rather unjustified."

RULE 166. Fairly is used with positive degree only - fairly good, fairly beautiful etc.

Rather is used with positive and comparative degree - rather bad, rather difficult, rather hotter etc.

Note. Use of 'Fairly too..... ' is incorrect, 'Rather..... too......' is correct and should be used

Error. Fairly too good

Correct. Rather too good

RULE 167. 'Hardly' denotes barely or scarcely, whereas 'hard' means 'firm/ tough'.

Example. He works hard.

He hardly works. (means "He barely works.")

Error. This hardly-won supremacy was not to be lost.

Correct. This hard-won supremacy was not to be lost.

RULE 168. 'Since' is used with 'ever' as an adverb. The proper way should be 'ever since'.

Error. I met her about ten years ago and have remembered her ever for.

Correct. I met her about ten years ago and have remembered her ever since.

RULE 169. Uses of 'Else' and 'Other'.

'Else' should be followed by 'but'

'other' and 'otherwise' are followed by 'than'

Example. He has no other choice than leaving the room.

RULE 170. We should not use negative adverbs like seldom, nowhere, never, nothing, barely, hardly, merely, neither, rarely etc with the negative meaning words. Two negative words should be avoided.

Example. They hardly know anybody in the college

RULE 171.

Very- Very modifies present participle used as an adjective, adverb, and adjective in a positive degree.

Example. It is a very beautiful place.

I was very happy after getting the job.

RULE 172.

Much- Much is used in comparative degree and past participle.

Example. He is much taller than his brother.

They completed the mission much faster.

RULE 173.

So and Too- We should not use 'so' and 'too' without 'that' (adverb clause) and 'to' (infinitive) respectively.

Example. He is so strong that no one mess with him.

She is too good to do this job.

RULE 174.

Enough- 'Enough' is both an adjective and adverb.

As an adverb, it is always used after the adjective and

As an adjective, it is used before a noun.

Example. They have enough time to play.

He is good enough to get admission.

RULE 175.

Rule of Adverb. Main verb + adv (Manner) + adv (Place) + adv(Time)

IN CASE OF MOVEMENT. go, come, arrive, reach, return, leave

Main verb + adv (Place) + adv (Manner) + adv(Time)

Spot the error

Error. She beautifully danced yesterday in her school.

Correct. She danced beautifully in her school yesterday.

Spot the error

Error. They returned happily home yesterday.

Correct. They returned home happily yesterday.

RULE 176.

Rule of Adverb. Helping Verb + Adv(frequency) + Main Verb

Spot the error

Error. He has completed never his work on time.

Correct. He has never completed his work on time.

RULE 177.

Rule of Adverb. too +......+ to +V1

EXAMPLE. He is too weak to walk.

Error. The box is too heavy for me to lift.

Correct. The box is too heavy to lift for me

CROWN – 13

(Collection of Result Oriented Worksheet by Neharika)

1. He was exceedingly paid (1) / for how skilful he (2) / handled (3) / the crowd. (4) / No Error (5)
2. I met her (1) / about ten years ago (2) / and have remembered her (3) / ever for. (4) / No Error (5)
3. He is very senior (1) / to me (2) / so I dare not (3) / disrespect him. (4) / No Error (5)
4. He said (1) / it was (2) / quite all right (3) / to reject the offer. (4) / No Error (5)
5. She was (1) / heavily fined (2) / last month (3) / for coming lately. (4) / No Error (5)
6. I am too glad (1) / to receive (2) / the offer letter (3) / of this company. (4) / No Error (5)
7. Her failure (1) / is too much (2) / painful (3) / for our family. (4) / No Error (5)
8. The amount which (1) / the Company has paid (2) / to dependents of the dead worker(3) / is fairly unjustified. (4) / No Error (5)
9. She was (1) / hardly-hit (2) / by her (3) / father›s death. (4) / No Error (5)
10. When carefully examined, (1) / it was found (2) / that there (3) / were some missing pieces.(4) / No Error (5)

SOLUTIONS - CROWN – 13

(Collection of Result Oriented Worksheet by Neharika)

1. Replace '*skilful*' with '*skilfully*'.
2. Replace '*for*' with ‹*since*›.
3. Replace '*very*' with '*much*'.
4. 'Quite all' cannot be used together.
5. Replace '*lately*' with '*late*'.
6. Replace '*too*' with '*very*'.

7. Replace '*too much*' with '*much too*'.
8. Replace '*fairly*' with ‹*rather*›.
9. Replace '*hardly*' with '*hard*'.
10. '*Carefully*' will come after '*examined*'.

CROWN – 14

(Collection of Result Oriented Worksheet by Neharika)

1. Shivangi and Shweta (1)/ are (2)/ coward girls (3)/ no error
2. Meera had hardly (1)/ reached the airport (2)/ when the flight took off (3)/ no error
3. So quickly shivangi (1)/ ran that she (2)/ caught the bus (3)/ no error
4. One should face (1)/ the challenges posed by (2)/ life manly (3)/ no error
5. I hardly find (1)/ something in her character (2)/ that I can admire (3)/ no error
6. Sneha acted (1)/ nobler than all (2)/ of her friends (3)/ no error
7. It was much hot (1)/ day before yesterday and (2)/ we didn't go out (3)/ no error
8. I meet Shivangi often (1)/ near the (2)/ cafe shop (3)/ no error
9. I told her as blunt as (1)/ I could but (2)/ she was not convinced (3)/ no error
10. The description (1)/ of the incident (2)/ is fairly boring (3)/ no error

SOLUTIONS - CROWN – 14

(Collection of Result Oriented Worksheet by Neharika)

1. 'cowardly ' instead of coward. Coward is a noun while cowardly is an adjective. So either use 'shivangi and Shweta are cowards' or 'Shivangi and Shweta are cowardly girls'.
2. no error
3. 'so quickly did shivangi run' is the right usage. If a sentence is introduced by an adverb, inversion takes place. So 'did run' will be used instead of 'ran'.
4. 'Manfully' in place of 'manly. Manly is an adjective while manfully is an adverb.
5. anything instead of something. 'Hardly' is an adverb used in negative meaning so something/everything can't be used with it.
6. 'more nobly' instead of 'nobler'. 'Nobler' is comparative degree of adjective 'noble' while 'more nobly' is comparative form of adverb 'nobly'.Here we need an adverb to qualify the verb 'act'.
7. either use very instead of much or 'much hotter'. Much is used with comparative degree while very is used with positive degree.
8. 'I often meet Shivangi' is the correct usage. Adverb of time (always, never, ever, hardly, often, seldom etc) are used before the verbs that they modify.
9. 'As bluntly as' instead of 'as blunt as'.
10. 'rather ' instead of fairly.

CONJUNCTIONS

Conjunctions are words that link other words, phrases, or clauses together.

I like cooking and *eating,* but *I don't like washing dishes afterward.*

List of Conjunctions

for, and, nor, but, or, yet, so

both/and, either/or, neither/nor, not only/but, whether/or

after, although, as, as if, as long as, as much as, as soon as, as though, because, before, by the time, even if, even though, if, in order that, in case, in the event that, lest , now that, once, only, only if, provided that, since, so, supposing, that, than, though, till, unless, until, when, whenever, where, whereas, wherever, whether or not, while

RULE 178.

Make sure that the phrases joined by conjunctions are parallel (share the same structure.)

Error. I work quickly and am careful.

Correct. I work quickly and carefully.

RULE 179. The conjunction **both** is followed by **and**

Error. He is both intelligent or hard working.

Correct. He is **both** intelligent **and** hard working.

RULE 180. The conjunction **so.... as / as....as** is used to make comparison between two persons and things. so as is used in negative sentences.

But as....as is used in both affirmative and negative sentences

Correct. He is not **so** good **as** you.

Correct. He is **as** good **as** you.

Correct. He is not **as** good **as** you.

RULE 181. Although/ Though is followed by **yet** or a **comma(,)**

Error. Though he worked hard he failed.

Correct. **Though** he worked hard, he failed.

Error. Although these books are costly but the students buy them because these are useful.

Correct. **Although** these books are costly **yet** the students buy them because these are useful.

RULE 182 . Always use the correct pair No sooner........than

Hardly.... when or before

Scarcely.... when or before Barely.... when or before

Error. No sooner had he solved the riddle and he was applauded.

Correct. **No sooner** had he solved the riddle than he was applauded.

Error. Hardly had I come out of the room while I saw him dying.

Correct. **Hardly** had I come out of the room **before** I saw him dying.

Error. Scarcely had he asked the question while Agnes slapped him.

Correct. **Scarcely** had he asked the question **when** Agnes slapped him.

Error. Barely had he bought the car as it was stolen.

Correct. **Barely** had he bought the car **before** it was stolen.

Hardly, scarcely, and barely are negative words. Do not use not, no, never with the clause containing these words.

RULE 183. Lest is followed by **should** or first from of verb. Lest is a negative word. Do not use not, never, no with lest.

Error. Walk carefully lest he will fall.

Correct. Walk carefully **lest** he **should** fall.

Error. Walk carefully lest he don't fall.

Correct. Walk carefully **lest** he fall.

RULE 184. Until is time oriented and **unless** is action oriented. Until and unless are negative words.

Do not use not, never , no, with the clause containing these words.

Error. Wait here until I don't return.

Correct. Wait here **until** I return.

Error. Unless you will not work hard, you will not pass.

Correct. **Unless** you work hard, you will not pass.

RULE 185. In affirmative sentences **doubt** and **doubtful** are followed by **if / whether**. In negative or interrogative sentences **doubt** and **doubtful** are followed by **that.**

Error. I doubt that he will come.

Correct. I doubt **if** he will come.

Error. I do not doubt whether he will come.

Correct. I do not doubt **that** he will come.

RULE 186. Always use the correct pair **not only....but also.**

Error. He cheated not only his friends but his parents.

Correct. He cheated **not only** his friends **but also** his parents.

RULE 187. Between is followed by **and, from** is followed by **to.**

Error. You will have to choose between good or bad.

Correct. You will have to choose **between** good **and** bad.

Error. She keeps singing from morning and evening.

Correct. She keeps singing **from** morning **to** evening.

RULE 188. Neither of means **none of the two**. when more than two person or things are present **none of** is used.

Either of means **one of the two.** when more than two person or things are present **one of** is used.

Error. Neither of his friends helped him.

Correct. **None of** his friends helped him.

Error. One of the student of your class is responsible for this loss.

Correct. **One of** the students of your class is responsible for this loss.

RULE 189. Do not use seldom or ever in place of **seldom or never.**

Error. The national network seldom or ever telecasts good programmers.

Correct. The national network **seldom or never** telecasts good programmers.

RULE 190. After **rather /other**, the subordinating conjunction **than** should be used.

Error. He has no other object so as to get a handsome job.

Correct. He has no **other** object **than** to get a handsome job.

Error. I would rather buy a scooter but a cycle.

Correct. I would **rather** buy a scooter **than** a cycle.

List of Conjunctions	
Coordinating Conjunction Words	**Sentences – Conjunction Examples**
For	He needs to find a job, for he is unemployed.
And	Maria loves both ice cream and pizza.
Nor	Neither Tuesday nor Wednesday is good for the party.
But	She scored good marks but she is not satisfied.
Or	Which fruit do you like. mango or apple?

Yet	She dances well yet she hesitates to take part in the competition.
So	He is unwell so he will not come for the movie.
After	She went to the parlour after lunch.
Although	Although the sun was shining it wasn't warm.
As	She can do her hairstyle as she wants.
As if	He behaved as if he has lost it.
As long as	The dog would be cooperative as long as you fed him.
As much as	He likes football as much as he likes cricket.
As soon as	As soon as I get the details I will send the mail.
As though	The virus is spreading as though it will end the world.
Because	He did the task because he felt it was his duty.
Before	The baby sleeps before the massage.
Even	He has never even heard the name of the city Ohio.
Even if	Even if you perform your best, you won't be appreciated.
Even though	She doesn't want to give up even though she knows it won't better the relation.
If	They will party in the garden if the weather is good.
If only	She will feel better, if only she sees her son for a moment.
If then	If it rains then we will be stuck in traffic.
In order that	She will leave the party early in order that I get a cab.
Just as	It began to rain just as we got home.
Lest	He spent whole days in his room, wearing headphones lest he disturbs anyone.
Now	Boston is now a big city while earlier it was a small town.
Now since	Let's discuss the issue now since the manager is right here.
Now that	Now that everything is under control, the lockdown can be lifted.
Once	Once I pick you up from school we can go to the restaurant.
Provided	He will behave properly provided you be polite to him.
Provided that	I will go to the party provided that she comes.
Rather than	Better, ignore her questions rather than lie.

Since	its a long time since they met.
So that	He joined foreign language classes so that he could learn French.
Supposing	He was bluffed into believing his competitors were not prepared.
Than	The old man lived more than a 100 years.
That	The yellow building you are seeing there, that is my house.
Though	Though they were whispering, their voices echoed in the hall.
Till	She waited at the coffee shop till 11 pm.
Unless	He will not buy you a scooter unless you score good marks.
Until	You will not get a driving licence until you turn 18.
When	When is your mother coming from Canada?
Whenever	Please share the details of your friend, whenever you get time.
Where	Where is the bakery store?
Where is	If Ram is with this girl, where is his wife?
Whereas	The north has a hot climate whereas the south is cold.
Wherever	Eat healthy meals wherever possible.
Whether	She seemed undecided whether to stay or go.
Which	Which is your favourite colour?
While	He did my task while I was away from the office.
Who	Do you know the person who is standing near the bookstore?
Whoever	Whoever wins will get a cash prize.
Why	Why do people throw garbage on the streets?

CROWN – 15

(Collection of Result Oriented Worksheet by Neharika)

1. As soon as the watchman (1)/ rings the bell, then all (2) / the workers (3) / assemble in the hall. (4) / No Error (5)
2. No sooner (1) / did the monkey (2) / see the tiger (3) / when it jumped. (4) / No Error (5)
3. No sooner (1) / did I reach the office (2) / then (3) / it started raining. (4) / No Error (5)
4. Hardly had she (1) / seen her aunt (2) / than she stopped (3) / fighting. (4) / No Error (5)
5. Hardly (1) / we had reached (2) / the platform (3) / when the train started. (4) / No Error (5)
6. Scarcely had the nurse left (1) / after examining (2) / him than (3) / the patient died. (4) / No Error (5)

7. She had scarcely (1) / finished writing (2) / while she fell (3) / asleep. (4) / No Error (5)
8. That store (1) / hadnot hardly (2) / any of the (3) / required products. (4) / No Error (5)
9. Annie is (1) / either (2) / intelligent (3) / but hard-working. (4) / No Error (5)
9. Either you (1) /and he (2) / will have (3) / to pay. (4) / No Error (5)

SOLUTIONS - CROWN – 15

(Collection of Result Oriented Worksheet by Neharika)

1. Remove '*then*'.
2. Replace '*when*' with '*than*'. '*No sooner*' is **always** followed by '*than*'.
3. 'No sooner' is **always** followed by '***than***›
4. '*Hardly*' is **always** followed by ‹*when*›.
5. Hardly is followed by 'had' and 'third' form of verb. Proper way should be '*had we reached*'.
6. 'Scarcely' is **always** followed by 'when'.
7. Replace ‹*while*' with '*when*'.
8. 'Hardly' itself conveys a *negative sense*. Use of 'had not' is **not** required in this case.
9. Replace ‹*but*' with '*or*'.
10. Replace '*and*' with '*or*'.

CROWN – 16

(Collection of Result Oriented Worksheet by Neharika)

1. You must admire (1) / the artwork (2) / when your brother (3) / has done it. (4) / No Error (5)
2. She would not (1) / have suffered (2) / when you had (3) / helped her in time. (4) / No Error (5)
3. I can't allow (1) / you to go out of the class (2) / unless they provide (3) / further instructions. (4) / No Error (5)
4. Unless you do not give (1) / the keys to (2) / the locker (3) / you will be killed. (4) / No Error (5)
5. I could not (1) / go to school (2) / as I was (3) / seriously ill. (4) / No Error (5)
6. I did not (1) / go to college (2) / because it was (3) / raining.(4) / No Error (5)
7. He has been (1) / studying with me (2) / as he (3) / came here. (4) / No Error (5)
8. Till I am alive (1) / nobody can (2) / ever harm (3) / you. (4) / No Error (5)
9. So long (1) / you work (2) / honestly, no one (3) / can fire you. (4) / No Error (5)
10. Our destination (1) / was about (2) / fifty and sixty (3) / kilometers to the west. (4) / No Error (5)

SOLUTIONS - CROWN – 16

(Collection of Result Oriented Worksheet by Neharika)

1. Replace '*when*' with '*if*'.
2. Replace '*when*' with '*if*'.
3. Replace '*unless*' with '*until*'.
4. Remove '*do not*'. 'Unless' itself conveys a negative sense. Use of 'do not' is **not** required in this case.
5. Replace ‹*as*' with '*because*'.
6. Replace '*because*' with '*as*'.
7. Replace '*as*' with '*since*'.
8. Replace '*till*' with '*as long as*'.
9. Add '*as*' after '*so long*'.
10. Replace '*and*' with '*or*'.

PREPOSITION

Rule 191. We always place the objective case after preposition only.

Example.

I do not depend on he. (Incorrect)

I do not depend on him. (Correct)

Rule 192. When two words are connected by and/or, the prepositions after these words must be made clear.

Example.

He is conscious and engaged in his work. (Incorrect)

He is conscious of and engaged in his work. (Correct)

Rule 193. Some words like suggest/ say/ propose/ reply/ explain/ talk/ listen/ write/ speak is followed by "to" preposition, if there is a person in the object form.

Example.

He did not reply me. (Incorrect)

He did not reply to me. (Correct)

Rule194. Some prepositions like **On, in, at,** are not used before **today, tomorrow, yesterday, the following day, the next day** etc.

Example.

She will go there on tomorrow (Incorrect)

She will go there tomorrow. (Correct)

Rule 195. We directly use the object and no preposition is used after transitive verbs like **discuss, reach, describe, tell, order, attack, resemble, ridicule, demand** etc.

Example.

The poet describes about the beauty of nature in his poem. (Incorrect)

The poet describes the beauty of nature in his poem. (Correct)

Rule 196. The preposition across is used in different cases.

Examples.

1. My uncle lives across the river. (across = on the opposite side of)

2. The girl swam across the river (across = from one side to another)

3. She threw the luggage across her shoulders (across = both sides)

4. I came across him (come across= accidentally/ suddenly meet)

Rule 197. Preposition between **is used for** two things **or** two persons.

Example.

He is standing between Haseena and Manju

Rule 198. The preposition among **is used for persons or things more than two.**

Example.

The Chairman distributed prizes among the winners.

Rule 199. The preposition **Amidst** or Amid **used for persons or things (groups)**

Example.

Amid her friends.

Rule 200. Dispose of means sell away

Example.

She disposed of her scooty.

Rule 201. The preposition **From is applied to past/ future tenses.**

Example.

She stayed here from Tuesday to Friday.

Rule 202. Preposition during **is used to denote duration**

Example.

During the second world war, many people suffered.

Rule 203. Preposition of is used to denote origin or cause.

Example.

He comes of **a poor family** (Indicates – origin)

She died of **cancer (Indicates – cause)**

Rule 204. Preposition off used to denote separation.

Example.

A button has come off.

Rule 205. We should not use the preposition with the noun **"Home"**. Only we can use preposition for home when it is followed by an adjective in the possessive form.

Example.

She went to his home.

I decided to go to Ramya's home.

Rule 206. The preposition "Since – Used to denote the point of time, and For – used to denote the period of time. Both are applicable in the perfect tense forms.

Example.

I have known him since 2014.

She has been waiting at the bus stop for past 2 hours.

Rule 207. Sometimes preposition "into" after the verb "enter" should not be used, except in case with reference to an agreement.

Example.

1. He entered into the office premises without permission (Incorrect)

He entered the office premises without permission (Correct)

2.Thegroupenteredahotdiscussion.(Incorrect)
The group entered into a hot discussion (Correct)

Rule 208. Preposition Await means wait for and Despite means inspite of.

Example.

Sheisawaitingthereply.(awaiting=waitingfor)
Despite her hard work she failed in the entrance test.(Despite = inspite of)

Rule 209. The verbs like consists, comprises always followed by preposition "of".

Example.

The group comprises of / consists of 6 members.

RULE 210. Entered

They have entered into the room. (wrong)

They entered the room.(correct)

Now, we have entered the new syllabus of C+ course. (Wrong)

Now, we have entered into the new syllabus of C+ course. (correct)

RULE 211. ATTACK

The people attacked on the buses (wrong)

The people attacked the buses (correct)

Today, I have heard the news of attack Pakistan. (wrong)
Today, I have heard the news of attack on Pakistan. (correct)

RULE 212. DISCUSS

We have discussed about the issue related to the class. (wrong)

We have discussed the issue related to the class.(correct)

RULE 213. COMPRISES

The book comprises of many chapters related to human brain. (wrong)

The book comprises many chapters related to human brain. (correct)

RULE 214. USE OF 'AT' & 'IN'

I live in Delhi in India (wrong)

I live at Delhi in India.(correct)

I live in Delhi in India in Asia. (wrong)

I live at Delhi at India in Asia. (correct)

I live in Delhi street. (wrong)

I live at Delhi street. (correct)

RULE 215. 'At'is used before 'Rate/Price' expressing words.

Milk sells by ₹ 50 a litre. (wrong)

Milk sells at ₹ 50 a litre..(correct)

RULE 216.

'At' is used to express 'temporary action'.

I am at bank and it will take around 2 hours to reach at the counter. (wrong)

I am in the bank and at time , I get bored while working with old versioned computers. (correct)

RULE 217.

Other Usages

At morning	in the morning
At noon	in the noon
At evening	in the evening
At night	in the night
At dawn	in the dawn
At dusk	in the dusk

RULE 218.

'At'is used to express 'age' and 'stage'.

Akbar became the ruler in the age of 12. (wrong)

Akbar became the ruler at the age of 12.(correct)

RULE 219.

'In' is used before month, week, season, year expressing words.

They went to China in March. (correct)

I was born in 1623. (correct)

RULE 220.

'In' is used before the phrasal structure 'A/an + vehicle name (car/taxi/jeep).

He goes to college in the car. (wrong)

He goes to college in car. (wrong)

He goes to college in a car. (correct)

RULE 221. 'Into'

It is used to express the sense of 'motion inside anything'.

The Child fell into the well. (correct)

They jumped into the river. (correct)

It is used to express the change from one medium to another medium.

We can not translate it into English language. (correct)

Water converts into water vapour when it heats. (correct)

RULE 222. Use of 'between'

Between is used in the sense of 'in the middle of' for 'two' persons or things.

Distribute the notes between Aman and Karan.(correct)

He was sitting between his brother and father. (correct)

Generally 'each' and 'every' is not used with 'between'

Distribute the notes between each student. (wrong)

Each/every + noun(singular) + and the next.

Distribute the notes between each student and the next. (correct)

RULE 223. Use of 'between'

It is used with 'distinct' and 'individual' items even if they are 'more than two of them'.

What are the differences among SBI, NABARD and SIDBI. (wrong)

What are the differences between SBI, NABARD and SIDBI. (correct)

What are the differences between these five firms ? (wrong)

What are the differences among these five firms ? (correct)

Note. The names of the different firms are not mentioned here.

RULE 224. Use of 'among'

It is used with the sense of 'in the middle of' for more than 'two persons or things'

Distribute these notes among the students. (correct)

RULE 225. Use of 'amongst'

It is used with the sense of 'in the middle of' for more than 'two persons or things' before vowel starting.

Distribute these notes amongst our students. (correct)

It is used with the sense of 'in the middle of' for more than 'two persons or things' before 'the + Noun(plural)'

Distribute these notes amongst the students. (correct)

Distribute these notes among the students. (correct)

RULE 226.

Among/Amongst ------ countable nouns_

Amid/Amidst -------- countable/ uncountable nouns

I found this ring among the scraps of food (wrong).

I found this ring amongst the scraps of food (wrong).

I found this ring amid the scraps of food (correct).

I found this ring amidst the scraps of food (correct).

The bird was disappeared among the trees of jungles. (correct)

The bird was disappeared amongst the trees of jungles. (correct)

The bird was disappeared amid the trees of jungles. (correct)

The bird was disappeared amidst the trees of jungles. (correct)

RULE 227.

'Besides' is used to express the sense of 'in addition to'

Besides working in the factory, I teach in the school. (correct).

'Beside' is used to express the sense of 'by the side of'.

You must go and sit beside him. (correct)

RULE 228.

AGREE

Error. He will agree for his proposal.

Correct. He will agree to his proposal.

Error. He will agree to him.

Correct. He will agree with him.

RULE 229.

ANGRY

Error. He is angry to me.

Correct. He is angry with me.

Error. He felt angry with the injustice of the situation.

Correct. He felt angry at the injustice of the situation.

RULE 230.

AFRAID

Error. He is afraid to lizards.

Correct. He is afraid of lizards.

Error. He is afraid for operating the laptop.

Correct. He is afraid to operate the laptop.

RULE 231.

DREAMT

Error. I dreamt of my mother last night.

Correct. I dreamt about my mother last night.

Error. I dream about running my own business.

Correct. I dream of running my own business.

Common Prepositions List

Preposition	Type	Example Sentence
above	position	There was a display of fireworks **above** the town.
across	position	His dog lay **across** his lap.
	direction	The vendor walked **across** the street to sell fruits.
after	time	Shortly **after** their marriage, they moved to Texas.
against	position	The grasscutter was kept **against** the fence.
	direction	My aunt threw the painting **against** the wall.
along	direction	The road led **along** the forest.
among	position	The child hid **among** the trees.
around	position	The fence **around** the house is necessary for safety.

at	location	They have a dishwasher **at** home.
	time	Today the meeting is at 6 p.m.
away from	direction	The hospital staff led the body **away from** the other patients.
before	time	I go to the gym **before** college.
behind	position	We parked the car **behind** the school building.
below	position	Just **below** the pocket was a stain.
beneath	position	There is a tunnel **beneath** the Alps.
beside	position	He sat **beside** her in the front seat.
between	position	The garden **between** the two houses is beautiful
by	position	Go **by** the road to reach your destination.
	time	**By** the time the guests arrived, the snacks were over.
down	direction	He goes up and **down** the stairs for a workout.
during	time	His phone rang **during** the meeting with the CEO.
for	time	They went to Dubai **for** a week.
from	direction	He came running **from** home to catch the bus.
	time	The show will run from 10 p.m to 12 p.m.
in	position	His mother kept his clothes **in** the cupboard.
	location	My parents are living **in** Japan.
	time	The play will end **in** some minutes.
in front of	position	He was waiting for his friend **in front of** the pub.
inside	position	The cat hid **inside** the drawer.
into	direction	Put the food **into** the fridge.
near	position	The car was parked **near** the mall.
next to	position	The best friends sat **next to** each other.
off	direction	She rolled **off** the stairs.
on	position	The jug is **on** the shelf.
	location	Her house is **on** the main road
	time	My vacation begins **on** Tuesday.
onto	direction	The dog jumped **onto** his lap.
out of	direction	The cab arrived the moment they walked **out of** the hotel.
outside	location	There was an old man **outside** the temple.
over	position	He saw flames **over** the school building.
	direction	She jumped **over** the rat.
through	position	A long tunnel goes **through** these mountains.
	direction	He chose to walk **through** the subway.
till	time	They waited **till** the guests arrived to cut the cake.
to	direction	She prefers walking **to** work.
	time	The party is from 9 **to** 11.
toward(s)	direction	The steamer sailed **towards** the riverbank.
under	position	The rat is under my bed.
	direction	The fish swam **under** the ship.

underneath	position	Their bedroom is right **underneath** ours.
until	time	She can't wait **until** next month for the treatment.
up	direction	We climbed **up** the mountains to see the serene view.

CROWN – 17

(Collection of Result Oriented Worksheet by Neharika)

1. They will put on (1) / a note in this (2) / regard for (3) / your consideration. (4) / No Error (5)
2. Children always (1) / quarrel above (2) / petty issues. (3) / No Error (4)
3. After opening the door (1) / we entered into (2) / the room (3) / next to the balcony. (4) / No Error (5)
4. Most of the UP (1) / is a fertile plain (2) / between which (3) / the river Ganga flows. (4) / No Error (5)
5. He freed himself (1) / from the burglar's hold (2) /and ran on (3) / the road.(4) / No Error (5)
6. Having come to Mumbai (1) / he had found that there (2) / was nothing pessimistic (3) / in people. (4) / No Error (5)
7. Although the pain (1) / was behind (2) / his capacity (3) / yet he didn't complain. (4) / No Error (5)
8. Several prominent celebrities (1) / involved in the scandal (2) / are required to appear (3) / to the investigation committee.(4) / No Error (5)

SOLUTIONS - CROWN – 17

(Collection of Result Oriented Worksheet by Neharika)

1. Replace 'on' with 'up']
2. Replace 'above' with 'over'
3. Remove 'into'
4. Replace 'between' with 'through'
5. Replace 'on' with 'across'
6. Replace 'in' with 'about'
7. Replace 'behind' with 'beyond'
8. Replace 'to' with 'before'

CROWN – 18

(Collection of Result Oriented Worksheet by Neharika)

1. She ordered for cook's dismissal.
2. This girl resembles to my sister.
3. He will inform to your brother.
4. This lesson has benefited to me much.
5. Has he disposed the application?.
6. He must compensate this loss.
7. Don't boast your success.
8. Don't violate against the rules.
9. Don't sign on the contract.
10. She dispensed my services.

SOLUTIONS - CROWN – 18

(Collection of Result Oriented Worksheet by Neharika)

1. She ordered the cook's dismissal.
2. This girl resembles my sister.
3. He will inform your brother.
4. This lesson has benefited me much.
5. Has he disposed of the application?
6. He must compensate me for this loss.
7. Don't boast of your success.
8. Don't violate the rules.
9. Don't sign the contract.
10. She dispensed with my services.

TIME AND TENSE

Tense is that form of a verb which shows not only the time of an actions, but also the state of an action or event.

Tense and Time.

- Time is a natural Concept.
- Tense is a Grammatical concept.

She is coming tomorrow.
Time. Future time
Tense. Present Tense
Persons.

I PERSON	II PERSON	III PERSON
I, WE	YOU	HE, SHE, IT, THEY, NAME etc.

PRESENT TENSE.

- PRESENT INDEFINITE
- PRESENT CONTINUOUS
- PRESENT PERFECT
- PRESENT PERFECT CONTINUOUS

Example.

- He plays.
- He is playing.
- He has played.
- He has been playing for three hours.

RULE 232.
PRESENT INDEFINITE TENSE

SUBJECT + V-I (s or es) + OBJECT
I play.
He writes.
The sun rises in the East.
NEGATIVE SENTENCES.
SUBJECT + DO/DOES NOT + V-I + OBJECT
He does not go to office.
INTERROGATIVE SENTENCES.
DO/DOES + SUBJECT + V-I + OBJECT ?
Does he go to office ?
INTERROGATIVE - NEGATIVE SENTENCES.
DO/DOES + SUBJECT + NOT + V-I (s or es) + OBJECT ?
DON'T/DOESN'T + SUBJECT + V-I + OBJECT ?
Does he not go to office ?
Doesn't he go to office ?

RULE 233.
PRESENT CONTINUOUS TENSE

SUBJECT + is/am/are + V-I + ing + OBJECT
He is reading.
The students are fighting.
NEGATIVE SENTENCES.
SUBJECT + is/am/are + not + V +ing + OBJECT
I am not writing.
INTERROGATIVE SENTENCES.
is/am/are + SUBJECT + V + ing + OBJECT ?
Are they playing?
INTERROGATIVE - NEGATIVE SENTENCES.
Is/am/are + SUBJECT + Not + V-I + ing + OBJECT ?
Isn't/ Aren't + SUBJECT + V-I + ing + OBJECT ?
Am I not going to hospital ?
Aren't I going to hospital ?
NOTE. " Aren't I " is used in place of " Am I not " in interrogative negative sentences.

RULE 234.

PRESENT PERFECT TENSE

SUBJECT + has/have + V-III + OBJECT

Mahesh has completed his work.

I have taken bath.

NEGATIVE SENTENCES.

SUBJECT + has/have + not + V-III + OBJECT

I have not taken lunch.

INTERROGATIVE SENTENCES.

has/have + SUBJECT + V-III + OBJECT ?

Has he gone ?

INTERROGATIVE - NEGATIVE SENTENCES.

has/have + SUBJECT + not + V-III + OBJECT?

Hasn't/haven't + SUBJECT +V-III + OBJECT ?

Has he not taken food ?

Hasn't he taken food ?

RULE 235.

PRESENT PERFECT CONTINUOUS TENSE

SUBJECT + has/have been + V + ing + OBJECT + since/for....

It has been raining for a long time.

NEGATIVE SENTENCES.

SUBJECT + has/have + not + been + V + ing + OBJECT + since/for....

I have not been swimming for two hours.

INTERROGATIVE SENTENCES.

has/have + SUBJECT + been + V + ing + OBJECT + Since/for.... ?

Have I been swimming for two hours ?

INTERROGATIVE - NEGATIVE SENTENCES.

has/have + SUBJECT + not + been + V + ing + OBJECT + SINCE/FOR... ?

Hasn't/haven't + SUBJECT + been + V + ing + OBJECT + since/for .... ?

Has he not been playing for two hours ?

Hasn't he been playing for two hours ?

RULE 236.

FOR/SINCE.

FOR. "period of time"

For two hours, for the last 2 years,

for five days, for the last 2 months,

for 5 years, for the last 3 weeks.

SINCE. "from a particular time"

since morning, since the beginning,

since 2008, since time immemorial,

since 7 p.m. , since last year

SINCE → LAST/PAST 4 YEARS

FOR THE ↗

RULE 237.

- ◆ Simple present is used in routine work, not present continuous.
- ◆ If the work will continue for some time only, present continuous tense can be used.

SPOT THE ERROR.

Error. My father is working in a bank and my brother is studying in a school.

Correct. My father works in a bank and my brother studies in a school.

Correct. I am preparing for competitive exams now-a-days.

RULE 238.

SPOT THE ERROR.

Error. Tom works at the moment. Can I take a message?

Correct. Tom is working at the moment. Can I take a message?

- ◆ Use present continuous with action verbs such as 'work' with the time expression 'at the moment'.

Error. I am often playing Tennis on Saturdays.

Correct. I often play tennis on Saturdays.

- ◆ Use present simple with adverbs of frequency such as usually, often, sometimes, etc.

RULE 239.

SPOT THE ERROR.

Error. We rarely go out for dinner, but this week we go out on Saturday.

Correct. We rarely go out for dinner, but this week we are going out on Saturday.

- Use the present continuous to discuss future plans.

Error. He is believing every word she says.

Correct. He believes every word she says.

- Never use the continuous form with a stative verb (a verb that expresses a state, feeling, opinion etc.)

RULE 240. A desire is not an action and takes a stative verb.

SPOT THE ERROR.

Error. She is wanting to purchase a new computer.

Correct. She wants to purchase a new computer.

Error. I am working at my present job since the day my child was born.

Correct. I have been working at my present job since the day my child was born.

RULE 241.

Error. Peter is asking a lot of questions every day.

Correct. Peter asks a lot of questions every day.

Error. We attend a meeting in Chicago this weekend.

Correct. We are attending a meeting in Chicago this weekend.

- Present continuous is used to speak about scheduled events, especially when using buisness English.

RULE 242.

PAST TENSE.

- PAST INDEFINITE
- PAST CONTINUOUS
- PAST PERFECT
- PAST PERFECT CONTINUOUS

Example.

- She sang a song.
- She was singing a song.
- She had sung a song.
- She had been singing a song since 9 O'clock.

RULE 243.

PAST INDEFINITE TENSE

SUBJECT + V-II + OBJECT

I played

He wrote.

Radha made a mistake.

NEGATIVE SENTENCES.

SUBJECT + DID NOT + V-I + OBJECT

He did not play football.

INTERROGATIVE SENTENCES.

DID + SUBJECT + V-I + OBJECT ?

Did she make a mistake ?

INTERROGATIVE - NEGATIVE SENTENCES.

DID + SUBJECT + NOT + V-I + OBJECT ?

DIDN'T + SUBJECT + V-I + OBJECT ?

Did he not watch T.V. ?

Didn't he watch T.V. ?

RULE 244.

PAST CONTINUOUS TENSE

SUBJECT + was/were + V + ing + OBJECT

He was reading.

The students were fighting.

NEGATIVE SENTENCES.

SUBJECT + was/were + not + V +ing + OBJECT

He was not reading.

INTERROGATIVE SENTENCES.

was/were + SUBJECT + V + ing + OBJECT ?

Was I reading?

INTERROGATIVE - NEGATIVE SENTENCES.

Was/were + SUBJECT + Not + V + ing + OBJECT ?

Wasn't/Weren't + SUBJECT + V + ing + OBJECT ?

Was he not going to market ?

Wasn't he going to market?

RULE 245.

PAST PERFECT TENSE

SUBJECT + had + V-III + (before/after) + ... PAST INDEFINITE + ...

The train had departed before I reached the station.

The students had left the class before he reached college.

NEGATIVE SENTENCES.

SUBJECT + had + not + V-III + OBJECT

I had not played a match.

INTERROGATIVE SENTENCES.

Had + SUBJECT + V-III + OBJECT ?

Had she written a novel ?

INTERROGATIVE - NEGATIVE SENTENCES.

Had + SUBJECT + not + V-III + OBJECT ?

Hadn't + SUBJECT +V-III + OBJECT ?

Had I not already visited Goa ?

Hadn't I already visited Goa ?

RULE 246.

PAST PERFECT CONTINUOUS TENSE

SUBJECT + had been + V + ing + ... + since/for....

Ram had been watching T.V. for two hours.

NEGATIVE SENTENCES.

SUBJECT + had + not + been + V + ing + ... + since/for ....

He had not been waiting for her since morning.

INTERROGATIVE SENTENCES.

had + SUBJECT + been + V + ing + ... Since/for .... ?

Had he been waiting for her since morning ?

INTERROGATIVE - NEGATIVE SENTENCES.

Had + SUBJECT + not + been + V + ing + OBJECT + since/for + time ?

Hadn't + SUBJECT + been + V + ing + OBJECT + since/for + time ?

Had I not been flying kites since morning ?

Hadn't I been flying kites since morning ?

Usage (Past indefinite/simple past)

RULE 247.

Habitual action in the past.

Every/per + time

Error. They were organizing this function every year in our college.

Correct. They organized this function every year in our college.

RULE 248.

Some words which show the sentence must be in the past tense.

last/past + time, yesterday, day before yesterday, ago and any adverb of past time.

Error. They have created this web page last year.

Correct. They created this web page last year.

RULE 249.

It is time, it is high time, it is about time, it is peak time etc.

TO + V1

SUBJECT + V2

Error. It is high time you should start reading newspaper.

Correct. It is high time you started reading newspaper.

RULE 250.

We generally use past tense with these words.

wish, if, as if, as though, only if etc.

For 'be' verb --- use 'were'

Error. I wish I was your boss.

Correct. I wish I were your boss.

For other verbs --- use past form

Error. I wish the hurdles get away soon.

Correct. I wish the hurdles got away soon.

RULE 251.

Use of 'when' and 'while' in the past continuous tense.

when + continuous, simple

when + simple, continuous

Correct. When I was sleeping, someone knocked at the door.

Correct. When I saw him, he was playing with his brother.

RULE 252.

Rule 6. Use of 'when' and 'while' in the past continuous tense.

while + continuous, ...simple

while + continuous, ...continuous

Correct. While I was studying, my friends were playing.

Correct. While watching television, my mother prepared dinner.

RULE 253.

Subject + would rather + subject + past tense

- 'would rather' can be used to say that one person would prefer another or others to do something.
- Error. Would you like him to paint it ? I'd rather he didn't.
- Correct. no error.

RULE 254.

Two works in past. W1 happened first, then W2

w1. past perfect.

w2. simple past.

The crops had destroyed before it rained.

Error. The train left the station before I had reached there.

Correct. The train had left the station before I reached there.

Error. The patient had died after the doctor come.

Correct. The patient died after the doctor had come.

RULE 255.

Error. I have seen him yesterday.

Correct. I **saw** him yesterday.

Error. He has returned from London last week.

Correct. He **returned** from London last week.

RULE 256.

FUTURE TENSE.

- FUTURE INDEFINITE
- FUTURE CONTINUOUS
- FUTURE PERFECT
- FUTURE PERFECT CONTINUOUS

Example.

- She will write a letter.
- She will be writing a letter.

- He will have written a letter.
- He will have been writing a letter for an hour.

RULE 257.

FUTURE INDEFINITE TENSE

SUBJECT + WILL/SHALL/MAY/CAN + V-I + OBJECT

He will go to Jaipur.

NEGATIVE SENTENCES.

SUBJECT + WILL/SHALL + NOT + V-I + OBJECT

He will not write.

INTERROGATIVE SENTENCES.

WILL/SHALL + SUBJECT + V-I + OBJECT ?

Will she write ?

INTERROGATIVE - NEGATIVE SENTENCES

WILL/SHALL + SUBJECT + NOT + V-I + OBJECT ?

Won't/Shan't + SUBJECT + V-I + OBJECT?

Will he not go to market ?

Won't he go to market ?

RULE 258.

FUTURE CONTINUOUS TENSE

SUBJECT + will/shall + be + V + ing + OBJECT

They will be playing cricket in the evening.

NEGATIVE SENTENCES.

SUBJECT + will/shall + not + be + V +ing + OBJECT

She will not be washing the car.

INTERROGATIVE SENTENCES.

will/shall + SUBJECT + be + V + ing + OBJECT?

Will she be washing the car?

INTERROGATIVE - NEGATIVE SENTENCES.

Will/Shall + SUBJECT + Not + be + V + ing + OBJECT ?

Won't/Shan't + SUBJECT + be + V + ing + OBJECT ?

Shall I not be playing cricket tomorrow ?

Shan't I be playing cricket tomorrow ?

RULE 259.

FUTURE PERFECT TENSE

SUBJECT + will/shall + have + V-III + OBJECT

He will have completed this project by next year.

NEGATIVE SENTENCES.

SUBJECT + will/shall + not + have + V-III + OBJECT

He will not have completed his work by tomorrow.

INTERROGATIVE SENTENCES.

will/shall + SUBJECT + have + V-III + OBJECT ?

Will he have completed his work by tomorrow ?

INTERROGATIVE - NEGATIVE SENTENCES.

Will/shall + SUBJECT + have + not + V-III + OBJECT ?

Won't/shan't + SUBJECT + have + V-III + OBJECT ?

Shall I not have repaired the car by 5 p.m.?

Shan't I have repaired the car by 5 p.m. ?

RULE 260.

FUTURE PERFECT CONTINUOUS TENSE

SUBJECT + will/shall + have been + V + ing + ... + since/for....

They will have been playing for two hours by 7 o'clock.

NEGATIVE SENTENCES.

SUBJECT + will/shall + not + have been + V + ing + ... + since/for ....

They will not have been playing for two hours by 7 o'clock.

INTERROGATIVE SENTENCES.

will/shall + SUBJECT + have been + V + ing + ….. since/for …. Will they have been playing for two hours by 7 o'clock.

INTERROGATIVE - NEGATIVE SENTENCES.

will/shall + SUBJECT + not + have been + V + ing + OBJECT + since/for + time ?

Won't/shan't + SUBJECT + have been + V + ing + OBJECT + since/for + time ?

Will they not have been playing for two hours by 7 o'clock.

Won't they have been playing for two hours by 7 o'clock.

CROWN – 19

(Collection of Result Oriented Worksheet by Neharika)

1. After Sheetal will return (A)/ from Delhi(B) / I will go to meet her. (C) / No error(D)
2. My younger brother (A)/ has left (B) /for Bhopal last Saturday. (C) /No error(D)
3. I used to work (A) /till 11 pm and (B) / then I go to bed. (C) /No error (D)
4. Air pollution caused by industrial effluents has been studied (A)/ for years, but only recently has (B)/ the harmful effects of noise pollution become known. (C)/No error(D)
5. The judge asked the lady (A)/ if the bag she had lost(B)/ contain ten thousand rupees (C)/No error (D)
6. The ministry was considered several proposals (A)/ for the development of small and medium enterprises (B)/during Budget discussions.(C)/No error (D)
7. Having work(A)/ in both public and private sector banks(B)/she is the most suitable person to take over the post of the chairman.(C)/No error(D)
8. Rohit started a very small business two years ago (A)/ but it grew very fast (B)/as the country is experiencing a boom at that time.(C)/No error(D)
9. Keeping in mind the current market conditions (A)/ it has better for us (B)/ to invest in the infrastructure structure. (C)/ No error(D)
10. Since shivani had lived there for many years(A)/the villagers were very comfortable(B)/ talked to her about all their problems.(C)/No error(D)

SOLUTIONS - CROWN – 19

(Collection of Result Oriented Worksheet by Neharika)

1. omit will
2. b

   It is clearly mentioned that the activity is of last Saturday use simple past in part b. So omit 'has'.
3. c

   'Used to' is used for past habitual action. In part c change go to went.
4. b

   use have instead of has as harmful effects of noise pollution is plural.
5. c

   Replace contain with contained as the sentence is in past tense.
6. A

   Use simple past tense. (The ministry considered several proposals)
7. A

   Replace work by worked as the sentence is of past tense.
8. c

   The sentence is of past tense. So use was experiencing.

9. B

Replace it has better for us with 'it is better for us'. The sentence is in present tense.

10. C

Use talking instead of talked as the latter part of the sentence is in past continuous tense.

CROWN – 20

(Collection of Result Oriented Worksheet by Neharika)

1. Our equipment gets (A)/ damage very often in summer (B)/ because there are too many power cuts. (C)/No error (D)
2. Most children liked to rest in the afternoon (A)/ after they returned from school (B)/ but my son seems to have an inexhaustible source of energy. (C)/No error (D)
3. The cutting down on costs (A)/was the main reason for the firm to survive (B)/ even during a very difficult period. (C)/ No error (D)
4. I will go (A)/ for the dance classes tomorrow (B)/ if I have recovered from fever. (C)/No error. (D)
5. The principal announced (A)/ in the school assembly that the school fees (B)/ will be hiked from the beginning of the next academic session. (C)/No error(D)
6. The terrorist did not (A)/ confessed his crime even till the very end (B)/of his trail and said that he was innocent.(C) /No error (D)
7. If the industrial sector continues to grow(A)/ at the same rate for the next few months(B)/ I think it has a high growth rate this year.(C)/No error (D)
8. Results find that girls (A)/ played not only more than boys(B)/ but also performed better in many fields.(C)/No error (D)
9. Celebrating her fifteen long years in the film industry (A)/the actor announce that he would be doing a new show (B)/on television which would be done completely free of cost.(C)/No error (D)
10. Had I known (A)/ the weather forecast earlier (B)/I would not make plans to go out. (C)/ No error (D)

SOLUTIONS - CROWN – 20

(Collection of Result Oriented Worksheet by Neharika)

1. B

Use damaged instead of damage as the sentence is in passive voice. Third form of the verb is used in passive voice.

2. C

replace seems by seemed as the sentence is in past tense.

3. D (No error)

4. c

If I have recovered is to be replaced by if I recover. Sentences of future beginning with if should be in simple present.

5. C

Replace will with would. (The sentence is in indirect speech)

6. B

Replace confessed with confess. (We use first form of the verb with did).

7. c

replace I think it has with it will have as it is of the future tense.

8. A

replace find with found as the sentence is of past tense.

9. B

Replace announce with announced as the sentence is of past tense.

10. C

replace 'would not make' with would not have made. (for imaginary sentences of the past tense would have and third form of the verb is used). It's a conditional sentence.

CONDITIONAL SENTENCES

When the work done of first sentence, depend on second sentence that sentence is called is conditional sentence.

There are two parts of Conditional sentences

1. If Clause
2. Main clause

Mainly There are three types of conditional sentences

A. If clause in present tense

B. If clause in past tense

C. If clause in past perfect tense

D. Other types of conditional sentences

RULE 261.

IF CLAUSE IN PRESENT TENSE

If + Simple present, simple future

Error. If I will come to Delhi, I will meet you.

Correct. If I come to Delhi, I will meet you.

RULE 262.

If two work is in **future** back to back, and second work is depend on first work, then first work is in **Simple Present Tense** and second work is in **Simple Future Tense**.

Error. She will come to meet you as soon as you will reach Delhi.

Correct. She will come to meet you **as soon as** you reach Delhi.

Error. If the government will be become strict, corruption will surely finish.

Correct. **If** the government becomes strict, corruption will surely finish.

Error. I will help him provided he will mend his ways.

Correct. I will help him **provided** he mends his ways.

Error. Unless he will not take care of his health, he will not recover.

Correct. **Unless** he takes care of his health, he will not recover.

Error. There will be rush at the platform when the train will arrive.

Correct. There will be rush at the platform **when** the train arrives.

RULE 263.

If the sentence is in completely **present form** then it can be in'**Main clause' simple present**.

Example. If it rains, the schools remain closed.

RULE 264.

If there is **possibility** in sentence then in place of **will, 'may/might'** will be use.

Example. If it rains, the students **may** not come for class.

Example. If the fog doesn't clear, the plane **may** get late.

RULE 265.

If the sentence **shows order** then in place of **'will', 'May'** will use.

Example. If you finish your work, you **may** go home.

RULE 266.

If any sentence shows Advise/ suggestion then in place of will, should/must be use.

Example. If you want to remain healthy, you **should** exercise daily.

Example. If you do not know him, you **must** not open the door.

RULE 267.

If any sentence shows etiquette/manner then could, may will definitely be use.

Example. If you meet him, **could** you tell him to call me up?

Example. If you come to Delhi, **would** you come to meet me?

RULE 268.

In 'If clause' In place of simple present tense, present continuous tense can also be use.

Example. If you are waiting for the bus, you **should** better take a taxi.

Example. If you are not reading the newspaper, you **should** let others read it.

RULE 269.

IF CLAUSE IN PAST TENSE

If + Simple Past, Subject + would + V_1

Example. If I had money, I would lend it to you.

This type of sentence shows 'improbability'.

In above sentence **'If I had money'** clearly shows that **'there is no money**.

RULE 270.

'IF' CLAUSE IN PAST PERFECT TENSE

If + Past Perfect, Sub + would + have + V_3

Example. If I had seen you, I would have stopped my car.

In this type of sentence **'If'** can be replace by **'had'**.

Had + Subject + V_3 + obj, subject + would + have + V_3

Example. Had I seen you, I would have stopped my car.

RULE 271.

THREE IMPORTANT FORMULAE

If + Present Indefinite, Simple Future

If + S + had + V_3, S + would + have + V_3

If + S + V_2, S + would + V_1

RULE 272.

OTHER TYPES OF CONDITIONAL SENTENCES

Imaginative sentences

If + subject + were, subject + would + V_1

- For imaginative sentences with all subjects **'were'** will be use.

For below sentences **was** will not use.

Error. He scolded me as if he was my father.

Correct. He scolded me as if he were my father.

In **'If clause'** sentences **'Unless' so long, as soon as, when, provided, suppose, incase, but, for** can also be use.

e.g. (1) **Unless** you work hard, you will not pass.

Note. - with **Unless, 'not'** will not use. **Unless you work hard** we mean **'If you do not work hard.'**

Means **Unless + affirmative = If + negative.**

1. I shall support him **so long as** I am alive.
2. **As soon as** the train comes, there will be rush for seats.
3. **When** he comes to Delhi, I will go to meet him.

Error. We would have gone to the cinema with you if you (not be) ill.

Correct. We would have gone to the cinema with you if you **had not been** ill.

Error. If I (have) the chance, I would have hitch-hiked round the world.

Correct. If I **had had** the chance, I would have hitch-hiked round the world.

Error. We (not punish) by our teacher if we had completed our assignment.

Correct. We **would not have been punished** by our teacher if we had completed our assignment.

Error. If we climb higher, it (become) colder.

Correct. If we climb higher, it **becomes** colder.

Error. If you take a taxi, you (be) in time to catch the train.

Correct. If you take a taxi, you **will be** in time to catch the train.

Error. She'll be ill if she (drink) that dirty water.

Correct. She'll be ill if she **drinks** that dirty water.

Error. If they had really wanted to help her, they (say) so.

Correct. If they had really wanted to help her, they **would have said** so.

Error. We (not lose) the match if our goal-keeper had not slipped.

Correct. We **would not have lost** the match if

our goal-keeper had not slipped.

Error. She (insist) on going if you hadn›t interrupted her.

Correct. She **would have insisted** on going if you hadn't interrupted her.

Error. We ______ the meeting if there is not enough quorum. (postpone)

Correct. We **will postpone** the meeting if there is not enough quorum.

Error. No one _____ you anymore if you are still stubborn. (advise)

Correct. No one **will advise** you anymore if you are still stubborn.

Error. The workers› demonstration ______ if the manager had listened to their complaints. (avoid)

Correct. The workers› demonstration **would have been avoided** if the manager had listened to their complaints.

NON- FINITES

Gerund

RULE 273.

As the subject of the sentence.

Hunting tigers is dangerous.

Flying makes me nervous

RULE 274.

After a number of 'phrasal verbs' which are composed of a verb + preposition/adverb

Example. to look forward to, to give up, to be for/against, to take to, to put

off, to keep on.

I look forward to hearing from you soon. (at the end of a letter)

When are you going to give up smoking?

She always puts off going to the dentist.

He kept on asking for money.

RULE 275.

in compound nouns

Example.

a driving lesson,

a swimming pool, bird-watching, train-spotting

It is clear that the meaning is that of a noun, not of a continuous verb.

RULE 276.

After the expressions.

can't help, can't stand, it's no use/good, and

the adjective worth.

She couldn't help falling in love with him.

I can't stand being stuck in traffic jams.

It's no use/good trying to escape.

It might be worth phoning the station to check the time of the train.

Infinitives

What is the infinitive – The infinitive of a verb is its basic form with or without the particle to.

Examples. –

'do' or **'to do'**

'be' or **'to be'**

The infinitive without to is called **bare infinitive** (**'do'**, **'be'**)

The infinitive with to is called **full infinitive** (**'to do'**, **'to be'**)

RULE 277.

Verbs such as learn, remember, promise, swear, consent, neglect, refuse, purpose, try, endeavor, attempt, fail, carfe, hope, decide, hesitate, prepare, determine, undertake, manage, arrange, seem, forget, agree, regret etc. are followed by infinitives.

Examples.

We endeavor to invite such persons.

We promise to do this word soon.

RULE 278.

Verbs such as order, tell, invite, oblige, allow, permit, compel, teach, instruct, advise, tempt, encourage, urge, request, show, remind, forbid, warm etc. are followed by object and infinitives.

Examples.

The teacher instructed the students to go.

She told me to come there.

RULE 279.

Verbs of expression like- will, can, do, must, may, let are followed by infinitive without to.

Examples.

Let him do this work.

Let it be done.

RULE 280.

Expressions like would rather, would sooner, rather than, sooner than, had better are followed by infinitive without to.

Examples.

You had better tell him.

RULE 281.

See can be used with infinitive or without it.

Examples.

Go to see him.

Go and see him.

RULE 282.

The infinitive is used after adjectives like delight, angry, glad, and astonished.

Examples.

I was astonished to find him.

I was horrified to see the scene.

RULE 283.

The verb knows is never directly followed by the infinitive. It is followed by a conjunction and then the infinitive.

Examples.

Do you know to play the harmonium? (Wrong)

Do you know how to play the harmonium? (Right)

RULE 284.

……. had better is always followed by the infinitive without to.

Examples.

You had better to stop taking the medicine which has harmful side effects. (Wrong)

You had better stop taking the medicine which has harmful side effects. (Right)

RULE 285.

Infinitive is not used with to after verbs of perception like to see, to hear, to feel, to watch etc.

Examples.

I saw him cross the street.

She heard her come downstairs.

RULE 286.

Avoid using split-infinitive.

Examples.

He planned to not go on a vacation this year. (Wrong)

He planned not to go on a vacation this year. (Right)

RULE 287.

We can't use infinitive with to with model auxiliary verbs.

Sometimes we can see some auxiliary verbs i.e. can, could, may, might, shall, should, will, would, must in a sentence so we need to remove to from that sentence to correct that sentence.

You can to go there. (×) , You can go there. (√)

It may to rain today. (×) , It may rain today. (√)

He can to play Hockey. (×) , He can play Hockey. (√)

RULE 288.

We can't use infinitive with to after let + object.

Let me to go there. (×) , Let me go there. (√)

Let us to go to the park. (×) , Let us go to the park. (√)

RULE 289.

If we have make + obj. in an active sentence, we can't use infinitive with to.

They made me to laugh. (×) , They made me laugh. (√)

I was made laugh. (×) , I was made to laugh. (√)

RULE 290.

With some special words we can't use infinitive with to.

Had better, had sooner, had rather, would rather, would sooner after these words we can't use infinitive with to

Ex.

You had better to stop taking medicine which has harmful side-effects. (×),

You had better stop taking medicine which has harmful side-effects. (√)

You had better come now. (×) , You had better to come now. (√)

RULE 291.

In an active style sentence we can't use infinitive with to with these verbs.

If we have these verbs Feel, hear, see, notice, watch + obj. in a sentence we can't use infinitive with to

Ex.

He heard her to laugh. (×) , He heard her laugh. (√)

He watched the movie to enjoy. (×) , He watched the movie enjoy. (√)

RULE 292.

We can't use infinitive with to with do, does, did.

If we have do, does and did before but or except we can't infinitive with to

Ex.

He did nothing but to laugh. (×)

He did nothing but laugh. (√)

He does nothing but to play. (×)

He does nothing but play. (√)

PARTICIPLE

1. A participle is a verbal Adjectives.
2. Like a Verb it may govern a noun or pronoun. Such as;

   Hearing the noise, the girl woke up. (Here the noun 'noise' is governed by the participle 'hearing')
3. Like a Verb it may be modified by an adverb. Such as;

   Loudly *knocking* at the gate, she demanded admission. (Here the participle 'knocking' is modified by the adverb 'loudly')
4. Like an adjective the participle may qualify a noun or pronoun. Such as;

   Having rested, the women continued their journey.
5. Like an Adjective it may be compared. Such as;

   Education is the most *pressing* need of our time. (Here the participle 'pressing' is compared by prefixing 'most')

Use of Participle.

The use of present participle forms Continuous tenses (active voice) with tenses of the verb. Such as;

I am loving.

I was loving.

I shall be loving.

Types

Present Participle

Past Participle

RULE 293.

Present Participle

Participles

Here running is come alone without any helping verb, so from this we got to know that 'running ' is not a part of tense.

If we use only ' run ' instead of ' running ' it doesn't make any sense

So when v1 + ing comes alone, without them sentence doesn't make any sense is known as participle.

If it in the present tense (is, are is used) , then the participle is known as Present Participle.

Here participle is act as an adjective.

RULE 294.

Past Participle

Used for all perfect tense forms of a verb and in the passive voice.

Example. He hid the money in his recently gotten shirt.

Here gotten is past participle because.

1. It acts as adjective because it adds the quality or describes about noun. (Here

noun is shirt)

2. No helping verb is used with ‘ gotten ’ so it cannot be a part of tense.
3. It is third form of verb.

Example. He took the gun. He shot the tiger.
Having taken the gun, he shot the tiger.
[Active Voice]

Here past participle is used with having
So in the active voice past participle can come as

having + v3

Having been taken the gun, he shot the tiger.
[Passive Voice]

[He. Subject of Reference]

Example. He took the gun. He shot the tiger.
Having taken the gun, he shot the tiger.
[Active Voice]

Here past participle is used with having
So in the active voice past participle can come as

having + v3

Having been taken the gun, he shot the tiger.
[Passive Voice]

[He. Subject of Reference]

NARRATION

RULE 295.

Direct	Indirect
I	me/my/mine/myself
you	you/ your/ yours/ yourself/ yourselves
he	him/his/himself
she	her/hers/herself
they	them/ their/ theirs/ themselves
This	That
These	Those
Here	There
Now	Then
Ago	Before
Hence	Thence
Today	That day
Yesterday	The previous day/the day before
Tomorrow	The next day/the following day
Thus	The way/so
Come	Go (based on sense)

RULE 296.

If in direct narration, reporting verb is in present or future tense, then tense remains same.

RULE 297.

If reporting verb say, says, will say, or said are used in direct speech, then they will remian same in indirect. But if 'to' is used then.

say to tell
says to tells
said to told

RULE 298.

Object must be present after tell or told.

RULE 299.

If reporting verb is in past tense, then reported speech will be converted into past tense.

Present Indefinite Past indefinite
Present continuous Past continuous
Present perfect Past perfect
Present perfect continuous Past perfect continuous
Past indefinite Past perfect
Past continuous Past perfect continuous
Past perfect no change
Past perfect continuous no change

RULE 300.

Universal Truth / Habbits / Morality / Proverb / Mathematical Facts

He said, "Man is mortal"

He said that the man is mortal.

He said, "The sun sets in the west"

He said that the sun sets in the west.

He said to me, " I go for a walk daily."

He told me that he goes for a walk daily.

The saint said, " Man proposes and God disposes

The saint said that man proposes and God disposes.

The teacher said, "A stitch in times saves nine."

The teacher said that a stitch in times saves nine.

RULE 301.

Interrogative Sentences.

The the interrogative sentences which starts with an auxiliary verb and whose answer can be given in yes or no form when changed to indirect, we use 'if/whether' instead of 'that' is used.

RULE 302.

In indirect speech, interrogative sentence is change into assertive sentence and question mark is removed.

RULE 303.

Say, says, said are replaced by ask, asks, asked. Sometimes inquire/enquire of is used.

She said to me, "Are you going to college?"

She asked me whether I was going to college.

He said, "Am I looking smart ?"

He asked if he was looking smart.

He said to me, " Can you write a letter ?"

He asked me if I could write a letter.

She said to me, " Will you help me ?"

She asked me if I would help her.

RULE 304.

If interrogative sentence starts with 'wh' word, then conjunction (if/whether,that) is not used but the same 'wh' word is used.

He said to her, " What do you want ?"

he asked her what she wanted.

He said to me, " Why are you happy ?"

He asked me why I was happy.

Ram said to Shyam, " Who are you ?"

Ram asked shyam who he was.

RULE 305.

Special Type

a. "Shall I ever see her again ?", he said.

He wondered if he would ever see her again.

b. He said to the customer, "Shall we dispatch these letters ?"

He asked the customer if they should dispatch those letters.

c. "Shall I bring you something to eat ?" , She said.

She offered to bring me something to eat.

d. He said, " Will you be there on Monday?"

He asked if he would be there on Monday.

e. "Shall we meet again tomorrow?", he said.

He suggested to meet again the next day.

f. He shouted, "Will you keep silence ?"

He shouted at me to keep silence.

g. He said, "Would you like a lift ?"

He offered me a lift.

RULE 306.

Imperative Sentences-

She said to Ramu, " Please bring my book"

She requested Ramu to bring her book.

She said to me, "Have a glass of milk"

She asked me to have a glass of milk.

Ram said to Sita, "Take medicines regularly."

Ram advised Sita to take medicines regularly.

I said to Hari, "Don't pluck the flower."

I ordered Hari not to pluck the flowers.

The SP said to the SHO, "shoot the robber."

The SP ordered the SHO to shoot the robber.

The Principal said to the students, "Get out from office."

The principal ordered the students to get out from office.

He said, " Follow my instructions."

He ordered me to follow his instructions.

The teacher said to Hari, "Don't write on table."

The teacher forbade Hari to write on the table.

OR

The teacher instructed Hari not to write on the table.

She said to me, "Don't park your car here."

She forbade me to park my car there.

RULE 307.

Emphatic Imperative (Use of Do)

He said to me, " Do have a cup of coffee, please."

He requested me to have a cup of coffee.

She said to me, "Do come again."

She requested me to come again.

Rahim said to her, " Do have a seat, please."

Rahim requested het to have a seat.

RULE 308.

Tag Questions

He said to me, "Open the door, will you?"

He asked me to open the door.

She said to Ram, "Bring me a glass of water, won't you?"

She asked Ram to bring her a glass of water.

The leader said to us, "Caste your votes, will you ?"

The leader advised us to caste our votes.

RULE 309.

Sentences with LET –

She said to me, "Let us go to market."

She suggested to me to go to market. /or

She suggested to me that we should go to market.

He said to me, "Let us purchase that house."

He proposed to me to purchase that house./

He proposed to me that we should purchase that house.

She said, " Let him complete his work first."

He suggested that he should complete his work first.

The student said, " Let me take food."

The student wished that he should take food.

The lady said, "Let me have an ice-cream pack."

The lady wished that she should have an ice-cream pack.

The boy said to the teacher, "Let me go home now."

The boy requested the teacher to allow him to go home then.

The principal said to the peon, "Let the students come in."

The principal ordered the peon to allow the students come in.

I said to her, " Let me go to market."

I requested her to let me go to market.

She said to Shyam, " Let him go to Jaipur."

She requested Shyam to let him go to Jaipur.

RULE 310.

Optative Sentences (Good Wishes) –

My mother said to my friend, "May you live long !"

My mother wished my friend that he might live long.

She said to Sita, "May God bless you with a son."

She prayed that God might bless Sita with a son.

She said, "God grant you success!"

She prayed that God might grant me success.

He said to the teacher, "Good Morning."

He wished the teacher Good Morning.

He said to me, "Good Bye."

He bade me good bye.

The leader said, "Farewell my friends."

The leader bade his friends farewell.

RULE 311.

Exclamatory Sentences –

She said, " If I were a bird."

She wished that she would be a bird.

He said, "If I were young again."

He wished that he would be young again.

Ram said, "Alas! I have been ruined."

Ram exclaimed with sorrow that he had been ruined.

The lady said, "Oh! My dog is dead."

The lady exclaimed with sorrow that her dog was dead.

They said, "What a great fall!."

They Exclaimed with applause that it was a great fall.

RULE 312.

Incomplete Sentences –

He said to me, "Congratulations!"

He congratulated me.

The teacher said to the student, "stupid!"

The teacher called the student, stupid.

She said, "Thank You"

She thanked me.

They said to us, "Welcome!"

They welcomed us.

RULE 313.

Must – Had to

She said, " I must leave at once."

She said that she had to leave at once.

Ramesh said, "He must go to Jaipur tomorrow."

Ramesh said that he had to go to Jaipur the next day

RULE 314.

Must not / need not - no change.

He said, "You must not speak to anyone."

He said that I must not speak to anyone.

She said, "You need not purchase this book."

She said that I need not purchase that book.

RULE 315.

Had to - Had had to

The poet said, "After the function, I had to rush to my house."

The poet said that after the function he had had to rush to his house.

RULE 316.

Joint Sentences – [Added/ further added/ add are used as conjunctions]

She said, "I am a girl. I cannot stay here in night."

She said that she was a girl and added that she could not stay there in might.

He said, "Do you know, who is he ?"

He asked me if I know who he was.

She said, "Can you find, where are the keys?"

She asked me if I could find where the keys were.

He said, "Sarla is coming, wait here."

He said that Sarla was coming and asked me to wait there.

He said, "Where is your purse, I have lost mine."

He asked me where my purse was and added that he had lost his.

My father said, "I am going to office, where are you going."

My father said that he was going to office and wanted to know where I was going.

Sita said to Ram, "No,No. I can't play with you. My father has forbidden me to play with you."

Sita told Ram that she couldn't play with him as her father had forbidden her to play with him.

RULE 317.

Indirect Commands – (advice, invitation, request)

She said, "If I were you, I'd stop smoking."

She advised me to stop smoking.

He said, "Why don't you change your watch?"

He advised me to change my watch.

"Would/Could you show me your ticket please ?"

The TC asked me to show him my ticket.

His wife said, "Please, Please don't take risk."

His wife begged/implored him not to take risk.

Mrs. Jacob said, "Don't forget to order Pizza."

Mrs. Jacob reminded him to order Pizza.

RULE 318.

If complete action is not mentioned –

He said, "When I saw her, she was playing football."

He said that when he saw her, she was playing football.

She said, "When I saw them, they were swimming in the river."

She said that when she saw them, they were swimming in the river.

RULE 319.

Fact will remain same –

He said, "I decided not to purchase the house, because it was near the

Railway track."

He said that he had decided not to purchase the house because it was near the railway track

RULE 320.

Wish/ It is time –

He said, "I wish I didn't have to take exam."

He said he wished he didn't have to take exam.

It is time we began planning for our examinations.", he said.

He said that it was time they began planning for their examination

RULE 321.

I/ he/ she/ we/ they + had better → no change in tense

You had better → change in tense if 'advised' is used.

→ no change if 'advised' is not used.

"The children had better go to bed early.", said Ram.

Ram said that the children had better go to bed early.

Sita said, "You had better given up smoking."

Sita said that I had better given up smoking. Or/

Sita advised me to give up smoking.

RULE 322.

Conditional Sentences –

He said, " If I had a permit I could get this job."

He said that if he had a permit he could get the job.

He said, " If I had the tools I Could mend the car."

He said that if he had the tools he could mend the car.

Active and Passive Voice

The voice of a verb expresses whether the subject in the sentence has performed or received the action.

Active Voice – When an action performed by the subject is expressed by the verb, it is an active voice. Active voice is used when more straightforward relation and clarity is required between the subject and the verb.

Active Voice example.

- Hens lay eggs.
- Birds build nests.

Passive Voice – When the action expressed by the verb is received by the subject, it is passive voice. Passive voice is used when the doer of the action is not known and the focus of the sentence is on the action and not the subject.

Passive Voice Examples.

- Eggs are laid by hens.
- Nests are built by birds.

RULE 323.

- Subject and object interchanges.
- There is no change in Tense.

RULE 324.

Pronouns get changed when they change their positions in the following way -

I ↔ Me

We ↔ Us

You ↔ You

He ↔ Him

She ↔ Her

It ↔ It

They ↔ Them

RULE 325.

Present Indefinite -

Active Voice - Sub + V1+ s/es + Obj.

Passive Voice - Obj + is/am/are/ V3+ by + Sub.

Examples -

She helps the poor.

The poor are helped by her.

RULE 326.

Past Indefinite Tense -

- Active Voice - Sub + V2 + Obj.
- Passive Voice - Obj + was/were + V3+ by + Sub.

Examples -

They played football in the evening.

Football was played by them in the evening.

RULE 327.

Future Indefinite -

- Active Voice - Sub + will/shall + V1 + Obj.
- Passive Voice - Obj + will/shall + be + V3+ by + Sub.

Examples -

We will take lunch now.

Lunch shall be taken by us now.

RULE 328.

Present Continuous -

- Active Voice - Sub + is/am/are + V1+ ing + Obj.
- Passive Voice - Obj + is/am/are + being + V3+ by + Sub.

Examples -

She is singing a beautiful song this time.

A beautiful song is being sung by her this time.

RULE 329.

Voice of Past Continuous Tense -

- Active Voice - Sub + was/were + V1+ ing + Obj.
- Passive Voice - Obj + was/were + being + V3+ by + Sub.

Examples -

The teacher was reading newspaper.

Newspaper was being read by the teacher.

RULE 330.

Present Perfect -

- Active Voice - Sub + has/have + V3 + Obj.
- Passive Voice - Obj + has/have + been + V3+ by + Sub.

Examples -

Children have taken their breakfast.

RULE 331.

Past Perfect -

- Active Voice - Sub + had + V3 + Obj.
- Passive Voice - Obj + had + been + V3+ by + Sub.

Examples -

I had written a poem.

A poem had been written by me.

RULE 332.

Future Perfect -

- Active Voice - Sub + will/shall+ have + V3 + Obj.
- Passive Voice - Obj + will/shall+have + been + V3+ by + Sub.

Examples -

She will have completed her home work.

The home work will have been completed by her.

RULE 333.

Voice Related with Modals -

- Active Voice - Sub + any Modal + V1 + Obj.
- Passive Voice - Obj + same Modal + be + V3 + by + sub.

Examples -

Rudra can speak English.

English can be spoken by Rudra.

You need not read this book.

The book need not be read by you.

RULE 334.

Sentences with W-H Families (Interrogative Sentences) -

- Active Voice - What are you doing here ?
- Passive Voice - What is being done by you here ?

Rules of changing some Interrogative Pronouns -

Who is changed in to **By whom**

Whom in to **Who**

How many in to **By how many**

In some cases **What** into **By what**.

How many people attended the party ?

By how many people was the party attended ?

What brings you here?

By what are you brought here ?

RULE 335.

- **It is time to + v1+ obj. - Active Voice**
- **It is time for obj + to + be + v3. - Passive Voice**

Examples

It is time to tale tea.

It is time for tea to be taken.

a. How does she tell a lie ?

b. Don't wear my shirt.

c. Do it immediately.

d. She bade me go.

e. Let us rest here.

Answers

a. How is a lie told by her ?

b. You are forbidden to wear my shirt.

c. Let it be done immediately.

d. I was bidden to go.

e. It is suggested that we should rest here.

QUESTION TAG

What is a tag question?

A tag question is a statement followed by a small-question. We use tag questions to ask for confirmation. In a tag question a statement is made and a question is asked after that.

For an example-

a. You are busy, Arent't you?

Rule 336.

Basic Rules

1. The sentence and the question tag will be in the same tense.
2. If the sentence is an affirmative sentence, the question tag will be negative.

   If the sentence is a negative sentence the question tag will be positive.
3. The pronoun is always used in the question tag.
4. In negative question tags we use the contracted form of the helping verb. Eg- Hasn't , couldn't etc.

RULE 337.

In affirmative sentence the Tag question will be negative.

Examples -

a. A good student always works hard, doesn't he?
b. A teacher goes to school daily, doesn't he?
c. Madhu plucks flowers, doesn't she?
d. You appeared at the SSC examination, didn't you?
e. Helmet makes driving safe, isn't it?

RULE 338.

In Negative Sentence the Tag question will be Positive.

Examples –

a. All the children were not present, were they?
b. Everybody cannot be clever, can they?

RULE 339. For sentences having modal Auxiliary (can, could, will, would, may, might, must, shall, should, ought to, need, would rather, had better, dare) Tags will be shalln't , shan't, will not, won't, can't etc depending on whet ether positive or negative is needed.

Examples

a. A healthy body can achieve the impossible, can't it?
b. A student must be regular in studies, musn't he?
c. Everybody cannot drive, can they?
d. Everbody should wear a seat belt while driving, shouldn't they?
e. Water animals can breathe under water, can't they?

RULE 340. Everybody, everyone , no one, no body are singular. So we use a singular verb and singular pronoun with them. But in the question tag a plural verb and a plural pronoun will be used.

Examples –

a. Everybody has to pay his own bill, Haven't they?
b. None of your friends has arrived yet, Have they?

RULE 341. For Affirmative Imperative sentence we use will you or won't you in the question tag.

Examples –

a. Be assured of all co-operation, will you?
b. Switch on the cooler, will you?
c. Please give me the documents ,wont you?
d. Kindly take a seat, will you?

RULE 342. For Negative Imperative sentence we use will you as the question tag.

Examples –

a. Don't touch the wire, will you?
b. Don't litter here, will you?
c. Don't make a noise in the class, will you?

RULE 343. For Imperative sentences beginning with let us, when a suggestion or proposal is being made the question tag will be shall we.

Examples –

a. Let us go for a movie, shall we?

b. Let us help her to complete the work , shall we?

c. Let us go to meet her, shall we?

RULE 344. For Imperative sentences beginning with let but not followed by us, the question tag will be will you.

Examples –

a. Let Madhu go, will you?

b. Let them do their homework, will you?

c. Let the labourer go, will you?

RULE 345. For imperative sentences having nothing, anything, everything, something as the subject the question tag will have it as the pronoun.

Examples –

a. Everything has gone bad today, hasn't it?

b. Everything is clear, isn't it?

c. Nothing can revive this worse situation, can it?

d. Nothing comes from nothing, does it?

RULE 346. If any sentence has used to in it then the question tag will be usedn't/didn't.

Examples –

a. He used to come here,usedn't he?

b. He used to play the casio very well,didn't he?

RULE 347. Never, no, nobody, hardly, seldom, scarcely, few, little, not ,none ,rarely etc. are negative words. So the question tag will not be negative.

Examples –

a. A barking dog seldom bites, does it?

b. My son never stands still, does it?

c. He hardly came here, did he?

d. He hardly does his duties, does he?

RULE 348. In exclamatory sentences the question tag will contain the auxiliary verbs.

Examples –

a. How beautiful the garden is, isn't it?

b. How big the slide is, isn't it?

c. How nicely the bird sings, isn't it?

RULE 349. Moon, earth, river, motherland, country, ship, train are treated as feminine gender. In the tag question the Pronoun used will be "she".

Examples –

a. The Titanic was thought to be unsinkable, wasn't she?

b. India has never attacked any country, has she?

RULE 350. There is no contracted form of am not. So in question tags aren't is used.

Examples –

a. I am a little late today, aren't I?

b. I am confident, aren't I?

Note. But if the question tag to be used is not in contracted form then 'Am I' can be used.

Examples –

a. I am late today, Am I?

b. I am not busy, Am I?

RULE 351. If the subject of a sentence is there/one/this/that/these/those then the question tag will contain there/one/this etc as the pronoun.

Examples –

a. There is a book on the table, Isn't there?

b. One cannot find a solution to this problem, Can one?

RULE 352. Collective nouns are used in singular forms so the question tag will have a singular verb and a singular pronoun.

Examples –

a. The class has selected its monitor, hasn't it?

b. The team has played very well, hasn't it?

But if the collective noun is not treated as one unit, we use the plural verb and the plural pronoun.

Example

The team have to arrange for their own shoes, haven't they?

SECTION–B

1. SPOT THE ERRORS

Q.1. I saw the highway(A)/ was blocked because of(B)/ accident in the early morning.(C)/ No error(D)

Q.2. My grandfather is(A)/ a famous writer(B)/ which wrote this journal.(C) No error(D)

Q.3. I have pain(A)/ in my right knee(B)/ from three days.(C)/ No error(D)

Q.4. We went to(A)/ temple every morning(B)/ before breakfast.(C) No error(D)

Q.5. I like to see(A)/ sunrise in morning,(B)/ even I have clicked some pics.(C)/ No error(D)

Q.6. We can seen(A)/ stars only(B)/ in the moonlight.(C)/ No error(D)

Q.7. A flock of bird migrate(A)/ to another cool regions(B)/ in the summer season.(C)/ No error(D)

Q.8. I saw a herd of antelope(A)/ moving away(B)/ from the lion.(C)/ No error(D)

Q.9. I like(A)/ rabble of butterflies very much (B)/ in the spring season(C). No error(D)

Q.10. It is confirmed by the research(A)/ that people having sedentary lifestyle(B)/ are more prone to diseases.(C)/ No error(D)

Q.11. (A)Varun is not only eminent / (B)for his novels but also for his/ (C)paintings on cultural heritage./ (D)No error

Q.12. (A)When he went out he left/ (B)the radio on so that his parents shall think/ (C)that he was still in the house./ (D)No error

Q.13. (A)Nitin's nephew who lives in Bangalore/ (B)is eager to travel to Delhi in winter to have/ (C)a glimpse of the capital./ (D)No error

Q.14. (A)Are you aware that by making/ (B)me wait for a long time/ (C)my schedule is getting upset./ (D)No error

Q.15. (A)For he can not do a/ (B)lot of work at a time,/ (C)he rejects many offers./ (D)No error

Q.16. (A)Natural resources are a gift of the nature/ (B)and these are consumed by/ (C)the living organisms directly as well as indirectly./ (D) No error

Q.17. (A)I found/ (B)the two first chapters of the book/ (C)particularly interesting./ (D)No Error

Q.18. (A)Bacon, the father of the English essay/ (B)had a thirst/ (C)of knowledge./ (D)No Error

Q.19. (A)She is very sensitive/ (B)to have a bad/ (C)cough in this season./ (D)No error

Q.20. How many clothes(A)/ have you stuff(B)/ in your bag? (C)/ (D)No error

Q.21. The next generation must (A)/ learnt about the need (B)/ for hygiene and sanitation at school.(C)/ No error(D)

Q.22. More problematically for India (A)/ foreign investors say that (B)/ outflows also reflect rise economic concerns.(C) No error(D)

Q.23. Many official artist(A)/ are being allowed(B)/ to display their paintings.(C)/ No error (D)

Q.24. Young man developed headache(A)/ and began making(B)/ silly mistakes in arithmetic.(C)/ No error (D)

Q.25. Socio-economic reasons(A)/ plays a key role in the illegal(B)/ trade of child trafficking.(C)/ No error(D)

Q.26. The teacher asked his students (A)/ if they had gone through (B)/ either of three chapters included in the prescribed text.

(C)/ No error (D)

Q.27. It is hope (A)/ that a compromise (B)/ will be reached in the meeting. (C)/ No error (D)

Q.28. An employment (A)/ advertisement should contain (B)/ the number of vacancies. (C) No error (D)

Q.29. Major solar projects (A)/ that connects to the grid often (B)/ face the challenges.(D)

Q.30. A unique type of dance (A)/ from Andhra Pradesh, transports viewers (B)/ to another time and era.(C) No error (D)

Q.31. The pilot is (A)/ seriously injured, (B)/ he died within half an hour.(C)/ No error(D)

Q.32. My friend says that he drink tea (A)/ because it is the best beverage (B)/ in the world. (C)/ No error(D)

Q.33. He has not only cheated (A)/ his friends, (B)/ but also his parents. (C) No Error(D)

Q.34. By next year (A)/ Ramesh will take (B)/ his university degree (C)/ No error(D)

Q.35. I slept (a)/ rather late (B)/ last night. (C)/ No Error(D)

Q.36. If I saved money every month (A)/ I would be able to buy a vehicle of my choice (B)/ in time. (C)/ No Error(D)

Q.37. When I read his book (A)/ I implied from it (B)/ that he never understood me. (C)/ No Error(D)

Q.38. The boy laid in the shelter (A)/ for a long time before (B)/ somebody came to rescue him. (C)/No Error(D)

Q.39. The teacher was(A)/ angry at Paul as(B)/ he had not done the homework.(C)/ No error(D)

Q.40. Kids can start early(A)/ on skill-build routines(B)/ where having fun is an important element.(C)/ No error(D)

Q.41. The conference is to start(A)/ at 9. 30 am with the introductory(B)/ speech of the minister.(C)/ No error.

Q.42. She had offered a temporary assignment (A)/ but she turned it down saying (B)/ that she would accept only a permanent one (C)/ No error (D)

Q.43. He could neither clearly identify the man (A)/ who attacked him nor he could name the weapon (B)/with which he was attacked (C)/ No error (D).

Q.44. If Aruna would have come to me(A)/ I would have given her (B)/ some help she needed.(C)/ No error (D)

Q.45. Having acquired some experience, (A)/ she is no longer (B)/ one of those who believes every explanation. (C)/ No error (D)

Q.46. Governments and businesses must reduce (A)/ its own energy use (B)/ and promote conservation. (C)/ No error (D)

Q.47. Households across the state are either(A)/ opting for a more modest lifestyle or compromising(B)/ on the nutritional value of their food in efforts to negate the price rise.(C)/ No error(D)

Q.48. Samuel Smith had a little milk(A)/ in his refrigerator that(B)/ has been taken by his brother.(C)/ No error(D)

Q.49. We can access(A)/the World Wide Web and(B)/ we have internet connection.(C)/ No error(D)

Q.50. That little girl has(A)/ covered nine and(B)/ quarter metre distance.(C)/ No error(D)

Q.51. When shall they (a) / arrive (b) to their destination? (c) / No error (d)

Q.52. The teacher was happy (a) / when he entered the class (b) / which comprised of a hundred students. (c) / No error (d)

Q.53. Females (a) / are not appointed (b) / in our college. (c) / No error (d)

Q.54. The officer (a) / is angry, on the clerk (b) / for not attending to the work. (c) / No error (d)

Q.55. No sooner (a) / She had spoken (b) than he left. (c) / No error (d)

Q.56. What is your opinion? (a) /I am sure the accused (b) / is not guilty of the offence. (c) / No error (d)

Q.57. You will be persecuted (a) / for bringing seeds (b) / into Sydney. (c) / No error (d)

Q.58. You must either tell me (a) / the whole story or, at least (b) / the first half of it. (c) / No error (d)

Q.59. My new neighbours (a) / had been living in Jammu (b) / since twelve years before moving to their present flat. (c) / No error (d)

Q.60. When Shalu arrived (a) / she found them both sitting at the table (b) / waiting on her. (c) / No error (d)

Q.61. The rate off growth for India (A)/is the highest among(B)/ international students in the US.(C)/no error(D)

Q.62. Though Chinese students account for(A)/ near one-third of (B)/ foreign students in the US. (C)/no error(D

Q.63. Thousands of aspirant(A)/ appear in the(B)/ civil service exam. (C)/no error(D)

Q.64. According to official data released(A)/ a total of 186,267 Indians (B)/ was studying in the US universities. (C)/no error(D)

Q.65. Indian students' flow(A)/ to US for higher education(B)/ rose 12.3% in 2016-17. (C)/ no error(D)

Q.66. While the cumulative student population(A)/ has grown, the flow of fresh students(B)/ have reported a negative growth. (C)/no error(D)

Q.67. Experts at the agency's jet propulsion laboratory(A)/ decided to turned to (B)/ four backup thrusters. (C)/no error(D)

Q.68. Overall, an cumulative(A)/ 1.08 million foreign students(B)/ were pursuing higher education.(C)/no error(D)

Q.69. The blood report(A)/ of a cancer patient (B)/ is under examination. (C)/no error(D)

Q.70. The Voyager team got more excited(A)/ each time with each milestone(B)/ in the thruster test. (C)/ no error (D)

Q.71. The chairman(A)/ and retired IAS officer (B)/ reviewed the scheme. (C)/no error(D)

Q.72. Astronomy textbooks were rewritten (A)/ on a wide scale, thanks(B)/ to the newly spacecraft. (C)/no error(D)

Q.73. The committee (A)/ had submitted their report(B)/ to the Union Public Service Commission. (C)/no error(D)

Q.74. The small adjustments is(A)/needed to turn spacecraft antenna(B)/ toward the earth. (C)/no error(D)

Q.75. The committee has recommend(A)/ reduction in upper age limit (B)/ to appear in the examination. (C)/no error(D)

Q.76. The recommendations(A)/ have been made by (B)/ the organisation. (C)/no error(D)

Q.77. Higher education (A)/leaders have (B)/ been in alert. (C)/no error(D)

Q.78. A seven-day time frame has been fixed (A)/ for candidates to report discrepancies (B)/ in questions asked on the examination. (C)/no error(D)

Q.79. The twin spacecraft Voyager 1 and Voyager 2 was launched to (A)/explore the outer planets (B)/ of our solar system. (C)/no error(D)

Q.80. NASA plans to switch(A)/ over to the formerly (B)/ dormant thrusters.(C)/no error(D)

Q.81. The Manager put forward (a) / a number of criterions (b) / for the post. (c) / No error (d)

Q.82. The Railways have made (a) / crossing the tracks (b) / a punished offence. (c) / No error (d)

Q.83. A member shall be required (a) / to pay interest at such rate (b) / as is fixed by the committee. (c) / No error (d)

Q.84. Citizens cannot afford (a) / to take the law (b) / out of their hands. (c) / No error (d)

Q.85. The relatives of the deceased (a) / threatened to revenge (b) / his death, (c) / No error (d)

Q.86. I remember (a) / meet him (b) / five years ago. (c) / No error (d)

Q.87. He asked (a) / that how long (b) / you would be absent. (c) / No error (d)

Q.88. He ate (a) / nothing (b) / since yesterday. (c) / No error (d)

Q.89. Madhuri Dixit is having (a) / a large (b) / fan following. (c) / No error (d)

Q.90. She (a) / is working here (b) / since 2016. (c) / No error (d)

Q.91. I found (A)/ the two first chapters of the book (B)/ particularly interesting. (C)/No Error (D)

Q.92. Education plays a very important role(A)/ in the modern technology world and there are many ways(B)/ to enhance the education level nowadays.(C)/ No error(D)

Q.93. Bacon, the father of English essay (A)/ had a thirst (B)/ of knowledge. (C)/ No Error (D)

Q.94. When the moon comes(A)/ between the earth and the sun,(B)/ her shadow causes a solar eclipse. (C)/ No error(D)

Q.95. Socio-economic reasons(A)/ play a key role in the illegal trade from(B)/ child trafficking within India.(C)/ No error(D)

Q.96. He bought me(A)/ an English grammar book and a pen(B)/ which was very expensive those days.(C)/ No error(D)

Q.97. Heaven or hell make(A)/ little difference for the man(B)/ who believes only in life on earth. (C)/ No error(D)

Q.98. A telephone is(A)/ a convenience to those in(B)/ constant need for communication from a far. (C) No error(D)

Q.99. Strength of a team(A)/ is in its ability(B)/ to maintain harmony.(C)/ No error(D)

Q.100. After watching(A)/ three generations of human beings(B)/ he has collected much information.(C)/ No error(D)

Q.101. We asked them (A)/ why did they want to enter into a business (B)/ with which they were less familiar (C)/ No error (D)

Q.102. She had offered a temporary assignment (A)/ but she turned it down saying (B)/ that she would accept only a permanent one (C)/ No error (D).

Q.103. I do not understand (A)/ what to make employees so agitated (B)/ on such trivial issues (C)/ No error (D).

Q.104. The conference is to start (A)/ at 9. 30 am with the introductory (B)/ speech of the minister (C)/ No error. (D)

Q.105. He could neither clearly identify the man (A)/ who attacked him nor he could name the weapon (B)/with which he was attacked (C)/ No error (D).

Q.106. England achieved(A)/ its primary objectives but(B)/ at a high cost than desired.(C)/ No error(D)

Q.107. The forensic report revealed that(A)/ she had accidentally injured(B)/ follow loss of consciousness.(C)/ No error(D)

Q.108. His car is smaller(A)/ than her (B)/ however very attractive.(C)/ No error(D)

Q.109. The NIA would receive(A)/ financial aid under Nirbhaya Fund(B)/ for safety of women.(C)/ No error(D)

Q.110. The first-in-class molecule shuts down(A)/ oestrogen-sensitive cancer(B)/ in new way, researchers said.(C)/ No error(D)

Q.111. America achieved(A)/ its primary objectives but(B)/ at a high cost than desired.(C)/ No error(D)

Q.112. The forensic report revealed that(A)/ he had accidentally injured(B)/ follow loss of consciousness.(C)/ No error(D)

Q.113. His car is smaller(A)/ than her (B)/ however very attractive.(C)/ No error(D)

Q.114. The organisation would receive(A)/ financial aid under the Fund(B)/ for safety of women.(C)/ No error(D)

Q.115. The first-in-class molecule shuts down(A)/ oestrogen-sensitive cancer(B)/ in new way, researchers said.(C)/ No error(D)

Q.116. One of his elder brothers give him(A)/ butter with bread(B)/ in the breakfast everyday.(C)/ No error(D)

Q.117. The International Treasury recent placed(A)/ India on the watch-list(B)/ on the issue of currency manipulation.(C)/ No error(D)

Q.118. Public transport in our cities(A)/ seems to grown(B)/ more crowded all the time. (C)/ No error(D)

Q.119. The educated unemployment should be given(A)/ some kind of financial relief(B)/ in the form of unemployment allowance. (C)/ No error(D)

Q.120. We have to distribute(A)/ some clothes (B)/ among the poor people.(C)/ No error(D)

Q.121. We sent call letters (A)/ to many candidates (B)/ but a few had reported so far. (C)/ No error (D)

Q.122. For ages India has been (A)/ a champion of peace (B) and non-violent. (C)/ No error (D)

Q.123. A big personality (A)/ had never been invited (B)/ to the ceremony. (C)/ No error (D)

Q.124. The lion was wild and (A)/ that is the reason (B)/ it released in the forest. (C)/ No error (D)

Q.125. Businessmen know that (A)/ decisions are the coin (B)/ of the realm in business. (C)/ No error (D)

Q.126. A company's managers often (A)/ focuses on individual (B)/ components of success. (C)/ No error (D)

Q.127. In life we come across with several things (A)/ and persons that are entirely different (B)/ from what they look like. (C)/ No error (D)

Q.128. Knowledge is a rich (A)/ and unique possessions (B)/ that cannot be stolen or plundered. (C)/ No error (D)

Q.129. Will power helps us (A)/ get through (B)/ all the difficulties in our life. (C)/ No error (D)

Q.130. Failure is a stepping stone to success (A)/ but we wish to keep (B)/ to success avoiding the steps. (C)/ No error (D)

Q.131. The Board indicated that to refrain (A)/ with saying about others is (B) a form of self-censorship. (C)/ No error (D)

Q.132. They who have (A)/ gone to Agra (B)/ are my relatives. (C)/ No error (D)

Q.133. The hotels of Kanpur (A) / are more (B) / costly than Rampur. (C) / No error (D)

Q.134. The Indian way of thinking (A)/ is superior to most of the (B)/ countries of the world. (C)/ No error (D)

Q.135. If I was you (A) / would have told (B) / the chairman to keep his mouth shut (C) / No error (D)

Q.136. Two-thirds of hotels (A) / has been (B) / painted. (C) / No error (D)

Q.137. When she was (A) / returning from college (B) / a ruffian attacked on her (C) / No error (D)

Q.138. Had they have anything like my condition (A)/ they would have felt (B)/ miserable and thought of committing suicide. (C)/ No error (D)

Q.139. This machine looks good (A)/ but is very badly designed (B)/ and doesn't work good. (C)/ No error (D)

Q.140. Like most young women living at homes (A)/ I can't really talk about my ideas (B)/ or what I really feel to my parents. (C)/ No error (D)

Q.141. When he lent me (A)/ some books, he asked (B)/ me to return them back by the end of the month. (C)/ No error (D)

Q.142. One of the most (A)/ intelligent student (B)/ who scored full marks is Ankur. (C)/ No error (D)

Q.143. The patient is comparatively better today (A)/ and I hope that he will (B)/ recover soon, said the doctor. (C)/ No error (D)

Q.144. Neither his father (A)/ nor his mother (B)/ plays chess. (C)/ No error (D)

Q.145. The idea of the Chief Minister's has (A)/ surprised the intellectuals (B)/ to a great extent. (C)/ No error (D)

Q.146. The only one of these (A)/ most intelligent candidates (B)/ who is under 18 is Peter. (C)/ No error (D)

Q.147. His father would have been pleased (A)/ to get him a wrist watch if he would have (B)/ secured higher marks in the exam. (C)/ No error (D)

Q.148. Have you turned (A)/ detective that you keep (B)/ your eye on me like this? (C)/ No error (D)

Q.149. One of these most intelligent students whose example is being followed is Marshall. No error (D)

Q.150. He was congratulated by his teacher (A)/ on his brilliant success (B)/ in the recent examination. (C)/ No error (D)

Q.151. One day they will (A)/ arrive at their destination (C)/ and be considered successful. No error. (D)

Q.152. According to the reports, (A)/ we can conclude that (B)/ many accidents caused by reckless driving. (C)/ No error. (D)

Q.153. The several consequences of (A)/ the decision taken by the (B)/ finance ministry was not foreseen by the bureaucrats. (C)/ No error (D)

Q.154. I never considered him to be a person who would (A)/ go back on his promise and (B)/ then do not even apologise. (C)/ No error (D)

Q.155. Having finished at school (A)/ Mahesh thought/ of going to Goa in (B)/ search some job. (C)/ No error (D)

Q.156. Unless it is acceptable to both the girls, (A)/ an arbitrator would be of no (B)/ use to settle this dispute. (C)/ No error (D)

Q.157. Although the accountant was keen on getting the work (A)/ done through Ravi yesterday, (B)/ he tries to avoid it (C)/ No error (D)

Q.158. Females (A)/ are not appointed (B)/ in our college. (C)/ No error. (D)

Q.159. The officer (A)/ is angry with the clerk (B)/ for not attending to the work. (C)/ No error. (D)

Q.160. No sooner (A)/ I had spoken, (B) than he left. (C)/ No error. (D)

Q.161. It is a truth that (1)/ those who are jealous of others (2)/ never get peace in life. (3)/ No error (4)

Q162. Walking along (1)/the bank of the river (2)/ the road begins to rise. (3)/ No error (4)

Q163. He is telling (1)/ that I have (2)/ stolen his pen. (3)/ No error (4)

Q164. The driver showed (1)/ great talent in keeping (2)/ the damaged car under control. (3)/ No error (4)

Q165. If it were possible to get near when (1)/ one of the volcanic eruptions take place (2)/ we should see a grand sight. (3)/ No error (4)

Q166. Tea grows (1)/ both in Assam (2)/ and Ceylon. (3)/ No error (4)

Q167. He described about (1)/ the unpleasant experiences (2)/ he had in the jail. (3)/ No error (4)

Q168. I shall avail (1)/ of this opportunity (2)/ to meet you there. (3)/ No error (4)

Q169. If I got rich (1)/ I would travel (2)/ around the world. (3) /No error (4)

Q170. Engines used in space shuttles (1)/ are much larger (2)/ and more strong than the ones used in Jet planes. (3) / No error (4)

Q.171. Mistry's office issued a statement(A)/ saying, "A caveat are a notice filed(B)/ by a party fearing legal action."(C)/No error(D)

Q.172. Describing failure of the state health administration(A)/ in protecting life of citizens dying(B)/ of dengue fever as constitutional failure.(C)/No error(D)

Q.173. The death of a seriously ill professor(A)/ while he awaited for six hours (B)/ for an ambulance to be arranged has sparked protests.(C)/No error(D)

Q.174. Jihadi outfit posters announcement funeral prayers(A)/ in absentia raises questions over Pakistan's denial(B)/ that the strike was sourced from its soil.(C)/ No error(D)

Q.175. India moved up only one position(A)/ in the international Finance Corporation's (B)/ ease of doing business rankings.(C)/ No error(D)

Q.176. Addressing CEOs of the group's companies(A)/ Tata hinted that decisions took(B)/ by his predecessor might be reviewed.(C)/No error(D)

Q.177. Responding to state government counsel's(A)/ suggestion to constitution a panel(B)/ of experts to deal with the situation.(C)/No error(D)

Q.178. Rallying around their beloved Chieftains,(A)/ the residents of a place the sun(B)/ of the soil are worried about the party.(C)/No error(D)

Q.179. Many have decided (A)/ to organise the puja(B)/ to ward of (C)/No error(D)

Q.180. Many a time, when the jeep's engine (A)/ developed a snag Raju himself used(B)/ to give the vehicle a push.(C)/No error(D)

Q.181. The communist party of India (A)/ has blamed the district administration and the police (B)/ for the post wednessday developments. (C)/ No error (D)

Q.182. There news agencies (A)/ give us much information on the (B)/ matter of racial discrimination. (C)/ No error (D)

Q.183. The nation health insurance (A)/ scheme for unorganised labourers will be launched in the (B)/ seven divisional headquarters. (C)/ No error (D)

Q.184. Among the other charges against Mr. John was (A)/ the support being taken from the antisocial (B)/ and undersirable elements in his constituency. (C)/ No error (D)

Q.185. A five members team of doctors from Sawai Man Singh hospital (A)/ here started the autopsies at the Bharatpur (B)/ government hospital in the afternoon. (C)/ No error (D)

Q.186. John besides the (A)/ members of the committee were (B)/ not sure about the result of the strike. (C)/ No error (D)

Q.187. He is charged of (A)/his brother's murder (B)/ by the judge. (C)/ No error (D)

Q.188. The MP had been (A)/ debarred of (B)/ attending the party meeting and programmes. (C)/ No error (D)

Q.189. The assembly had maintained (A)/ special diginity of conduct and (B)/ established high standards at debate. (C)/ No error (D)

Q.190. 'Enactment of law is (A)/ not as one think', (B)/ said the judge to the lawyer. (C)/ No error (D)

Q.191. We found (a)/ that a wolf slow (b)/came near to us.(c)/No error(d)

Q.192. The former (a)/ aim was noble (b)/but latter was achievable.(c)/No error(d)

Q.193. Between major cities (a)/ you can still find a train but (b)/ their running status is becoming less frequent. (c)/No error(d)

Q.194. In one of his (a)/ ideas, Garuna suggested (b)/the idea of evolution. (c)/No error(d)

Q.195. Amitank joined a group (a)/ of young sportsmen and gave (b)/ attention of the riches and marksmanship.(c)/No error(d)

Q.196. A novel is (a)/ only a abridge (b)/ version of events.(c)/ No error(d)

Q.197. It is clear that (a)/ the decline of a language must (b)/ultimately has political and economic causes.(c)/No error(d)

Q.198. If one get (a)/ rid of bad habits, one (b)/ can think more clearly.(c)/No error(d)

Q.199. Ansh was so (a)/ tall because he could talk (b)/ to the stars in the sky.(c)/No error(d)

Q.200. In the mountains (a)/ it is the weather (b)/ that ruled over everything. (c)/No error(d)

Q.201. Senior officers (a)/confirmation the contents(b)/ of the document. (c)/No error(d)

Q.202. They succeeded(a)/ in play (b)/games of chess. (c)/No error(d)

Q.203. Plastic containers(a)/ are cheap (b)/and lighting. (c)/No error(d)

Q.204. These conclusions(a)/ made the detectives (b)/to think that it was a fake theft. (c)/No error(d)

Q.205. The role of precious(a)/ yellow metal is undergoing(b)/ dramatic change. (c)/No error(d)

Q.206. When the investigators(a)/ tried to reconstruct the crime, (b)/ they come down against facts. (c)/No error(d)

Q.207. Thick clouds of (a)/expectation charge the atmosphere (b)/with voluminous advertisements. (c)/No error(d)

Q.208. He said that (a)/free alternation are not(b)/ possible without a receipt. (c)/No error(d)

Q.209. The motor car(a)/ is one of the useful gift (b)/of modern science. (c)/No error(d)

Q.210. Leave the (a)/pram outside, he disappeared (b)/inside the bar.(c)/No error(d)

Q.211. Two miles beyond the field (A)/ was seen (B)/ hundreds of sheep including some Deer. (C)/ No error (D)

Q.212. More than (A)/ one idea are (B)/ needed to deal with such a situation. (C)/ No error (D)

Q.213. One of the issues (A)/ which was discussed (B)/ in the meeting was raised by me. (C)/ No error (D)

Q.214. Now a days (A)/ he is teaching Physics (B)/ because the teacher of Physics is absent. (C)/ No error (D)

Q.215. Her beauty (A)/ is (B)/ most unmatched. (C)/ No error (D)

Q.216. John's performance in the drama (A)/ was best than (B)/ Smith's but not as good as Wayn's. (C)/ No error (D)

Q.217. Out of these two players (A)/, John is (B)/ the luckiest as he got the prize. (C)/ No error (D)

Q.218. John besides (A)/ his friends and relatives (B)/ were absent at the meeting. (C)/ No error (D)

Q.219. Can you tell me (A)/ how many eggs and milk he (B)/ has bought home? (C)/ No error (D)

Q.220. A lots of books (A)/ on English Grammar and Composition (B)/ are available in the market. (C)/ No error (D)

Q.221. Different personality theorists(a)/ present their own (b)/definitions of any word base on their theoretical positions. (c)/No error. (d)

Q.222. the concepts of modernity interprets(a)/ the general meaning of such events (b)/and seek explanations for major developments. (c)/No error. (d)

Q.223. once you(a)/ learnt to drive, (b)/you will never forget it. (c)/No error. (d)

Q.224. The scientist could (a)/not hardly complete(b)/ all the experiments. (c)/No error. (d)

Q.225. My brother (a)/asked me that (b)/how long I would stay there. (c)/No error. (d)

Q.226. He is very (a)/angry on me because(b)/ I failed to return his book. (c)/No error. (d)

Q.227. I have (a)/resigned for(b)/ my post. (c)/No error. (d)

Q.228. Mathematics(a)/ is indeed a (b)/difficult subject. (c)/No error. (d)

Q.229. I shall (a)/wait till you(b)/ will finish your lunch. (c)/No error. (d)

Q.230. Many a student(a)/ have stared the(b)/ same work. (c)/No error.(d)

Q.231. I was one of the (A)/ happiest souls (B)/ on the earth. (C)/ No error (D)

Q.232. She caught (A)/ the child (B)/ with the ear. (C)/ No error (D)

Q.233. An one eyed man (A)/ is standing (B)/ outside your house. (C)/ No error (D)

Q.234. The widow who lives (A)/ near his house (B)/ has been facing many crisis. (C)/ No error (D)

Q.235. Some people consider (A)/ wealth superior (B)/ than wisdom. (C)/ No error (D)

Q.236. Many socialogists (A)/ has argued that there is a functional relationship (B)/ between education and economic system. (C)/ No error (D)

Q.237. Probably there was more unity and harmony (A)/ in the human personality (B)/ in the old days. (C)/ No error (D)

Q.238. He being a police officer, (A)/ he should not (B)/ help a murderer. (C)/ No error (D)

Q.239. Scarcely had the servant finished washing the car (A)/ than the master came (B)/ and asked him to clean the office. (C)/ No error (D)

Q.240. The reason why Pakistan (A)/ has not been able to build up its trade (B)/ is due to her poor economic condition. (C)/ No error (D)

2. SENTENCE IMPROVEMENT

Q.1. We are going **upon** vacation.
(A) At
(B) With
(C) On
(D) No improvement

Q.2. Don't tell me that you can't go **onto** us.
(A) By
(B) With
(C) At
(D) No improvement

Q.3. Anybody who says it won't be fun has no clue **what they are talk** about.
(A) What they are talking
(B) What they are been talked
(C) What they has been taking
(D) No improvement

Q.4. These are **terrible steep** stairs.
(A) terrible steeping
(B) terribly steep
(C) terribly was steep
(D) No improvement

Q.5. We **talked into** each other at the mall.
(A) Walked into
(B) Met into
(C) Ran into
(D) No improvement

Q.6. I'm **not surely** which is worse. rain or snow.
(A) Not sure
(B) Ensure
(C) Surely
(D) No improvement

Q.7. It is **one of nice** Italian restaurants in town.
(A) One of the nicest
(B) one of nicely
(C) one the nice
(D) No improvement

Q.8. Richard **stared at himself** in the mirror.
(A) Started himself
(B) Starting himself
(C) Started him
(D) No improvement

Q.9. The laundry isn't going **to did itself**.
(A) to doing itself
(B) to do itself
(C) to doing it
(D) No improvement

Q.10. Someone spilled orange juice **all in over** the countertop!
(A) Over all
(B) All over
(C) All on over
(D) No improvement

Q.11. It's very **difficulty to hiking** across the Rocky Mountains.
(A) difficulty to hike
(B) difficult to hike

(C) difficult to hiking

(D) no improvement

Q.12. I **listened complete speech** of the president on teacher's day.

(A) listened completely speech

(B) listen complete speak

(C) listened completion speech

(D) no improvement

Q.13. One of the cricketers **belong** the Philippines.

(A) belong to

(B) belongs to

(C) belongs

(D) no improvement

Q.14. The Statue of Liberty **is located in** New York.

(A) located in

(B) is located on

(C) locates in

(D) no improvement

Q.15. John's mother is really ill and **need some urgent care.**

(A) needs some urgent care

(B) needs few urgent care

(C) needs some urgently care

(D) no improvement

Q.16. His colleague is very nice man but he **can come** in the meeting today.

(A) could not come

(B) could have not come

(C) cannot come

(D) no improvement

Q.17. Chronic illness **without** treatment is a death's door.

(A) with

(B) of

(C) from

(D) no improvement

Q.18. This is my grandmother's stick which supports her **when walking at the road.**

(A) when walk on the road

(B) while walking at the road

(C) while walking on the road

(D) no improvement

Q.19. Brave soldier always protect their country **by stand right** on the borders.

(A) by stood right

(B) by standing rightly

(C) by standing right

(D) no improvement

Q.20. I have won number of trophies **for** football match.

(A) from

(B) by

(C) with

(D) no improvement

Q.21. The principle was annoyed **at** all the staff of the college as they had not followed him.

A. at

B. on

C. with

D. no Improvement

Q.22. Officials were asked to examine the **likelihood** of providing banking facilities in the area.

A. probability

B. possibility

C. profit

D. no Improvement

Q.23. The storage of fuel has **obstacle** interstate transportation.

A. facilitated

B. hampered

C. burdened

D. no Improvement

Q.24. Rahul gave me **an old scissor**.

A. an old scissors

B. a pair of old scissors

C. a pair of old scissor

D. no Improvement

Q.25. She **gave** most of her time to dance.

A. lent

B. spend

C. devoted

D. no Improvement

Q.26. Please do not **refuse** an offer made by the manager.

A. refrain

B. abstain

C. avoid

D. no Improvement

Q.27. The government is confident that the standard of living will begin to revive again soon.

A. increase

B. rise

C. survive

D. no Improvement

Q.28. Everyone was relaxed by a surprise when she announced her resignation from the company.

A. made

B. moved

C. taken aback

D. shook

Q.29. In view of the gravity of the situation, the police adopted decisive measures.

A. in pursuit of

B. in order

C. in spite

D. the sake of

Q.30. This car is well-styled **whenever** that one is old fashioned.

A. whereas

B. because

C. so

D. how

Q.31. They watched the lions **is being fed**.

(a) has been fed

(b) are being fed

(c) have been fed

(d) No improvement

Q.32. He struggled hard **to** get equality.

(A) for

(b) with

(c) at

(d) No improvement

Q.33. Sarika will try to succeed in business **by fair means or foul**.

(A) by fair means or by foul

(B) by fair or foul means

(C) by any means

(D) No improvement

Q.34. Despite her old age, her movements were as spirited as **a young man**.

(A) a young man's

(B) if a young man

(C) those of a young man

(D) No improvement

Q.35. The quality of food served here is so poor that nobody **would want to eat** over here.

(A) will want to eat

(B) will want to have eaten

(C) will have wanted to eat

(D) No improvement

Q.36. Let us **begin this song**.

(A) this song begin us

(B) us begin with this song

(C) us beginning this song

(D) No improvement

Q.37. Gaurika does not give any cognizance **on** what he says.

(A) to

(B) about

(C) for

(D) No improvement

Q.38. **All, but her**, had made an attempt.

(A) All, but she
(B) All, but herself
(C) All, but she herself
(D) No improvement

Q.39. Prabhat did not **obey to his orders.**
(A) obey his orders
(B) obey him
(C) obey to him
(D) No improvement

Q.40. **The child** is father of **the man**.
(A) A child, man
(B) Child a man
(C) Child, man
(D) No improvement

Q.41. Icy patches **are like on** untreated roads and cycle paths.
(a) is likely on
(b) are likely on
(c) are likely in
(d) no improvement

Q.42. People **will be surprised into** almost all bottled water appears to be contaminated.
(A) will be surprise that
(b) will surprised that
(c) will be surprised that
(d) no improvement

Q.43. There was no **noticeable change in** his behaviour.
(A) notice change in
(b) noticeable changeable in
(c) notices changes in
(d) no improvement

Q.44. When he arrived, he found his friends **had slept**.
(A) sleeping
(b) was sleeping
(c) has been sleeping
(d) No correction required

Q.45. I shall try to record a new song by the end of **this present month**.
(A) this current month
(b) this month
(c) this very month
(d) No improvement

Q.46. He found it difficult to **adapt to** the changed circumstances.
(A) adapt himself to
(b) adapt with
(c) adapt according to
(d) No improvement

Q.47. Is journey by air **preferable than** that of by train?
(A) much more preferable than
(b) preferable to
(c) more preferable to
(d) No correction required

Q.48. The floor of my room is **covered by** a carpet.
(A) covered with
(b) covered upon
(c) covered in
(d) No improvement

Q.49. He glanced at the painting thrice **in** the past five minutes.
(A) within
(b) during
(c) since
(d) No improvement

Q.50. Taxes are high in India, **aren't they**?
(A) aren't taxes?
(b) don't they?
(c) do they?
(d) No correction required

Q.51. My father has made **big garden** in front of the house.
A. a bigger garden
B. a big garden

C. the biggest garden

D. no improvement required

Q.52. She and her sister **had saw baboons** and Black Panther at the zoo yesterday.

A. saw balloons

B. was seen balloons

C. see balloons

D. no improvement required

Q.53. My car is **too big** in which my whole family members can sit.

A. so big

B. very big

C. to big

D. no improvement required

Q.54. **Sometimes peacocks coming into my yard** especially in the rainy season.

A. Sometime peacocks comes into my yard

B. Sometimes peacocks come in my yard

C. Sometimes peacocks come into my yard

D. no improvement required

Q.55. I always eat **hard boiled egg** in my breakfast.

A. an hard boiled egg

B. a hard boiled egg

C. hardened boiled egg

D. no improvement required

Q.56. There is a special quality which makes him **who he is**.

A. where he is

B. what he is

C. whom he is

D. No improvement

Q.57. To learn a language well, one must have patience and **readiness to work hard**.

A. readiness to working

B. be ready to working

C. ready to working

D. No improvement

Q.58. **We should be** bound by a code of conduct isn't it?

A. shouldn't we

B. shouldn't we be

C. aren't we

D. No improvement

Q.59. We **might not be** able to change the situation quickly but we should continue our efforts in that direction.

A. could not be

B. did not

C. had not been

D. No improvement

Q.60. He **shook hand with me** after receiving the prize.

A. shook my hand

B. shook hands with me

C. shook my hands

D. No improvement

Q.61. Please report to me when **you return back from** Delhi.

A. you have returned back from

B. you return from

C. you returned back from

D. No improvement

Q.62. Ravi has been demanding a lot more marks, **doesn›t he**?

A. hasn't he?

B. isn't he?

C. isn't it?

D. No improvement

Q.63. Exercise is **benevolent** to good health.

A. beneficial

B. beneficent

C. bounteous

D. No improvement

Q.64. He parked his vehicle **under** the shade of a tree.

A. on

B. in

C. beneath

D. No improvement

Q.65. **In ease if** it rains, I shall not visit you.

A. If so

B. In case of

C. If

D. No improvement

Q.66. TV sets have become costlier, thanks to the sudden rise in the prices of imported **compounds**.

A. tub

B. components

C. things

D. No improvement

Q.67. The enemy had a reputation for engaging in sneak attacks, we were **frequently** on the alert.

A. occasionally

B. inevitably

C. constantly

D. No improvement

Q.68. Less people came to watch cricket matches to year, so the gate receipts were **lesser** than last year.

A. Many

B. Fewer

C. Lot of

D. No improvement

Q.69. God has **bestowed man** unusual gifts.

A. bestowed with man

B. bestowed for man

C. bestowed on man

D. No improvement

Q.70. Many workers were being **held hostages**.

A. held to be hostages

B. held as hostages

C. held like hostages

D. No improvement

Q.71. **Does not expect** quick results when you start learning a language.

(A) Expect not

(B) Do not expect

(C) Either could be used here

(D) No improvement

Q.72. You seldom work on Saturdays, **don't you?**

(A) do you

(B) don›t you

(C) have you

(D) No improvement

Q.73. There is little point in doing anything about it, **isn't there?**

(A) was there

(B) is there

(C) does there

(D) No improvement

Q.74. He has few reasons for staying, **hasn't he?**

(A) does he

(B) doesn›t he

(C) has he

(D) No improvement

Q.75. **I need have** watered the flowers. Just after I finished it started raining.

(A) don't need to water

(B) needn't have watered

(C) didn't need to water

(D) No improvement

Q.76. She is **no anymore** a great dancer than I am.

(A) no more

(B) not more

(C) Either could be used here

(D) No improvement

Q.77. **Not of my friends** wished me a happy birthday.

(A) None of my friends

(B) Not one of my friends

(C) Both (A) and (B)

(D) No improvement

Q.78. Mother suggested **me to** a dentist.

(A) me seeing

(B) that I should see

(C) Both (A) and (B)

(D) No improvement

Q.79. I didn't ask **you to paid** for the meal.

(A) that you pay

(B) you to pay

(C) to pay

(D) No improvement

Q.80. After putting it off many times, we **on the end** managed to have a holiday in France.

(A) finally

(B) in the end

(C) at the end

(D) No improvement

Q.81. You have to persevere **on** difficult students.

A. with

B. off

C. to

D. No improvement

Q.82. They have **persistent deny** claims of illegal dealing.

A. persistently denying

B. persistently denied

C. persistent denied

D. No improvement

Q.83. You have you **been doing** your homework regularly?

A. had been doing

B. have doing

C. has you being doing

D. No improvement

Q.84. You **will be hold** personally responsible for aid loss.

A. will hold

B. will be held

C. will be holding

D. No improvement

Q.85. I must find out some means **to balance** my budget.

A. to meet

B. to get

C. to achieve

D. No improvement

Q.86. The comments in pencil have not photocopied **very good**.

A. very well

B. a very well

C. the better

D. No improvement

Q.87. The streets are so wet, it **should have** rained last night.

A. could have

B. would have

C. indeed have

D. No improvement

Q.88. I can still picture the house I **grow up** into.

A. grew up with

B. grew up in

C. have grown

D. No improvement

Q.89. He is angry **on me** because I failed to return his book

A. by me

B. with me

C. at me

D. No improvement

Q.90. I complimented him **for** his success in the examination.

A. about

B. on

C. at

D. No improvement

Q.91. He will not buy **some** apples.

(A) a little

(B) much

(C) any

(D) No improvement

Q.92. She **would surely assist him** if he had requested her to do so.

(A) would surely assisted him

(B) would have surely assisted him

(C) will have surely assisted him

(D) No improvement

Q.93. The **alarming report** of the plane crash left everyone in a state of shock.

(1) alarmed report

(2) alarmed reporting

(3) reported alarm

(4) No improvement

Q.94. They were **not** the wiser after hearing the explanation.

(1) none

(2) neither

(3) nevertheless

(4) No improvement

Q.95. Mamta's sister had ribbons **on** her hair.

(1) in

(2) over

(3) through

(4) No improvement

Q.96. He has an **ability** for Economics.

(1) attitude

(2) aptitude

(3) altitude

(4) No improvement

Q.97. They were impressed **of** it.

(1) by

(2) on

(3) for

(4) No improvement

Q.98. Only high officials have access **with** the Prime Minister.

(1) to

(2) for

(3) from

(4) No improvement

Q.99. No other snake **is as poisonous as** this one.

(1) are as poisonous as

(2) is more poisonous as

(3) is poisonous than

(4) No improvement

Q.100. He likes to drive his car at a speed of eighty kilometres **each hour**.

(1) every hour

(2) an hour

(3) hourly

(4) No improvement

Q.101. He is staying with some relatives who **are owning** a farm.

A. will be owning

B. own

C. have been owning

D. No improvement

Q.102. Her **argument** against her competitors duly brought jeers from the crowd.

A. invective

B. praise

C. controversy

D. No improvement

Q.103. An old friend, may I **give you an advice?**

A. give you some advice

B. give you an advise

C. offer you an advice

D. No improvement

Q.104. Practically **every** part of the coconut tree is used by man.

A. each

B. most

C. any

D. No improvement

Q.105. The more they earn, **more they spend**.

A. The more they spend.

B. more they spent.

C. much they spend.

D. No improvement

Q.106. The offerings were placed **on the alter**.

A. on the altar.

B. on the steps.

C. on the platform.

D. No improvement

Q.107. The principal congratulated the student **for his** success in the examination.

A. in his

B. on his

C. over his

D. No improvement

Q.108. **Really** speaking, no man is perfect

A. Strictly

B. Slightly

C. Vaguely

D. No improvement

Q.109. Mankind **does** not know this.

A. do

B. had

C. is

D. No improvement

Q.110. I am sorry but I **will not believe** the story you have told me.

A. do not believe

B. am not believed

C. have not believed

D. No improvement

Q.111. Ideas have **much larger** impact than violence.

(A) a much large

(B) much largest

(C) a much larger

(D) No improvement

Q.112. Success is basically about how you **might turn adverse** situations in your favour.

(A) must turn adverse

(B) can turn adverse

(C) could have turned adverse

(D) No improvement

Q.113. A bank draft is a payment on behalf of a payer that **is guarantee by** the issuing bank.

(A) is guaranteed by

(B) was guaranteed by

(C) is a guaranteed by

(D) No improvement

Q.114. Babies like milk, **isn't it**?

(A) don't they?

(B) aren't it?

(C) do they?

(D) No improvement

Q.115. The police caught **the victim** red handed.

(A) thief

(B) the prisoner

(C) the thief

(D) No improvement

Q.116. This house belongs to **the blind**.

(A) blinds

(B) the blind people

(C) blind

(D) No improvement

Q.117. **I am having** more than five hundred books.

(A) had

(B) have

(C) have had

(D) No improvement

Q.118. She is **enough mature** to take her own decisions.

(A) mature enough

(B) enough old

(C) enough

(D) No improvement

Q.119. She is **happiest of all**.

(A) more happier than all

(B) the happiest of all

(C) most happiest of all

(D) No improvement

Q.120. Force is **incapable of changing** the ideas and beliefs of the people.

(A) incapability of change

(B) an incapable of changing

(C) incapable of changed

(D) No improvement

Q.121. I **take my hat off to** all those who donate

blood regularly.

(A) welcome

(B) admire

(C) congratulate

(D) encourage

Q.122. Kindly tell him **by word of mouth** that I shall be dining with her tonight.

(A) orally

(B) using gestures

(C) jargons

(D) No improvement

Q.123. You better learn **to toe the line** to avoid consequences.

(A) to disobey rule

(B) to be indifferent to rule

(C) to make your own rule

(D) To follow the lead

Q.124. Hari was **taken to task** by the teacher for making a noise in the class.

(A) scolded

(B) rewarded

(C) appreciated

(D) No improvement

Q.125. The teacher announced that she had no **blue-eyed boys** in class.

(A) favourites

(B) young boys

(C) royal children

(D) foreigners

Q.126. The passing of anti-defection law **struck a chill to the heart** of every opportunistic legislator.

(A) caused anger

(B) caused relief

(C) aroused fear

(D) awakened bitterness

Q.127. Winslet was **over head and ears** in love with Leonardo.

(A) cautiously

(B) carefully

(C) brilliantly

(D) completely

Q.128. Who would not **look blue**, having to pay those heavy bills of entertainment every months?

(A) upset

(B) enjoy

(C) sad

(D) No improvement

Q.129. It was on the **tip my tongue** when you also proposed that we should go to the auditorium.

(A) slip of tongue

(B) on lips

(C) about to say

(D) None

Q.130. The step mother **shed crocodile tears** on the death of her step son.

(A) to cry for no reason

(B) felt sorry for the son

(C) shed tears of blood

(D) false tears of sorrows

Q131. In these circumstances, they will not be able to meet the **assign target** to them.

A. targeted assignment

B. assign target

C. target assigned

D. No improvement

Q132. It took a long time for him to realise, **what was truth**?

A. what is truth?

B. what the truth was?

C. what was the truth?

D. No improvement

Q133. Roads are wet, it **must have** rained last night

A. must had

B. might has

C. must has

D. No improvement

Q134. If one works hard, **you have got** rewards

A. one gets

B. one has got

C. one will get

D. No improvement

Q135. His reasons can be good. **Is it not?**

A. Can they?

B. Isn't he?

C. Can't they

D. No improvement

Q136. Matthew is **addicted to gamble.**

A. is addicted for gamble

B. is addicted to gambling

C. is addicted on gamble

D. No improvement

Q137. Despite of applying for many jobs, he is still jobless.

A. Despite for applying for many jobs

B. Despite to apply for many job

C. Despite applying for many jobs

D. No improvement

Q138. He asked me **what I was named**.

A. what is my name

B. what my name was

C. what my name is

D. No improvement

Q139. You should never **put off** till tomorrow what you can do today.

A. does

B. desires

C. postpones

D. No improvement

Q140. He is busy now **he has decided to write** the letter later.

A. he can write

B. he will writes

C. he will be writing

D. No improvement

Q.141. If he **would have stolen** the money, he would have done wrong.

(A) had stolen

(B) would steal

(C) stole

(D) No improvement

Q.142. You seem to be **enough rich** to buy anything you like.

(A) too rich

(B) very rich

(C) rich enough

(D) No improvement

Q.143. If I had accepted his invitation the years ago, I would have become a millionaire by now.

(A) If I was to accept

(B) If I were to accept

(C) If I did accept

(D) No improvement

Q.144. Yesterday **I have received** a legal notice from the Bank from repayment of the loan I had taken from it.

(A) I did receive

(B) I had received

(C) I received

(D) No improvement

Q.145. The Desais soon **got used to live** in the country.

(A) were used to live

(B) got used to living

(C) had used to live

(D) No improvement

Q.146. We **usual have** a meeting of all department heads every Friday.

A. as usual has

B. as usually have

C. usually have

D. unusually have

Q.147. Over fifty per cent of people in the country **not have any** access to banking services.

A. have not any

B. are having not

C. does not have

D. do not have any

Q.148. Anil's friends have convinced him **withdrawn his** resignation.

A. in withdrawing him

B. for withdrawal of

C. to withdraw from his

D. to withdraw his

Q.149. India and China have **many large number** of educated workers than Brazil.

A. a larger number

B. the largest number

C. large numbers

D. very larger number

Q.150. Many accidents at the factory **are caused of** workers do not read warning signs.

A. is the cause of

B. are caused by

C. are caused because

D. are a cause of

Q151. He was weary of failure, **didn't he** ?

(1) isn't he?

(2) wasn't he?

(3) doesn't he?

(4) No improvement

Q152. What **you have been** doing in the workshop since last month ?

(1) have you done

(2) you have done

(3) have you been doing

(4) No improvement

Q153. Keats **says** the idea very well in his poems.

(1) speaks

(2) describes

(3) expresses

(4) No improvement

Q154. The enemy soldiers **went back** hastily.

(1) returned

(2) retreated

(3) retrenched

(4) No improvement

Q155. No sooner had the teacher entered the room **and** the boys rushed to their seats.

(1) when

(2) than

(3) but

(4) No improvement

Q156. We have already **disposed our** old house.

(1) disposed off

(2) disposed out

(3) disposed of

(4) No improvement

Q157. We can buy anything in this shop, **can we** ?

(1) isn't it?

(2) can't we?

(3) don' t we?

(4) No improvement

Q158. If I had followed your advice, I **would not regret** today.

(1) will not regret

(2) had not regretted

(3) would not have regretted

(4) No improvement

Q159. Somebody must be made to answer **for** the securities scam.

(1) to

(2) after

(3) upon

(4) No improvement

Q160. Corruption is **the most serious** problem in India.

(1) the more serious

(2) the seriouser

(3) serious

(4) No improvement

Q161. In the desert, the sun is the master, all else **resigns** before its merciless rays.

(1) collapses

(2) falls

(3) retires
(4) No improvement

Q162. I intend **to learn** French next year.
(1) learning
(2) learn
(3) have learnt
(4) No improvement

Q163. The police **needed him** for armed robbery.
(1) liked
(2) was after
(3) were looking to
(4) No improvement

Q164. There is **no more room** for you in this compartment.
(1) no seat
(2) no more space
(3) no more accommodation
(4) No improvement

Q165. It is easy to see why cities grew **on the river banks**.
(1) along the river banks
(2) in the river banks
(3) upon the river banks
(4) No improvement

Q166. The only way to solve the racial problem **is by** education
(1) because of
(2) thanks to
(3) on account of
(4) No improvement

Q167. He may be poor now but he appears **to be rich**.
(1) to seem rich
(2) rich to be
(3) to have been rich
(4) No improvement

Q168. The suspected couple was **taken away** from the airport through a side entrance to the police station for interrogation.
(1) whisked
(2) rushed
(3) guided
(4) No improvement

Q169. She left the room feeling **contrite**.
(1) sorry for what she had done
(2) rather ill
(3) extremely irritated
(4) No improvement

Q170. The transport workers have organised a strike **asking** for more salary.
(1) demanding
(2) begging
(3) requesting
(4) No improvement

Q171. Obviously he isn't **cut up** to be a good teacher.
(1) cut out
(2) cut in
(3) cut for
(4) No improvement

Q172. Power got with money is the most **craved for** today.
(1) sought after
(2) wished for
(3) welcomed for
(4) No improvement

Q173. The brown shirt **wants washing**.
(1) has to wash
(2) is in need of a wash
(3) requires a wash
(4) No improvement

Q174. You are asked to copy this letter **word by word**.
(1) word for word
(2) word with word
(3) word to word
(4) No improvement

Q175. The weak man is a slave to his **sensuous** pleasures.
(1) sensory
(2) sensual

(3) secondary
(4) No improvement

Q176. To get into the building I'll **disguise as a** reporter.
(1) disguise to be
(2) disguise as one
(3) disguise myself
(4) No improvement

Q177. He denied that he **had not forged** my signature.
(1) would not forge
(2) had forged
(3) did not forge
(4) No improvement

Q178. If **I had played well**, I would have won the match.
(1) I played well
(2) I play well
(3) I am playing will
(4) No improvement

Q179. Since the records are missing, the possibility of paying more than one compensation for the same piece of land cannot be ruled **aside**.
(1) out
(2) off
(3) away
(4) No improvement

Q180. A callous system **generates** nothing but a misanthrope.
(1) develops
(2) induces
(3) produces
(4) No improvement

Q181. Who **you said was** coming to see me this morning ?
(1) you did say
(2) did you say
(3) did you say that
(4) No improvement

Q182. He is **not only known for his wealth** but also for his learning.
(1) not only known for his learning
(2) only known for his wealth
(3) known not only for his wealth
(4) No improvement

Q183. Owing to the close **affinity** of the architect and the builder, the project was completed ahead of schedule.
(1) termination
(2) cooperation
(3) collaboration
(4) No improvement

Q184. The servant was disturbed as her son was now **out of sight** due to bad company.
(1) out of bounds
(2) out of control
(3) out of reach
(4) No improvement

Q185. **Whenever I doubt** about the meaning of a word, I look up my dictionary.
(1) Whenever I have a doubt
(2) Whenever I am in doubt
(3) The moment I doubt
(4) No improvement

Q186. He behaves **like coward**.
(1) cowardly
(2) in a cowardly manner
(3) as if he was a coward
(4) No improvement

Q187. **Neither of them went** to the cinema.
(1) Both of them did not go
(2) Both did not go
(3) Neither went
(4) No improvement

Q188. **I used to have** very thick hair.
(1) use to have
(2) used to having
(3) used to had
(4) No improvement

Q189. They **reached at Calcutta** on Monday last.

(1) reached to Calcutta
(2) reached on Calcutta
(3) reached Calcutta
(4) No improvement

Q190. I **did not saw** my cousin in Madras.
(1) not seen
(2) did not see
(3) did not seen
(4) No improvement

Q191. Several disciples **follow** the footsteps of their guru.
(1) follow in
(2) follow on
(3) are following
(4) No improvement

Q192. I **did not see him** since he wrote last.
(1) I could not see him
(2) I shall not see him
(3) I have not seen him
(4) No improvement

Q193. Who will provide **relief** to the poor in this country ?
(1) money
(2) succour
(3) shelter
(4) No improvement

Q194. Most of the non-Western countries **have been subject either to** total colonial rule or varying degrees of economic control and their native population has either been destroyed or Westernised.
(1) has been subject to either
(2) either have been subject to
(3) have been either subjected to
(4) No improvement

Q195. **Strenuous as it was,** they went on with their task.
(1) since it was
(2) because it was
(3) although it was
(4) No improvement

Q196. **The strong breeze** blew his hat away.
(1) The strong air
(2) The strong breath
(3) The strong wind
(4) No improvement

Q197. The Japanese are **hardly working people.**
(1) a hard working people
(2) a hardly working people
(3) hard working people
(4) No improvement

Q198. The monkey was seated at the **foot** of a tree.
(1) bottom
(2) end
(3) root
(4) No improvement

Q199. My father lives **on Delhi.**
(1) in Delhi
(2) at Delhi
(3) inside Delhi
(4) No improvement

Q200. He will come **instantaneously.**
(1) just now
(2) presently
(3) instantly
(4) No improvement

Q201. He has been growing weaker and his life now hangs **with a** thread.
(1) on
(2) to
(3) by
(4) No improvement

Q202. The passengers were afraid, but the captain **consoled** them that there was no danger.
(1) guaranteed
(2) assured
(3) confided
(4) No improvement

Q203. **Would you** like some water ?
(1) Can
(2) Do
(3) Shall
(4) No improvement

Q204. The injured man had been shot **from his back**.
(1) in the back
(2) to the back
(3) by his back
(4) No improvement

Q205. Luckily we've got **the few** minutes to spare.
(1) quite few
(2) a little
(3) a few
(4) No improvement

Q206. We hurried to the door, but **nobody is there**.
(1) nobody was there
(2) nobody are there
(3) nobody were there
(4) No improvement

Q207. I cannot say it to you right now. We will **discuss** it tomorrow.
(1) demand
(2) expect
(3) explain
(4) No improvement

Q208. Let's buy a new sari with the annual bonus, **can we** ?
(1) shall we
(2) could we
(3) isn't it
(4) No improvement

Q209. He is not only a good teacher **but** a good man.
(1) instead also
(2) but seldom
(3) but also
(4) No improvement

Q210. The position **gives** an excellent remuneration.
(1) offers
(2) carries
(3) holds
(4) No improvement

Q211. The trek is difficult but it is **worth well the endeavour**.
(1) well worth the endeavour
(2) worth the endeavour well
(3) the endeavour well worth
(4) No improvement

Q212. The manager was given a holiday and so he decided to go **to the hitch-hiking**.
(1) for the hitch-hiking
(2) for hitch-hiking
(3) hitch-hiking
(4) No improvement

Q213. Goaded to frenzy, **the bull charged its tormentors**.
(1) the tormentors were charged by the bull
(2) the tormentors were being charged by the bull
(3) the bull charged on its tormentors
(4) No improvement

Q214. The war was a time of **tribulations** for all of us.
(1) intimacy
(2) placidity
(3) stupidity
(4) No improvement

Q215. The temptations that **bestow** young people today are ruining them.
(1) appeal
(2) beset
(3) confront
(4) No improvement

Q216. We kept all the old paintings in a place where they **would remain safe** from harm or danger.

(1) will remain safe

(2) are safe

(3) may remain safe

(4) No improvement

Q217. The tragedy is **reflection** of an episode that took place a decade ago.

(1) rendition

(2) reincarnation

(3) reminiscent

(4) No improvement

Q218. He **makes** excellent portraits.

(1) paints

(2) portrays

(3) illustrates

(4) No improvement

Q219. The dog **bite him.**

(1) beat him

(2) bit him

(3) bitten him

(4) No improvement

Q220. Students will have to **take the test again** tomorrow.

(1) apply the test

(2) avoid the test

(3) retain the test

(4) No improvement

Q221. The innocence of the child was **obliterated** due to hard labour.

(1) maintained

(2) increased

(3) destroyed

(4) No improvement

Q222. He was **given a lot of pressure** to sign the deed.

(1) told

(2) forced

(3) asked

(4) No improvement

Q223. **Presently**, she is busy composing the music for her next play.

(1) At the present

(2) In the present

(3) At present

(4) No improvement

Q224. Modern medicine **promotes** good health.

(1) means

(2) preaches about

(3) praises

(4) No improvement

Q225. Despite having many other opportunities, he **went** for Police Service.

(1) liked

(2) opted

(3) selected

(4) No improvement

Q226. I love him because he is a good man **by heart.**

(1) at heart

(2) of heart

(3) in heart

(4) No improvement

Q227. The editor gave me **a time line** to finish the article.

(1) guideline

(2) deadline

(3) decline

(4) No improvement

Q228. **Since she directing** the play for quite some time, she knows the actors really well.

(1) Since she has directed

(2) Since she has been directing

(3) Since she was directing

(4) No improvement

Q229. She **is scrutinising** hard for the final examination.

(1) recollecting

(2) recapitulating

(3) revising

(4) No improvement

Q230. This is the **late** edition of the Shakespearean play which was originally published in 1603.

(1) later

(2) latest

(3) latter

(4) No improvement

Q231. You can borrow my laptop **as long as** you promise not to misuse it.

(1) only long as

(2) too long as

(3) so long as

(4) No improvement

Q232. On receiving his appointment letter, Ravi **treated us with** a sumptuous meal.

(1) treated us to

(2) treated us for

(3) treated us by

(4) No improvement

Q233. He proved himself unique for he refused **to go with the tide**.

(1) go in the tide

(2) go against the tide

(3) go by the tide

(4) No improvement

Q234. The building you are talking about **is not existing**.

(1) have not been existing

(2) does not exist

(3) has not been existing

(4) No improvement

Q235. His lecture was **banned** because of the bandh.

(1) called off

(2) disturbed

(3) interrupted

(4) No improvement

Q236. Some people garner new **experiences** after retirement.

(1) episodes

(2) events

(3) happenings

(4) No improvement

Q237. The deaf man asked me to **speak up**.

(1) speak in

(2) speak into

(3) speak down

(4) No improvement

Q238. The **difficulty** level of this problem is extremely great.

(1) perplexity

(2) hindrance

(3) intricacy

(4) No improvement

Q239. **The cooking soup on the stove got burnt.**

(1) The soup cooking on the stove got burnt.

(2) The soup which has been cooking on the stove gets burnt.

(3) The soup which have been cooking on the stove got burnt

(4) No improvement

Q240. Diamonds are **eternal**.

(1) enduring

(2) forever

(3) imperishable

(4) No improvement

Q241. I have studied such characters at **close hand**.

(1) close to hand

(2) at close quarters

(3) close off hand

(4) No improvement

Q242. **I must quit the job now if I prefer a better one.**

(1) It's time I quit the job if I prefer a better one

(2) It's time I quit the better job if I prefer

(3) It's time the job quits me before I get the better job

(4) No improvement

Q243. The workers were **bent at getting** their dues.

(1) bent for getting
(2) bent upon getting
(3) bent in getting
(4) No improvement

Q244. Jatin's case against Jagat was **trivial**.

(1) insignificant
(2) harmful
(3) tolerable
(4) No improvement

Q245. How can one adjust among **a passive lot**?

(1) people who are cold and without feeling
(2) A lot of crowd
(3) Indolent people
(4) No improvement

Q246. Her activities are **limited only to** cooking and washing clothes.

(1) limited by
(2) limited to
(3) not limited to
(4) No improvement

Q247. **My sister doesn't have as much jewellery as my mother.**

(1) My mother has jewellery but not more than my sister.
(2) My sister has too much jewellery.
(3) My mother has more jewellery than my sister.
(4) No improvement

Q248. She prefers **tea than** coffee.

(1) tea to
(2) tea over
(3) tea more than
(4) No improvement

Q249. **Mutual shakes of hands was exchanged.**

(1) Both shakes of hands was carried.
(2) The hand shakes were exchanged.
(3) They shook hands with each other.
(4) No improvement.

Q250. The incident **made** a deep impression on me.

(1) rounded
(2) profound
(3) slight
(4) No improvement

Q251. **He, I, She and They cooked the food.**

(1) I, He, She and They cooked the food.
(2) They, I, He and She cooked the food.
(3) He, She, They and I cooked the food.
(4) No improvement.

Q252. The newspaper report of the killing **verified** with the police findings.

(1) authenticated
(2) corroborated
(3) confirmed
(4) No improvement

Q253. The saint **said that men are mortal**.

(1) said that men is mortal.
(2) advised men are mortal.
(3) said that men were mortal.
(4) No improvement.

Q254. There is no **alternate** offered to us.

(1) way
(2) solution
(3) choice
(4) No improvement

Q255. The voluntary organization appealed to the people to come forward to help the victims and said that **each may contribute what they can.**

(1) each may contribute what he can
(2) each may contribute what one can
(3) each may contribute what each one can
(4) No improvement

Q256. There is no **escape** in the container for the water to flow.

(1) outlet
(2) inlet
(3) drainage
(4) No improvement

Q257. The problem was **so** complicated to be solved in a day.
(1) too
(2) very
(3) much
(4) No improvement

Q258. **They left the hotel by car where they had been staying.**
(1) They left the hotel where they had been staying, by car.
(2) They left where they were staying in a hotel by car.
(3) In a car they left where they were staying in a hotel
(4) No improvement

Q259. Will you **lend me few rupees** in this hour of need ?
(1) lend me a little rupees
(2) borrow me a few rupees
(3) lend me a few rupees
(4) No improvement

Q260. Five years ago today, **I am sitting** in a small Japanese car, driving across Poland towards Berlin.
(1) was sitting
(2) sat
(3) have been sitting
(4) No improvement

Q261. He could not **look** anything in the dark room.
(1) look at
(2) see
(3) see through
(4) No improvement

Q262. No one could explain how a calm and balanced person like him could **penetrate** such a mindless act on his friends.
(1) perpetuate
(2) perpetrate
(3) precipitate
(4) No improvement

Q263. **Anyone who would speak** with authority on the poets of the Renaissance must have a broad acquaintance with the writers of classical antiquity.
(1) Anyone who will speak
(2) If one would speak
(3) Anyone desirous for speaking
(4) No improvement

Q264. He found a **wooden broken chair** in the room,
(1) wooden and broken chair
(2) broken wooden chair
(3) broken and wooden chair
(4) No improvement

Q265. The starving and crawling people in the television programme **looked** more like beasts than tiring creatures.
(1) posed
(2) resembled
(3) seemed
(4) No improvement

Q266. I took the cycle **which he bought yesterday.**
(1) that he bought yesterday.
(2) which he had bought yesterday.
(3) that he has bought yesterday.
(4) No improvement

Q267. Having only a few hours left, she wondered **as** she would finish the assignment.
(1) that if
(2) whether
(3) that
(4) No improvement

Q268. It became clear that the strangers were heading **into** a serious disaster.
(1) along
(2) towards

(3) on

(4) No improvement

Q269. Twenty kms **are not a great distance** in these days of fast moving vehicles.

(1) is not a great distance

(2) are not too great a distance

(3) aren't proving a great distance

(4) No improvement

Q270. **I adapted** a new method to solve the problem.

(1) I have been adopted

(2) I adopted

(3) I was adapted

(4) No improvement

Q271. Hoping not to be disturbed, I sat down in my easy chair to read the book, **I won as a prize**.

(1) I had won as a prize

(2) I have won as prize

(3) I had to win as a prize

(4) No improvement

Q272. If you are living near a market place you should be ready to **bear the disturbances** caused by traffic.

(1) to bear upon

(2) to bear with

(3) to bear away

(4) No improvement

Q273. The more they earn, **more they spend** on luxury items.

(1) more they should spend

(2) the more they spend

(3) the more they ought to spend

(4) No improvement

Q274. You have come here with a view **to insult me**.

(1) to insulting me

(2) of insulting me

(3) for insulting me

(4) No improvement

Q275. A little rail-road engine **was employed by a station yard** for doing small pieces of work.

(1) was made by a station yard

(2) was used at the station yard

(3) was employed at the station yard

(4) No improvement

Q276. **From an aesthetic point of view, the painting did not appeal to me.**

(1) From the viewpoint of aesthetics, the painting did not appeal to me

(2) The painting had no aesthetic appeal to me

(3) From an aesthetic point of view, the painting had a little appeal to me

(4) No improvement

Q277. **The child tossed in bed burning with fever.**

(1) The child in bed, burning with fever tossed

(2) The child burning with fever, tossed in bed

(3) The child burning in bed tossed with fever

(4) No improvement

Q278. He may have grown taller **when I last saw him**.

(1) from when I last saw him

(2) since I last saw him

(3) before I last saw him

(4) No improvement

Q279. While crossing the highway, a five year old child was knocked **out** by a passing car.

(1) away

(2) up

(3) down

(4) No improvement

Q280. We are **looking forward to see** you tomorrow.

(1) looking forward towards seeing

(2) looking forward for seeing

(3) looking forward to seeing
(4) No improvement

Q281. The clients **are waiting** outside since morning and will continue to wait until you meet them.
(1) have waited
(2) have been waiting
(3) were waiting
(4) No improvement

Q282. The workers are **hell bent at getting** what is due to them.
(1) hell bent on getting
(2) hell bent for getting
(3) hell bent upon getting
(4) No improvement

Q283. During his long discourse, he did not **touch that** point.
(1) touch upon
(2) touch in
(3) touch of
(4) No improvement

Q284. They could not tell me **why did he not eat his lunch**.
(1) why not had he eaten
(2) why he did not eat
(3) why had he not eaten
(4) No improvement

Q285. He **who will bid the highest** will get the product.
(1) who bids the highest
(2) who the highest bids
(3) who would bid the highest
(4) No improvement

Q286. If he had time **he will** call you.
(1) would have
(2) would have had
(3) has
(4) No improvement

Q287. John **had told** me that he hasn't done it yet.
(1) told
(2) tells
(3) was telling
(4) No improvement

Q288. The disparity of the GDP between the rich and the poor **has broadened in the last some decades**.
(1) have widened in the last some decades
(2) has widened in the last few decades
(3) have broadened in the last few decades
(4) No improvement

Q289. **How, is beyond my understanding, the boy could fall into the ditch.**
(1) How the boy could fall into the ditch is beyond my understanding
(2) Beyond my understanding is how the boy could fall into the ditch
(3) How could the boy fall into the ditch is beyond my understanding
(4) No improvement

Q290. The pioneer spacecraft **went beyond** Pluto.
(1) made its way past
(2) went across
(3) went after
(4) No improvement

Q291. The firm buys frozen seafood in bulk, packs it into smaller pouches and then **they sell them** to the local grocery stores.
(1) it sells them
(2) sell them
(3) they sell the pouches
(4) No improvement

Q292. The learners **are intended** to read the sources at home.
(1) are meant
(2) are suggested
(3) are expected
(4) No improvement

Q293. Fuji's invention of super computer **will be enable to make Japan** supercede America in computer technology.

(1) will make Japan
(2) will enable Japan
(3) can make Japan
(4) No improvement

Q294. I could never repay the debt I owe to my **place of study**.
(1) Alma Mater
(2) Motherland
(3) Place of worship
(4) No improvement

Q295. She cries **all the time**.
(1) mostly everytime
(2) day in and day out
(3) pretty frequently
(4) No improvement

Q296. For a week last month, the team's 20 players were stranded because the **Government issued passport is not up to international standards,**
(1) Government-issued passports were not up to international standards
(2) Government-issued passports are not up to international standards
(3) the passports issued by the government were not up to international standards
(4) No improvement

Q297. Since July 2008, our customers **will be able to use** the ATM network of BBY Bank, the bank that was acquired by us during that year.
(1) have been able to use
(2) were using
(3) will have been able to use
(4) No improvement

Q298. It has been raining **since** morning.
(1) from
(2) for
(3) during
(4) No improvement

Q299. I am neither a poet **nor philosopher**.
(1) not philosopher
(2) nor the philosopher
(3) nor a philosopher
(4) No improvement

Q300. He was **hung** for murder.
(1) hang
(2) hanged
(3) hanging
(4) No improvement

FILL IN THE BLANKS

Q.1. It is politician's greediness which _______ country financially empty.
(A) constructs
(B) makes
(C) develops
(D) builds

Q.2. I have to go on James's shop _______ some needed things.
(A) to bring
(B) to bringing
(C) bring
(D) brought

Q.3. I _______ to the Agra's Taj Mahal last year but it was raining.
(A) arrive
(B) reached
(C) went
(D) gone

Q.4. This is my brother's favourite dish _______ I will not give him.
(A) and
(B) as well as
(C) but
(D) provided

Q.5. I have to come first in exam _______ this

is the matter of my parent's reputation.

(A) but
(B) as
(C) yet
(D) soon

Q.6. My friend's home has _______ playground where we can play cricket.

(A) biggest
(B) more big
(C) bigger
(D) big

Q.7. A girl of class tenth was _______ for her honesty.

(A) reward
(B) devotion
(C) rewarded
(D) devote

Q.8. Mom _______ me an apple and milk in the breakfast.

(A) takes
(B) was given
(C) gives
(D) is given

Q.9. We should not delay in getting medicine _______ we get ill.

(A) whenever
(B) where
(C) when
(D) wherever

Q.10. Greenery in the environment is the _______ of nature.

(A) nice
(B) beauty
(C) gorgeous
(D) beautiful

Q.11. It is confirmed by the research that people having sedentary lifestyle are more ________ to diseases.

(A) flexible
(B) prone
(C) rigid
(D) complex

Q.12. I know the leader of a well-known gang ________ criminals.

(A) with
(B) from
(C) on
(D) of

Q.13. __________ is the tool to remove all problems.

(A) Work hardly
(B) Happiness
(C) Ambitious
(D) Hardly work

Q.14. We should not late in _________ medicine whenever we get ill.

(A) get
(B) got
(C) getting
(D) getting up

Q.15. My father always gives us _________ fruits in the morning.

(A) importance
(B) seasonal
(C) authorised
(D) strengthen

Q.16. I _________ 'Hichki' movie the first time in cinema hall yesterday.

(A) had seen
(B) saw
(C) have seen
(D) see

Q.17. My final exams will start _________ Friday.

(A) on
(B) at
(C) in
(D) from

Q.18. We will _________ abroad in December.

(A) go to
(B) gone to

(C) go

(D) went

Q.19. I ________ a son named Haider and a daughter named Adeeba.

(A) am having

(B) have

(C) was

(D) were

Q.20. She _________ in Goa with her friends.

(A) was been traveling

(B) had been traveling

(C) was traveling

(D) travel

Q.21. It is difficult at this stage to forecast the _______ of results of the ongoing research on Cancer.

A. importance

B. measure

C. magnitude

D. consequence

Q.22. There was a look of __________ on his face during the interrogation.

A. disfavour

B. disguise

C. dejection

D. disgrace

Q.23. The serious __________ with her is that she does not know typing.

A. disadvantage

B. inconvenience

C. handicap

D. obstacles

Q.24. A prejudiced person who is intolerant of any opinion ___________ from his own.

A. depreciate

B. differing

C. catering

D. disparate

Q.25. Brookfield is on the _______ of signing the deal for the property situated in the district.

A. voracious

B. verge

C. candid

D. surge

Q.26. He was ------------of playing -------------and loose with the sentiments of his dearest friends.

A. innocent; false

B. guilty; fast

C. accused; tight

D. complained; thick

Q.27. Raising _________ over the funding to media houses, Zee group chairman sought ________ of media licences before they are issued.

A. burden, opinion

B. concern, scrutiny

C. matter, opinion

D. charges, regulation

Q.28. Everyone even _______________ familiar with serious theatre and the effort that it takes to process Shakespearean language ________________ live.

A. remotely; performed

B. comically; restrained

C. hardly; directing

D. so; bring

Q.29. The government has decided not to make any ____________ changes in the country's tax ____________.

A. sweeping; regime

B. Transparent; hike

C. drastically; net

D. constitution; revenue

Q.30. If criminals are...............to join electoral fray,................is likely to increase.

A. compelled, brotherhood

B. encouraged, harmony

C. allowed, extortion

D. deterred, corruption

Q.31. Ravindar saw a _____ of cattle grazing in the meadow.

(a) bunch
(b) litter
(c) group
(d) herd

Q.32. My flight was _____ from Lucknow to Delhi airport.

(a) deflected
(b) diverted
(c) reverted
(d) shifted

Q.33. For the days of inflation we all have to _____ our belts.

(a) lesson
(b) strengthen
(c) tighten
(d) shorten

Q.34. People continue to keep an open mind and don't _____ all cryptocurrencies with the same brush.

(a) tar
(b) war
(c) jar
(d) mar

Q.35. The patient's condition has been ____ for many days.

(a) putting
(b) buried
(c) burning
(d) deteriorating

Q.36. Look who has been ____ the issue!

(a) pushing
(b) learnt
(c) earning
(d) bought

Q.37. The mobile, if used properly, helps you develop___.

(a) discernment
(b) concerns
(c) simulate
(d) originality

Q.38. Have you ever____ that laptops are getting under your skin?

(a) express
(b) felt
(c) think
(d) dealt

Q.39. Soldiers are comparatively____ and defenceless.

(a) ocular
(b) powerful
(c) fragile
(d) strange

Q.40. Gaurav is in a dilemma ____ the choice of career.

(a) at
(b) in
(c) on
(d) over

Q.41. The __________of welfare support for small and marginal farmers cannot be overstated, given the vagaries of the monsoon.

(a) important
(b) importance
(c) collection
(d) thinking

Q.42. Everyone is _________by her zeal and enthusiasm.

(a) impressed
(b) affect
(c) happiness
(d) altered

Q.43. Garima used to like it _________now I do not enjoy it.

(a) and
(b) or
(c) still
(d) but

Q.44. If you had contacted Sachin everyday on phone, he _________have helped you.

(a) will

(b) should

(c) must have

(d) would

Q.45. The Supreme Court ____________to pass any fresh order to stop cockfights in Andhra Pradesh.

(a) attacked

(b) compiled

(c) refused

(d) order

Q.46. The novel is very important for me _________it is a present from my mother.

(a) as if

(b) because

(c) nevertheless

(d) unless

Q.47. Two thousand kilometres ________ Patna to Goa is a long distance.

(a) between

(b) across

(c) from

(d) side

Q.48. Abhinav is planning to travel across America _________music on a month long road trip.

(a) creating

(b) manage

(c) finishing

(d) damaging

Q.49. Both the boys _________ late in the hall and sat beside me.

(a) goes

(b) attended

(c) came

(d) joins

Q.50. A music and dance show has been ____________to raise funds.

(a) organised

(b) created

(c) arrange

(d) formed

Q.51. She was musing....... memories of the past.

A. over

B. about

C. on

D. from

Q.52. Each school has its own set of rules....... all good pupils should follow them.

A. but

B. or

C. so

D. and

Q.53. On my return from a long holiday, I had to....... with a lot of work.

A. catch on

B. catch up

C. makes up

D. take up

Q.54. I appealed him not....... from the main issue.

A. prevent

B. abstain

C. digress

D. dissent

Q.55. Our appeal to public has met....... a good response.

A. for

B. with

C. against

D. upon

Q.56. Hopes of a settlement depends on the....... of the discussion.

A. conclude

B. outcome

C. break through

D. resolutions

Q.57. We must avail ourselves....... every opportunity that comes in our way.

A. of

B. on

C. against

D. to

Q.58. It is time we....... with determination

A. act

B. acted

C. have acted

D. will act

Q.59. He is so....... that he will not utter a single word against his father.

A. possessive

B. meek

C. gifted

D. arrogant

Q.60. Seven hundred men worked for 10 years to....... the Borobudur temple in Java to its former glory.

A. restore

B. give

C. create

D. revive

Q.61. The audience _________ at the end of the drama.

A. applauded

B. appraised

C. appreciated

D. praised

Q.62. This room is very exquisite but ______ small to accommodate all of you.

A. much too

B. too much

C. very much

D. much

Q.63. The prisoner was released on _______ for good behaviour.

A. probation

B. bail

C. parole

D. grounds

Q.64. The Man who was blind _____ right eye was a notorious criminal.

A. with the

B. in the

C. of the

D. into the

Q.65. ________ between labour and management is inevitable.

A. Controversy

B. Friction

C. Competition

D. Association

Q.66. The prize was given to the girl ______ they said stood first.

A. whom

B. which

C. who

D. whose

Q.67. His companions prevailed upon him not to _______ violence.

A. refer

B. prone

C. resort

D. provoke

Q.68. The team ______ fighting among them selves.

A. was

B. were

C. is

D. will

Q.69. The peasant's produce was _________ in lieu of his previous year's rent.

A. quelled

B. vanquished

C. projection

D. confiscated

Q.70. Hardly had he gone out of the office _____ the manager called him.

A. then

B. than

C. when

D. at once

Q.71. Health is too important to be ________.

A. neglected

B. detested

C. despised

D. discarded

Q.72. It was his __________ that saved him from the coming danger.

A. prediction

B. presage

C. foresight

D. detection

Q.73. The doctor ________ the patient from taking certain medicine.

A. banned

B. prohibited

C. prescribed

D. proscribed

Q.74. Parliamentary Democracy postulated a discipline and ________ to the rules.

A. liability

B. commitment

C. obligation

D. subjection

Q.75. I have often ______________ why he went to live abroad.

A. puzzled

B. thought

C. wondered

D. surprised

Q.76. Priya is not _______ for this kind of job.

A. acquire

B. besides

C. capacity

D. capable

Q.77. He was annoyed ________ my brother.

A. for

B. with

C. at

D. to

Q.78. It is no use _______ to come now because he is very busy.

A. to ask him

B. that you ask him

C. if you asked him

D. asking him

Q.79. He is so bad tempered that he has _____ friends.

A. lot of

B. a lot of

C. few

D. a few

Q.80. A woman came in with a baby who she said, ____ a safety pin.

A. swallowed

B. just swallowed

C. had just swallowed

D. was just swallowing

Q.81. The court ordered the electronic and print media not to report any ________ made by the Justice.

(a) account

(b) remarks

(c) presentation

(d) statements

Q.82. Ramu has the _______ of an honest man and nobody wants to appreciate that.

(a) character

(b) quality

(c) condition

(d) factor

Q.83. Sometimes, after I finish my day's work, I go home and think a particular scene or _______.

(a) break

(b) opportunity

(c) shot

(d) occasion

Q.84. We could see change in the nature of warfare and its _______ on society.

(a) effects

(b) goods

(c) affects

(d) holdings

Q.85. The driving force is the generation of wealth certain types of economic ________.

(a) regulation

(b) doctrine

(c) instruction

(d) heterodoxy

Q.86. we must ________ the substance of which life is made.

(a) forget

(b) elicited

(c) remember

(d) illicit

Q.87. The relationship between chronic stress disease and aging is another area of ________.

(a) research

(b) discovery

(c) ignorance

(d) enquiry

Q.88. Ravi Shankar has a large circle of friends and is very ________ at parties.

(a) social

(b) popular

(c) obscure

(d) conscious

Q.89. We don't know _________ the machines are the masters or we are.

(a) however

(b) although

(c) whether

(d) nevertheless

Q90. Every society must develop in its people a social _________.

(a) subjection

(b) Importance

(c) exemption

(d) responsibility

Q.91. The boy was ____ of cheating in the examination.

(A) condemned

(B) accused

(C) charged

(D) punished

Q.92. We will have to atone ____ our misdeeds.

(A) at

(B) on

(C) for

(D) with

Q.93. I got used ____on the right when I was in the U.S. for two years.

(A) driving

(B) to drive

(C) to driving

(D) by driving

Q.94. Had you told me earlier I ___the meeting.

(A) had attended

(B) have attended

(C) attended

(D) would have attended

Q.95. The climate is not conducive ___ good health.

(A) with

(B) from

(C) in

(D) to

Q.96. We ____the picture on the wall.

(A) hung

(B) hanged

(C) hang

(D) hanging

Q.97. We thought the banner would look better with.............change in colour combination.

(A) every

(B) all

(C) each

(D) some

Q.98. Prices................during the war.

(A) raise

(B) risen

(C) rise

(D) raising

Q.99. I shall go and................down.

(A) lied

(B) lie

(C) lay

(D) layed

Q.100. The story about her unhappy childhood turned ______ to be a pack of lies.

(A) out

(B) in

(C) with s

(D) for

Q.101. To celebrate the____________, the team's supporters went out and enjoyed a lively evening in bars, night-clubs.

A. procession

B. victory

C. campaign

D. evening

Q.102. Long-term deployment of soldiers inevitably _______ to friction with local communities.

A. projects

B. produces

C. manages

D. leads

Q.103. As a politician, _________ is he competent, but he has the gift of the gab too!

A. only not

B. only none

C. not only

D. not if

Q.104. We need volunteers to _________ an eye out for gate crashers tonight.

A. keep

B. watch

C. prevent

D. state

Q.105. ________ works of reference are valuable as Encyclopaedia, Britannica.

A. A few

B. Few

C. The few

D. Fewer

Q.106. You cannot devise a method which ________ all possibility of errors.

A. excludes

B. includes

C. avoids

D. ignores

Q.107. Find the ________ that accompany these cartoons.

A. topics

B. titles

C. captions

D. headings

Q.108. About twenty clerks were made _________ when the banks introduced computers.

A. dispensable

B. redundant

C. expandable

D. obsolete

Q.109. A sanguine outlook is associated with the ________.

A. rationalist

B. socialist

C. philanthropist

D. optimist

Q.110. My uncle was awaiting me _______ the bus stop Yesterday.

A. on

B. at

C. upon

D. by

Q.111. The ___________ of puppies is fond of milk.

A. Gang

B. Group

C. Litre

D. Litter

Q.112. He __________ his father.

A. Takes back

B. Takes off

C. Takes after

D. Takes out

Q.113. We shall go for a picnic if the weather _____ good.

A. Has been

B. Was

C. Had been

D. Is

Q.114. Mr. and Mrs. Joshi go for a _____ walk Just before dinner.

A. Brisk

B. Vibrant

C. Vivacious

D. Slow

Q.115. __________ weight gain or weight loss is not good for your body.

A. Excessive

B. Extensive

C. Expressive

D. Explosive

Q.116. India will ________ arch rival Pakistan in the finals.

A. take on

B. taken back

C. looks after

D. takes after

Q.117. The shepherd was looking after the ______ of sheep.

A. crew

B. gang

C. fleet

D. flock

Q.118. Many of us believe that science is something modern _______ the truth is otherwise.

A. If

B. Unless

C. But

D. As if

Q.119. _________ my food and my repose were salted.

A. Both of

B. Both

C. All of

D. None of

Q.120. I _____ your parents that I would take care of you.

A. promised

B. alerted

C. said

D. forced

Q.121. Although the warring parties had settled a number of disputes, past experience made them _____ to express optimism that the talks would be a success.

A. rash

B. ambivalent

C. reticent

D. overjoyed

Q.122. Davis is an opprobrious and ____ speaker, equally caustic toward friend or foe–a true curmudgeon.

A. lofty

B. vituperative

C. unstinting

D. retiring

Q.123. Wilson ____ that human beings inherit a tendency to feel an affinity and awe for other living things, in the same way that we are ____ to be inquisitive or to protect our young at all costs.

A. argues – encouraged

B. maintains – trained

C. contends – predisposed

D. fears – taught

Q.124. The cricket match seemed ____ to our guests; they were used to watching sports in which the action is over in a couple of hours at the most.

A. unintelligible

B. inconsequential

C. interminable

D. implausible

Q. 125. The subtle shades of meaning, and still subtler echoes of association, make language an instrument which scarcely anything short of genius can wield with ____ and ____.

A. confidence – aloofness

B. definiteness – certainty

C. sincerity – hope

D. conservatism – alacrity

Q. 126. Research suggests there will be an annual rise in ____ until 2042, before a decline sets in.

A. whole

B. fatalities

C. vital

D. healthful

Q.127. At the moment Ms. Clinton's strong delegate count puts in the shadow her only Democratic ____ the self-declared socialist Bernie Sanders.

A. associate

B. rival

C. revival

D. supporting

Q.128. A true celebrity is one who is able to bring a certain spirit into daily life, inspiring and ____ joy to those around.

A. radiating

B. clouding

C. inspiring

D. increasing

Q.129. We become so anesthetized that it almost seems normal, and we don't even question the choices we make or the values we are ________.

A. facing

B. promoting

C. permitting

D. pretending

Q.130. The challenge of warding off __________ inflationary pressures in the early stages of the tax's implementation will require enlightened policies.

A. developed

B. incipient

C. predicate

D. prescribe

Q.131. Chetan, where are you?_____ up this tree.

(A) Here I am

(B) Here am I

(C) There I am

(D) There am I

Q.132. I don't know the time _____.

(A) at which the accident happened

(B) the accident happened

(C) when the accident happened

(D) when the accident had happened

Q.133. Siddharth seized control of country _____.

(A) by being a diplomat and forceful

(B) not only because of diplomacy but force

(C) by using diplomacy and force

(D) by diplomacy and being forceful

Q.134. It is unfortunate that ______.

(A) you lost your mobile phone.

(B) you have lost your mobile phone

(C) you lose your mobile phone

(D) your mobile phone was lost

Q.135. If you are unable to pay the debt within the period _____.

(A) your name strike off our register
(B) however your name will be strike off our registers
(C) and your name will be struck off our register
(D) your name will be struck off our register

Q.136. With great difficulty _____.
(A) he could not tolerate his nonsense
(B) he could lose his temper
(C) he could keep his cool
(D) he could get annoyed

Q.137. 'Where is my key?' _____.
(A) Here is it, on the table!
(B) There is it, on the table!
(C) Here it is, on the table!
(D) There it is, on the table!

Q.138. My parents are so poor _____.
(A) to send me to school
(B) because they will not work.
(C) to get medical help for my brother
(D) that they can not buy food for us

Q.139. One of you must help me _____.
(A) shan't you?
(B) wouldn't you?
(C) won't you?
(D) mustn't you?

Q.140. _____ at all is doubtful.
(A) He will come
(B) His coming
(C) Will he come
(D) Whether he will come

Q.151. Your father doesn't object ______ you to the party at Pat's on Saturday.
(A) to drive
(B) drives
(C) to driving
(D) none of the above

Q.152. I'm looking forward to ______ him again when he's back from the USA.
(A) see
(B) seen
(C) seeing
(D) none of the above

Q.153. I'm awfully sorry, but I'm totally opposed to ____________ him my car for the weekend!
(A) lends
(B) lent
(C) lend
(D) lending

Q.154. He doesn't want you __________ her offer!
(A) accept
(B) accepts
(C) accepted
(D) to accept

Q.155. I wouldn't like him to take ______ alcohol after the terrible disappointment he's had.
(A) to drink
(B) drinks
(C) to drinking
(D) drunk

Q.156. He only came to see her with a view to ____________ some money from her.
(A) borrow
(B) borrowed
(C) borrows
(D) borrowing

Q.157. Ansh didn't expect to ________ such a fast answer.
(A) receive
(B) received
(C) receiving
(D) in receiving

Q.158. Don't drive me to school… I'm used to __________ there with my friends.
(A) walking
(B) walks
(C) walk

(D) walked

Q.159. When will you get around ______ that report? It will just take you an hour.

(A) to writing

(B) to write

(C) writing

(D) write

Q.160. Even if everyone knew it, he didn't admit ____________ to the police.

(A) to lying

(B) lie

(C) lying

(D) none of the above

Q161. Shivali hadn't eaten all day, and by the time she got home she was______.

a. blighted

b. confutation

c. ravenous

d.ostentatious

Q162. The movie offended many of the parents of its younger viewers by including unnecessary ______ in the dialogue.

a. vulgarity

b. verbosity

c. vocalizations

d. garishness

Q163. Prateek's neighbors found his ______ manner bossy and irritating, and they stopped inviting him to their functions.

a. insentient

b. magisterial

c. reparation

d. restorative

Q164. Sashtaang is always ______ about showing up for work because he feels that tardiness is a sign of irresponsibility.

a. legible

b. tolerable

c. punctual

d. literal

Q165. Mayank would ______ his little sister into an argument by teasing her and calling her names.

a. advocate

b. provoke

c. perforate

d. expunge

Q166. The dress Anu wore ______ with small, glassy beads, creating a shimmering effect.

a. titillated

b. reiterated

c. scintillated

d. enthralled

Q167. Being able to afford this luxury car will ______ getting a better paying job.

a. maximize

b. recombinant

c. reiterate

d. necessitate

Q168. Levina unknowingly ______ the thief by holding open the elevator doors and ensuring his escape.

a. coerced

b. proclaimed

c. abetted

d. sanctioned

Q169. Shakespeare, a(n) ______ writer, entertained audiences by writing many tragic and comic plays.

a. numeric

b. obstinate

c. dutiful

d. prolific

Q170. I had the ______ experience of sitting next to an over-talkative passenger on my flight home from Dubai.

a. satisfactory

b. commendable

c. galling

d. acute

Q171. Prince had to choose. marry the woman

he loved and ______ his right to the throne.

a. reprimand

b. upbraid

c. abdicate

d. extol

Q172. If you will not do your work of your own ______, I have no choice but to penalize you.

a. predilection

b. coercion

c. excursion

d. volition

Q173. After lying in the sink for several days, the dirty, food-encrusted dishes became ______.

a. malodorous

b. prevalent

c. imposing

d. perforated

Q174. Gitika soon discovered the source of the ______ smell in the room. a week-old sandwich that one of the children had hidden in the almirah.

a. weird

b. fastidious

c. clandestine

d. laconic

Q175. After making ______ remarks to the President, the reporter was not invited to return to the White House pressroom.

a. hospitable

b. itinerant

c. enterprising

d. irreverent

Q176. With her ______ eyesight, Krishna spotted a pair of deer on the hillside and she reduced the speed of her car.

a. inferior

b. keen

c. impressionable

d. ductile

Q177. With a(n) ______ grin, the boy quickly slipped the candy into his pocket without his mother's knowledge.

a. jaundiced

b. nefarious

c. stereotypical

d. sentimental

Q178. Shreya's ______ display of tears at work did not impress her new boss.

a. excessive

b. meritorious

c. precarious

d. plausible

Q179. Jatin argued, "If you know about a crime but don't report it, you are ______ in that crime because you allowed it to happen."

a. acquitted

b. steadfast

c. tenuous

d. accomplice

Q180. The authorities, fearing a ______ of their power, called for a military state in the hopes of restoring order.

a. subversion

b. premonition

c. predilection

d. infusion

Q.181. The Lucknow ______ of _____ Allahabad High Court has directed the state government to provide a ______ women helpline number for rape and sexual _____ victims.

(A) branch, the, universal, assault

(B) bench, a, universal, assault

(C) bench, the, universal, assault

(D) bench, the, unique, suffering

Q.182. The government has put 77 foreign NGO's on _____ global ____, _____ it difficult for their officials to get visas ____ India.

(A) their, watch-list, making, to

(B) its, waitlists, making, to

(C) its, watch-list, making, on

(D) its, watch-list, making, to

Q.183. Government _______ Tuesday moved the Supreme Court _____ ______ of one of its 2G Spectrum scam ruling that ___ for prosecution of a public servant in a corruption case can be sought even before filing of a complaint.

(A) at, seeking, review, sanction

(B) on, seeking, review, sanction

(C) on, wanting, review, sanction

(D) on, seeking, reviewing, sanction

Q.184. He promised to ____ the contract, and they ____ his honour _____ its fulfilment.

(A) abide on, relied on, for

(B) abide by, relied on, for

(C) abide by, relied at, for

(D) abide by, relied on, in

Q.185. I hope you will be ____ _____ the _____ entailed ______ you.

(A) compensation, for, annoyance, upon

(B) compensated, on, annoyance, upon

(C) compensated, of, annoyance, upon

(D) compensated, for, annoyance, upon

Q.186. He ______ ______ a simple minded people, _____ the Kalpi village _____ the Northen part of the district.

(A) dwell, among, at, in

(B) dwells, between, at, on

(C) dwells, among, in, in

(D) dwells, among, at, in

Q.187. A_____ ______ this letter will _______ you of its _______ that he is grasping at your money.

(A) look, in, convince, contents

(B) look, at, convinced, contents

(C) glance, at, convince, ideas

(D) glance, at, convince, contents

Q.188. He _____ ______ this place ______ the outer part _____ the day.

(A) moved, about, for, of

(B) loitered, into, for, of

(C) loitered, about, for, of

(D) loitered, about, of, in

Q.189. You may _____ some people for _____ time and ______all people for ____ time.

(A) cheat, this, even, some

(B) cheat, some, even, some

(C) cheat, some, except, some

(D) cheat, some, even, all

Q.190. _____ is a ____ in disguise. It is a nice training for our heart, mind and ____.

(A) Adversity, blessing, sole

(B) Adversities, blessing, soul

(C) Adversity, blessing, soul

(D) Adversity, curse, soul

Q191. Net neutrality .... rules of the road for a free and open Internet.

(a)comprehensive

(b)denoted

(c) creates

(d)modifying

Q192. In the face of the .... cross examination, the accused remained stoic.

(a) solid

(b) terrible

(c) tedious

(d) grueling

Q193. His success is worthy of ....

(a) copying

(b) aping

(c) simulation

(d) emulation

Q194. He had never been of a .... constitution, and after a little more than a week's illness he died.

(a) superb

(b) energetic

(c) dynamic

(d) robust

Q195. The priest called upon the families to .... their differences and agree to the wedding.

(a) sink

(b) abolish

(c) immerse

(d) lower

Q196. To understand the nature of electromagnetic radiation, it is imperative that we grasp the .... nature of light.

(a) twice

(b) dual

(c) double

(d) dichotomous

Q197. State laws .... the sale of alcoholic beverages inside the stadium.

(a) freeze

(b) inhibit

(c) prohibit

(d) impede

Q198. Even if two horses may look ...., they may not be of the same age.

(a) comparable

(b) alike

(c) on par

(d) only same

Q199. The .... with which she manages the task is remarkable.

(a) calm

(b) comfort

(c) ease

(d) satisfaction

Q200. The security for the Prime Minister has been .... up following the shoot out.

(a) secured

(b) fortified

(c) strengthened

(d) beefed

Q201. _______ your instructions, we have closed your bank account.

(1) In lieu of

(2) With regard to

(3) In accordance with

(4) On account of

Q202. _______ she is clever, she often makes mistakes.

(1) Despite

(2) Since

(3) Although

(4) Yet

Q203. Do you prefer _____ or traditional art forms ?

(1) archaic

(2) contemporary

(3) foreign

(4) simultaneous

Q204. The farmers _______ their farms, if they had known that a thunderstorm was approaching.

(1) will leave

(2) would leave

(3) will have left

(4) would have left

Q205. The Paralympics is a competition for the ____.

(1) disadvantaged

(2) discouraged

(3) disabled

(4) despised

Q206. She made her stepson her ____ to her large fortune.

(1) hare

(2) heir

(3) hair

(4) here

Q207. The stewardess showed the passenger __

(1) when to start travelling

(2) where to land the plane
(3) how to fasten the seat belt
(4) how to judge the altitude of the plane

Q208. Many people reported _____a noise in the night.
(1) to hear
(2) having heard
(3) to have heard
(4) been hearing

Q209. I am exhausted; let's ____ a day.
(1) call it
(2) call at
(3) call off
(4) call in

Q210. The worker used _____ to patch up the hole in the wall.
(1) sand
(2) cement
(3) soil
(4) grass

Q211. How did these things come ________ ?
(1) about
(2) into
(3) at
(4) down

Q212. The news was _______ good to be true.
(1) very
(2) too
(3) so
(4) as

Q213. How much longer _______ this book ?
(1) you are needing
(2) will you be needing
(3) will you have needed
(4) have you needed

Q214. ______ you hear the President's speech ?
(1) Have
(2) Has
(3) Had
(4) Did

Q215. I ______ to the movie with some friends last night.
(1) have gone
(2) went
(3) am gone
(4) am going

Q216. She has only__________friends.
(1) fewer
(2) less
(3) more
(4) a few

Q217. If I ____ a doctor, I would serve the poor.
(1) am
(2) had been
(3) were
(4) was

Q218. He is weak ___ he does a lot of work.
(1) and
(2) yet
(3) because
(4) so

Q219. Mahesh showed an _____ for sports at a very early stage.
(1) attitude
(2) aptitude
(3) imagination
(4) intuition

Q220. For_______ sake don't tell it to others.
(1) haven
(2) heaven
(3) heavens
(4) heaven's

Q221. Napoleon's army ___ to the Russian soldiers without any fight.
(1) evaded
(2) decimated
(3) capitulated
(4) cordoned

Q222. The work was _____ by the rains.
(1) restricted
(2) prevented

(3) hampered

(4) obstructed

Q223. He knows French and German _____ Russian.

(1) beside

(2) besides

(3) aside

(4) except

Q224. His reputation has been _____ by his foolish acts.

(1) increased

(2) decreased

(3) retrieved

(4) tainted

Q225. Meditation is _____ way to calm your nerves.

(1) a best

(2) one of the best

(3) the best

(4) an best

Q226. The Prime Minister of England called _____ the President of America.

(1) in

(2) out

(3) on

(4) at

Q227. Many a man _____ imprisoned without trial in Fascist countries.

(1) are

(2) were

(3) is

(4) have been

Q228. The plane will take off when the thunderstorm ______.

(1) stops

(2) stopped

(3) would stop

(4) will stop

Q229. When the doctor _____, the patient was already ______.

(1) arrived ; died

(2) arrived ; dead

(3) arrive ; dead

(4) arriving ; dying

Q230. Age and experience________ wisdom to man.

(1) bring

(2) have brought

(3) are bringing

(4) brings

Q231. He drove from Maharashtra _____ Karnataka without stopping to rest.

(1) is

(2) to

(3) into

(4) towards

Q232. If you litter, you _____ to pay a fine.

(1) will have

(2) would have

(3) will had

(4) would had

Q233. Most animals which are nocturnal have a sharper ____ at night, than in the morning.

(1) vision

(2) sight

(3) view

(4) eye

Q234. If I were ____, I wouldn't accept such treatment,

(1) him

(2) them

(3) he

(4) one

Q235. I know to ____ you are alluding.

(1) who

(2) which

(3) where

(4) whom

Q236. Each man and each woman ____ a vote.

(1) have

(2) has

(3) can
(4) must

Q237. You may bring your dog where _______.
(1) you have to pay
(2) there is no water
(3) pets are allowed
(4) pets can sleep

Q238. The chef was wondering _____.
(1) when to brush his teeth
(2) what to prepare for the important dinner
(3) how to wash the dishes
(4) when to take the dog for a walk

Q239. I have brought some books _______, you to examine.
(1) to
(2) for
(3) with
(4) over

Q240. The speaker did not properly space out his speech, but went on _______ one point only.
(1) stressing
(2) avoiding
(3) devoting
(4) decrying

Q241. The usher showed us _____.
(1) how to take photographs
(2) where to sit
(3) when to comb our hair
(4) how to dance

242. The explosion that ___________ the bus killed twelve people.
(1) wrecked
(2) deflated
(3) stalled
(4) hindered

Q243. There was some __________ between the member's version and the committee's version.
(1) discourse
(2) discrepancy
(3) certainty
(4) recurrence

Q244. We have talked a lot ; now let us ________ to work.
(1) get down
(2) set off
(3) take off
(4) sit up

Q245. The life-guard would not let the children _________ at the deep end of the pool.
(1) swims
(2) swim
(3) swam
(4) to swim

Q246. The audience watched the clowns _________ their act.
(1) performs
(2) perform
(3) performed
(4) are performing

Q247. He was accused of bringing money into the country in _____ of foreign exchange rules.
(1) anticipation
(2) compensation
(3) perpetration
(4) violation

Q248. One of the players forgot to ___.
(1) turn up for practice
(2) run away from school
(3) buy shoes for the exam
(4) bring his books for the match

Q249. Today students should be reconciled _____ the way things are changing.
(1) with
(2) to
(3) for
(4) at

Q250. The country's economic growth was adversely _____ by political instability.
(1) reflected
(2) effected
(3) affected
(4) expected

Q251. The agenda for the meeting is _____ the notice.
(1) forwarded in
(2) subscribed to
(3) enclosed with
(4) delivered as

Q252. We shall go for a picnic if the weather _____ good.
(1) is
(2) was
(3) has been
(4) had been

Q253. Mr. and Mrs. Joshi go for a ____ walk just before dinner.
(1) vibrant
(2) brisk
(3) vivacious
(4) slow

Q254. _____ weight gain or weight loss is not good for your body.
(1) Explosive
(2) Expressive
(3) Extensive
(4) Excessive

Q255. John must have the ____ to stick to his diet, if he wants to lose weight.
(1) obstinacy
(2) determination
(3) decision
(4) obligation

Q256. There was an ____ response for the marathon.
(1) overwhelming
(2) overriding
(3) excessive
(4) extreme

Q257. Some animals have unique ____ that allow them to survive in extreme weather conditions.
(1) characteristics
(2) problems
(3) feelings
(4) conditions

Q258. Did the boys turn _____ for football practice?
(1) up
(2) on
(3) back
(4) in

Q259. The fireman managed to put _____ the fire.
(1) away
(2) down
(3) out
(4) off

Q260. The pupil was asked to write ____ his name on the front page of the exercise book.
(1) back
(2) in
(3) down
(4) about

Q261. The teacher found many mistakes in my composition, when she went ______ it.
(1) into
(2) about
(3) for
(4) through

Q262. We must ________ help to the people hit by the cyclone.
(1) contribute
(2) summon
(3) impart
(4) render

Q263. The metals and minerals sector________ currently highly volatile.
(1) are

(2) is

(3) was

(4) were

Q264. We should not mix with those people who have an________ reputation.

(1) unsavoury

(2) unsteady

(3) unsafe

(4) unsanctified

Q265. It was said of Akbar that he rarely ________ more than three hours a day.

(1) sleeps

(2) is sleeping

(3) had slept

(4) slept

Q266. As the bare mountains turned green, the people found _______ looking forward to spring.

(1) they

(2) them

(3) their

(4) themselves

Q267. The sparrows took no ____ the bread.

(1) notice of

(2) notice about

(3) notice from

(4) notice to

Q268. He shows great ability ____ Mathematics.

(1) at

(2) for

(3) about

(4) in

Q269. There ____ any message from my teacher since she moved to London.

(1) isn't

(2) wasn't.

(3) hasn't been

(4) hadn't been

Q270. May I give you ____ advice?

(1) an

(2) some

(3) little

(4) one

Q271. She has been supporting her family ____ her husband's death.

(1) on

(2) at

(3) from

(4) since

Q272. The telephone kept ______ ringing, but no one attended.

(1) off

(2) on

(3) up

(4) up with

Q273. She is sad, because her father turned ______ her request.

(1) up

(2) off

(3) out

(4) down

Q274. You should not confide _____ a stranger.

(1) in

(2) to

(3) with

(4) by

Q275. Poets have compared this world ______ a stage.

(1) with

(2) to

(3) by

(4) on

Q276. I prevailed _______ him to contest the election.

(1) on

(2) off

(3) over

(4) of

Q277. The government must _____ all resources of energy.

(1) collect

(2) gather
(3) muster
(4) harness

Q278. A.R. Rahman ____ the music for Commonwealth Games 2010.
(1) sang
(2) made
(3) composed
(4) produced

Q279. Appearances are _____.
(1) deceptive
(2) deception
(3) deceptively
(4) deceive

Q280. Girls generally ____ in their mother.
(1) confide
(2) confident
(3) confidential
(4) confidence

Q281. Children below the age of fourteen should be ______ sent to school.
(1) compel
(2) compulsory
(3) compulsively
(4) compulsorily

Q282. The headmaster congratulated Rajan ____ getting the merit scholarship.
(1) for
(2) about
(3) with
(4) on

Q283. Smallpox has been eradicated ____ India.
(1) in
(2) from
(3) within
(4) out of

Q284. The police offered a ____ for information about the stolen money.
(1) reward
(2) award
(3) profit
(4) prize

Q285. There is no possibility of _____ coming late.
(1) they
(2) their
(3) them
(4) theirs

Q286. His friend ____ unexpectedly.
(1) returned to
(2) come back
(3) turned up
(4) get down

Q287. Have you got any idea as to what has happened to Akila ? I haven't seen her ______.
(1) lately
(2) later on
(3) late
(4) later

Q288. I _____ hard to establish the validity of the theory since morning.
(1) have been trying
(2) had tried
(3) tried
(4) am trying

Q289. _____ of defence personnel would be given transfers to their place of choice.
(1) Friends
(2) Wives
(3) Husbands
(4) Spouses

Q290. Sachin was standing ____ me.
(1) aside
(2) next
(3) beside
(4) besides

291. My sister and _____ are pleased to accept your invitation.
(1) I
(2) me

(3) myself
(4) I myself

Q292. For a child, a blow _____ selfesteem is a terrible thing.
(1) of
(2) with
(3) to
(4) on

Q293. The Greenland ice sheet is _____ at the rate of about 12 cubic miles a year.
(1) smelting
(2) condensing
(3) melting
(4) freezing

Q294. The Principal called _____ an explanation from the clerks.
(1) on
(2) out
(3) for
(4) in

Q295. The ______ crowd gave the victorious team a tumultuous welcome.
(1) jubilant
(2) troublesome
(3) noisy
(4) arrogant

Q296. It is our duty to get ____ the truth.
(1) to
(2) over
(3) into
(4) at

Q297. A thorough search of the aircraft was carried _____ in the airport.
(1) out
(2) off
(3) on
(4) along

Q298. Discrimination _____ any form should be avoided.
(1) of
(2) by
(3) from
(4) in

Q299. My friend's father died _____ cancer.
(1) by
(2) of
(3) from
(4) with

Q300. I can't make both ends ______ on my small salary.
(1) meet
(2) unite
(3) join
(4) touch

Q301. His manners____him.
(1) speak of
(2) speak out
(3) speak up
(4) speak for

Q302. The aim of education is to ______ the best in students.
(1) bring on
(2) bring in
(3) bring about
(4) bring out

Q303. I have known him ______ a long time.
(1) since
(2) for
(3) before
(4) from

Q304. I wish I ______ her to clean the room.
(1) have asking
(2) have asked
(3) asked
(4) had asked

Q305. He always takes full _______of the mistakes made by his friends.
(1) benefit
(2) advantage
(3) profit

(4) use

Q306. He drained what was left __________ his drink.

(1) from
(2) in
(3) of
(4) off

Q307. Our teacher___several points before the exams.

(1) cleared off
(2) cleared away
(3) cleared up
(4) cleared out

Q308. Let me give you ___.

(1) an advise
(2) any advice
(3) some advice
(4) some advises

Q309. The cart was driven ___ bullocks.

(1) with
(2) off
(3) to
(4) by

Q310. Simon ___ very polite at the moment, because he wants to make a good impression.

(1) was being
(2) has been
(3) is behaving
(4) is being.

Q311. If I don't ____advantage of this platform, then how dare I be a film maker ?

(1) make
(2) take
(3) bring
(4) find

Q312. The old gentleman _____ to be a very good friend of my grand father.

(1) turned in
(2) turned over
(3) turned out
(4) turned up

Q313. It's a ______, that young people are inspired by celebrities.

(1) lie
(2) myth
(3) bluff
(4) mistake

Q314. Had I saved money, I _____ a new car.

(1) will purchase
(2) would purchase
(3) would have purchased
(4) purchased

Q315. He decided to ____ for his matric examination in order to get a higher score.

(1) redo
(2) reappear
(3) rewrite
(4) remake

Q316. The police pushed the people back to make _____ for Prime Minister's car to pass.

(1) passage
(2) way
(3) place
(4) area

Q317. The Chairman is ill and we'll have to _________ the meeting for a few days.

(1) put on
(2) put of
(3) put away
(4) put off

Q318. He told me that he ______the movie.

(1) is finished
(2) was finished
(3) had finished
(4) not finished

Q319. I do my work ______ carefully to make mistakes.

(1) so
(2) very

(3) too
(4) more

Q320. The cat and the dog have a ______ enemy in the rat.
(1) same
(2) common
(3) mutual
(4) similar

Q321. He is very good ______ making stories.
(1) in
(2) about
(3) at
(4) for

Q322. That farmer may be old but he is ________.
(1) less energetic
(2) more energetic
(3) most energetic
(4) energetic

Q323. The monitor takes care ______the class _______ the absence of the teacher.
(1) in; at
(2) of; in
(3) during; in
(4) of; for

Q324. When he saw the fish swimming ______ the river, he was extremely happy.
(1) on
(2) besides
(3) in
(4) at

Q325. The railway coaches______by the Integral Coach Factory, Chennai.
(1) is manufactured
(2) are manufactured
(3) are manufacture
(4) is being manufactured

Q326. The truck was _______ when the bus rammed into it.
(1) stationery
(2) machinary
(3) machinery
(4) stationary

Q327. I haven't ________ butter but I have a lot of bread.
(1) a lot of
(2) little
(3) much
(4) some

Q328. People from ________ and near came to see the final match of the tournament yesterday.
(1) distance
(2) long
(3) above
(4) far

Q329. The student ________ book I still have, can take it from me.
(1) that
(2) whose
(3) which
(4) his

Q330. Corruption should be ________ out with the utmost vigour.
(1) talked
(2) left
(3) rooted
(4) brought

Q331. Books are a great source ______ happiness.
(1) of
(2) for
(3) into
(4) with

Q332. He spoke ________ his travels.
(1) of
(2) on
(3) about
(4) along

Q333. Man is essentially a _____ animal and

tends to associate with others.

(1) sentimental

(2) gregarious

(3) selfish

(4) perverse

Q334. Why do we always have to submit ______ his authority ?

(1) under

(2) with

(3) for

(4) to

Q335. The master assured her _____ success in the examination.

(1) of

(2) in

(3) for

(4) with

Q336. The child was so spoiled by her indulgent parents that she became _____ when she did not receive all of their attention.

(1) sullen

(2) elated

(3) discreet

(4) suspicious

Q337. His directions to the driver were ______ , and helped him to reach on time.

(1) expletive

(2) implicate

(3) explicit

(4) implicit

Q338. My windows look __________the garden.

(1) up on

(2) out on

(3) in

(4) at

Q339. I have made a rough__________of the report.

(1) drapht

(2) draught

(3) drought

(4) draft

Q340. The reward was not commensurate __________the work done by us.

(1) for

(2) on

(3) with

(4) upon

Q341. I don't care________ the expense; I want the party to be a real success.

(1) of

(2) with

(3) about

(4) at

Q342. Vinay does not play cricket, and __________does Yeshwant.

(1) so

(2) also

(3) either

(4) neither

Q343. The department head insisted that he ____ absolute authority to regulate office work.

(1) gives

(2) is given

(3) would give

(4) would be given

Q344. Vinod, two of___brothers attend primary school, wishes to be a school teacher after his graduation from the University.

(1) whom

(2) them

(3) whose

(4) which

Q345. The deadline was near by, so Mrs. Sweth had her students ____ their essays.

(1) complete

(2) to complete

(3) completing

(4) completed

Q346. Our new digital photo-print machine, the manual ____ is lost awaits to be set up properly.

(1) of what
(2) where
(3) by whom
(4) of which

Q347. Ramu is in the habit of revising just once, but Suresh never understands a subject _____ he revises it for at least three times.
(1) in case
(2) thus
(3) although
(4) unless

Q348. He was sorry _______ late last night.
(1) about coming
(2) to come
(3) to coming
(4) from coming

Q349. Our rich culture inspires us to take ______ in our heritage.
(1) prided
(2) proudly
(3) pride
(4) proud

Q350. The car broke down and we ___ get a taxi.
(1) were to
(2) are to
(3) had to
(4) have to

ACTIVE/ PASSIVE VOICE

1. They have published all the details of the invention.
(1) All the details of the inventionhave been published bythem.
(2) The publication of the detailsof invention was doneby them.
(3) All the details have been inventedby the publishers.
(4) All the inventions have been detailed by them.

2. He teaches us grammar.
(1) Grammar was taught to us by him
(2) We are taught grammar by him
(3) Grammar will be taught to us by him
(4) We were teached grammar by him

3. The manager could not accept the union leader's proposals.
(1) The union leader's proposals could not be accepted by the manager.
(2) The union leader's proposals were not accepted by the manager.
(3) The union leader's proposals will not be accepted by the manager.
(4) The union leader's proposals would not be accepted by the manager.

4. Prepare yourself for the worst.
(1) You be prepared for the worst.
(2) The worst should be prepared by yourself.
(3) Be prepared for the worst.
(4) For the worst, preparation should be made by you.

5. Please shut the door and go to sleep.
(1) The door is to be shut and you are to go to sleep.
(2) Let the door be shut and you be asleep.
(3) You are requested to shut the door and go to sleep.
(4) The door is to be shut and you are requested to sleep.

6. It is impossible to do this.
(1) Doing this is impossible.
(2) This is impossible to be done.
(3) This must not be done.
(4) This can't be done.

7. We must take care of all living species on Earth.

(1) All living species on Earth are taken care of by us.
(2) All living species on Earth must be taken care of by us.
(3) All living species on Earth had been taken care of by us.
(4) All living species on Earth will be taken care of by us.

8. People call him a fool.
(1) He has been called a fool.
(2) He is called a fool by the people.
(3) The people have been calling him a fool.
(4) We all people have called him a fool.

9. It is being read by us.
(1) We are reading it.
(2) It will be read by us.
(3) We can read it.
(4) We have to read it.

10. He had committed a mistake.
(1) A mistake had committed by him.
(2) A mistake was committed by him.
(3) A mistake had been committed by him.
(4) A mistake has been committed by him.

11. The most useful training of my career was given to me by my boss.
(1) My boss has been giving me the most useful training of my career.
(2) My boss gives me the most useful training.
(3) My boss is giving me the most useful training.
(4) My boss gave me the most useful training of my career.

12. We have decided to open a new branch.
(1) To open a new branch was decided by us.
(2) To be opened a new branch has been decided.
(3) It has been decided to open a new branch.
(4) It may be decided to open a new branch by us.

13. The loan will be sanctioned by the bank.
(1) The bank sanctioned the loan.
(2) The bank is going to sanction the loan.
(3) The bank would sanction the loan.
(4) The bank will sanction the loan.

14. Paint the windows.
(1) Windows should be painted.
(2) Let the windows be painted.
(3) Let be the windows painted.
(4) Windows are let to be painted.

15. The traitors should be shot dead by them.
(1) They should have shot the traitors dead.
(2) They shall shoot the traitors dead.
(3) They should shoot the traitors dead.
(4) They shot the traitors dead.

16. Rahul is teaching the children in the slum areas.
(1) The children in the slum areas are taught by Rahul.
(2) The children are taught by Rahul in the slum area.
(3) In the slum areas the children are learning from Rahul.
(4) The children in the slum areas are being taught by Rahul.

17. One cannot expect children to understand these problems.
(1) Children cannot be expected to understand these problems.
(2) Children to understand these problems cannot be expected.
(3) Children cannot be expected to be understood these problems.
(4) To understand these problems cannot be expected from children by one.

18. Why did she break the garden wall ?

(1) Why the garden wall was broken by her ?
(2) Why had the garden wall been broken by her ?
(3) Why was the garden wall broken by her ?
(4) Why will the garden wall be broken by her ?

19. The students were laughing at the old man.
(1) The old man was being laughed at by the students.
(2) The old man was laughed at by the students.
(3) The old man was being laughed by the students.
(4) The old man is laughing at the students.

20. He admonished her for the error.
(1) She was admonished by him for the error.
(2) She has been admonished by him for the error.
(3) She would be admonished by him for the error.
(4) She is admonished by him for the error.

21. Can we send this big parcel by air ?
(1) Can this big parcel be sent by air ?
(2) Can this big parcel sent by air ?
(3) Could this big parcel be sent by air?
(4) Could this big parcel sent by us by air ?

22. The boys saved many elders from being drowned.
(1) Many elders are saved from being drowned by the boys.
(2) Many elders are being saved from being drowned by the boys.
(3) Many elders were saved from being drowned by the boys.
(4) Many elders have been saved from being drowned by the boys.

23. We found him a good wife.
(1) He was found a good wife by us.
(2) A good wife was found out by them.
(3) A good wife found him.
(4) A good wife was being found by us.

24. You will be taken care of by me.
(1) I will be taking care of you.
(2) I would take care of you.
(3) I will take care of you.
(4) I will being take care of you.

25. Promises should be kept.
(1) You must keep promises.
(2) We must keep promises.
(3) Keep promises.
(4) One should keep promises.

26. Circumstances forced him to resign his post.
(1) Circumstances make him to resign his post.
(2) He was forced to resign his post.
(3) He is forced to resign his post.
(4) He is forced and resigned his post.

27. He would have written this essay in time.
(1) The essay was written on time.
(2) This essay would have been written by him in time.
(3) The essay was written by him in time.
(4) He wrote the essay on time.

28. He completed the story on time.
(1) The story was completed by him on time.
(2) The story was being completed by him on time.
(3) The story completed by him on time.
(4) The story had completed by him on time.

29. Sheela painted the house green.
(1) The house was painted green by Sheela.

(2) The house will be painted green by Sheela.

(3) The house is painted green by Sheela,

(4) The house has been painted green by Sheela.

30. An American scientist has won the Nobel Prize for Physics.

(1) The Nobel Physics Prize has been won by an American scientist.

(2) The Nobel Prize has been won by an American scientist.

(3) The Nobel Prize for Physics is won by an American scientist.

(4) The Nobel Prize for Physics has been won by an American scientist.

31. By now the winners will have been felicitated.

(1) They will fel icitate the winners now.

(2) They have felicitated the winners by now.

(3) They will have been felicitated the winners by now.

(4) They will have felicitated the winners by now.

32. I was sanctioned the loan by the office.

(1) The office had sanctioned the loan to me.

(2) The office sanctioned loan to me.

(3) The office sanctioned me the loan.

(4) The office was sanctioned me the loan.

33. Open the window.

(1) Open window.

(2) Someone opens the window.

(3) Window is opened.

(4) Let the window be opened.

34. Deforestation has reduced rainfall in the tropical lands.

(1) Rainfall has been reduced and caused deforestation.

(2) Reduced rainfall deforested the tropical lands.

(3) Rainfall has been reduced due to deforestation in tropical lands.

(4) Tropical lands have been reduced by rainfall.

35. The doctor bandaged the arm of the injured man.

(1) The arm of the injured man was bandaged by the doctor.

(2) The injured man bandaged his arm.

(3) The injured man made the doctor injure his arm.

(4) The doctor injured and bandaged the arm of a man.

36. The ringing of the alarm clock startled me from the deep depths of slumber.

(1) The alarm clock rang, startled and awakened me from sleep.

(2) I was startled from the deep depths of slumber by the ringing of the alarm clock.

(3) The alarm clock rang and startled me from the depths of slumber.

(4) The ringing of the alarm clock made me awake.

37. One of the girls in the class will sing the national anthem at the end of the function.

(1) The function will end, a girl will sing national anthem at the end of the function.

(2) The national anthem will be sung by one of the girls in the class at the end of the function.

(3) There is a girl in the class who sings national anthem.

(4) A girl to sing national anthem is there in the class.

38. Robin would draw a picture in the competition.

(1) In the competition Robin would have to draw a picture.

(2) A picture in the competition would have been drawn by Robin.

(3) In the competition Robin would be drawn a picture.
(4) A picture would be drawn by Robin in the competition.

39. Who gave you ice-cream ?
(1) Who has given you icecream?
(2) By whom were you given ice-cream ?
(3) By whom was you given icecream ?
(4) Who had given you icecream?

40. Are you not revising your lessons?
(1) Are your lessons not be revised by you ?
(2) Are your lessons not being revised by you?
(3) Are not your lessons revised by you ?
(4) Are you not being revising your lessons ?

41. We should not encourage indiscipline.
(1) Indiscipline should have not encouraged by us.
(2) Indiscipline should not be encouraged by us.
(3) Indiscipline should not being encouraged.
(4) Indiscipline should not been encouraged.

42. Our Almighty will bless wise men.
(1) Wise men will be blessed by our Almighty.
(2) Wise men should be blessed by our Almighty.
(3) Wise men have been blessed by our Almighty.
(4) Wise men would be blessed by our Almighty.

43. The Army chief punished his subordinate.
(1) His subordinate is punished by the Army chief.
(2) His subordinate is being punished by the Army chief.
(3) His subordinate was punished by the Army chief.
(4) His subordinate was being punished by the Army chief.

44. One must keep one's promises.
(1) One's promises are kept.
(2) Promises must be kept.
(3) One's promises were kept.
(4) One's promises must kept.

45. They have cut all the telephone wires.
(1) All the telephone wires will be cut.
(2) All the telephone wires had been cut.
(3) All the telephone wires have been cut.
(4) All the telephone wires shall be cut.

46. I shall write a letter.
(1) A letter is written by me.
(2) A letter will be written by me.
(3) A letter has written to me.
(4) A letter has been written by me.

47. Will Motin be helped by us ?
(1) Will Motin help us ?
(2) Shall we help Motin ?
(3) Shall Motin be helped?
(4) We shall helped Motin ?

48. A letter has been written by me.
(1) I have been writing a letter.
(2) I has written a letter.
(3) I had written a letter.
(4) I have written a letter.

49. I cannot draw this picture.
(1) This picture cannot be drawn by me.
(2) This picture cannot be drawn by I.
(3) This picture could not be drawn by me.
(4) This picture could not be drawn by I.

50. The men had constructed the bridge.
(1) The bridge has been constructed by the men.
(2) The bridge was constructed by the men.

(3) The bridge was being constructed by the men.

(4) The bridge had been constructed by the men.

51. Do not inform the police about the robbery.

(1) The police do not be informed about the robbery.

(2) Let not the police be informed about the robbery.

(3) Let the police be informed about the robbery.

(4) The police need to be informed by the robbery.

52. They have spotted me in the crowd.

(1) I am spotted by them in the crowd.

(2) I will have been spotted by them in the crowd.

(3) I would have been spotted by them in the crowd.

(4) I have been spotted by them in the crowd.

53. He made us work.

(1) We were made to work by him.

(2) We would work by him.

(3) We might work by him.

(4) We have to work by him.

54. Leo Tolstoy wrote 'War and Peace'.

(1) 'War and Peace' was written by Leo Tolstoy.

(2) 'War and Peace' is written by Leo Tolstoy.

(3) 'War and Peace' will be written by Leo Tolstoy.

(4) 'War and Peace' was being written by Leo Tolstoy.

55. Rita rescued three puppies.

(1) Three puppies are rescued by Rita.

(2) Three puppies were rescued by Rita.

(3) Three puppies will be rescued by Rita.

(4) Three puppies are being rescued by Rita.

56. Will he have written a letter ?

(1) Will a letter have written by him ?

(2) Will a letter be written by him?

(3) Will a letter to be written by him ?

(4) Will a letter have been written by him ?

57. The doctor advised me to give up sweets.

(1) To me give up sweets was advised by doctor.

(2) The doctor advised to give up sweets me.

(3) I was advised by the doctor to give up sweets.

(4) I was advised to give up eat sweets by the doctor.

58. They will laugh at you.

(1) You will have been laughed at by them.

(2) You can be laughed at by them.

(3) You may be laughed at by them.

(4) You will be laughed at by them.

59. Trespassers shall be prosecuted.

(1) The authorities might prosecute trespassers

(2) The authorities can prosecute trespassers

(3) The authorities shall prosecute trespassers.

(4) The authorities may prosecute trespassers.

60. The waiter filled the glasses with water.

(1) The water were filled in the glasses by waiter.

(2) The glasses filled with water by the waiter.

(3) The glasses were filled with water by the waiter.

(4) The waiter was filled the glasses with water.

61. She took the dog for a walk.

(1) The dog took a walk by her.

(2) The dog was taken for a walk by her.

(3) The dog took her for a walk.

(4) The dog was took for a walk.

62. He was driving the car so fast that it skidded on the snowy road.

(1) The car has been driven by him so fast that it skidded on the snowy road.

(2) The car was driven by him so fast that it skidded on the snowy road.

(3) The car was being driven by him so fast that it skidded on the snowy road.

(4) The car had been driven by him so fast that it skidded on the snowy road.

63. I don't like people telling me what to do.

(1) I don't like it when people are telling me what to do.

(2) I don't like being told what to do.

(3) Telling me what to do is what I don't like.

(4) I don't like people when they tell me what to do.

64. Aditya saw Dinesh shopping at the mall.

(1) Dinesh is seen shopping at the mall by Aditya.

(2) Dinesh was seen shopping at the mall by Aditya.

(3) Dinesh was being seen shopping at the mall by Aditya.

(4) Dinesh is being seen shopping at the mall by Aditya.

65. He wasn't given the information he needed.

(1) Somebody was not given the information he needed.

(2) The information he needed wasn't given to him.

(3) He needed the information he wasn't given.

(4) They didn't give him the information he needed.

66. Bipin was not told about the meeting.

(1) Somebody did not tell Bipin about the meeting.

(2) There was nobody who could tell Bipin about the meeting.

(3) Nobody told Bipin about the meeting.

(4) The meeting was not told about to Bipin.

67. Have you been shown what to do ?

(1) Have anybody been shown by you what to do ?

(2) Have anybody been showing you-what to do ?

(3) Has you been shown what to do?

(4) Has anybody shown you what to do?

68. They proposed to hold a meeting.

(1) A meeting had to be proposed to be held by them.

(2) It was proposed by them to hold a meeting.

(3) A meeting should be proposed to be held.

(4) It had been proposed by them to hold a meeting.

69. Her manners pleased us very much.

(1) We were very much pleased on her manners.

(2) We are very much pleased with her manners.

(3) We pleased her very much with manners.

(4) We were very much pleased with her manners.

70. The driver was blowing the horn.

(1) The horn was blown by the driver.

(2) The horn was being blown by the driver.

(3) The horn has been blown by the driver.

(4) The horn is being blown by the driver.

71. I shall post these letters tomorrow.
(1) These letters would be posted tomorrow.
(2) These letters will be posted tomorrow.
(3) These letters are to be posted tomorrow.
(4) These letters have to be posted tomorrow.

72. A massive search operation has been launched to nab the suspects.
(1) The police had launched a massive search operation to nab the suspects.
(2) The police have launched a massive search operation to nab the suspects.
(3) The police launched a massive search operation to nab the suspects.
(4) The police had been launched a massive search operation to nab the suspects.

73. A fresh batch of eggs was collected by the farmer's wife.
(1) The farmer's wife had collected a fresh batch of eggs.
(2) The farmer's wife will be collecting a fresh batch of eggs.
(3) The farmer's wife was collecting a fresh batch of eggs.
(4) The farmer's wife collected a fresh batch of eggs.

74. I shall have written the letter.
(1) The letter is being written by me.
(2) The letter will have been written by me.
(3) The letter will be written by me.
(4) The letter has been written by me.

75. Then her face was bowed.
(1) Then she bowed her face.
(2) Then her face has been bowed.
(3) Then she was being bowed her face.
(4) Her face was bowed by then.

76. The walls had not been decorated by us.
(1) We have not decorated the walls.
(2) We had not decorated the walls.
(3) We have not been decorating the walls.
(4) We had not been decorating the walls.

77. We must endure what we cannot cure.
(1) What cannot cured must endured.
(2) What could be cure must be endured.
(3) What we cure must be endured.
(4) What cannot be cured must be endured.

78. Did everybody miss the first bus?
(1) The first bus was missed by everybody ?
(2) Was the first bus missed by everybody ?
(3) Everybody missed the first bus ?
(4) Had the first bus been missed by everybody ?

79. We will not allow them to run away.
(1) They will not be allowed to run away by us.
(2) They would not be allowed to run away.
(3) They are not allowed to run away.
(4) They were not allowed to run away.

80. Everyone must read this book.
(1) This book should be read by everyone.
(2) This book has to be read by everyone.
(3) This book is to be read by everyone.
(4) This book must be read by everyone.

81. He knew that his own life was unjust.
(1) It was known to him that his own life had been unjust.
(2) It was known by him that his own life was unjust.

(3) It was known to him that his own life was unjust.
(4) It was known by him that life was unjust.

82. The student has learnt the answer by heart.
(1) The answer was learnt by the student by heart.
(2) The answer is learnt by heart by the student.
(3) The answer by the student was learnt by heart.
(4) The answer has been learnt by heart by the student.

83. The old lady touched and patted the cow.
(1) The cow patted and touched the old lady.
(2) The cow was touched by the old lady patting her.
(3) The cow was touched and patted by the old lady.
(4) The patted cow touched the old lady.

84. This watch was given to me by my grandfather.
(1) My grandfather gave me this watch.
(2) My grandfather gives me this watch.
(3) My grandfather had given this watch to me.
(4) My grandfather has given this watch to me.

85. By whom is the child being fed?
(1) Who is feeding the child ?
(2) Who has fed the child ?
(3) Who was feeding the child ?
(4) Who has been feeding the child ?

86. Alexander expected to conquer the world.
(1) It was expected by Alexander that he should conquer the world.
(2) It was expected by Alexander that he would conquer the world.
(3) It was expected by Alexander that he will conquer the world.
(4) It had been expected by Alexander that he would conquer the world.

87. She begins her day with a cup of coffee.
(1) Her day is being begun with a cup of coffee.
(2) Her day is begun with a cup of coffee.
(3) A cup of coffee is beginning her day.
(4) A cup of coffee has begun her day.

88. Cacao is bitter when it is tasted.
(1) Cacao is bitter.
(2) Cacao tastes bitter.
(3) Cacao's taste is bitter.
(4) Cacao tasted bitter.

89. A great man acknowledged me as a flatterer to him.
(1) I was acknowledged by a great man to be a flatterer.
(2) I was acknowledged by a great man to have been a flatterer.
(3) I am acknowledged as a flatterer by a great man.
(4) I was acknowledged as a flatterer to a great man.

90. Let us help him.
(1) Let him help us.
(2) Let he is helped.
(3) Let he be helped.
(4) Let him be helped by us.

91. Can those happy moments be ever forgotten by me ?"
(1) Shall I ever forget those happy moments ?
(2) Can I ever forget those happy moments ?
(3) Will I ever forget those happy moments ?
(4) Could I ever forget those happy moments ?

92. You have to do this immediately.
(1) This has been done by you immediately.
(2) This is being done by you immediately.

(3) This was being done by you immediately.
(4) This has to be done by you immediately.

93. The labourers were digging a canal.
(1) A canal is being digged by the labourers.
(2) A canal was dug by the labourers.
(3) A canal was being dug by the labourers.
(4) A canal had been dug by the labourers.

94. The watchman switched on the lights before it began to grow dark.
(1) The 1 ights were only switched on before it began to grow dark.
(2) The lights are being switched on before it' began to grow dark.
(3) The lights were being switched on by the watchman before it began to grow dark.
(4) The lights were switched on by the watchman before it began to grow dark.

95. Where do you keep the current magazines ?
(1) Where were the current magazines kept ?
(2) Where have the current magazines been kept ?
(3) Where are the current magazines being kept ?
(4) Where are the current magazines kept by you ?

96. She will be rewarded for her kind deed.
(1) Her kind deed will reward her.
(2) Her kind deed will have rewarded her.
(3) Her kind deed will be her reward.
(4) Her kind deed will have been her reward.

97. God gives us happiness.
(1) Happiness is given by God.
(2) Happiness is being given to us by God.
(3) Happiness has been given by God.
(4) Happiness will be given by God.

98. The gardener ought to water the plants daily.
(1) The plants have been watered daily by the gardener.
(2) The plants ought to water daily by the gardener.
(3) The plants are ought to water daily by the gardener.
(4) The plants ought to be watered daily by the gardener.

99. Who wrote it ?
(1) By who will it be written ?
(2) By whom was it written ?
(3) By who might it be written?
(4) By who would it be written ?

100. The principal will announce the results.
(1) The results were announced by the principal.
(2) The results are announced by the principal.
(3) The results will have announced by the pripcipal.
(4) The results will be announced by the principal.

101. Some people were helping the wounded woman.
(1) The wounded woman is being helped by some people.
(2) The wounded woman was being helped by some people.
(3) The wounded is helped by some people.
(4) The wounded woman was helped by some people.

102. The servant will execute all orders promptly.
(1) All orders will have to be executed promptly by the servant.
(2) All orders would be executed

promptly by the servant.

(3) All orders should be executed promptly by the servant.

(4) All orders will be executed promptly by the servant.

103. I was obliged to go.

(1) Circumstances obliges me to go.

(2) Circumstances oblige I should go.

(3) Circumstances oblige me to go.

(4) Circumstances obliged me to go.

104. They established this club in 2000.

(1) This club was being established in 2000.

(2) This club was established in 2000.

(3) This club had been established in 2000.

(4) This club is being established in 2000.

105. For a long time people believed the earth to be flat.

(1) The earth was believed to be flat for a long time.

(2) The earth had been believed to be flat for a long time.

(3) The earth was being believed to be flat for a long time.

(4) The earth is believed to be flat for a long time.

106. The boy did not break the glass.

(1) The glass was not broken by the boy.

(2) The glass has not been broken by the boy.

(3) The glass is not broken by the boy.

(4) The glass had not been broken by the boy.

107. They fund schools for girls.

(1) Schools for girls was funded by them.

(2) Schools for girls will be funded by them.

(3) Schools for girls are funded by them

(4) Schools for girls are being funded by them.

108. The lady of the house was furnishing the mansion.

(1) The mansion is being furnished by the lady of the house.

(2) The mansion was being furnished by the lady of the house.

(3) The mansion is furnished by the lady of the house.

(4) The mansion has been furnished by the lady of the house.

109. The convict was found guilty by the jury.

(1) The jury found that the convict was guilty.

(2) The jury convicted him.

(3) The jury found the convict guilty.

(4) The jury finds the convict guilty.

110. I have lost my book.

(1) My book had been lost.

(2) My book must have been lost.

(3) My book has been lost.

(4) My book have been lost.

111. Open the door.

(1) Let the door shall be opened.

(2) The door shall be opened.

(3) The door was opened.

(4) Let the door be opened.

112. My father has promised me a bicycle.

(1) I have promising a bicycle by my father.

(2) I have been promised by my father a bicycle.

(3) I promised a bicycle by my father.

(4) I have been promised a bicycle by my father.

113. My mother bakes cakes.

(1) A cake was baked by my mother.

(2) My mother is baking a cake.

(3) A cake is being baked by my mother.

(4) Cakes are baked by my mother.

114. My father will write a letter.

(1) A letter will be written by my father.

(2) A letter is written by my father.

(3) A letter was written by my father.
(4) A letter will have been written by my father.

115. My brilliant niece is speaking Italian.
(1) Italian is spoken by my brilliant niece.
(2) Italian was being spoken by my brilliant niece.
(3) Italian is being spoken by my brilliant niece.
(4) Italian has been spoken by my brilliant niece.

116. She is putting in many hours of work.
(1) Many hours of work would be put in by her.
(2) Many hours of work is being put by her.
(3) Many hours of work are being put in by her.
(4) Many hours of work will be put in by her.

117. Everyone praises good men.
(1) Good men are being given praises by everyone.
(2) Good men are praised by everyone.
(3) Everyone give praises to good men.
(4) Good men are given praises by everyone.

118. Children make a noise.
(1) A noise was being made by the children
(2) Noise is made by children
(3) A noise was made by the children
(4) A noise is being made by the children

119. She taunted her husband with the memory of his early promise.
(1) Her husband is taunted by her with the memory of his early promise
(2) Her husband was taunted with the memory of his early promise
(3) Her husband was taunted by her with the memory of his early promise
(4) The husband was taunted by her with the memory of his early promise

120. He impresses his boss with his performance.
(1) His boss is impressed by his performance.
(2) His performance impresses his boss
(3) His boss is impressed at his performance
(4) His boss is impressed in his performance

121. How was it managed by you?
(1) How have you managed it ?
(2) Did you manage it ?
(3) How did you manage it ?
(4) Was it managed by you ?

122. I was astonished at his behaviour.
(1) His behaviour is astonishing to me
(2) His behaviour astonished me
(3) His behaviour astonishes me
(4) His behaviour had astonished me

123. All his friends laughed at him.
(1) He was laughed at by all his friends
(2) He was laughed by all his friends
(3) He was being laughed by all his friends
(4) He was being laughed at by all his friends

124. Every disaster affected victim has been compensated by the government.
(1) The government has compensated every disaster affected victim
(2) The government had compensated every disaster affected victim
(3) The government has been compensating every disaster affected victim
(4) The government have been compensating every disaster affected victim

125. Indiscipline should not be encouraged.
(1) We are not encouraging indiscipline
(2) We have not encouraging indiscipline

(3) We should not encourage indiscipline
(4) We must not encouraged indiscipline

126. This house is used very rarely by us.
(1) We are using this house very rarely
(2) We use this house very rarely
(3) We used this house very rarely
(4) We uses this house very rarely

127. The box can contain no more.
(1) No more this box can contain
(2) No more could be contained in this box
(3) No more can be contained in this box
(4) Nothing can be contained in this box

128. They held a meeting and delivered speeches.
(1) A meeting was held and delivered speeches
(2) A meeting will be held and speeches delivered
(3) A meeting is held and speeches delivered
(4) A meeting was held and speeches delivered

129. It is time for food to be eaten.
(1) It is time to eat our food
(2) It is time for eating food
(3) It is time to eat
(4) Food is to be eaten now

130. The teacher may punish you.
(1) You should be punished by the teacher
(2) You shall have been punished by the teacher
(3) You will be punished by the teacher
(4) You may be punished by the teacher

131. None likes him.
(1) He is liked by none
(2) He was not liked by anyone
(3) He has not been liked by anyone
(4) He is not liked by anyone

132. You are requested to keep the book on the table.
(1) You should keep the book on the table
(2) You must keep the book on the table
(3) Please kept the book on the table
(4) Please keep the book on the table

133. He was being chased by the dogs.
(1) The dogs are chasing him
(2) The dogs chased him
(3) The dogs chase him
(4) The dogs were chasing him

134. She wrote a letter.
(1) A letter is being written by her
(2) A letter is written by her
(3) A letter was written by her
(4) A letter was being written by her

135. My mother mustn't be disturbed.
(1) You mustn't disturb my mother
(2) You shouldn't disturb my mother
(3) You must be disturbing my mother
(4) You have disturbed my mother

136. His lordship soon found me to be unfit for the service.
(1) I had been found by his lordship to be unfit for the service
(2) I was soon found by his lordship to be unfit for the service
(3) I was found by his lordship to be unfit for the service
(4) I was soon found out by his lordship to be unfit for the service

137. They have not been submitting their class work regularly.
(1) The class work have not been submitted regularly by them
(2) The class work has not been submitted regularly by them
(3) The class work are not being submitted regularly
(4) The class work is not being submitted regularly by them

138. One should keep ones promises.
(1) Promises should be kept by someone.
(2) One promise should be kept.
(3) Once a promise should be kept.
(4) Promises should be kept.

139. People in Egypt speak Arabic.
(1) Arabic was spoken by people in Egypt.
(2) Arabic is spoken in Egypt.
(3) In Egypt Arabic is spoken.
(4) Arabic is being spoken by people in Egypt.

140. The poor must be looked after by society.
(1) Society must have looked after the poor.
(2) Society must look after the poor.
(3) Society must be looked after the poor.
(4) Society must looked after the poor.

141. We should respect elders.
(1) Elders should have respected.
(2) Elders are to be respected.
(3) Elders have been respected.
(4) Elders should be respected.

142. Can we rely on him ?
(1) Can he be relied on ?
(2) Can we be relied by him ?
(3) Can he be relied by us ?
(4) Can we be relied on by him?

143. Who teaches you English ?
(1) By whom you are taught English ?
(2) By whom English is taught to you ?
(3) By whom was you taught English ?
(4) By whom are you taught English ?

144. Do not insult the poor.
(1) Let the poor not to insult.
(2) Let not the poor be insulted.
(3) Let the poor to be not insulted.
(4) Let us not insulted the poor.

145. It interests me.
(1) I have been interested in it.
(2) I am interested in it.
(3) I will be interested in it.
(4) I was interested in it.

146. The boy laughed at the lame man.
(1) The boy laughed seeing the lame man.
(2) The lame man was laughed at by the boy.
(3) The boy laughed when he saw the lame man.
(4) The lame man was laughed by the boy.

147. Rohit was taken to the hospital by the villagers.
(1) Rohit was helped by the villagers to reach the hospital.
(2) The villagers took Rohit to the hospital.
(3) The hospital was reached by the villagers with Rohit.
(4) The villagers reached the hospital with Rohit.

148. Complete the minutes of the last meeting.
(1) The last meeting's minutes are completed.
(2) The completed minutes of last meeting is to be tabled
(3) Minutes of the last meeting are to be completed.
(4) The meeting's last minutes are completed.

149. Grandfather was digging the flowerbeds.
(1) The grandfather was digging flowerbeds.
(2) The flowerbeds were digging grandfather.
(3) Grandfather's flowerbeds were being dug.
(4) The flowerbeds were being dug by grandfather.

150. I will complete my project next week.
(1) Next week my project I will complete.
(2) Next week my project will be

completed.

(3) My project will be completed by me next week.

(4) My project I will complete next week.

151. God helps those who help themselves.

(1) Those who help themselves help God.

(2) Those who help themselves are helped by God.

(3) Those who help God help themselves.

(4) Those who are helped by themselves are helped by God.

152. He will object to my proposal.

(1) My proposal will be objected to by him.

(2) The objection to my proposal will come from him.

(3) His objection will be to my proposal.

(4) There will be an objection to my proposal by him.

153. Father called up Angela on her birthday.

(1) On her birthday Angela was called up by her father.

(2) Angela called up her father on her birthday.

(3) Angela received a call from her father on her birthday.

(4) Angela was called up by father on her birthday.

154. Why didn't you bring the matter to my notice ?

(1) Why wasn't the matter brought to my notice ?

(2) Why isn't the matter brought by you to my notice ?

(3) Why isn't the matter brought to my notice ?

(4) Why wasn't the matter brought by you to my notice ?

155. Why was he refused admittance?

(1) Why were they refusing him admittance ?

(2) Why did they refuse him admittance?

(3) Why are they refusing him admittance ?

(4) Why do they refuse him admittance?

156. People say that he is a spy.

(1) It was said that he is a spy.

(2) It is said by people that he is a spy.

(3) It has been said that he is a spy.

(4) It is said that he is a spy.

157. Finish the game.

(1) The game had to be finished.

(2) Let the game finish.

(3) Let the game be finished

(4) The game should be finished

158. The task should have been completed by the student.

(1) The student should have completed the task.

(2) The student should complete the task.

(3) The student should be completing the task.

(4) The student should have complete the task.

159. He was caught by the police for littering up the streets.

(1) The police has caught him littering up the street.

(2) The police was catching him littering up the street.

(3) The police caught him for littering up the street.

(4) The police catches him littering up the street.

160. Let the window be opened.

(1) Window be opened.

(2) Leave the window open

(3) Open the window.

(4) Don't close the window.

161. I know that he did the work.

(1) That the work was done by him is

known to me.

(2) That the work is done by him is known to me.

(3) That he did the work is known by me.

(4) That he did the work is known to me.

162. Many factors within our nation affect the economy.

(1) The economy was affected by many factors within our nation.

(2) The economy has affected by many factors within our nation.

(3) The economy is being affected by many factors within our nation.

(4) The economy is affected by many factors within our nation.

163. The child upset the salt over everything.

(1) The child is upset about the salt over everything.

(2) The salt is upset over everything by the child.

(3) The salt is upsetted by the child over everything.

(4) The salt was upset over everything by the child.

164. He opens the door.

(1) The door is opened by him.

(2) The door was opened by him.

(3) The door shall be opened by him.

(4) The door will be opened by him.

165. I am going to bring him here.

(1) He is going to bring here by me.

(2) He is being brought here by me.

(3) He is going to be brought here by me.

(4) He is being gone to be brought here by me.

166. He has sent me a present.

(1) I have been sent to him a present.

(2) A present will be sent to me by him.

(3) A present have been sent to me.

(4) A present has been sent to me by him.

167. Parents love their children.

(1) Children have been loved by their parents.

(2) Children will be loved by their parents.

(3) Children are loved by their parents.

(4) Children are being loved by their parents.

168. The painting would have been stolen if he hadn't helped.

(1) Someone had stolen the painting if he hadn't helped.

(2) Someone stole the painting if he hadn't helped.

(3) Someone would have stolen the painting if he hadn't helped.

(4) Someone may have stolen the painting if he hadn't helped.

169. They believe Veerappan to be dangerous.

(1) Veerappan has been believed to be dangerous.

(2) Veerappan could be believed to be dangerous.

(3) Veerappan is believed to be dangerous.

(4) Veerappan can be believed to be dangerous.

170. My last venture undid me completely.

(1) I was completely undone by my last venture

(2) I was incompletely done by my last venture

(3) I was not done completely by my last venture.

(4) I was not being undone completely by my last venture.

171. Your promises are to be kept by you

(1) Promises must be kept by you.

(2) You are to keep your promises.

(3) You may keep your promises.

(4) You should keep your promises.

172. Many types of fish were being sold by them at the market.
   (1) They are selling many types of fish at the market.
   (2) They were sel ling many types of fish at the market.
   (3) They have sold many types of fish at the market.
   (4) They sell many types of fish at the market.

173. We have cycled more than ten kilometers.
   (1) More than ten kilometers have been cycled by us.
   (2) None of the above.
   (3) We have been cycling for more than ten kilometers.
   (4) Both of the above.

174. The lady is treading on the flowers.
   (1) The flowers are being treaden on by the lady.
   (2) The flowers are being trodden on by the lady.
   (3) The flowers are being trod on by the lady.
   (4) The flowers are being treaded on by the lady.

175. The historical society built the museum.
   (1) The museum was built by the historical society.
   (2) The museum has been built by the historical society.
   (3) The museum is built by the historical society.
   (4) The museum was being built by the historical society.

176. Let him be told to do it.
   (1) He is told to do it.
   (2) He should be told to do it.
   (3) Tell him to do it.
   (4) Tell him about doing it.

177. Please see that the room is swept and mopped before I return.
   (1) Please see that somebody will sweeps and mop the room before I return.
   (2) Please see that somebody has swept and mopped the room before I return.
   (3) Please see that somebody sweeps and mops the room before I return.
   (4) Please see that somebody is sweeping and mops the room before I return.

178. The Swiss regarded him as an imposter and called him a Villain.
   (1) He has been regarded as an imposter and called a Villain by the Swiss.
   (2) He was regarded as an imposter and is called a Villain by the Swiss.
   (3) He is regarded as an imposter and called a Villain by the Swiss.
   (4) He was regarded as an imposter and was called a villain by the Swiss.

179. That too many cooks spoil the broth is known to all.
   (1) All knew that too many cooks spoilt the broth.
   (2) All knows that the broth is spoilt by too many cooks.
   (3) All know that too many cooks spoil the broth.
   (4) All know that the broth is spoilt by too many cooks.

180. Did he plan an excursion to mountains ?
   (1) Has an excursion to mountains planned by him ?
   (2) Had an excursion to mountains planned by him?
   (3) Was an excursion to mountains planned by him ?
   (4) Is an excursion to mountains planned by him ?

181. The judge ordered the murderer to be hanged.
   (1) The order was given by the judge to hang the murderer.

(2) The murderer was to be hanged according to the order of the judge.
(3) The murderer was ordered by the judge to be hanged.
(4) It was ordered by the judge to hang the murderer.

182. Kindly offer your remarks.
(1) You have been requested to offer your remarks.
(2) You were requested to offer your remarks.
(3) You are requested to offer your remarks.
(4) You are being requested to offer your remarks.

183. Ratan is performing an experiment.
(1) An experiment is performed by Ratan.
(2) An experiment is being performed by Ratan.
(3) An experiment was performed by Ratan.
(4) Experiments were performed by Ratan.

184. I shall be obliged to go.
(1) Circumstances could oblige me to go.
(2) Circumstances will oblige me to go.
(3) Circumstances would oblige me to go.
(4) Circumstances may oblige me to go.

185. Who gave you the money ?
(1) By whom was you given the money ?
(2) By whom were you given the money ?
(3) Who was given the money by you ?
(4) Who gave the money to you?

186. I didn't speak even a single word in the meeting.
(1) Even a single word had not been spoken by me in the meeting.
(2) Even a single word have not been spoken by me in the meeting.
(3) Even a single word was not spoken by me in the meeting.
(4) Even a single word has not been spoken by me in the meeting.

187. We shall write a novel.
(1) A novel will have been written by us.
(2) A novel will be written by us.
(3) A novel is written by us.
(4) A novel would be written by us.

188. Our vehicle had been stolen from our garage by the same burglary team.
(1) The same burglary team has stolen our vehicle from our garage.
(2) The same burglary team had stolen our vehicle from our garage.
(3) The same burglary team is stealing our vehicle from our garage.
(4) The same burglary team will have stolen our vehicle from our garage.

189. Sita learns her lessons daily.
(1) Her lessons is learnt daily by Sita.
(2) Her lessons are learnt daily by Sita.
(3) Her lessons was learnt daily by Sita.
(4) Her lessons were learnt daily by Sita.

190. It is time to water the plants.
(1) The plants should be watered.
(2) It is time when plants are watered.
(3) It is time the plants be watered.
(4) It is time for the plants to be watered.

191. These days most of the students do their assignments with the help of the internet.
(1) These days most of the students are doing their assignments with the help of the internet.
(2) These days most of the assignments are done with the help of the internet by the students.
(3) These days the assignments are being done with the help of the internet by most of the students.
(4) These days the assignments are done with the help of the internet by most of the students.

192. Who tore the curtains yesterday ?

(1) By whom were the curtains teared yesterday ?

(2) By whom were the curtains torn yesterday ?

(3) By whom are the curtains torn yesterday ?

(4) By whom were the curtains tore yesterday ?

193. Shut the door.

(1) Let door be shut.

(2) Let the door be shut.

(3) Let door be shut by you.

(4) Let the door be shutted.

194. Rajesh could not complete his paper because he had a headache.

(1) Rajesh's paper would not be completed because he had a headache.

(2) The paper could not be completed by Rajesh because he had a headache.

(3) The paper of Rajesh could not be completed by him because he had a headache.

(4) Rajesh's paper could not be completed because he had a headache.

195. The situation could hardly have been altered by the interference of the police force.

(1) The interference of the police force can hardly alter the situation.

(2) The interference of the police force could alter the situation with hardness.

(3) The interference of the police force could hardly have altered the situation.

(4) The interference of the police force had altered the situation.

196. Who had laughed at you ?

(1) By whom had you been laughed at ?

(2) Who had you been laughed at ?

(3) By whom you had been laughed at ?

(4) By whom were you been laughed at ?

197. We prohibit smoking.

(1) Smoking is being prohibited.

(2) Smoking has been prohibited.

(3) Smoking will be prohibited.

(4) Smoking is prohibited.

198. I cannot trust him any more.

(1) He cannot trust by me any more.

(2) He may not be trusted by me any more.

(3) He cannot be trusted by me any more.

(4) He could not be trusted by me any more.

199. Take the medicine.

(1) Let the medicine be taken.

(2) The medicine must take you.

(3) The medicine is to be taken by you.

(4) You are requested to take the medicine.

200. People say that he is a spy.

(1) A spy that he is said the people.

(2) It has been said by the people that he is a spy.

(3) It is said that he is a spy.

(4) He is a spy was said by people.

201. Has he completed the assignments ?

(1) Has the assignments being completed by him ?

(2) Have the assignments been completed by him ?

(3) Have the assignments completed by him ?

(4) Has the assignments been completed by him ?

202. The boys were making kites.

(1) Kites are being made by the boys.

(2) Kites were being made by the boys.

(3) Kites are made by the boys.

(4) The boys had made kites.

203. He will not use the computer.

(1) By him the computer will not be used.

(2) The computer will not be used by him.

(3) The use of the computer will not be by him.

(4) The computer he will not use.

204. I was obliged to leave.

(1) Circumstances have obliged me to leave.

(2) Circumstances obliged me to leave.

(3) Circumstance will oblige me to leave.

(4) Circumstance was obliged me to leave.

205. Close the door.

(1) Let the door be closed.

(2) Let the door closed.

(3) Let the door is closed.

(4) Let the door is being closed.

206. We must take care of our parents.

(1) Our parents are taken care of by us.

(2) Our parents will be taken care of by us.

(3) Our parents had been taken care of by us.

(4) Our parents must be taken cared for by us.

207. Please close the door.

(1) You please close the door.

(2) You close the door yourself.

(3) Let the door be closed by you.

(4) Please be the door closed by you.

208. The agreement between the management and the workers was drafted by an advisory board.

(1) The agreement between the management and the workers is being drafted by an advisory board.

(2) An advisory board drafted the agreement between the management and the workers.

(3) An advisory board is drafting the agreement between the management and the workers.

(4) An advisory board had drafted the agreement between the management and the workers.

209. Put up the tent.

(1) Let the tent be put up.

(2) The tent is being put up.

(3) The tent has been put up.

(4) Let the tent being put up.

210. Please give me your pen and take your seat.

(1) Let your pen given me and take your seat.

(2) You are requested to give me your pen and take your seat.

(3) You are warned to give me your pen and take your seat.

(4) You are ordered to give me your pen and take your seat.

211. The prisoner is known to have assaulted warden earlier too.

(1) It is known that the prisoner has assaulted the warden earlier too.

(2) The warden was assaulted by the prisoner earlier too.

(3) It is known that the warden has been assaulted by the prisoner earlier too.

(4) It is known that the warden has assaulted the prisoner earlier too.

212. Can she write an interesting story ?

(1) Can an interesting story be written for her ?

(2) Can an interesting story be written to her ?

(3) Can an interesting story be written by her ?

(4) Could an interesting story be written by her ?

213. The poet, Blake, wrote many poems for children.

(1) Many poems were written for children by the poet, Blake.

(2) Many poems were written by children for the poet, Blake.

(3) Many are the poems written by children for the poet Blake.

(4) Children wrote many poems by the poet Blake.

214. Each person exhibited various facial expressions.

(1) Various facial expressions are exhibited by each person.

(2) Various facial expressions were exhibited by each person.

(3) Various facial expressions were being exhibited by each person.

(4) Various facial expressions have been used by each person.

215. The girls ate a mango yesterday.

(1) A mango is eaten by the girls yesterday.

(2) A mango was eaten by the girls yesterday.

(3) A mango is being eaten by the girls yesterday.

(4) A mango has been eaten by the girls yesterday.

216. Your manners irritate me.

(1) I am irritated by my manners.

(2) Manners are irritating me.

(3) I am being irritated by your manners.

(4) I am irritated by your manners.

217. The boys laughed at the old man.

(1) The old man was laughed by the boys.

(2) The old man was being laughed by the boys.

(3) The old man was being laughed at by the boys.

(4) The old man was laughed at by the boys.

218. Ideas are generated by Group discussions.

(1) Group discussions generated idea.

(2) Group discussions generate ideas.

(3) Group discussions have generated ideas.

(4) Group discussions generates ideas.

219. Who is singing such a sweet song?

(1) By whom is such a sweet song sang?

(2) By whom has such a sweet song sung?

(3) By whom is such a sweet song sung?

(4) By whom is such a sweet song being sung?

220. Please give me your pen and take your seat.

(1) Let your pen given me and take your seat.

(2) You are requested to give me your pen and take your seat.

(3) You are warned to give me your pen and take your seat.

(4) You are ordered to give me your pen and take your seat.

221. The prisoner is known to have assaulted the warden earlier too.

(1) It is known that the prisoner has assaulted the warden earlier too.

(2) The warden was assaulted by the prisoner earlier too.

(3) It is known that the warden has been assaulted by the prisoner earlier too.

(4) It is known that the warden has assaulted the prisoner earlier too.

222. Can she write an interesting story?

(1) Can an interesting story be written for her ?

(2) Can an interesting story be written to her ?

(3) Can an interesting story be written by her ?

(4) Could an interesting story be written by her ?

223. The poet, Blake, wrote many poems for children.

(1) Many poems were written for children by the poet, Blake.

(2) Many poems were written by

children for the poet, Blake.

(3) Many are the poems written by children for the poet Blake.

(4) Children wrote many poems by the poet Blake.

224. Each person exhibited various facial expressions.

(1) Various facial expressions are exhibited by each person.

(2) Various facial expressions were exhibited by each person.

(3) Various facial expressions were being exhibited by each person.

(4) Various facial expressions have been used by each person.

225. The girls ate a mango yesterday.

(1) A mango is eaten by the girls yesterday.

(2) A mango was eaten by the girls yesterday.

(3) A mango is being eaten by the girls yesterday.

(4) A mango has been eaten by the girls yesterday.

226. Your manners irritate me.

(1) I am irritated by my manners.

(2) Manners are irritating me.

(3) I am being irritated by your manners.

(4) I am irritated by your manners.

227. I will send the papers to the officer.

a) The papers would be sent to the officer by me.

b) The papers were sent to the officer by me.

c) The papers are sent to the officer by me.

d) The papers will be sent to the officer by me.

228. The doctor advised the child not to eat junk food.

a) The child was advised by the doctor to not to eat junk food.

b) The child was advised by the doctor that he should not eat junk food.

c) The child was being advised that he should not eat junk food by the doctor.

d) The child has been advised not to eat junk food by the doctor.

229. You cannot deny the fact.

a) The fact can not denied by you.

b) You cannot be denied by the fact.

c) The fact cannot be denied by you.

d) The fact shouldn't be denied.

230. Our parents have taught us to behave properly.

(1) We were taught how to behave properly by our parents.

(2) Our parents taught us how to behave properly.

(3) Our parents have been teaching us how to behave properly.

(4) We have been taught to behave properly by our parents.

231. Why did your father refuse such an honourable job ?

(1) Why does your father refused such an honourable job ?

(2) Why is such an honourable job refused by your father ?

(3) Why was such an honourable job refused by your father ?

(4) Why was such an honourable job denied by your father ?

232. James Cameron directed the Titanic.

(1) The Titanic was directed by James Cameron.

(2) James Cameron had directed the Titanic.

(3) James Cameron had been directing the Titanic.

(4) The Titanic has been directed by James Cameron.

233. Mr. Dutta teaches us English.

(1) We are being taught English by Mr.

Dutta.

(2) By Mr. Dutta we are taught English.

(3) We have been taught English by Mr. Dutta.

(4) English is taught to us by Mr. Dutta.

234. Has the postman not delivered the letter ?

(1) Has the letter not been delivered by the postman ?

(2) Is the letter delivered by the postman ?

(3) The postman hasn't delivered the letter,

(4) Has the letter been delivered by the postman ?

235. John is building a new cupboard.

(1) A new cupboard is being built by John.

(2) A new cupboard is been built by John.

(3) John's new cupboard is being built.

(4) John has been building a new cupboard.

236. Someone will pay you next Monday.

(1) Someone will be paying you next Monday.

(2) You will be paid next Monday.

(3) Someone is going to pay you next Monday.

(4) You would be paid next Monday.

237. Drinking was ruining his life gradually.

(1) His life is ruined by gradual drinking.

(2) Gradually, his life is ruined because of drinking problems.

(3) Drinking problems caused the gradual ruin of his life.

(4) His life was being ruined gradually by drinking.

238. A small epitaph had been laid out by them in his memory.

(1) They had laid out a small epitaph in his memory.

(2) They were laying out, in his memory, a small epitaph.

(3) They lay out a small epitaph in his memory.

(4) They laid out a small epitaph.

239. The nurse is giving food to the sick boy.

(1) The sick boy gets food from the nurse.

(2) The sick boy is being given food by the nurse.

(3) Food is given to the sick boy by the nurse.

(4) The sick boy is given food by the nurse.

240. He could have solved the problem.

(1) The problem could be solved by him.

(2) The problem could have solved by him.

(3) The problem could have been solved by him.

(4) The problem could solve by him.

241. Do not insult the poor.

(1) The poor are not insulted.

(2) The poor is not insulted.

(3) Let the poor be not insulted.

(4) Let the poor not be insulted.

242. Do not disturb me.

(1) Let me be disturbed not.

(2) Let me not disturbed.

(3) Let me not be disturbed.

(4) Let I not be disturbed.

243. Who will help me?

(1) By whom I shall be helped?

(2) By whom will I be helped?

(3) By whom would I be helped?

(4) By whom I will be helped?

244. Who has destroyed Nagasaki?

(1) By whom Nagasaki have been destroyed?

(2) By whom has Nagasaki been destroyed?

(3) By whom Nagasaki had been destroyed?

(4) By whom Nagasaki has been

destroyed?

245. Arun has written a newspaper report on the inauguration of Delhi Metro Railways.
   (1) A newspaper report on the inauguration of Delhi Metro Railways have been written by Arun.
   (2) A newspaper report on the inauguration of Delhi Metro Railways had been written by Arun.
   (3) A newspaper report on the inauguration of Delhi Metro Railways is written by Arun.
   (4) A newspaper report on the inauguration of Delhi Metro Railways has been written by Arun.

246. The students have dedicated an issue of magazine to him.
   (1) An issue of magazine had been dedicated to him by the students.
   (2) An issue of magazine has been dedicated to him by the students.
   (3) An issue of magazine have been dedicated to him by the students.
   (4) An issue of magazine is dedicated to him by the students.

247. The old owl will listen to the squirrel's problems, patiently.
   (1) The squirrel's problems shall be listened patiently by the old owl.
   (2) The squarrel's problems will be listened to patiently by the old owl.
   (3) The squirrel's problems would be listened patiently by the old owl.
   (4) The squirrel's problems should be listened patiently by the old owl.

248. Parents elected him the chairman of PTA as he was the only talented contestant.
   (1) He was elected the chairman of PTA by parents as he was the only talented contestant.
   (2) He had been elected the chairman of PTA by parents as he was the only talented contestant.
   (3) He have been elected the chairman of PTA by parents as he is the only talented contestant.
   (4) He is elected the chairman of PTA by parents as he was the only talented contestant.

249. The movie will create tension in the Indian society.
   (1) Tension would be created in the Indian society by the movie.
   (2) The tension shall be created in the Indian society by the movie.
   (3) Tension will be created in the Indian society by the movie.
   (4) The tension can be created in the Indian society by the movie.

250. Late arrival of the Gomati Express created confusion among the passengers.
   (1) Confusion has been created among passengers due to the late arrival of the Gomati Express.
   (2) Confusion have been created among passengers due to the late arrival of the Gomati Express.
   (3) Confusion was created among passengers due to the late arrival of the Gomati Express.
   (4) Confusion is created among passengers due to the late arrival of the Gomati Express.

251. The scorpion stung the farmer.
   (1) The farmer was stung by the scorpion.
   (2) The farmer had been stung by the scorpion.
   (3) The farmer is stung by the scorpion.
   (4) The farmer has been stung by the scorpion.

252. Let Sumita help him.
   (1) Let them be helped by Sumita.
   (2) Let him be helped by Sumita.
   (3) Let him helped by Sumita.

(4) He should help by Sumita.

253. I found the box last night in a ditch near my house.

(1) The box I found last night in a ditch near my house.

(2) The box was found last night in a ditch near my house.

(3) Last night I found the box in a ditch near my house.

(4) The box is found last night in a ditch near my house.

254. The government has launched a programme to improve the performance of the ministries.

(1) To improve the performance of the ministries, a programme has been launched by the government.

(2) For the improvement of performance by the ministries, a programme has been launched by the government.

(3) A programme has been launched for the improvement of ministries by the government.

(4) The programme launched by the government was for the improvement of performance of the ministries.

255. A hundred carefully–screened people were invited to dinner by the Prime Minister.

(1) The Prime Minister invited a hundred people after screening them to dinner.

(2) The Prime Minister invited a hundred carefully screened people to have dinner with him.

(3) The Prime Minister invited a hundred carefullyscreened people to dinner.

(4) The Prime Minister invited to dinner a hundred persons who were carefully screened.

256. It is good that your ideas can be expressed with such clarity by you.

(1) It is good that you can express your ideas with such clarity.

(2) It is good that such clarity can be expressed by you through your ideas.

(3) It is good that you could have expressed your ideas with such clarity.

(4) It is good that you could express yourself with such clarity.

257. A good deal of money will be made by that investment.

(1) That investment has made a good deal of money.

(2) That investment will be making a good deal of money.

(3) That investment has been making a good deal of money.

(4) That investment will make a good deal of money.

258. He had transported all his equipment to his factory.

(1) All his equipment are transported to his factory by him.

(2) All his equipment were transported to his factory by him.

(3) All his equipment have transported by him to his factory.

(4) All his equipment had been transported by him to his factory.

259. Marketing professionals play a major role in the development of business sectors.

(1) A major role is played by the marketing professionals in the development of business sectors.

(2) A major role is being played by the marketing professionals in the development of business sectors.

(3) In the development of business sectors, a major role was played by the marketing professionals.

(4) In the development of business sectors, a major role has been played by the marketing professionals.

260. The enemies have destroyed the 'Ajooba' town.
(1) The 'Ajooba' town was destroyed by the enemies.
(2) The 'Ajooba' town had been destroyed by the enemies.
(3) The 'Ajooba' town have been destroyed by the enemies.
(4) The 'Ajooba' town has been destroyed by the enemies.

261. Rohit had written an essay on 'pollution'.
(1) An essay on 'pollution' was written by Rohit.
(2) An essay on 'pollution' had been written by Rohit.
(3) An essay on 'pollution' wrote by Rohit.
(4) An essay on 'pollution' have been written by Rohit.

262. He had already torn the pages of the book.
(1) The pages of the book has already been torn by him.
(2) The pages of the book have already been torn by him.
(3) The pages of the book had already been torn by him.
(4) The pages of the book had already torn by him.

263. This word cannot be uttered by a sane man.
(1) A sane man did not utter this word.
(2) A sane man will not utter this word.
(3) A sane man cannot utter the word.
(4) A sane man cannot utter this word.

264. The national anthem is being sung by Jason.
(1) Jason was singing the national anthem.
(2) Jason is singing the national anthem.
(3) Jason sings the national anthem.
(4) Jason has sung the national anthem.

265. Can he complete the job in three weeks?
(1) Can he in three weeks complete the job?
(2) Can't the job be completed by him in three weeks?
(3) Can the job be completed by him in three weeks?
(4) He cannot complete the job in three weeks?

266. Grid failure brings five hundred trains to a halt.
(1) Five hundred trains are being brought to a halt by grid failure.
(2) Five hundred trains are brought to a halt by grid failure.
(3) Five hundred trains were brought to a halt by grid failure.
(4) Five hundred trains had been brought to a halt by grid failure.

267. The teacher was pleased with his recitation.
(1) His recitation pleases the teacher.
(2) His recitation pleased the teacher.
(3) His recitation will please the teacher.
(4) His recitation has pleased the teacher.

268. We saw her singing at her work.
(1) Her singing was seen by us at her work.
(2) Her singing was seen at her work by us.
(3) She was seen being sung at her work by us.
(4) She was seen singing at her work.

269. They will help us with money.
(1) We will be helped by them with money.
(2) We should be helped by them with money.
(3) We must be helped by them with money.
(4) We could be helped by them with money.

270. I was asked my name.

(1) My name was asked for.
(2) They asked me my name.
(3) They asked my name from me.
(4) My name was asked.

271. Kamala was told the bad news as soon as she arrived.
(1) Someone had told Kamala the bad news as soon as she arrived.
(2) Some is telling Kamala the bad news as soon as she arrived.
(3) Someone told Kamala the bad news as soon as she arrived.
(4) Someone has told Kamala the bad news as soon as she arrived.

272. The girl's death has opened a can of worms.
(1) A can of worms is being opened by the girl's death.
(2) A can of worms has been opened by the girl's death.
(3) A can of worms are being opened by the girl's death.
(4) A can of worms were being opened by the girl's death.

273. By that time tomorrow, they would have completed the work allotted to them.
(1) By that time tomorrow, the work allotted to them would be completed by them.
(2) By that time tomorrow, the work allotted to them would complete by them.
(3) By that time tomorrow, the work allotted to them would be complete by them.
(4) By that time tomorrow, the work allotted to them would have been completed by them.

274. While I was on holiday, my camera was stolen from my hotel room.
(1) While I was on holiday, somebody stole my camera from my hotel room.
(2) While I was on holiday, my camera had been stolen from my hotel room.
(3) While I was on holiday, they steal my camera from my hotel room.
(4) While I was on holiday, they had stolen my camera from my hotel room.

275. By 1829 British goods worth seven crore rupees were being exported to India by Britain.
(1) India was exporting British goods worth seven crore rupees to Britain, by 1829.
(2) By 1829, Britain exported British goods worth seven crore rupees to India.
(3) By 1829, Britain was exporting British goods worth seven crore rupees to India.
(4) Britain exported British goods to India worth seven crore rupees by 1829.

276. Do all the necessary tests soon.
(1) All the necessary tests may be done soon.
(2) Let all the necessary tests be done soon.
(3) Let all the necessary tests were done soon.
(4) All the necessary tests have to be done soon.

277. She had locked the door, before she left.
(1) She locks the door, before she leaves.
(2) She locked the door and left.
(3) The door was locked by her, before she took leave.
(4) The door had been locked by her, before she left.

278. Bravery and loyalty were rewarded by the king.
(1) Reward was given for bravery and loyalty.
(2) The king rewarded bravery and

loyalty.

(3) The king gave a reward for a bravery and loyalty.

(4) For loyalty and bravery it is said that the king gave reward.

279. I remember them taking me to the Zoo.

(1) I remember having being taken to the Zoo.

(2) I remember to be taken to the Zoo.

(3) I remember being taken to the Zoo.

(4) I remember I was taken to the Zoo.

280. The news surprised us.

(1) We are surprised at the news

(2) We were surprised by the news

(3) We are surprised by the news

(4) We were surprised at the news

281. Mahmud gave me a pen.

(1) I was given a pen by Mahmud

(2) I am given a pen by Mahmud

(3) I had given a pen by Mahmud

(4) A pen is given to me by Mahmud

282. Mr. Mukerjee teaches us English.

(1) English was taught us by Mr. Mukerjee

(2) We were taught English by Mr. Mukerjee

(3) We have taught English by Mr. Mukerjee

(4) We are taught English by Mr. Mukerjee

283. Somebody has stolen his purse.

(1) His purse has been stolen

(2) His purse had been stolen

(3) His purse had been stealing

(4) His purse have been stolen

284. She looks after the child.

(1) The child are looked after by her

(2) The child were looked after by her

(3) The child is looked after by her

(4) None of these

285. Honey is made by bees.

(1) Bees made honey

(2) Bees are making honey

(3) Bees make honey

(4) Bees makes honey

286. The walls had not been decorated by us.

(1) We has not decorated the walls

(2) We had not decorated the walls

(3) We have not been decorating the walls

(4) We had not been decorating the walls

287. I can teach Nalini.

(1) Nalini can taught by me

(2) Nalini could be taught by me

(3) Nalini can be teach by me

(4) Nalini can be taught by me

288. Hamlet was written by Shakespeare.

(1) Shakespeare had written Hamlet

(2) Shakespeare wrote Hamlet

(3) Shakespeare writes Hamlet

(4) Shakespeare has wrote Hamlet

289. This book contains pictures.

(1) Pictures are contained by this book

(2) Pictures were contained in this book

(3) Pictures are contained to this book

(4) Pictures are contained in this book

290. I like him.

(1) He was liked by me

(2) He is being liked by me

(3) He was being liked by me

(4) He is liked by me

291. Jatinder can help Gurdeep.

(1) Gurdeep can be helped by Jatinder

(2) Gurdeep could be helped by Jatinder

(3) Gurdeep can be help by Jatinder

(4) Gurdeep could be help by Jatinder

292. She is calling me.

(1) I was being called by her

(2) I am being called by her

(3) I have been called by her

(4) None of these

293. A retail store was inaugurated by Sanju.
(1) Sanju had inaugurated a retail store
(2) Sanju has inaugurated retail store
(3) Sanju inaugurate a retail store
(4) Sanju inaugurated a retail store

294. Who stole your pen?
(1) Who was stolen your pen?
(2) By whom is your pen stolen?
(3) By whom was your pen stolen?
(4) By whom did your pen steal?

295. I can help you.
(1) You could be helped by me
(2) You can be helped by me
(3) You can be help by me
(4) You could be help by me

296. You are teasing them.
(1) They were being teased by you
(2) They are teasing by you
(3) They have been teasing by you
(4) They are being teased by you

297. She often praises me.
(1) I was often praised by her
(2) I have been often praised by her
(3) I am often praises by her
(4) I am often praised by her

298. Did he buy that house?
(1) Is that house bought by him?
(2) Were that house bought by him?
(3) Was that house bought by him?
(4) Are that house bought by him?

299. She has taught him.
(1) He has taught by her
(2) He had been taught by her
(3) He has been taught by her
(4) He has been teach by her

300. The payment was collected by the hardworking salesman.
(1) The hardworking salesman collected the payment.
(2) The salesman who worked hard was able to collect the payment.
(3) To collect the payment the salesman had to work hard.
(4) The hardworking salesman was able to collect the payment.

301. I had to stop all my work to complete this project.
(1) All other work had to be stopped to complete this project by me.
(2) For completing this project all other work must be stopped.
(3) For completing this project I had to stop all my work.
(4) To complete this project all other work had been stopped by me.

DIRECT-INDIRECT NARRATION

1. He said to me, "I am ready".
(a) He told to me that he is ready.
(b) He told me that he was ready.
(c) He told me that I am ready.
(d) He told me that I will ready.

2. Sonia said, "You help my sister".
(a) Sonia said that I helps her sister.
(b) Sonia said to me that I helped her sister.
(c) Sonia said that I helped her sister.
(d) Sonia says that I helped her sister.

3. They said, "We can not live without oxygen".
(a) They said that we can not live without oxygen.
(b) They said that they can not live without oxygen.
(c) They said that they would not live without oxygen.
(d) They says that they can not live without oxygen.

4. Rahul said to me, "We are mortal".

(a) Rahul said to me that we are mortal.
(b) Rahul says to me that we are mortal.
(c) Rahul said to me that we all are mortal.
(d) Rahul said to me that he and I are mortal.

5. The Indian express says, "We shall issue a astrology section in our Thursday's paper".
(a) The Indian express says that it will issue a astrology section in their Thursday's paper.
(b) The Indian express says that they will issue a astrology section in their Thursday's paper.
(b) The Indian express said that it will issue a astrology section in its Thursday's paper.
(d) The Indian express says that it will issue a astrology section in its Thursday's paper.

6. John says, "I shall go there".
(a) John said that he went there.
(b) John says that he will go there.
(c) John says that he went there.
(d) John said that I will go there.

7. Robert will say to me, "I am your classmate".
(a) Robert will tell me that he is my classmate.
(b) Robert will tell me that he was my classmate.
(c) Robert will tell me that he will be my classmate.
(d) Robert said me that he is my classmate.

8. Sushant said to him, "I have been helping your son for years".
(a) Sushant told him that he has helped his son for years.
(b) Sushant told him that he have been helping his son for years.
(c) Sushant told him that he had been helping his son for years.
(d) Sushant told him that he has been helping his son for years.

9. He said to me, "I shall write an essay".
(a) He said to me that he will be writing an essay.
(b) He told me that he would write an essay.
(c) He said to me that he will write an essay.
(d) He told me that he would write an essay.

10. He said to me, "I shall be writing an essay".
(a) He told me that he would have been writing an essay.
(b) He told me that he would be writing an essay.
(c) He told me that he will be writing an essay.
(d) He told me that he shall be writing an essay.

11. Sita said to Geeta, "You can learn piano".
(a) Sita told Geeta that she can be learn piano.
(b) Sita told Geeta that you can learn piano.
(c) Sita told Geeta that she could learn piano.
(d) Sita told Geeta that she can learn piano.

12. He said to you, "You may go out".
(a) He told you that you might be go out.
(b) He said you that you might be go out.
(c) He told you that you may go out.
(d) He told you that you might go out.

13. Ram said to Rahul, "You are a good player of cricket".
(a) Ram told Rahul that he was a good player of cricket.

(b) Ram told Rahul that he were a good player of cricket.

(c) Ram told Rahul that he would a good player of cricket.

(d) Ram told Rahul that he could be a good player of cricket.

14. Shahekant said to me, "I have no time for you".

(a) Shahekant said that he had no time for me.

(b) Shahekant told me that he had no time for me.

(c) Shahekant told me that he has no time for me.

(c) Shahekant told me that he was having no time for me.

15. Sahil said to Deepu, "I was going to buy milk".

(a) Sahil told Deepu that he were going to buy milk.

(b) Sahil told Deepu that he would going to buy milk.

(c) Sahil told Deepu that he had been going to buy milk.

(d) Sahil told Deepu that he was going to buy milk.

16. She said, "You were missing from the picnic".

(a) She told me that I had been missing from the picnic.

(b) She told me that I has been missing from the picnic.

(c) She told me that I were missing from the picnic.

(d) She told me that I had been missed from the picnic.

17. Reeta said Shivani, "You have to go to school".

(a) Reeta told Shivani that she would have to go to school.

(b) Reeta told Shivani that she has to go to school.

(c) Reeta told Shivani that she have to go to school.

(d) Reeta told Shivani that she had to go to school.

18. You said to her, "She has to cook food for you".

(a) You told her that she has to cook food for you.

(b) You told her that she had to cook food for you.

(c) You told her that she needs to cook food for you.

(d) You told her that she would have to cook food for you.

19. He said to me, " I had to finish this first."

(a) He told me that he has to finish this first.

(b) He told me that he have to finish this first.

(c) He told me that he had had to finish this first.

(d) He told me that he had to finish this first.

20. Rahul said to Shusheela, "I had to reach there".

(a) Rahul told Susheela that he has to reach there.

(b) Rahul told Susheela that he would have to reach there.

(c) Rahul told Susheela that he had to reach there.

(d) Rahul told Susheela that he had had to reach there.

21. She said to me, "I could reach there easily".

(a) She told me that she could reach there easily.

(b) She told me that she could have reach there easily.

(c) She told me that she had reach there easily.

(d) She told me that she had been reach

there easily.

22. Reema said to Jitender, "You would not fight with me."
    (a) Reema told to Jitender that he has not to fight with her.
    (b) Reema told to Jitender that he would not fight with her.
    (c) Reema told to Jitender that he will not fight with her.
    (d) Reema told to Jitender that he should not fight with her.
23. My father said to me, "It might rain yesterday".
    (a) My father told me that it may have rain the previous day.
    (b) My father told me that it would rain the previous day.
    (c) My father told me that it might rain the previous day.
    (d) My father told me that it could rain the previous day.
24. He said, "I went to Rajesthan yesterday."
    (a) He told that he had gone to Rajesthan the day before.
    (b) He told that he has gone to Rajesthan the day before.
    (c) He told that he has went to Rajesthan the day before.
    (d) He told that he had went to Rajesthan the day before.
25. Raju said to me, "He worked hard".
    (a) Raju told me that he had worked hard.
    (b) Raju told me that he has worked hard.
    (c) Raju told me that he had been worked hard.
    (d) Raju told me that he has been worked hard.
26. Rahul said, " He was walking."
    (a) Rahul said that he had been walking.
    (b) Rahul said that he was walking.
    (c) Rahul said that he had walking.
    (d) Rahul said that he had walked.
27. Sheela said to me, "Munni is dancing better than me."
    (a) Sheela told me that Munni have been dancing better than her.
    (b) Sheela told me that Munni was dancing better than her.
    (c) Sheela told me that Munni had been dancing better than her.
    (d) Sheela told me that Munni had dancing better than her.
28. She said, "He was trying to help me".
    (a) She said that he tried to help her.
    (b) She said that he had been trying to help her.
    (c) She said that he has been trying to help her.
    (d) She said that he was trying to help her.
29. Deepak said to me, "I had finished the coffee."
    (a) Deepak told me that he had finished the coffee.
    (b) Deepak told me that he had been finished the coffee.
    (c) Deepak told me that he had finish the coffee.
    (d) Deepak told me that he finished the coffee.
30. Rahul said to me, " I had gone through it."
    (a) Rahul told me that he have went through it.
    (b) Rahul told me that he have gone through it.
    (c) Rahul told me that he had went through it.
    (d) Rahul told me that he had gone through it.
31. Baljider said to me, "I had been working on it for 5 days."
    (a) Baljinder told me that he had been

working on it for 5 days.

(b) Baljinder told me that he has been working on it for 5 days.

(c) Baljinder told me that he had worked on it for 5 days.

(d) Baljinder told me that he was working on it for 5 days.

32. Sweety said to me, "I had been writing an essay for 3 hours."

(a) Sweety told me that she has been writing an essay for 3 hours.

(b) Sweety told me that she had been writing an essay for 3 hours.

(c) Sweety told me that she was writing an essay for 3 hours.

(d) Sweety told me that she had written an essay for 3 hours.

33. Rahul said, "I can buy that watch."

(a) Rahul said that he can buy that watch.

(b) Rahul said that he could buy that watch.

(c) Rahul said that he was able to buy that watch.

(d) Rahul said that he can be buy that watch.

34. He said, "Honesty is the best policy."

(a) He said that Honesty is the best policy.

(b) He said that Honesty was the best policy.

(c) He said that Honesty would be the best policy.

(d) He said that Honesty will be the best policy.

35. He remarked, "Two and two makes four."

(a) He remarked that two and two would make four.

(b) He remarked that two and two made four.

(c) He remarked that two and two makes four.

(d) He advised that two and two makes four.

36. My father said, "All that glitters is not gold."

(a) My father said that all that glitters was not gold.

(b) My father advised that all that glitters is not gold.

(c) My father remarked that all that glitters is not gold.

(d) My father said that all that glitters is not gold.

37. Rahul said, "We must obey our parents."

(a) Rahul remarked that we must obey our parents.

(b) Rahul advised that we must obey our parents.

(c) Rahul said that we must obey our parents.

(d) Rahul said that we should obey our parents.

38. Sheela said, "I must go."

(a) Sheela said that she had to go.

(b) Sheela said that I must go.

(c) Sheela said that she need to go.

(d) Sheela said that she must went.

39. Rakhi says to him, "You must come back home in time."

(a) Rakhi tells him that he has to come come back home in time.

(b) Rakhi tells him that he had to come come back home in time.

(c) Rakhi tells him that he will have to come come back home in time.

(d) Rakhi tells him that he must come come back home in time.

40. The MLA said to people, "Ladies and gentlemen, your vote is my real power."

(a) The MLA said that people your vote will my real power.

(b) The MLA addressed the people as ladies and gentlemen and said that your vote will be my real power.

(c) The MLA addressed the people as ladies and gentlemen and said that their vote is my real power.

(d) The MLA addressed the people as ladies and gentlemen and said that their vote was his real power.

41. She said, "Well, Rahul, You have done this work."

(a) She told Rahul that you had done this work.

(b) She told Rahul that you had done that work.

(c) She told Rahul that he had done that work.

(d) She told Rahul that he has done that work.

42. Salma said to me, "Have you a LED TV ?"

(a) Salma asked me if I have a LED TV.

(b) Salma asked me have you a LED TV.

(c) Salma told me have you a LED TV.

(d) Salma asked me if I had a LED TV.

43. He said to us, "Are you going to market today?"

(a) He asked us if we were going to market that day.

(b) He asked us if you are going to market that day.

(c) He asked us if we went to market that day.

(d) He asked us if we had gone to market that day.

44. I said to my brother, "What are you playing today ?"

(a) I asked my brother what he will be playing that day.

(b) I asked my brother what he was playing that day.

(c) I asked my brother if he was playing that day.

(d) I asked my brother what he would be playing that day.

45. I asked, "What happened?"

(a) I enquired what happened.

(b) I asked what happened.

(c) I enquired that what happened.

(d) I asked what had happened.

46. Rahul said to Shilpa, "How are you ?"

(a) Rahul asked Shilpa how she was.

(b) Rahul asked Shilpa how she were.

(c) Rahul asked Shilpa how is she.

(d) Rahul enquired Shilpa how she was.

47. He said to me, "You are rich, aren't you ?"

(a) He asked me if I had rich.

(b) He asked me if I had been rich.

(c) He asked me if I was rich.

(d) He asked me if I was rich, wasn't me.

48. Rohit said to Sunita, "Will you love me."

(a) Rohit asked Sunita if she would love him.

(b) Rohit asked Sunita if you would love me.

(c) Rohit asked Sunita if she will love him.

(d) Rohit asked Sunita if she should love him.

49. The Judge said to inspector, "Call the thieves."

(a) The Judge urged inspector to call the thieves.

(b) The Judge ordered inspector to get the thieves.

(c) The Judge requested inspector to call the thieves.

(d) The Judge ordered inspector to call the thieves.

50. She said, "Madam, I have done homework."

(a) She said respectfully that she had been done homework.

(b) She said respectfully that she has done homework.

(c) She said respectfully that she had done homework.

(d) She said respectfully to her teacher that she had done homework

51. He said to me, "Do read the holy Gita daily."

(a) He asked to me to read the holy Gita daily.

(b) He asked me to do read the holy Gita daily.

(c) He asked me to read the holy Gita daily.

(d) He requested me to read the holy Gita daily.

52. Sahil said to his friends, "Lets go to the park."

(a) Sahil suggested to his friends that we should go to the park.

(b) Sahil requested to his friends that we should go to the park.

(c) Sahil suggested to his friends that we would go to the park.

(d) Sahil suggested to his friends that we have to go to the park.

53. The children said, "Let us complete homework together."

(a) The children told that let them complete homework together.

(b) The children told that they should complete homework together.

(c) The children suggested that they should complete homework together.

(d) The children asked that they should complete homework together.

54. He said, "May God bless you."

(a) He prayed that God bless him.

(b) He prayed that may God bless him.

(c) He told that may God bless him.

(d) He prayed that might God bless him.

55. They said to me, "May you live long."

(a) They prayed for me that I might live long.

(b) They blessed me that I might live long.

(c) They blessed me that I may live long.

(d) They blessed me that may I live long.

56. Captain said, "Bravo ! We have won the match."

(a) Captain exclaimed with joy that they have won the match.

(b) Captain exclaimed that they had won the match.

(c) Captain exclaimed with joy that they had won the match.

(d) Captain exclaimed with surprise that they had won the match.

57. She said, " Ugh! I have hated him."

(a) She exclaimed with disgust that she had been hated him.

(b) She exclaimed with disgust that she had hated him.

(c) She exclaimed with sorrow that she had hated him.

(d) She exclaimed with disgust that I had hated him.

58. Shakshi said, "How clever I am!"

(a) Shakshi exclaimed that she was very clever.

(b) Shakshi exclaimed with joy that she was very clever.

(c) Shakshi exclaimed that she is very clever.

(d) Shakshi said that she was very clever.

59. Mr. Bajaj said, "How foolish of me!"

(a) Mr. Bajaj confessed with regret that he had been very foolish.

(b) Mr. Bajaj confessed with regret that he is very foolish.

(c) Mr. Bajaj confessed with sorrow that he was very foolish.

(d) Mr. Bajaj confessed with regret that he was very foolish.

60. Bhaskar said to Kapil, "Please do come some time."

(a) Bhaskar requested Kapil to do come

sometime.

(b) Bhaskar requested Kapil to come sometime.

(c) Bhaskar asked Kapil to come sometime.

(d) Bhaskar requested Kapil to please come sometime.

61. I said her, "Could you please help me ?"

(a) I requested her to help me.

(b) I asked her to help me.

(c) I told her if she can help me.

(d) I asked her if she can help me.

62. The man to who I sold my house was a cheat.

(a) to who I sell

(b) to whom I sell

(c) to whom I sold

(d) who was sold to

63. He is too important for tolerating any delay.

(a) to tolerate

(b) with tolerating

(c) to tolerating

(d) at tolerating

64. I need not offer any explanation regarding this incident - my behaviour is speaking itself.

(a) will speak to itself

(b) speaks for itself

(c) has been speaking

(d) speaks about itself

Q65. Deepak said to Mona, "You are punctual".

(a) Deepak told Mona that she is punctual.

(b) Deepak told Mona that she was punctual.

(c) Deepak said to Mona that she was punctual.

(d) Deepak told that Mona was punctual.

Q66. I said to him, "Let us go out for a walk."

(a) I proposed to him to go out for a walk.

(b) I proposed to him that let's go out for a walk.

(c) I proposed him that we should go out for a walk.

(d) I proposed to him that we should go out for a walk.

Q67. He said to Akash, "Don't move".

(a) He told Akash not to move.

(b) He told Akash don't move.

(c) He said to Akash not to move.

(d) He told Akash to not to move.

Q68. Ram said to his boss, "Let me go home."

(a) Ram requested his boss to allow him to go home.

(b) Ram requested to his boss to allow him to go home.

(c) Ram requested his boss that he should go home.

(d) Ram requested his boss to allow him for going home.

Q69. He said to me, "Don't go out".

(a) He forbade me to not to go out.

(b) He forbade me to go out.

(c) He forbade me not to go out.

(d) He forbade me to not go out.

Q70. You said to your mother, "Stop working".

(a) You prohibited your mother from working.

(b) You prohibited your mother to work.

(c) You prohibited your mother by asking to stop working.

(d) You asked your mother to let the work stop.

Q71. He said, "I saw him here".

(a) He said that he saw him there.

(b) He said that he has seen him there.

(c) He said that he had seen him there.

(d) He said he had seen him there.

Q72. He said, "I had gone to New Delhi".

(a) He said that he had gone to New

Delhi.

(b) He said that he had to go to New Delhi.

(c) He said that he was gone to New Delhi.

(d) He said that he had been going to New Delhi.

Q73. Sonia said to me, "I will do it now or never."

(a) Sonia told me that she would do it now or never.

(b) Sonia told me that she would do it then or never.

(c) Sonia told that she would do it then or never.

(d) Sonia told to me she would do it then or never.

Q74. He said to them, "Don't make a noise."

(a) He told them to not make noise.

(b) He asked them not to make a noise.

(c) He asked them to not to make a noise.

(d) He begged them not to make a noise.

Q75. He said, "I clean my teeth twice a day."

(a) He said that he cleaned his teeth twice a day.

(b) He said that he cleans his teeth twice a day.

(c) He said that he was to clean his teeth twice a day.

(d) He said he cleans his teeth twice a day.

Q76. The boys said, "Hurrah! we have won the match".

(a) The boys exclaimed with joy that they won the match.

(b) The boys exclaimed with joy that had to win the match.

(c) The boys exclaimed with shock that they had won the match.

(d) The boys exclaimed with joy that they had won the match.

Q77. She said, "Let's go for a walk."

(a) She suggested that they should go for a walk.

(b) She suggested going for a walk.

(c) She suggested to go for a walk.

(d) She suggested that they should go on a walk.

Q78. You said to your wife, "What are you doing"?

(a) You asked your wife that what she was doing.

(b) You asked your wife what she was doing.

(c) You told your wife what she was doing.

(d) You asked your wife what was she doing.

Q79. Pressed by his students, the Principal suddenly said I am in no way responsible for the quarrel.

(a) Pressed by his students, the Principal suddenly said that he was in no way responsible for the quarrel.

(b) Pressed by his students, the Principal suddenly told that he was in no way responsible for the quarrel.

(c) The Principal suddenly said he was in no way responsible for the quarrel, pressed by his students.

(d) Pressed by his students, the Principal suddenly said that he is in no way responsible for the quarrel.

Q80. I said to my sister, "Where were you this evening?"

(a) I asked my sister where she was that evening.

(b) I asked my sister where she had been that evening.

(c) I asked my sister where she was this evening.

(d) I asked my sister where she has been that evening.

Q81. The intern said to the manager, "Can I

go?"

(a) The intern asked the manger if he could go.

(b) The intern asked the manger whether he can go.

(c) The intern asked the manger whether he can be going.

(d) The intern asked the manger whether if he could go.

Q82. He said to me, "Don't go out".

(a) He forbade me to not to go out.

(b) He forbade me to go out.

(c) He forbade me not to go out.

(d) He forbade me to not go out.

Q83. He said, "I had gone to New Delhi".

(a) He said that he had gone to New Delhi.

(b) He said that he had to go to New Delhi.

(c) He said that he was gone to New Delhi.

(d) He said that he had been going to New Delhi.

Q84. "Do you have anything to say on behalf of the accused?" said the judge finally.

(a) The judge finally asked if he had anything to say on behalf of the accused.

(b) The judge finally ask that whether he had anything to say on behalf of the accused.

(c) The judge finally asked that if he has anything to say on behalf of the accused.

(d) The judge finally asked that if he has had anything to say on behalf of the accused.

Q85. Sita said to her mother, "Do you always get up early?"

(a) Sita asked her mother that whether she always got up early.

(b) Sita asked her mother that whether she has been always getting up early.

(c) Sita asked her mother that if she has been always getting up early.

(d) Sita asked her mother if she always got up early.

Q86. Mother said, "Lie down, Arjun."

(a) Mother told lie down Arjun.

(b) Mother told Arjun for lying down.

(c) Mother asked Arjun to lie down.

(d) Mother asked Arjun to be lied down

Q87. "Alas! I have broken my grandfather's watch" said Amit.

(a) Amit was sorrowful that he broke his grandfather's watch.

(b) Amit exclaimed sorrowfully that he has broken his grandfather's watch.

(c) Amit was sorrowful that he had broken his grandfather's watch.

(d) Amit exclaimed sorrowfully that he had broken his grandfather's watch.

Q88. The coach said, "Don't move, boys."

(a) The coach told to the boys don't move.

(b) The coach said to the boys not to be moving.

(c) The coach asked the boys not to move.

(d) The coach told to them, don't move boys.

Q89. Kunal said, "Tanu is coming this week."

(a) Kunal says that Tanu was coming that week.

(b) Kunal says that Tanu was coming this week.

(c) Kunal said that Tanu was going to be come this week.

(d) Kunal said that Tanu was coming that week.

Q90. "Are you coming with us?" Isha asked Nisha.

(a) Isha asked Nisha whether she would be going with them.

(b) Isha asked Nisha if she was going with them.

(c) Isha asked Nisha whether she would go with them.

(d) Isha asked Nisha whether she would come with us.

Q91. Teacher said to children, "Have you prepared well for the finals?"

(a) Teacher asked the children whether they have prepared well for the finals.

(b) Teacher asked the children whether they have been preparing well for the finals.

(c) Teacher asked the children if they did prepare well for the finals.

(d) Teacher asked the children if they had prepared well for the finals.

92. Jyoti said to her sister, "The RBI is India's central bank".

(a) Jyoti told her sister the RBI was India's central bank.

(b) Jyoti told her sister that the RBI was India's central bank.

(c) Jyoti told her sister that the RBI is India's central bank.

(d) Jyoti told her sister the RBI is India's central bank.

Q93. Jay says, "I eat a guava".

(a) Jay said that he ate a guava.

(b) Jay said that he has been eating guavas.

(c) Jay says that he eats a guava.

(d) Jay said he ate a guava.

Q94. Mother said to you, "When will you come from Pune?"

(a) Mother asked you when you would come from Pune.

(b) Mother asked you when you will come from Pune.

(c) Mother asked you when you will be coming from Pune.

(d) Mother asked you when you will have come from Pune.

Q95. She said to me, "It has been raining heavily and you cannot go."

A) She told me that it had been raining heavily and I could not go.

B) She told me that it was raining heavily and I could not go.

C) She told me that it has been raining heavily and I could not go.

D) She told me that it is raining heavily and I could not go.

96. John said to me, "Where have you been last night?"

A) John asked me where had I been the previous night.

B) John asked me where have I been the previous night.

C) John asked me where I am the previous night.

D) John asked me where I had been the previous night.

Q97. "I am taking my children to the zoo tomorrow ,"she said "to see the baby white tiger."

A) She said that she will take the children to the zoo to see the baby white tiger tomorrow.

B) She said that she would take the children to the zoo the next day to see the baby white tiger.

C) She said that she was taking her children to the zoo the next day to see the baby white tiger.

D) She said that she was taking the children to the zoo that day to see the baby white tiger.

Q98. She said, "Mother , please cook me something nice today."

A) She told her mother to cook her something nice today.

B) She ordered her mother to cook her something nice that day.

C) She requested her mother to cook her

something nice that day.

D) She asked her mother if she could cook her something nice that day.

Q99. John said ,"I shall be 21 tomorrow."

A) John said that he would be 21 tomorrow.

B) John said that he would be 21 the following day.

C) John said that he should be 21 the following day.

D) John said that I shall be 21 tomorrow.

Q100. She asked ,"Is the secretary coming to the meeting?"

A) She asked that the secretary was coming to the meeting.

B) She asked that if the secretary was coming to the meeting.

C) She asked if the secretary is coming to the meeting.

D) She asked if the secretary was coming to the meeting.

Q101. The convict said ,"Let me speak freely please."

A) The convict suggested that he must be allowed to speak freely.

B) The convict requested that he must be allowed to speak freely.

C) The convict requested that he be allowed to speak freely.

D) The convict proposed that he might be allowed to speak freely.

Q102. Nisha told Monica, "What a beautiful dress you are wearing?"

A) Nisha exclaimed that Monica was wearing a very beautiful dress.

B) Nisha exclaimed that it is a very beautiful dress.

C) Nisha exclaimed that Monica is wearing a very beautiful dress.

D) Nisha told Monica that was a beautiful dress.

Q103. "Call the witness ,"said the magistrate.

A) The magistrate requested to call the witness.

B) The magistrate begged for calling the witness.

C) The magistrate ordered to call the witness.

D) The magistrate prayed to call the witness.

Q104. "Have you done this sort of work before?"said his new employer.

A) His new employer asked him whether he has done that sort of work before.

B) His new employer asked him whether he has done this sort of work before.

C) His new employer asked him whether he had done that sort of work before.

D) His new employer asked him whether he had done this sort of work before.

105) Rahul says that Azhar loves cricket.

A) Rahul said ,"Azhar loves cricket."

B) Rahul said ,"Azhar loved cricket."

C) Rahul says ,"Azhar loved cricket."

D) Rahul says ,"Azhar loves cricket."

Q106. "I came home last night,"said he.

A) He told that he had come home last night.

B) He said that he came home last night.

C) He said that he had come home the previous night.

D) He says that he came home the previous night.

Q107. The beggar said,"Poverty is a great curse."

A) The beggar said poverty has a great curse.

B) The beggar said that poverty is a great curse.

C) The beggar said that poverty as a great curse.

D) The beggar said that poverty had been a great curse.

Q108. "If you want to smoke you will have to go

out," said the conductor.

A) The conductor ordered me to go out and smoke.

B) The conductor said that if I/he wanted to smoke I/he would have to go out.

C) The conductor said told me that smoking is not permitted in the bus.

D) The conductor told me that I will have to go out and smoke.

Q109. "Be careful ,the steps are very slippery ,"I warned him.

A) I warned him to be careful as the steps were very slippery.

B) I warned him to be careful as the steps are very slippery.

C) I warned him to be careful and steps were very slippery.

D) I told him to be careful and the steps are very slippery.

Q110. The old lady declared that she was going to walk where she pleased.They had the liberty.

A) The old lady said that,"I am going to walk where I pleased. They have the liberty."

B) The old lady said ,"I am going to walk where I please. We have the liberty."

C) The old lady. "I am going to walk where I pleased.They have the liberty."

D) The old lady. "I am going to walk where I pleased. They had the liberty."

Q111. The teacher asked me why I had been absent the day before.

A) The teacher asked me ,"Why were you absent yesterday?"

B) The teacher asked me ,"Why are you absent yesterday?"

C) The teacher asked me ,"Why are you absent the day before?"

D) The teacher asked me ,"Were you absent the day before?"

Q112. Mr Robinson asked his son what he wanted to be when he grew up.

A) "My son ,"said Mr Robinson ,"What will you be when you grow up?"

B) "My son ,"said Mr Robinson ,"What do you want to be when you grow up?"

C) Mr Robinson said ,"My son,what did you want to be when you grew up."

D) Mr Robinson said ,"My son ,what would you be when you grow up."

Q113. The boys respectfully wished their teacher good morning.

A) "Good morning," said the boys to their teacher.

B) "Good morning," said the boys to the teacher.

C) "Good morning , Madam" said the boys to the teacher.

D) "Good morning , Madam" said the boys to their teacher.

Q114. She said ,"I am sorry ,I will not be able to submit those papers."

A) She said she was sorry ,she is not able to submit those papers.

B) She said that she was sorry and she would not be able to submit those papers.

C) She apologized for not being able to submit those papers.

D) She exclaimed with sorrow that she as sorry and she will not be able to submit those papers.

Q115. The girl wondered where the sparrows had gone.

A) The girl said ,"Oh ! Where the sparrows have gone?"

B) The girl said ,"Oh! Where are the sparrows?"

C) The girl said,"Oh! Where had the

sparrows gone?"

D) The girl said,"Oh! Where have the sparrows gone?"

Q116. She said to me,"I am going shopping. Can I get you something?"

A) She said she was going shopping and said to me if I wanted something.

B) She said she was going shopping and asked if I wanted something.

C) She said she was going shopping and asked if she could get me something.

D) She said she is going shopping and asked if she could get me something.

Q117. Ramesh informed his friend that he could make use of his car while he was away.

A) Ramesh said to his friend ,"You will make use of my car while I was away."

B) Ramesh said to his friend ,"Use my car while I go away."

C) Ramesh said to his friend ,"You can make use of my car while I am away."

D) Ramesh asked his friend ,"Will you make use of my car while I am away."

Q118. Kala said to Radha, "Who were you speaking to over the phone?"

A) Kala asked Radha who she had been speaking to over the phone.

B) Kala asked Radha who she has been speaking to over the phone.

C) Kala asked Radha that who she was speaking to over the phone.

D) Kala asked Radha that who she had been speaking to over the phone.

Q119. The king said to his men,"Do not be afraid of the enemy. Face them bravely."

A) The king ordered his men to not be afraid of the enemy and that they had to be faced bravely.

B) The king asked his men to not be afraid of the enemy but they should be faced bravely.

C) The king advised his men not to be afraid of the enemy but to face them bravely.

D) The king told his men not to be afraid of the enemy and they had faced them bravely.

Q120. Kanan said to Subha ,"I 'll return the book after I have read it."

A) Kanan told Subha that he will return the book after he has read it.

B) Kanan told Subha that he would return the book after he has read it.

C) Kanan told Subha that he will return the book after he read it.

D) Kanan told Subha that he would return the book after he had read it.

Q121. The boss said to his secretary ,"Did you discuss the matter with the manager?"

A) The boss asked his secretary whether he discussed that matter with the manager.

B) The boss asked his secretary if you have discussed that matter with the manager.

C) The boss asked his secretary if he had discussed that matter with the manager.

D) The boss asked his secretary whether he has discussed that matter with the manager.

Q122. Socrates said,"Virtue is its own reward."

A) Socrates said that virtue had its own rewards.

B) Socrates says that virtue is its own reward.

C) Socrates said that virtue is its own reward.

D) Socrates said that virtue as its own reward.

Q123. Gopan said to me,"Can you do these sums for me?"

A) Gopan asked me if I could do those sums for him.

B) Gopan asked me if I can do those sums for him.

C) Gopan asked me if I can do those sums for he.

D) Gopan asked if I could do these sums for him.

Q124. He said,"We have done our work."

A) He said that he had done his work.

B) He said that they have done their work.

C) He said that they had done their work.

D) He said that they should do their work.

Q125. "What did you eat for breakfast today ?" the doctor asked the patient.

(A) The doctor asked the patient whether he had eaten breakfast that day

(B) The doctor asked the patient what he had eaten for breakfast that day

(C) The doctor asked the patient whether he has eaten breakfast that day

(D) The doctor asked the patient whether he was eaten breakfast that day

Q126. The employer said to him, "I shall pay your wages tomorrow."

(A) The employer said that he shall pay your wages the next day

(B) The employer told him that he would pay his wages the next day

(C) The employer said that I shall pay my wages the next day

(D) The employer said that he shall pay his wages the next day

Q127. "Why are you looking through the key hole ?" I said.

(A) I asked him why he was looking through the key hole

(B) I said to him why he is looking through the key hole

(C) I said to him that way he was looking through the key hole

(D) I asked you why you are looking through the key hole

Q128. "How cruel the boss is!" said the clerk.

(A) The clerk said that the boss was very cruel

(B) The clerk said that the boss is very cruel

(C) The clerk exclaimed that the boss was very cruel

(D) The clerk exclaimed that the boss is very cruel

Q129. My husband said to me, "Wait for me outside."

(A) My husband told me to wait for him outside

(B) My husband said that I have to wait for him outside

(C) My husband wanted me to wait for him only outside

(D) My husband angrily asked me to wait outside

Q130. "Please could you tell me the way ?" he said.

(A) He asked me please could I tell him the way

(B) He asked me to please tell him the way

(C) He requested me to tell him the way, please

(D) He requested me to tell him the way

Q131. They said to him, "we will destroy your homestead".

(A) They said to him they will destroy his homestead

(B) They told him they would destroy their homestead

(C) They told him that they can destroy his homestead

(D) They told him that they would destroy his homestead

Q132. "You can phone from my office," he said.

(A) He said that he could phone from his office

(B) He said you could phone from his office

(C) He said that I can phone from your office

(D) He said I can phone from my office

Q133. "Please sit down," he said.

(A) He asked her to sit down

(B) He said that she could sit down

(C) He told her that sit down

(D) He said her to sit down

Q134. Keats wrote "a thing of beauty is a joy forever".

(A) Keats wrote that a thing of beauty is a joy forever

(B) Keats wrote that a thing of beauty was a joy forever

(C) A thing of beauty was a joy forever is written by Keats

(D) Keats has written that a beautiful thing is always joyful

Q135. Socrates said, "Virtue is its own reward."

(A) Socrates said that virtue had its own rewards

(B) Socrates says that virtue is its own reward

(C) Socrates said that virtue is its own reward

(D) Socrates said that virtue was its own reward

Q136. He said to the interviewer, "Could you please repeat the question?"

(A) He requested the interviewer if he could please repeat the question

(B) He requested the interviewer to please repeat the question

(C) He requested the interviewer to repeat the question

(D) He requested the interviewer if he could repeat the question

Q137. He said, "it used to be a lovely, quiet street."

(A) He said that it used to be a lovely, quiet street

(B) He pointed out that it had used to be a lovely, quiet street

(C) He said that there used to be a lovely, quiet street

(D) He inquired whether there was a lovely, quiet street

138. The Prime Minister said that no one would be allowed to disturb the peace.

(A) The Prime Minister said, "We shall not allow anyone to disturb the peace."

(B) The Prime Minister said, "We would not allow no one to disturb the peace."

(C) The Prime Minister said, "No one will disturb the peace."

(D) The Prime Minister said, "No one can disturb the peace."

Q139. The spectators said, "Bravo! Well done, players."

(A) The spectators shouted that the players were doing very well

(B) The spectators exclaimed with joy that the players were doing very well

(C) The spectators applauded the players saying that they had done well

(D) The spectators applauded the players joyfully to do well

Q140. I said to my friend, "Good Morning. Let us go for a picnic today."

(A) I told good morning to my friend, and asked to go for a picnic that day

(B) I wished my friend good morning and proposed that we should go for a picnic that day

(C) I wished my friend good morning and proposed that should go for a picnic that day

(D) I told good morning to my friend and suggested to go for a picnic today

Q141. The new student asked the old one, "Do you know my name?"

(A) The new student asked the old one if he knew his name

(B) The new student asked the old one that whether he knew his name

(C) The new student asked the old one did he know his name

(D) The new student asked the old one if he knows his name

Q142. I warned her that I could no longer tolerate her coming late.

(A) I said to her, "You can no longer tolerate my coming late."

(B) I said to her, "I can no longer tolerate your coming late."

(C) I said to her, "He can no longer tolerate her coming late."

(D) I said to her, "I can no longer tolerate she coming late."

Q143. I said to my mother, "I will certainly take you to Bangalore this week."

(A) I told my mother he would certainly take her to Bangalore that week

(B) I told my mother that I would certainly take her to Bangalore that week

(C) I told my mother that she would certainly take her to Bangalore that week

(D) I told to my mother that I would take you to Bangalore that week

Q144. "How long does the Journey take?", my co-passenger asked me.

(A) My co-passenger asked me how long does the journey take

(B) I asked my co-passenger how long the journey would take

(C) My co-passenger wanted to know how long the journey would take

(D) My co-passenger asked me how long the journey did take

Q145. "How clever of you to have solved the puzzle so quickly," said the mother.

(A) The mother exclaimed admiringly that it was very clever of him to have solved the puzzle so quickly

(B) The mother expressed that he was so clever to have solved the puzzle quickly

(C) The mother expressed that he was so clever in solving the puzzle so quickly

(D) The mother exclaimed with joy that he was clever enough to solve the puzzle so quickly

Q146. He said he goes for a walk every morning.

(A) He said, "I went for a walk every morning".

(B) He said, "I go for a walk every morning".

(C) He said, "I will go for a walk-every morning".

(D) He said, "He goes for a walk every morning".

Q147. I reiterated, "I don't care about the job".

(A) I reiterated I didn't care about the job

(B) I said again and again I didn't care about the job

(C) I reiterated that I did not care about the job

(D) I repeatedly said that I cared about the job

Q148. I said to my brother, "Let us go to some hill station for a change."

(A) I suggested to my brother that they should go to some hill station for a change

(B) I suggested to my brother that we should go to some hill station for a change

(C) I suggested to my brother that let us go to some hill station for a change

(D) I suggested to my brother that let them go to some hill station for a change

Q149. I wondered how many discoveries went unheeded.

(A) I said, "How many discoveries have gone unheeded?"

(B) I said, "How many discoveries went unheeded?"

(C) I said, "Do discoveries go unheeded?"

(D) I said, "How many discoveries go unheeded?"

Q150. Gopan said to me, "Can you do these sums for me?"

(A) Gopan asked me if I could do those sums for him

(B) Gopan asked me if I can do those sums for him

(C) Gopan asked me if I can do these sums for him

(D) Gopan asked if I could do these sums for him

Q151. The boss said, "It's time we began planning our work".

(A) The boss said that it was time they had begun planning their work

(B) The boss said that it was time we had begun planning our work

(C) The boss said that it was time they began planning their work

(D) The boss said that it was time we began planning his work

Q152. He said to the judge, "I did not commit this crime,"

(A) He told the judge that he had not committed that crime

(B) He told the judge that he did not commit the crime

(C) He told the judge that he had not committed the crime

(D) He told the judge that he had not committed this crime

Q153. Rahul said, "I will do it now or never".

(A) Rahul said that he will do it now or never

(B) Rahul said that he will now or never do it

(C) Rahul said that he would do it then or never

(D) Rahul said that he would now or never do it

Q154. My father once said to me, "If I can't trust my people, then I don't want to be doing this."

(A) His father once told him that if he couldn't trust his people then he didn't want to be doing that

(B) My father once told me that if he couldn't trust his people then he didn't want to be doing that

(C) My father once told me that if he couldn't trust my people then he didn't want to be doing that

(D) My father once told me that if he couldn't trust his people then he didn't want to be doing this

Q155. Doshi said to his wife, "Please select one of these necklace."

(A) Doshi requested his wife to select one of those necklaces

(B) Doshi said to his wife to please select one of these necklaces

(C) Doshi told his wife to please select one of those necklaces

(D) Doshi pleased his wife to selects one of those necklaces

Q156. He wrote in his report, "The rainfall has been scanty till now."

(A) He reported that the rainfall has been scanty till now

(B) He reported that the rainfall had been scanty till now

(C) He reported that the rainfall has been scanty till then

(D) He reported that the rainfall had been scanty till then

Q157. "Govind," said the manager sternly, "I command you tell me what the old man said."

(A) The manager sternly told Govind that he commanded him to tell V him what the old man had said

(B) The manager sternly commanded sternly to Govind to tell him what the old man had said

(C) The manager commanded Govind to tell him what the old man said

(D) The manager sternly commanded Govind to tell him what the old man had said

Q158. I said to him, "Where have you lost the pen I brought for you yesterday?"

(A) I asked him where he had lost the pen I had brought for him the day before

(B) I asked him where he had lost the pen I had brought for him the previous day

(C) I asked him where he had lost the pen I had brought for him the next day

(D) I asked him where he had lost the pen I brought for him the previous day

Q159. She said to Rita, "Please help me with my homework."

(A) She requested Rita to help her in her homework

(B) Rita requested her to help her with her homework

(C) She requested Rita to help her with her homework

(D) She requested Rita to help her homework.

Q160. "Call the first witness", said the Judge.

(A) The judge commanded to call the first witness.

(B) The judge commanded them to call the first witness.

(C) The judge commanded that the first witness be called.

(D) The judge commanded the first witness to be called.

Q161. The queen said to her son, "You must go to the forest and remain there till your father calls you back."

(A) The queen ordered her son to go to the forest and remain there till his father calls him back

(B) The queen told her son that he must go to the forest and remain there till his father called him back

(C) The queen told his son that you must go to the forest and remain there till your father called you back

(D) The queen told her son to go to the forest and remained there till his father called him back.

Q162. I said to her, "All your faults will be pardoned if you confess them."

(A) I told her that all her faults will be pardoned if you confess them

(B) I told her that all her faults would be pardoned if she confessed them

(C) I told her all her faults will have to be pardoned if she confessed them

(D) I told her that all her faults would has to be pardoned if she confessed them

Q163. He said to Sita, "When do you intend to pay back the money you borrowed from them

(A) He enquired Sita when did she intend to pay back the money she borrowed from him

(B) He enquired Sita when she intended to pay back the money she borrowed from him

(C) He enquired Sita when she intended to pay back the money she had borrowed from him

(D) He enquired when Sita intended to pay back the money she borrowed from him

Q164. "Let's give a party", said Jaya. "Let's not", said her husband.

(A) Jaya suggested giving a party but her husband answered in the negative.

(B) Jaya suggested giving a party but her husband opposed the idea.

(C) Jaya suggested giving a party but her husband contradicted her.

(D) Jaya suggested giving a party but her husband refused.

165. The old man Latur said, "Alas, my only son is dead!"

(A) The old man of Latur exclaimed with sorrow that his only son was dead

(B) The old man of Latur told with pain that his only son was dead

(C) The old man of Latur expressed with anguish that his only son was dead

(D) The old man of Latur sorrowfully narrated that his only son was dead

Q166. The Chief Minister said, "What a terrible disaster the earthquake is!"

(A) The Chief Minister cried that the earthquake was a terrible disaster

(B) The Chief Minister expressed with surprise that the earthquake was a terrible disaster

(C) The Chief Minister exclaimed with sorrow that the earthquake was a terrible disaster

(D) The Chief Minister told in pain that the earthquake was a terrible disaster

Q167. "Many happy returns of your birthday", we said.

(A) We greeted him on his birthday

(B) We said that many happy returns of your birthday

(C) We wished him many happy returns of his birthday

(D) We prayed for many happy returns of his birthday

Q168. Shanker said to his friend, "Look out! There is a snake behind you."

(A) Shanker told his friend to look out as there was a snake behind him

(B) Shanker exclaimed to his friend with surprise that there was a snake behind him

(C) Seeing a snake behind him, Shanker asked his friend to look out

(D) Shanker warned his friend that there was a snake behind him

Q169. "Doctor", the patient cried, "please tell me how much time I have."

(A) The patient pleaded the doctor how much time she will have

(B) The patient exclaimed to the doctor that how much time she had

(C) The patient pleaded with the doctor to tell her how much time she had

(D) The patient cried to the doctor that how much time had she

Q170. "So help me Heaven!" he cried , "I never steal again."

(A) He wanted Heaven to help him so that he would never steal again

(B) He exclaimed to Heaven that he would never steal again

(C) He exclaimed Heaven to help him that he would never steal again

(D) He called upon Heaven to witness his resolve never to steal again

Q171. She said, "I'II give you Rs. 100/- to keep your mouth shut."

(A) She said that she would give him Rs. 100/- to keep his mouth shut

(B) She offered him Rs. 100/- to keep his mouth shut

(C) She suggested to him that she would give him Rs. 100/- to keep his mouth shut

(D) She proposed that she would given him Rs. 100/- to keep his mouth shut

Q172. "From one of the windows of my flat I can see the Qutub Minar", said my friend.

(A) My friend told that from one of the windows of his flat he could see the Qutub Minar

(B) My friend said that from one of the windows of his flat he can see the Qutub Minar

(C) My friend said that from one of the windows of his flat he could see the Qutub Minar

(D) My friend told that from one of the windows of his flat he can see the Qutub Minar

Q173. The teacher said to the students, "Why were you absent yesterday?

(A) The teacher asked the student why had been he absent the previous day

(B) The teacher asked the student why had he been absent the previous day

(C) The teacher informed the student that why he had been absent the next day

(D) The teacher asked the student why he had been absent the previous day

Q174. The teacher said to Ashok, "I shall report the matter to the Principal if you misbehave again."

(A) The teacher told Ashok that he would be reporting the matter to the Principal if he misbehaved again

(B) The teacher warned Ashok that he would report the matter to the Principal if he misbehaved again

(C) The teacher threatened Ashok to report the matter to the Principal if he would misbehave again

(D) The teacher cautioned Ashok about reporting the matter to the Principal if he misbehaved again

Q175 Sweta requested me to lend her some money.

(A) Sweta said to me, "Please lend me some money."

(B) Sweta said me, "Please lend me some money."

(C) Sweta said to me, "Please lent me some money."

(D) Sweta said to me to please lend me some money."

Q176. The teacher said, "Where there is will, there is way."

(A) The teacher said that Where there is will, there is way.

(B) The teacher say that Where there is will, there is way.

(C) The teacher said that Where there was will, there was way.

(D) The teacher has said that Where there is will, there is way.

Q177. Vivek said, "When I came to your home, You were sleeping."

(A) Vivek told me to that when he came to my home, I was sleeping.

(B) Vivek told me when he came to my home, I was sleeping.

(C) Vivek told me that when he came to my home, I was sleeping.

(D) Vivek told me when he had come to my home, I was sleeping.

Q178. The teacher said to me, "Dogs bark at strangers."

(A) The teacher told me that dogs barked at strangers.

(B) The teacher told me that dogs bark at strangers.

(C) The teacher told to me that dogs bark at strangers.

(D) The teacher told me that dogs have bark at strangers.

Q179. Anita said to me, "Would you like to have a cup of tea with me?" I said, "NO."

(A) Anita asked me if I would like to have a cup of tea with her. Anita replied no.

(B) Anita asked me if I would be liking to have a cup of tea with her. Anita replied in negative.

(C) Anita asked me that if I would like to have a cup of tea with her. Anita replied in negative.

(D) Anita asked me if I would like to have a cup of tea with her. Anita replied in negative.

Q180. "You had better leave the snake alone," the man said.

(A) The man had warned me to leave the snake alone.

(B) The man warned me to leave the snake alone.

(C) The man warned me to leave the snake.

(D) The man warned me that to leave the snake alone.

Q181. "You can't bathe in this pond," he said to me, "It is very rough."

(A) He told me that I cannot bathe in that pond as it was very rough.

(B) He told me that I could not bathe in that pond as it is very rough.

(C) He told me that I could not bathe in that pond as it was very rough.

(D) He told me that I could not been bathe in that pond as it was very rough.

Q182. The manager told the peon not to send anyone in his cabin.

(A) The manager said to the peon, "Don't send anyone in his cabin."

(B) The manager said to the peon, that "Don't send anyone in his cabin."

(C) The manager said to the peon, "Don't sent anyone in his cabin."

(D) The manager said to the peon, "Don't send noone in his cabin."

Q183 Suresh said, "Wait here till I return."

(A) Suresh told us to wait there till he returns.

(B) Suresh told us to wait here till he returned.

(C) Suresh told to us to wait there till he returned.

(D) Suresh told us to wait there till he returned.

Q184. Raju said, "Where do you live?"

(A) Raju asked me where I did live.

(B) Raju asked me where did I lived.

(C) Raju asked me where I lived.

(D) Raju asked me that where I lived.

Q185. "Mohan made this mess. Let him clear it up", said his father.

(A) Mohan's father said that Mohan had made the mess and proposed that he clear it up

(B) Mohan's father said that Mohan had made the mess and that he was to clear it

(C) Mohan's father said that Mohan had made the mess and suggested that he clear it

(D) Mohan's father said that Mohan had made the mess and that he should clear it

Q186. "Fie! A soldier and afraid of fighting!" said Babar.

(A) Babar exclaimed with surprise that a soldier should be afraid of fighting

(B) Addressing a soldier, Babar cursed him that he should be afraid of fighting

(C) Babar cursed the soldier who was afraid of fighting

(D) Babar cursed and exclaimed that a soldier should not be afraid of fighting

Q187. He said to her, "Did it shake you up as much as it shook me?"

(A) He asked her if it had shaken her up as much as it shook him

(B) He enquired of her if it shook her up as it shook him

(C) He enquired of her if it shook her up as much as it had shaken him

(D) He asked her if it had shaken her up as much as it had shaken him

Q188. The teacher said to Ram, "Would you like to go on a trip to Kashmir ?" Ram said, "Yes."

(A) The teacher asked if Ram would like

to go on a trip to Kashmir and Ram replied yes
(B) The teacher asked Ram if he would like to go on a trip to Kashmir and Ram replied yes
(C) The teacher asked Ram if he would have like to go on a trip to Kashmir and Ram replied in the affirmative
(D) The teacher asked Ram if he would like to go on a trip to Kashmir and Ram replied in the affirmative

Q189. Everybody said, "How well she sings!"
(A) Everybody told us that she sings very well
(B) Everybody exclaimed that she sings very well
(C) Everybody exclaimed that she sang very well
(D) Everybody told us that how she sang very well

Q190. "Suppose you children go out for a nice long walk", she said.
(A) She proposed that the children went out for a nice long walk
(B) She advised that the children go out for a nice long walk
(C) She suggested that the children go out for a nice long walk
(D) She suggested that the children should go out for a nice long walk

Q191. "Do as you wish, but don't come and ask me for help if you get into difficulties."
(A) He told me to do as he wished or he wouldn't come and help me if I got into difficulties
(B) He told me to do as I wished, but not to go and ask him for help if I got into difficulties
(C) He ordered me to do as I wished, but not to go and ask him for help if I got into difficulties
(D) He told me that unless I did as I wished he would not come and help me if I got into difficulties

Q192. I said, "Let Mohan do his worst, he cannot harm me."
(A) I suggested to Mohan to do his worst, he could not harm me
(B) I told that if Mohan did his his worst, he could not harm me
(C) I declared that Mohan might do his worst, he could not harm me
(D) I declared that Mohan might do his worst, he could not harm me

Q193. I said, "When it gets dark, light the lantern and hang it out."
(A) I said that when it got dark he light the lantern and hung it out.
(B) I requested that when it got dark he may light the lantern and hang it out.
(C) I said that when it got dark he should light the lantern and hang it out.
(D) I told that when it got dark he should light the lantern and hang it out.

Q194. "May you live long and prosper", said the old lady to her son.
(A) The old lady blessed her son with long life and wished him prosperity
(B) The old lady prayed for her son's long life and prosperity
(C) The old lady prayed for her son and said that he might live long and prosper
(D) The old lady blessed her son and prayed for his long life and prosperity

Q195. "Do you want balloons ?" he said to the child.
(A) He asked the child if it wanted balloons
(B) He asked the child whether it had wanted balloons
(C) He asked the child did if it would want balloons
(D) He asked the child if it would want

balloons

Q196. She said, "How ugly I look in this dress !"

(A) She said that how ugly she was looking in that dress

(B) She exclaimed how ugly she looked in that dress

(C) She expressed how ugly she looked in that dress

(D) She exclaimed that she looked very ugly in that dress

Q197. She said, "You can leave the books here."

(A) She said that they can leave the books there

(B) She said that they could leave the books there

(C) She said that they can leave the books here

(D) She said that they could leave the books here

Q198. My friend said, "I am leaving today."

(A) My friend said that he is leaving today

(B) My friend said that he was leaving today

(C) My friend said that he leaves today

(D) My friend said that he was leaving that day

Q199. Mukta said to Puneet, "My mother is a good cook."

(A) Mukta told Puneet that her mother was a good cook

(B) Mukta told Puneet that my mother was a good cook

(C) Mukta told to Puneet that her mother is a good cook

(D) Mukta asked Puneet that her mother is a good cook

Q200. The commander said to the army, "March forward".

(A) The commander asked the army march forward

(B) The commander ordered the army to march forward

(C) The commander requested the army to go forward

(D) The army requested the commander to march

Q201. He promised, "I will do it tomorrow."

(A) He promised that he will do it tomorrow

(B) He promised that he will do it the next day

(C) He promised that he would do it tomorrow

(D) He promised that he would do it the next day

Q202. Geeta said, "I did not do this deliberately."

(A) Geeta said that I had not done that deliberately

(B) Geeta said that she had not done that deliberately

(C) Geeta said that she has not done this deliberately

(D) Geeta said that I have not done this deliberately

Q203. She exclaimed, "I'm afraid we are rather late !"

(A) She exclaimed that they were frightened of being late

(B) She exclaimed that she was afraid that they were rather late

(C) She shouted that they were scared that they would be late

(D) She screamed that she was worried that they would all be late

Q204. She said to me, "What can I do for you?"

(A) She asked me what she could do for me

(B) She asked me what can she do for me

(C) She asked me what she can do for me

(D) She asked me whether she can do anything for me

Q205. "Do you want balloons ?" he said to the child.

(A) He asked the child if it wanted balloons

(B) He asked the child whether it had wanted balloons

(C) He asked the child did if it would want balloons

(D) He asked the child if it would want balloons

Q206. She said, "How ugly I look in this dress !"

(A) She said that how ugly she was looking in that dress

(B) She exclaimed how ugly she looked in that dress

(C) She expressed how ugly she looked in that dress

(D) She exclaimed that she looked very ugly in that dress

Q207. She said, "You can leave the books here."

(A)She said that they can leave the books there

(B)She said that they could leave the books there

(C)She said that they can leave the books here

(D)She said that they could leave the books here

Q208. My friend said, "I am leaving today."

(A)My friend said that he is leaving today

(B)My friend said that he was leaving today

(C)My friend said that he leaves today

(D)My friend said that he was leaving that day

Q209. Mukta said to Puneet, "My mother is a good cook."

(A)Mukta told Puneet that her mother was a good cook

(B)Mukta told Puneet that my mother was a good cook

(C)Mukta told to Puneet that her mother is a good cook

(D)Mukta asked Puneet that her mother is a good cook

Q210. The commander said to the army, "March forward".

(A)The commander asked the army march forward

(B)The commander ordered the army to march forward

(C)The commander requested the army to go forward

(D)The army requested the commander to march

Q211. He promised, "I will do it tomorrow."

(A)He promised that he will do it tomorrow

(B)He promised that he will do it the next day

(C)He promised that he would do it tomorrow

(D)He promised that he would do it the next day

Q212. Geeta said, "I did not do this deliberately."

(A)Geeta said that I had not done that deliberately

(B)Geeta said that she had not done that deliberately

(C)Geeta said that she has not done this deliberately

(D)Geeta said that I have not done this deliberately

Q213. She exclaimed, "I'm afraid we are rather late !"

(A)She exclaimed that they were frightened of being late

(B)She exclaimed that she was afraid that they were rather late

(C)She shouted that they were scared that they would be late

(D)She screamed that she was worried that they would all be late

Q214. She said to me, "What can I do for you?"

(A)She asked me what she could do for me

(B)She asked me what can she do for me

(C)She asked me what she can do for me

(D)She asked me whether she can do anything for me

Q215. Mrs. Shankar said, "I know what it is to be depressed."

(1) Mrs. Shankar said that she was knowing what it was to be depressed.

(2) Mrs. Shankar said that she knew what it was to be depressed.

(3) Mrs. Shankar knows what it is to be depressed.

(4) Mrs. Shankar is depressed she said.

Q216. "Who now," they had asked, "will listen to our troubles and protect us from the crocodiles ?"

(1) They wanted to know who will listen to their troubles and protect them from the crocodiles.

(2) They had wanted to know who would listen to their troubles and protect them from the crocodiles.

(3) They had wanted to know who then would listen to their troubles and protect them from the crocodiles.

(4) They had wanted to know who will now listen to their troubles and protect them from the crocodiles.

Q217. Moti asked Gangu whether the latter was in his senses.

(1) "Are you senseless, Gangu?" asked Moti.

(2) "Hey Gangu, are you in your senses now ?" asked Moti

(3) "Gangu, have you lost your senses" asked Moti.

(4) "Gangu, are you in your senses?" asked Moti

Q218. He said that we are all born to die.

(1) He said, "We have all been born to die."

(2) He exclaimed, "We were all born to die."

(3) He said, "We were all born to die."

(4) He said, "We are all born to die."

Q219. He said to me, "I grew these carrots myself."

(1) He told me that he grew those carrots himself.

(2) He told me I grew these carrots myself.

(3) He told me that he grew these carrots himself.

(4) He told me that he had grown those carrots himself.

Q220. Israt said to Irfat, "Let's go to Puri for a change."

(1) Israt proposed to Irfat to go to Puri for a change.

(2) Israt suggested to Irfat to go to Puri for a change.

(3) Israt asked Irfat to go to Puri for a change.

(4) Israt proposed to Irfat that they should go to Puri for a change.

Q221. The poor beggar said, "0h God, have mercy on my soul".

(1) The poor beggar prayed to God to have mercy on his soul.

(2) The poor beggar, invoking God, implored him to have mercy on his soul.

(3) The poor beggar exclaimed that God, have mercy on his soul.

(4) The poor beggar told God to have mercy on his soul.

Q222. He said to her, "Why didn't you put on the brakes ?

(1) He asked her why she hadn't put on the brakes.

(2) He asked her why she didn't put on the brake.

(3) He asked her that why she hadn't put on the brake.

(4) He told her that why she hadn't put on

the brake.

Q223. She said to me, "I took breakfast in the morning."

(1) She told me that she took breakfast in the morning.

(2) She told me that she had taken breakfast in the morning.

(3) She told me that she has taken breakfast in the morning.

(4) She said to me that she was taking breakfast in the morning.

Q224. John's father reminded him to take his umbrella.

(1) John's father said, "Remember your umbrella John ?"

(2) "Here, is your umbrella John," said his father.

(3) "Are you going to take your umbrella or not ?" said John to his father.

(4) "Don't forget to take your umbrella, John" said his father.

Q225. He said, "He took tea in the morning".

(1) He said that he did take in the morning.

(2) He said that he had taken tea in the morning.

(3) He said that he took in the morning.

(4) He said that he would take tea in the morning.

Q226. He requested the boss to let him go on with his project.

(1) He said to the boss, "You better let me go on with my project".

(2) He told the boss, "Please go on with my project".

(3) He said to the boss, "Let me go on with my project please".

(4) He told the boss, "Go on with my project please".

Q227. I told her, "It was raining last night when you left".

(1) I told her that it had been raining the previous night when she had left.

(2) I told her that it has raining last night when she left.

(3) I told her that it has been raining the night before when she left.

(4) I told her that it had been raining last nght when she had left.

Q228. He said, "I shall try to bring you the books tomorrow".

(1) He said that he should try to bring me the books the next day.

(2) He said that he would try to bring me the books the next day.

(3) He said that he would try to bring me the books tomorrow.

(4) He said that he should try to bring me the books tomorrow.

Q229. He said, "Alas ! The little puppy is run over by the car".

(1) He exclaimed, alas, the little puppy was run over by the the car.

(2) He exclaimed sadly that the little puppy was run over by the car.

(3) He exclaimed sadly that the little puppy had been run over by the car.

(4) He exclaimed sadly that the little puppy is run over by the car.

Q230. Suresh asked Prasad whether he had watched the cricket match on television the previous night.

(1) Suresh said to Prasad, "Did you watched the cricket match on television last night?"

(2) Suresh asked Prasad, "Did you watch the cricket match on television previous night?"

(3) Suresh asked Prasad, "Have you watched the cricket match on television last night?"

(4) Suresh said to Prasad, "Did you watch the cricket match on television last night?"

Q231. Father said to me, "You are idling away your time."

(1) Father told me that you were idling away your time.

(2) Father told me that I was idling away my time.

(3) Father told me that I am idling away my time.

(4) Father told me that you are idling away your time.

Q232. The captain said to his men, "Fall into line."

(1) The captain said to his men that they can fall into line.

(2) The captain commanded his men to fall into line.

(3) The captain warned his men to fall into line.

(4) The captain told his men that they should fall into line.

Q233. The priest said, "May God pardon this sinner !"

(1) The priest prayed that God would pardon this sinner.

(2) The priest prayed that God might pardon that sinner.

(3) The priest prayed if God will pardon that sinner.

(4) The priest said that God might pardon the sinner.

Q234. Ashmita advised me to go and see a doctor.

(1) "Shouldn't you go and see a doctor ?" asked Ashmita.

(2) "You should go and see a doctor," said Ashmita.

(3) Ashmita asked me, "Will you go and see a doctor ?"

(4) Ashmita told me, "Go and see a doctor."

235. She said to me, "It has been raining heavily and you cannot go".

(1) She told me that it had been raining heavily and I could not go.

(2) She told me that it was raining heavily and I could not go.

(3) She told me that it has been raining heavily and I could not go.

(4) She told me that it is raining heavily and I could not go.

Q236. John said to me, "Where have you been last night ?"

(1) John asked me where had I been the previous night.

(2) John asked me where I have been the previous night.

(3) John asked me where I am the previous night.

(4) John asked me where I had been the previous night.

Q237. "I'm taking my children to the zoo tomorrow", she said, "to see the baby white tiger".

(1) She said that she will take the children to the zoo to see the baby white tiger tomorrow.

(2) She said that she would take the children to the zoo the next day to see the baby white tiger.

(3) She said that she was taking her children to the zoo the next day to see the baby white tiger.

(4) She said that she was taking the children to the zoo that day to see the baby white tiger.

Q238. She said, "Mother, please cook me something nice today".

(1) She told her mother to cook her something nice today.

(2) She ordered her mother to cook her something nice that day.

(3) She requested her mother to cook her something nice that day.

(4) She asked her mother if she could cook her something nice that day.

Q239. John said, "I shall be 21 tomorrow".

(1) John said that he would be 21 tomorrow.

(2) John said that he would be 21 the following day.

(3) John said that he should be 21 the following day.

(4) John said that I shall be 21 tomorrow.

Q240. She asked, "Is the secretary coming to the meeting ?"

(1) She asked that the secretary was coming to the meeting.

(2) She asked that if the secretary was coming to the meeting.

(3) She asked if the secretary is coming to the meeting.

(4) She asked if the secretary was coming to the meeting.

Q241. The convict said, "Let me speak freely please".

(1) The convict suggested that he must be allowed to speak freely.

(2) The convict requested that he must be allowed to speak freely.

(3) The convict requested that hebe allowed to speak freely.

(4) The convict proposed that he might be allowed to speak freely.

Q242. Nisha told Monica, "What a beautiful dress you are wearing!"

(1) Nisha exclaimed that Monica was wearing a very beautiful dress.

(2) Nisha exclaimed that it is a very beautiful dress.

(3) Nisha exclaimed that Monica is wearing a very beautiful dress.

(4) Nisha told Monica that was a beautiful dress.

Q243. "Call the witness", said the magistrate.

(1) The magistrate requested to call the witness.

(2) The magistrate begged for calling the witness.

(3) The magistrate ordered to call the witness.

(4) The magistrate prayed to call the witness.

Q244. "Have you done this sort of work before ?" said his new employer.

(1) His new employer asked him whether he has done that sort of work before.

(2) His new employer asked him whether he has done this sort of work before.

(3) His new employer asked him whether he had done that sort of work before.

(4) His new employer asked him whether he had done this sort of work before.

Q245. Rahul says that Azhar loves cricket.

(1) Rahul said, "Azhar loves cricket".

(2) Rahul said, "Azhar loved cricket".

(3) Rahul says, "Azhar loved cricket".

(4) Rahul says, "Azhar loves cricket".

Q246. "I came home last night", said he.

(1) He told that he had come home last night.

(2) He said that he came home last night.

(3) He said that he had come home the previous night.

(4) He says that he came home the previous night.

Q247. The beggar said, "Poverty is a great curse".

(1) The beggar said poverty has a great curse.

(2) The beggar said that poverty is a great curse.

(3) The beggar said that poverty was a great curse.

(4) The beggar said that poverty had been a great curse.

Q248. "If you want to smoke, you'll have to go out", said the conductor.

(1) The conductor ordered me to go out and smoke.

(2) The conductor said that if I/ he

wanted to smoke, I/he would have to go out.

(3) The conductor told me that smoking is not permitted in the bus.

(4) The conductor told me that I will have to go out and smoke.

249. "Be careful; the steps are very slippery", I warned him.

(1) I warned him to be careful as the steps were very slippery.

(2) I warned him to be careful as the steps are very slippery.

(3) I warned him to be careful and steps were very slippery.

(4) I told him to be careful and the steps are very slippery.

Q250. The old lady declared that she was going to walk where she pleased. They had the liberty.

(1) The old lady said that, "I was going to walk where I pleased. They have the liberty".

(2) The old lady. "1 am going to walk where I please. We have the liberty".

(3) The old lady. "I was going to walk where I pleased. They have the liberty".

(4) The old lady. "I am going to walk where I pleased. They had the liberty".

Q251. The teacher asked me why I had been absent the day before.

(1) The teacher asked me, "Why were you absent yesterday ?"

(2) The teacher asked me, "Why are you absent yesterday ?"

(3) The teacher asked me, "Why are you absent the day before ?"

(4) The teacher asked me, "Were you absent the day before ?"

Q252. Mr Robinson asked his son what he wanted to be when he grew up.

(1) "My son," said Mr Robinson, "what will you be when you grow up ?'

(2) "My son," said Mr Robinson, "what do you want to be when you grow up ?"

(3) Mr Robinson said, "My son, what did you want to be when you grew up ?"

(4) Mr Robinson said, "My son, what would you be when you grow up ?"

Q253. The boys respectfully wished their teacher good morning.

(1) "Good morning," said the boys to their teacher.

(2) "Good morning," said the boys to the teacher.

(3) "Good morning, Madam," said the boys to the teacher.

(4) "Good morning, Madam," said the boys to their teacher.

Q254. She said, "I am sorry, I am not able to submit those papers".

(1) She said she was sorry, she is not able to submit those papers.

(2) She said that she was sorry and she will not be able to submit those papers.

(3) She apologized for not being able to submit those papers.

(4) She exclaimed with sorrow that she was sorry and she will not be able to submit those papers.

Q255. The girl wondered where the sparrows had gone.

(1) The girl said, "Oh! Where the sparrows have gone ?"

(2) The girl said, "Oh ! Where are the sparrows ?"

(3) The girl said, "Oh ! Where had the sparrows gone ?"

(4) The girl said, "Oh ! Where have the sparrows gone ?"

Q256. She said to me, "I'm going shopping. Can I get you something ?"

(1) She said she was going shopping and

said to me if I wanted something.

(2) She said she was going shopping and asked if I wanted something.

(3) She said she was going shopping and asked if she could get me something.

(4) She said she is going shopping and asked if she could get me something.

Q257. Ramesh informed his friend that he could make use of his car while he was away.

(1) Ramesh said to his friend, "You will make use of my car while I was away".

(2) Ramesh said to his friend, "Use my car while I go away".

(3) Ramesh said to his friend, "You can make use of my car while I am away".

(4) Ramesh asked his friend, "Will you make use of my car while I am away ?"

Q258. Kala said to Radha, "Who were you speaking to over the phone ?"

(1) Kala asked Radha who she had been speaking to over the phone.

(2) Kala asked Radha who she has been speaking to over the phone.

(3) Kala asked Radha that who she was speaking to over the phone.

(4) Kala asked Radha that who she had been speaking to over the phone.

Q259. The king said to his men, "Do not be afraid of the enemy. Face them bravely."

(1) The king ordered his men to not be afraid of the enemy and that they had to be faced bravely.

(2) The king asked his men to not be afraid of the enemy but they should be faced bravely.

(3) The king advised his men not to be afraid of the enemy but to face them bravely.

(4) The king told his men not to be afraid of the enemy and they had faced them bravely.

Q260. Kannan said to Subha, "I'll return the book after I have read it".

(1) Kannan told Subha that he will return the book after he has read it.

(2) Kannan told Subha that he would return the book after he has read it.

(3) Kannan told Subha that he will return the book after he read it.

(4) Kannan told Subha that he would return the book after he had read it.

Q261. The boss said to his secretary, "Did you discuss this matter with the manager ?"

(1) The boss asked his secretary whether he discussed that matter with the manager.

(2) The boss asked his secretary if you have discussed that matter with the manager.

(3) The boss asked his secretary if he had discussed that matter with the manager.

(4) The boss asked his secretary whether he has discussed that matter with the manager.

Q262. I said to him, 'Will you go to Delhi ?'

(1) I asked him will he go to Delhi.

(2) I said to him would he go to Delhi.

(3) I asked him if he would go to Delhi.

(4) I said to him would you go to Delhi.

Q263. He said, 'I have read this novel.'

(1) He said that he has read this novel.

(2) He said that he had read that novel.

(3) He said that he read that novel.

(4) He said that he had read this novel.

Q264. Tania said to her friend, 'Can you lend me an umbrella ?'

(1) Please give me an umbrella Tania requested her friend.

(2) Will you lend me your umbrella, Tania asked her friend.

(3) Tania requested her friend to lend her an umbrella

(4) Tania asked her friend to give her an umbrella.

Q265. Sita said, 'I may go there.'

(1) Sita says that she may go there.

(2) Sita says that she is going there.

(3) Sita said that she will go there.

(4) Sita said that she might go there.

Q266. My friend requested me to bring him a sandwich.

(1) He said, 'My friend, please bring me a sandwich.'

(2) My friend said, 'Will you bring me a sandwich.'

(3) 'Please bring me a sandwich', said my friend.

(4) 'Please bring my friend a sandwich.', said he.

Q267. He said, 'If I had the tools I could mend the car.'

(1) He said that if he had the tools he could mend the car.

(2) He tells that he had the tools he could mend the car.

(3) He said I could mend the car if I have the tools.

(4) He told he could mend the car.

Q268. She said to the children, 'You mustn't play with fire.'

(1) She told the children they were not to play with fire.

(2) She told the children that they mustn't play with fire.

(3) She told the children not to play with fire.

(4) She told the children they are not to play with fire.

Q269. Everybody says, 'How well she sings !'

(1) Everybody comments that she sings well.

(2) Everybody says how well she sings.

(3) Everybody tells that she sang very well.

(4) Everybody says that she sang well.

Q270. He says that he is very sorry.

(1) He said, 'He was very sorry'.

(2) He says, 'I am very sorry'.

(3) He said, 'He is very sorry'.

(4) He told me, 'I felt sorry'.

271. Daman says, 'Priya is working in Ahmedabad.'

(1) Daman say that Priya was working in Ahmedabad.

(2) Daman said that Priya was working in Ahmedabad.

(3) Daman said that Priya works in Ahmedabad.

(4) Daman says that Priya is working in Ahmedabad.

Q272. Anne said, 'It is time to leave for the meeting.'

(1) Anne said that it was time to leave for the meeting.

(2) Anne told that it is time to leave for the meeting.

(3) Anne said its time to leave for the meeting.

(4) Anne said that it was time for the meeting.

Q273. The old man said that he would soon be leaving the world.

(1) The old man said, "I shall soon be leaving the world."

(2) The old man said, "I am soon leaving the world."

(3) The old man said, "I would soon leave the world."

(4) The old man said, "I am going to leave the world soon."

274. "Come home early" said MrMatthew to his clerk.

(1) Mr Matthew told his clerk to come home as early as possible.

(2) Mr Matthew asked his clerk to be home early.

(3) Mr Matthew ordered his clerk to come home early.

(4) Mr Matthew requested his clerk to come home a little early.

275. I said, "Water is essential for life."

(1) Water is essential for life was said by me.

(2) I told that water was essential for life.

(3) I exclaimed that water was essential for life.

(4) I said that water is essential for life.

276. She asked me if I was going to college.

(1) She said, "Am I going to college ?"

(2) She said to me, "Are you going to college ?"

(3) She asked me, "Will you go to college ?"

(4) She asked to me, "Was I going to college ?"

Q277. Iba said that she might go home the next day with her sister.

(1) Iba said, "I could go home tomorrow with my sister."

(2) Iba said, "I may just go home tomorrow with my sister."

(3) Iba said, "I can go home tomorrow with my sister."

(4) Iba said, "I will go home tomorrow with my sister."

Q278. He said, "I was doing it."

(1) He said that he had been doing it.

(2) He said that he had done it.

(3) He said that he has done it.

(4) He said that he did it.

Q279. The lady asked me how my uncle was.

(1) The lady said to me, "How is your uncle ?"

(2) The lady asked me, "How has your uncle been ?"

(3) The lady said to me, "How was your uncle ?"

(4) The lady asked me, "How is your uncle doing?"

Q280. He said, "Honesty is the best policy."

(1) He said that honesty is the best policy.

(2) He said that honesty was the best policy.

(3) He said that honesty had been the best policy.

(4) He said that honesty has been the best policy.

Q281. He said that he intended to leave for Surat that night.

(1) "I intend to leave for Surat that night" he said.

(2) "I intend to left for Surat that night" he said.

(3) "I intended to leave for Surat tonight" he said.

(4) "I intend to leave for Surat tonight" he said.

Q282. The teacher said to him, "Is poverty not a curse ?"

(1) The teacher asked him is poverty not a curse.

(2) The teacher asked him if poverty was not a curse.

(3) The teacher asked him was poverty not a curse.

(4) The teacher asked him whether poverty is not a curse.

Q283. The prisoner enquired if a lawyer had been arranged for him.

(1) The prisoner enquired, "Is there a lawyer for me ?"

(2) The prisoner asked, "Has a lawyer been arranged for me ?"

(3) The prisoner enquired, "Had a lawyer been arranged for me ?"

(4) The prisoner said, "Have you arranged a lawyer for me ?"

284. Phila ordered her brother to turn down the television and let her work in peace.

(1) Phila said to her brother, "Turn down the television that let me do my work in peace."

(2) Phila said to her brother, "Turn down the television and let me work in peace."

(3) Phila said to her brother, "Turn down the television to let me do my work in peace."

(4) Phila said to her brother, "Turned down the television and let me do my work in peace."

Q285. You will say, "I am ill."

(1) You will say that you are ill.

(2) You would say that you were ill.

(3) You would say that you are ill.

(4) You will say that you were ill.

286. He bade his friends goodbye.

(1) "I will see you later" he told his friends.

(2) "I am bidding you Goodbye."

(3) He said, "Goodbye, my friends."

(4) "Goodbye, my friends" he was saying to them.

Q287. He exclaimed with joy that their team had won the tournament.

(1) He said, "Our team has won the tournament."

(2) He said, "Wow ! Our team won the tournament."

(3) He exclaimed, "Hurrah ! Our team has won the tournament!"

(4) He said, "Our team won the tournament."

Q288. His father said that it was time he visited his uncle.

(1) "It was time you visited your uncle" said his father.

(2) "It is time you visited my uncle" said his father.

(3) "It is time you visit your uncle" said his father.

(4) "It is time you visited your uncle" said his father.

Q289. The project manager asked Vivek, "How much time will you take to finish this project ?"

(1) The project manager asked Vivek how much time would he take to finish that project.

(2) The project manager enquired of Vivek how much time he would take to finish that project.

(3) The project manager enquired of Vivek how much time he will be taking to finish that project.

(4) The project manager asked Vivek how much time he would take to finish this project.

Q290. The ox asked the dog not to sit there.

(1) The ox said to the dog, "Not to sit here."

(2) The ox said to the dog, "Do not sit here."

(3) The ox said to the dog, "Does not sit here."

(4) The ox said to the dog, "Did not sit here."

Q291. He said, "I am writing a poem."

(1) He said that I am writing a poem.

(2) He said that he is writing a poem.

(3) He said that the poem is being written.

(4) He said that he was writing a poem.

Q292. He said, "Asha washed the clothes."

(1) He said that Asha washed the clothes.

(2) He said that clothes were washed by Asha.

(3) He said that Asha had washed the clothes.

(4) He said that Asha has washed the clothes.

Q293. Martha said, "I am going to Mexico next year."

(1) Martha said that she had been going to Mexico next year.

(2) Martha said that she was going to Mexico next year.

(3) Martha said that she had gone to Mexico next year.

(4) Martha said that she will be going to Mexico next year.

Q294. My mother said to me, "Wish you a happy and prosperous life!"

(1) My mother wished me a happy and prosperous life.

(2) My mother told me that I should lead a happy and prosperous life.

(3) My mother wished that I enjoy a happy and prosperous life.

(4) My mother wished that I should be living a happy and prosperous life.

Q295. You said to me, "Why are you talking so much ?"

(1) You asked me why, he was talking so much.

(2) You asked me why I was talking so much.

(3) You asked me why was I talking so much.

(4) You asked me why I had been talking so much.

Q296. Sandy said, "I have already written a letter to my family."

(1) Sandy said that she had already written a letter to her family.

(2) Sandy said that she wrote a letter to her family.

(3) Sandy said that she was writing a letter to her family.

(4) Sandy said that she will write a letter to her family.

Q297. You said, "They were busy the whole day."

(1) You said that they had busy the whole day.

(2) You said that they were busy the whole day.

(3) You said that they had been busy the whole day.

(4) You said that they have been busy the whole day.

Q298. I said to her, "I will have written letters."

(1) I told her that she will have written letters.

(2) I told her that she would have written letters.

(3) I told her that I will have written letters.

(4) I told her that I would have written letters.

Q299. I asked him, "Will you go to Agra tomorrow ?"

(1) I asked him whether I would go to Agra the next day.

(2) I asked him whether he would go to Agra the next day.

(3) I asked him whether you would go to Agra the next day.

(4) I asked him whether he will go to Agra the next day.

Q300. I asked him where he would stay.

(1) I said to him, "Where you will stay ?"

(2) I asked him, "Where will you stay?"

(3) I said to him, "Where I will stay ?"

(4) I said to him, "Where will I stay ?"

SECTION–C
1000 Practice Questions

1. (a) Neither of them/ (b) are going to attend/ (c) the party on 10th October./ (d) No error
2. (a) He walked five miles which are really a great distance/ (b) for a man like him who is/ (c) not only old but also ill./ (d) No error
3. (a) Either my colleague/ (b) or a peon are coming home/ (c) with the material today./(d) No error
4. (a) The rise and fall/ (b) of the tide are due/ (c) to lunar influence./ (d) No error
5. (a) Many a man/ (b) have succumbed/ (c) to this temptation./ (d) No error
6. (a) The introduction of tea, coffee/ (b) and such other beverages/ (c) have not been without some effect./ (d) No error
7. (a) The newer type of automatic machines/ (b) wash/ (c) clothes faster./ (d) No error
8. (a) Each of the students in the computer class/ (b) has to type/ (c) their own research paper this semester./ (d) No error
9. (a) Everyone of the films/ (b) you suggested/ (c) are not worth seeing./ (d) No error
10. (a) The Secretary and Principal of the college/ (b) are attending/ (c) the District Development Council Meeting at the Collectorate./ (d) No error
11. (a) There is/ (b) only one of his novels/ (c) that are interesting./ (d) No error
12. (a) Knowledge of/ (b) at least two languages/ (c) are required to pass the examination./ (d) No error
13. (a) It is I/ (b) who is to blame/ (c) for this bad situation./ (d) No error
14. (a) Romanticism of melancholy/ (b) in art and literature are the reason/ (c) for insensitivity to those suffering from depression./ (d) No error
15. (a) Patience as well as perseverance (b) are necessary/ (c) for success./ (d) No error
16. (a) In Singapore/ (b) my brother-in-law with his wife/ (c) were present at the function./ (d) No error
17. (a) A hot and/ (b) a cold spring/ (c) was found near each other./ (d) No error
18. (a)Eitheroftheroads/(b)lead/(c)tothepark/ (d) No error
19. (a) One of my desires/ (b) are to become/ (c) a doctor./ (d) No error
20. (a) The whole block of flats/ (b) including two shops were/ (c) destroyed in fire./ (d) No error
21. (a) The sum and substance/ (b) of his poem/ (c) are as follows./ (d) No error
22. (a) Neither of the/ (b) five accused/ (c) could be convicted./ (d) No error
23. (a) The strain of all/ (b) the difficulties, vexations and anxieties/ (c) were more than he could beat./ (d) No error
24. (a) Everybody/ (b) it must be admitted/ (c) has their ups and downs./ (d) No error
25. (a) Every woman in the world/ (b) fervently hopes that their child/ (c) will be a normal and healthy baby/ (d) No error
26. (a) Neither of them/ (b) sent their papers/ (c) in time for the last seminar/ (d) No error
27. (a) This is a strange world/ (b) where each one pursues their own golden bubble/ (c) and laughs at others for doing the same./ (d) No error

28. (a) If it were possible to get near when/ (b) one of the volcanic eruptions take place/ (c) we would see a grand sight./ (d) No error

29. (a) A rise in rents and wages/ (b) have been found/ (c) to go together./ (d) No error

30. (a) He is one of those few post-colonial writer who believes/ (b) that this talk about colonialism has gone too far/ (c) and has turned into a cliche./ (d) No error

31. (a) One of the peculiarities/ (b) which distinguishes the present age/ (c) is the multiplication of books/ (d) No error

32. (a) Neither of them/ (b) are going to attend/ (c) the party on 10th October/ (d) No error

33. (a) Ten miles are/ (b) a long distance / (c) to cover on foot./ (d) No error

34. (a) If Mahatma Gandhi/ (b) was alive, he would feel sorry for the poor and downtrodden who/ (c) still struggle everyday to make both ends meet. / (d) No Error

35. (a) Having acquired some experience/ (b) she is no longer one of those who believes/ (c) every explanation they are given./ (d) No error

36. (a) With regard to implementation of the/ (b) details of the proposal, the committee was divided/ (c) in their opinion./ (d) No error

37. (a) Most of the funds/ (b) we get from/ (c) America is used to build roads and bridges./ (d) No error

38. (a) The tiger was not/ (b) the only dangerous animal/ (c) in the forest there was hyenas too./ (d) No error

39. (a) She immediately quit/ (b) the job in which/ (c) neither skill nor knowledge were required./ (d) No error

40. (a) The type of qualities you acquire/ (b) depend upon your company/ (c) and so you associate yourselves with simple and good natured people./ (d) No error

41. (a) Our success or our failure/ (b) largely depend/ (c) upon our actions./ (d) No error

42. (a) He is/ (b) one of the tallest boy/ (c) in the class./ (d) No error

43. (a) That day when they brought her back for the last time/ (b) there was many old timers/ (c) who were shocked and fearful./ (d) No error

44. (a) A computer virus works exactly/ (b) like the biological variety/ (c) which invade the human body./ (d) No error

45. (a) Many a boy/(b) have not done their/ (c) homework properly./ (d) No error

46. (a) Two miles beyond/ (b) that building was seen dozens/ (c) of antisocial elements/ (d) No error

47. (a) Along the northern frontier/ (b) of India is seen/ (c) the beautiful and mighty Himalayas./ (d) No error

48. (a) A body of volunteers/ (b) have helped in/ (c) making this celebration a great success/ (d) No error

49. (a) There appears/ (b) a number of problems/ (c) and I really do not know how to solve them. (d) No error

50. (a) Shingles are a disease/ (b) in which a person develops/ (c) lots of inflamed spots round the waist./ (d) No error

51. (a) Whether she should get married/ (b) or whether she should remain/ (c) single are her personal problem./ (d) No error

52. (a) Two and two/ (b) makes/ (c) four./ (d) No error.

53. (a) Many a men/ (b) attended the meeting/ (c) last night./ (d) No error.

54. (a) The perquisites/ (b) to this job makes it/ (c) even more attractive than the salary indicated/ (d) No error.

55. (a) Either you/ (b) or he/ (c) are happy./ (d) No error.

56. (a) Neither he/(b) nor his friends/(c)

is going out/(d) for the shooting of documentary./(e) NO ERROR

57. (a) Most of the girls/(b)has bought the apparatus home/(c) in order to perform the/(d) experiment of chemistry./(e) NO ERROR

58. (a) Indian politics currently/(b) seem to be a battle between/(c) a juggernaut and a footnote./(d) NO ERROR

59. (a) Electoral politics with its wide repertoire of tactics/(b) teach you that you can indeed make a/(c) silk purse out of sow's ear./(d) NO ERROR

60. (a) He is one of/(b) the soldiers who has/ (c) gone to kargil/(d) during the time of war./(e) NO ERROR

61. (a) The new tagline/(b) for the television sets/(c) are attracting more and more/(d) customers day by day./ (e) NO ERROR

62. (a) A lot of/(b) singers encourages the crowd/(c) to dance and to enjoy/(d) the moment up to the fullest./(e) NO ERROR

63. (a) The doctor with/(b) his two daughters/ (c) were unable to find/(d) the reason behind his son's sudden demise./(e) NO ERROR

64. (a) The no. of refugees/(b) residing in America/(c) are increasing/(d) day by day./(e) NO ERROR

65. (a) The candidates who/(b) have not given their/(c) payment till now/(d) is bound to be disqualified./(e) NO ERROR

66. The government has being specifically (a)/ told that the retired judge (b)/ would not be eligible in (c)/ the fresh selection process. (d)/ No error(e)

67. The high court could not even go at the (a)/ relevance of the material on the basis of which (b)/ the Governor made the appointments, (c)/ as there was no material bar candidates' resumes. (d)/ No error(e)

68. Although Pakistan has responded as if India has(a)/ an aggressive limited war strategy, there is no(b)/ public evidence that India remotely has the capability (c)/ to adopt or execute such that doctrine. (d)/ No error(e)

69. The veterans have had their (a)/ time and should gracefully exiting , (b)/ paving the way for the(c)/ young to take over. (d)/ No error(e)

70. The bad blood is bound (a)/ to tarnish the party's image (b)/ and results in a shift(c)/ in the vote bank. (d)/ No error(e)

71. There have to be systems in place (a)/ before customers and merchants (b)/ end on clashing (c)/ with each other. (d)/ No error(e)

72. There are no uniform policy across (a)/ banks and petroleum (b)/ companies on sharing (c)/ different transaction costs. (d)/ No error(e)

73. All need to understand that the ban is not to (a)/ safeguard the animals or against its (b)/ legal use for activities such as(c)/ farming, but instead to safeguard lives. (d)/ No error(e)

74. The ground reality (a)/ continues to be grimed (b)/ with regard to water (c)/ storage and management. (d)/ No error (e)

75. Man's craze to go to all length (a)/ to entertain himself at the (b)/ cost of inflicting pain on (c)/ other living creatures knows no bounds. (d)/ No error(e)

76. The families /(a) are living in Gulmohar Park / (b) for the last two decades./(c) No error./ (d)

77. Two lakhs of people /(a) attended the meeting/(b) held in Parade grounds./(c) No error./(d)

78. There is a Bach's violin concerto /(a) on the radio / (b) at 6 p.m. this evening./ (c) No error/(d)

79. Lay your books aside and / (a) lay down to rest / (b) for a while. / (c) No error / (d)

80. We went / (a) with Guptas to a /(b) movie called 'Deewar'. /(c) No error / (d)

81. Once an old hermit / (a) saw a cat /(b) pounce upon a rat./ (c) No error. /(d)

82. A computer virus works exactly / (a) like the biological variety / (b) which invade the human body/ (c) No error. / (d)

83. When I first started my school / (a) my boys had / (b) no evident love for music. / (c) No error / (d)

84. My uncle / (a) has left / (b) for Bombay last Saturday. / (c) No error. / (d)

85. Don't think / (a) you can deceive me / (b) like you did my brother. / (c) No error. /(d)

86. The reason for my taking up this profession (A) / is that this vast country of our has not (B) / a sufficient number of qualified doctors (C)/ No error (D)

87. Look at (A) / what I am doing (B) / and do like I do. (C)/ No error(D)

88. You should put your valuables in the bank (A) / while away from home (B)/ on holiday. (C) / No error (D)

89. The sailor realized (A) / that they had much far to go (B)/ to reach their destination in time. (C)/ No error (D)

90. One of the problem (A)/ with you (B)/ is that you do not (C)/ come in time. (D)/ No Error (E)

91. All the girls students (A)/ of the college are advised (B)/ to sit in the(C)/ girls' common room. (D)/ No Error (E)

92. The majority of the woman (A)/ teachers are persuading (B)/ the principal to consider (C)/ their demands. (D)/ No Error (E)

93. He said that (A)/ he always kept in his pocket (B)/ a bundle of one hundred (C)/ rupees notes. (D)/ No Error (E)

94. He gave me (A)/ two important informations (B)/ I had been waiting for (C)/ the previous two Month (D)/ No Error (E)

95. The class teacher (A)/ gave him a home work (B)/ and instructed him to do it (C)/ at night. (D)/ No Error (E)

96. I saw only (A)/ five police who (B)/ were running after (C)/ the bank robbers. (D)/ No Error (E)

97. The wall of this magnificent (A)/ building is (B)/ fifty foot high and its paintings (C)/ are very striking (D)/ No Error (E)

98. Wordsworth's poetries (A)/ is characterized by his subtle description (B)/ of the beauty and liveliness (C)/ of nature. (D)/ No Error (E)

99. When you see his (A)/ offsprings, you can't (B)/ believe that he is (C)/ above seventy.(D)/ No Error(E)

100. A thousand (A)/dollars(B)/ are(C)/ not a small sum.(D)

101. As much as four brokerages (a)/ downgraded Titan (b)/ after the company confirmed the policy action on gold import. (c)/ No error (d)

102. Besides the central agency FCI (a)/ wheat is also been (b)/ purchased from farmers. (c)/ No error (d)

103. He wasn't (a)/ at the last conference (b)/ and neither was you. (c)/ No error (d)

104. I remembered that (a)/ my application will becoming (b)/ invalid this month.

105. In any case (a)/ no capital punishment are given (b)/ to the children. (c)/ No error (d)

106. She maintained (a)/ her dignity (b)/ despite being annoyed. (c)/ No error (d)

107. Several years (a)/ have passed since (b)/ I visit the Salarjung museum. (c)/ No error (d)

108. My mother and myself (a)/ did the entire (b)/ household work yesterday. (c)/ No error (d)

109. You are as good as (a)/ if not better (b)/ than your brother. (c)/ No error (d)

110. Such huge discounts never have been (a)/ neither can be (b)/ and never will be offered again. (c)/ No error (d)

111. (a) You are not at all junior/(b) than her in terms of/(c) getting promotion./(d)NO ERROR
112. (a) She is the /(b) most bravest girl i /(c) have ever seen./(d)NO ERROR
113. (a) Of all the girls in /(b) the village she is /(c) the better./(d)NO ERROR
114. (a)Reema and Sheena are best /(b) friends. The later is/(c) very hardworking./(d)NO ERROR
115. (a)The two last rows /(b) of the hall were /(c) vacant for the persons with disabilities./(d)NO ERROR
116. (a)On her next birthday /(b) i am going to send her /(c) much chocolates of dairy milk. /(d)NO ERROR
117. (a)The chances of his passing the exam /(b) are more better than Riya /(c) as he is very laborious./(d)NO ERROR
118. (a)The brain drain problem explains that /(b) much students are migrating to developed countries for/(c) better job opportunities./(d)NO ERROR
119. (a) You are senior than most of /(b) the professors of this college /(c) and still you are behaving like a child./(d)NO ERROR
120. (a) I always prefer reading than /(b) playing games as i /(c) am a bookworm./(d)NO ERROR
121. There were (a) / no less than fifty persons (b) / present in the room (c) / No error (d)
122. Few remarks (a) / that he made were (b) / offensive to my friend (c) / No error (d)
123. It is a (a) / worth watching documentary (b) / & you must not miss it (c) / No error (d)
124. Of all the students (a) / Rita was less worried (b) / when the date for the annual examination was announced (c) / No error (d)
125. Even the most perfect person (a) / in the world is said to have erred (b) / when there was time to perform (c) / No error (d)
126. The meeting was postponed (a) / because only a few number of persons (b) / were present there (c) / No error (d)
127. In the opinion of everyone (a) / she is wiser (b) / than beautiful (c) / No error (d)
128. The tiger is (a) / as swift as (b) / any animal (c) / No error (d)
129. He had to cut a sorry figure (a) / when he realised that he had (b) / no any many in his purse (c) / No error (d)
130. Of the three ministers (a) / which do you think (b) / is going to prove more successful (c) / No error (d)
131. Neither she is intelligent (a) / nor hard working (b) / and still she expects to secure first class (c) / No error (d)
132. I requested him (a) / to lend me few books (b) / that might help me in my studies (c) / No error (d)
133. Your essay (a) / should not exceed more than (b) / hundred words (c) / No error (d)
134. He is the tallest (a) / than anybody (b) / in the school (c) / No error (d)
135. He was surprised (a) / to see her speak (b) / with somewhat anger (c) / No error (d)
136. My brother is elder (a) / than me although (b) / he looks younger (c) / No error (d)
137. Could you (a) / give me any money (b) / to buy food? (c) / No error (d)
138. Privatisation offers the most ideal situation (a) / for consumers because private sector (b) / is very conscious of quality (c) / No error (d)
139. Little care on your part (a) / would have made you (b) / more successful than your friend (c) / No error (d)
140. He is as intelligent if not more intelligent (a) / than his brother who has qualified (b) / for this post (c) / No error (d)
141. Although they listen to me (a)/ but their actions (b) / prove otherwise (c) / No error (d)
142. He treats (a) / us as (b) / slaves (c) / No

error (d)

143. Most of the girls are doing (a) / their post graduation because (b) / they may get good husbands (c) / No error (d)

144. Such was his pronunciation (a) / as (b) / I could not understand him (c) / No error (d)

145. He asked (a) / that who (b) / I was (c) / No error (d)

146. I am interested (a) / in such books (b) / that are interesting (c) / No error (d)

147. Each member of the alliance (a) / agree to take such action (b) / that it deems necessary (c) / No error (d)

148. She looked at him (a) / in such distress (b) / as he had to look away (c) / No error (d)

149. This films is interesting (a) / and the previous one (b) / was boring (c) / No error (d)

150. It is difficult to know (a) / whether (b) / you are selected or not (c) / No error (d)

151. He has no chance (a) / than to start (b) / his own business (c) / No error (d)

152. They had hardly finished (a) / their meals that at once (b) / they resumed their duty (c) / No error (d)

153. I don't know whether (a) / Raj is equally (b) / good as Vimal (c) / No error (d)

154. He (a) / will return (b) / on either Monday or Tuesday (c) / No error (d)

155. He is (a) / not honest and not (b) / truthful (c) / No error (d)

156. He has no other business (a) / but to play (b) / with computers (c) / No error (d)

157. Be smart (a) / not only in dress (b) / and also in action (c) / No error (d)

158. Hardly had I reached the airport (a) / where I learned about (b) / the powerful bomb explosion (c) / No error (d)

159. My book has been missing (a) / from my room (b) / till yesterday (c) / No error (d)

160. The manager of the bank was busy (a) / so he asked them to come and see him (b) / between two to three in the afternoon (c) / No error (d)

161. No sooner did the sun rise (a) / when we took a hasty breakfast (b) / and resumed the journey (c) / No error (d)

162. Because he is physically strong (a) / therefore he was selected (b) / for the school boxing team (c) / No error (d)

163. The reason for his failure (a) / is because (b) / he did not work hard (c) / No error (d)

164. Arjun asked him (a) / that which was the way (b) / to the post office (c) / No error (d)

165. Unless you do not listen to his advice (a) / I am not going (b) / to help you (c) / No error (d)

166. How do you say (a) / that neither he or Raj has qualified (b) / in the examination ? (c) / No error (d)

167. We are not sure (a) / if he is coming (b) / to the party (c) / No error (d)

168. Sooner than he had arrived (a) / his friends arranged a reception in his honour (b) / in the best hotel in the town (c) / No error (d)

169. Mrs Dhaka went to Delhi (a) / because she might (b) / see Mrs Rai (c) / No error (d)

170. He gave him no money (a) / nor he did help him (b) / in any way (c) / No error (d)

171. The managing director well as (a)/ the Board members was in (b)/ favour of taking strict action (c)/ against the striking workers. (d)/ No error (e)

172. Unless he does not return (a)/ all the library books (b)/ he will not be relieved (c)/ from the service.(d)/ No error (e)

173. You must either tell me (a)/ the whole story or (b)/, at least, the (c)/ first half of it. (d)/ No error (e)

174. The old woman has had the (a)/ best medical facilities available (b)/ but she will not be cured unless she does not have

(c)/ a strong desire to live.(d)/ No error (e)

175. Hardly had I reached (a)/ the airport where (b)/ I learnt about the powerful (c)/ bomb explosion.(d)/ No error (e)

176. The manager of the bank (a)/ was busy; so he asked them (b)/ to come and see him between two to (c)/ three in the afternoon. (d)/ No error (e)

177. Because he is physically (a)/ strong, therefore he was (b)/ selected for the school (c)/boxing team.(d)/ No error (e)

178. Being a strict (a)/ vegetarian he depended (b)/ on milk and fruit and (c)/ had to cook for himself.(d)/ No error (e)

179. Even though the shirt (a)/ is rather expensive but (b)/ I wish to purchase (c)/ it with my own money.(d)/ No error (e)

180. Unless Ashish does not (a)/ return all the library books, (b)/ he will not be awarded (c)/ the pass certificate. (d)/ No error (e)

181. The judgment /(A) has understandably caused /(B) great dismay with activists / (C). No error (D)

182. The SC panel probing /(A) the issue has found /(B) prima facie evidence of his guilt /(C). No error (D)

183. The controversy generated /(A) for the student's allegation has /(B) dented the Principal's prestige /(C). No error (D)

184. Political scientist David Easton had /(A) argued that political systems /(B) running on an input-output model /(C). No error (D)

185. The meaning of /(A) political rights has / (B) be reduced to the right to vote /(C). No error (D)

186. It is (A)/ a quarter to ten (B)/ by my watch. (C)/ No error (D)

187. My cousin with her parents (A)/ have gone (B)/ to Chennai (C)/ No error (D)

188. The problem of soil erosion (A)/ is one of the serious imports (B)/ in various countries. (C)/ No error (D)

189. Rabindranath Tagore was not (A)/ the first Nobel laureate (B)/ without a University Degree. (C)/ No error (D)

190. Supposing if (A)/ he tells the truth (B)/ he can escape punishment. (C)/ No error (D)

191. Linguistics (A)/ are (B)/ my favourite subject.(C) /No error (D)

192. It is raining (A)/ since 8 o'clock (B)/ this morning. (C)/ No error. (D)

193. He has (A)/ no affection (B)/ with any body. (C)/ No error (D)

194. Neither Ravi nor his brother (A)/ is willing to shoulder the responsibility (B)/ of caring for their old parents. (C)/ No error (D)

195. After my son had searched (A)/ for an hour (B)/ he realized that his pen had been laying on the table. (C)/ No error (D)

196. He teaches (A)/ us English, (B)/ is n't it? (C)/ No error (D)

197. Grapes (A)/ cannot gathered (B)/ from thistles (C)/ No error (D)

198. No samples of the dead animals (A)/ were sent (B)/ for analysis. (C)/ No error (D)

199. We were awaiting (A)/ for the arrival (B)/ of our father. (C)/ No error (D)

200. Saurabhs' eyes (A)/ reflect a hope (B)/ for a better future in Microsoft. (C)/ No error (D)

201. Some people get (a)/ used to change very (b)/ easily than others do. (c)/ No error (d)

202. She has been writing(a)/ that essay for two hours(b)/ but he still has not finished. (c)/ No error (d)

203. He was so emotional (a)/stable that he was not moved by (b)/ their decision to suspend her. (c)/ No error (d)

204. Hard had (a)/she thrown the ball (b)/ when it fell on the ground. (c)/ No error (d)

205. When the police approached (a)/him, he

held up his both hands, (b)/ to show that he was surrendering. (c)/ No error (d)

206. There is a beautiful(a)/ and old temple in (b)/ the centre of the town. (c)/ No error (d)

207. Sometimes she(a)/ weeps and sometimes she (b)/ laughs as though she were mad. (c)/ No error (d)

208. He encouraged (a)/me so I might(b)/ not lose heart. (c)/ No error (d)

209. His manners indicate(a)/ that he has no other intention (b)/ than to steal his money. (c)/ No error (d)

210. She continued(a)/ to be lazy, as long as she (b)/ was sixteen years old. (c)/ No error (d)

211. Live from the 'higher Self', (a)/ not from the (b)/ 'low self'. (c)/ No Error (d)

212. The government said it is developing five (a)/ industrial corridors in the country which (b)/ is at different stages of implementation. (c)/ No Error (d)

213. Prepaid, pooled expenditure (a)/ must the norm in health spending, not (b)/ out-of-pocket payments. (c)/ No Error (d)

214. Plants feel 'pleasure (a)/ and pain' just (b)/ as humans. (c)/ No Error (d)

215. Science says consciousness is fundamental (a)/ to know all about the world and cosmos, (b)/ including birth and death, objectively. (c)/ No Error (d)

216. One who desires worldly pleasures and the (a)/ one who desires to renounce them, stand (b)/ to the same footing, for they both nurture desire. (c)/ No Error (d)

217. Plants show their experience of (a)/ pleasure by turning to (b)/ the sun and flourishing. (c)/ No Error (d)

218. While perfection is an unachievable end, (a)/ imperfection is the means with strong (b)/ sign of reality. (c)/ No Error (d)

219. Tech giant Google has rolled out a new scanning apps (a)/- Google PhotoScan - that allows users to (b)/ scan and digitise physical photographs. (c)/ No Error (d)

220. India's trade has improved with different (a)/ country after signing of free trade (b)/ agreements (FTA), Parliament was informed. (c)/ No Error (d)

221. India has asked the United Kingdom (A)/ to return 57 fugitives(B)/, including liquor baron Vijay Mallya(C)/, member of some extremist groups.(D)

222. The decks were cleared on Monday(A)/ for the elevation of(B)/ Rahul Gandhi president of the Congress(C)/ with the Congress working committee.(D)

223. A day before the Supreme Court was(A)/ to hear NDTV's challenge(B)/ to the Government order imposing(C)/ one-day ban on its Hindi channel-NDTV India. (D)

224. Sunlight and wind on Monday helped(A)/ to lift the cover of smog over Delhi(B)/ slightly during the day(C)/ though average pollution levels remained severe. (D)

225. In the face of strong objections all the opposition parties (A)/ the Home Minister introduced in the Rajya Sabha (B)/ a Bill to restrict certainly right conferred by the(C)/ constitution to the member of the police. (D)

226. Under the scheme, Indian Nationals (A)/ who frequently come to the U. K. and contribute (B)/ to growth in both countries will face (C) a 'significantly easier' entry process. (D)

227. An internal investigation has identified (A)/ improper payment totalling approximate $5 million (B)/ related to its India facilities (C), Cognizant Technology Solutions said.(D)

228. ICICI Bank, he list now stood at (A)/ ₹34,490 crore, said MD and CEO. (B) the bank, moreover, did not give any guidance on (C) how much further the bad loans could raise. (D)

229. It takes a few months for (A) the child's features to take shape before (B)/ one

could convincingly say (C)/ the child has taken after his mother or father.(D)

230. At least 14 people have died(A)/ and 12 others were injured when(B)/ a major fire broke out at Thursday night(C)/ at a building in Kamala Mills Compound.(D)

231. Many a man (A)/ have gone to Dubai (B)/ in search of a job. (C)/ No error (D)

232. My friend dared (A)/ me walk (B)/ along the edge of a roof. (C)/ no error (D)

233. I have not (A)/ met my friend Amit (B)/ from times immemorial. (C)/ no error (D)

234. She talked (A)/ to me as if (B)/ we met before. (C)/ No error (D)

235. Each one of my roommates (A)/ were stuck in the traffic (B)/ on the 15th of August. (C)/ No error (D)

236. My brother lived in Lucknow (A)/ since 1990 to 2008 (B)/ but is now living in Delhi. (C)/ No error (D)

237. You need to learn (A)/ to adapt to (B)/ changing circumstances. (C)/ no error (D)

238. Virat Kohli is one of those player (A)/ who perform better (B)/ in tough conditions. (C)/ no error (D)

239. Had I known (A)/ you were visiting me today (B)/ I would meet you at the airport. (C)/ no error (D)

240. I am not familiar with (A)/ most of the people of this locality (B)/ although I had been living here for 5 years. (C)/ no error (D)

241. All my sister-in-laws (A)/ were present at the (B)/ wedding ceremony of my sister. (C)/ no error (D)

242. It is high time (A)/ we start studying (B)/ for our exams. (C)/ no error (D)

243. Someone, they don't know, (A)/ broke theirwindow (B)/last night (C)/ no error (D)

244. You have been (A)/ sleeping for the past two hours (B)/ aren't you? (C)/ no error (D)

245. None of the ministers (A)/ was able either to deny (B)/ or accept the allegations of corruption. (C)/ no error (D)

246. The cricket match (A)/ that was played the couple of days ago (B)/ was very exciting. (C)/ no error (D)

247. It was (A)/ me who called (B)/ the ambulance. (C)/ no error (D)

248. My laptop is (A)/ superior and (B)/ more expensive than yours. (C)/ no error (D)

249. Our coach (A)/ emphasized on (B)/the use of correct techniques. (C)/ no error (D)

250. While crossing the road (A)/ the child was run over (B)/ with the bus. (C)/ no error(D)

251. A scientist who convinces the world (A)/ gets the credit not the (B)/ one to whom the idea first occurs. (C)/ no error (D)

252. One should be true (A)/ to his promises in (B)/ order to earn name and fame in life.(C)/ no error (D)

253. Keeping in view (A)/ the public's demand,(B)/ the government has decided to improve the quality of roads in this city. (C)/ no error(D)

254. He takes good care (A)/ of his hair so (B)/ his hairs are black and attractive. (C)/ no error (D)

255. I saw only ten police (A)/ who were providing security (B)/ to the celebrity. (C)/ no error (D)

256. The five players (A)/ had each an (B)/ achievement of their own. (C)/ no error (D)

257. The coach has great power (A)/ of making some useful decisions (B)/ but the players have more greater ability to foil them. (C)/ no error (D)

258. We have to accept (A)/ that driving vehicles (B)/ require expertise. (C)/ No error (D)

259. Both the BJP along with (A)/ the Congress are responsible for (B)/India's declining growth rate. (C)/ no error (D)

260. There is renewed sense (A)/of urgency in (B)/completing the project.(C)/No error (D)

261. The girl (A)/ distributed chocolates (B)/ between all her classmates. (C)/ no error(D)

262. It was apparent for (A)/ everyone present that if (B)/ the ambulance didn't arrive on time, he would die. (C)/ no error (D)

263. The English teacher (A)/ said that we should (B)/ work hard if we didn't want to fail. (C)/ no error (D)

264. The teacher (A)/ objected my (B)/ entering the examination hall. (C)/ no error (D)

265. Let no one remain with doubt (A) / that the USA (B)/ is responsible for the destruction of Iraq. (C)/ no error (D)

266. With regard to implementation the details(A)/ of the proposal, the committee (B)/ was divided in its opinion. (C)/ No error (D)

267. On discovering that it was (A)/ a forgery he torn up (B)/ the agreement he had signed. (C)/ No error (D)

268. Literature remains the interest of a minority (A)/ and the majority has chosen to ignore those aspects of language (B)/ which, at school, they were told to value highly. (C)/ No Error (D)

269. Either a certified cheque on deposit, (A)/ or a valid major credit card is (B)/ required for one to bid. (C)/ No error (D)

270. If you have faith in Almighty (A)/ everything will turn out (B)/ to be all right. (C)/ No error (D)

271. We have been under (1) / a lot of pressure to (2) / to open fifty new stores (3) / by the ending of the year. (4) / No error (5).

272. One of the oldest car (1) / seen in India was a Serpollet (2) / a French car named (3) / after its inventor. (4) / No error (5).

273. We informed customers (1) / that there will be (2) / no interrupting in (3) / Our bank services tomorrow. (4) / No error (5).

274. Some of the world (1) / largest water bodies are (2) / drying up thus threatening (3) / the livelihood of millions. (4) / No error (5).

275. Psychologists have been documenting (1) / the emotional and physical (2) / effect of (3) / negative political advertisements. (4) / No error (5).

276. We are yet starting (1) / offering this facility to (2) / our customers as we are (3) / awaiting approval from the Board. (4) / No error (5).

277. The Chairmen of all large (1) / public sector banks met with (2) / senior RBI officials to give its (3) / suggestions about implementing the new policy. (4) / No error (5).

278. They have not fully considered (1) / the impact that relaxing (2) / these guidelines is likely (3)/ to have with the economy (4) / No error (5)

279. Had this notification (1) / been amended earlier, (2) / we could have stopped (3) / the transfer of funds. (4) / No error (5)

280. There are many insurance (1) / disputes nowadays because of (2) / most people do not fully (3) / understand the terms and conditions of their policies (4) / No error (5)

281. India demonstrates its supremacy (1) / in space when it successfully (2) / launched its third satellite (3) / into orbit yesterday. (4) / No error (5)

282. India needs a value education system (1) / who will inculcate values (2) / among the students and (3) / enrich their personalities. (4) / No error (5)

283. Driven by the desire to save trees (1) / residents of locality (2) / has started using solar appliances (3) / for their everyday

needs. (4) / No error (5)

284. A large number of unmanned aircrafts (1) / being used by the military (2) / are suspected of having (3) / unsafe radio links. (4) / no error (5)

285. Recent survey shows that (1) / 35 million children in the age group of (2) / 6 to 10 years have never (3) / attended no primary school. (4) / No error (5)

286. Coal mines constitute (1) / a major percentage of the (2) / sources which cause damage (3) / on the environment. (4) / No error (5)

287. A man who has been (1) / accused of fraud in (2) / an earlier job he will never be (3)/ welcome in any other organization. (4) / No error (5)

288. Worried about the continuing violence in the city (1)/ much students are set to migrate (2) / to other cities (3) / for higher education (4)/ No error (5)

289. Many organizations have been offering (1) / attractive incentives to (2)/ their employees in an attempt (3)/ to boosting employee retention. (4) / No error (5)

290. Some genuine issues exist (1) / with the newly adopted (2) / system and needs to (3) / be examined seriously. (4) / No error (5)

291. She is one of the (1)/ best mothers (2)/ that has ever lived. (3)/ No error (4).

292. John, I and Hari (1)/ have finished (2)/ our studies. (3)/ No error (4).

293. Neither the mouse (1)/ nor the lion (2)/ were caught. (3)/ No error (4)

294. After you will returns (1)/ from New Delhi (2)/ I will meet you (3)/ No error (4)

295. When I was young, (1)/ I used to collect stamps (2)/ as a hobby. (3)/ No error (4)

296. Pacific Ocean is (1) / the deepest ocean (2)/ in the world. (3)/ No error (4)

297. You will come (1) / to my sister's wedding tomorrow, (2)/ isn't it? (3)/ No error (4)

298. I am (1) / your's (2)/ affectionate son.(3)/ No error (4)

299. Beside Hindi, (1) / she knew (2)/ Bengali well. (3)/ No error (4)

300. He walks (1) / as if the earth (2)/ belonged to him. (3)/ No error (4)

301. He walked (1)/ten miles (2)/ by foot. (3)/ No error (4)

302. He is good (1)/ in mathematics (2)/ but his friend isn't.(3)/ No error (4)

303. By noon (1)/ the fog cleared (2)/ completely. (3)/No error (4)

304. Ahmed has been watching (1)/ the Oscar nominated film (2)/ three times. (3)/ No error (4)

305. The police (1)/ has arrested him (2)/ on the charge of theft. (3)/ No error (4)

306. The period (1)/ between 1991 to 1995 (2)/ was very significant in my life. (3)/ No error (4)

307. Both me (1)/ and my sister (2)/ went to a boarding school. (3)/ No error (4)

308. Time and tide (1)/ wait (2)/ for no man. (3)/ No error (4)

309. Christina's friends (1)/ preferred her remedies (2)/over the doctor's. (3)/ No error (4)

310. Those who are in power (1)/ have to be sensitive of (2)/ the sufferings of the poor. (3)/ No error (4)

311. There are (1) / no poetries (2)/ in my book.(3)/ No error (4)

312. That house (1)/is built of (2)/ stones. (3)/ No error (4)

313. He as well as (1)/ you like (2)/ to go.(3)/ No error (4)

314. Very soon (1)/ I realised (2)/ that he is at fault. (3)/ No error. (4)

315. We always complain that prices (a)/are too high and that we were (B)/not getting our money's worth. (C)/No Error (D)

316. Neither of these two documents (1)/ support your claim (2)/ on the property. (3)/ No error (4)

317. Get this book (1)/ be published (2)/ in time. (3)/ No error. (4)
318. He (1)/ is junior than (2)/ all his friends. (3)/ No error (4)
319. Had you (1)/ worked hard (2)/ you will have passed. (3)/ No error (4)
320. He works hardly (1)/ to make (2)/ both ends meet. (3)/ No error (4)
321. Supposing if (1)/ it rains (2)/ what shall we do? (3)/ No error. (4)
322. The captain along with his team (1)/ are practising very hard (2)/ for the forthcoming match. (3)/ No error. (4)
323. It was him (1)/ who came running (2)/ into the classroom. (3)/ No error. (4)
324. The capital of Yemen (1)/ is situating (2)/ 2190 metres above the sea level. (3)/ No error. (4)
325. Ram was (1)/ senior to (2)/ Sam in college. (3)/ No error. (4)
326. Even after requesting Ramesh (A)/he did not tell us (B)/that how he (C)/solved the problem. (D)
327. Ravi (1)/ told to his friend (2)/ to buy a car. (3)/ No error. (5)
328. I would (1)/ accept the offer (2)/ if I were you. (3)/ No error. (4)
329. I am more lonelier (1)/ here than (2)/ I was in the USA. (3)/ No error. (4)
330. May I know (1)/ to who (2)/ I am speaking ? (3)/ No error. (4)
331. This custom (1) / has come down (2)/ since times immemorial.(3)/ No error.(4)
332. This letter will reach him (1)/before he left (2)/ for Delhi. (3)/ No error.(4)
333. We stayed for (1)/ a short time(2)/ in the hotel.(3)/ No error. (4)
334. Students are prohibited (1)/ to bring cycles (2)/ into the college. (3)/ No error. (4)
335. Unless you are careful,(1)/ you are bound to make mistake (2)/ in your work.(3)/ No error. (4)
336. Due to the heavy rains (1)/ the ship drowned (2)/ in the middle of the ocean. (3)/ No error (4)
337. Death of (1)/ his only son (2)/ made Mohan desolate. (3)/ No error (4)
338. He fell heavily (1)/ and this caused (2)/ him great pain. (3)/ No error (4)
339. When I met him (1)/ the couple of days back (2)/ he was writing a new book. (3)/ No error (4)
340. In his old age, (1)/ a person is likely to get (2)/ more weak day by day. (3)/ No error (4)
341. You are (1)/ always doing (2)/ this mistake. (3)/ No error (4)
342. He has (1)/ a large family (2)/ to care. (3)/ No error (4)
343. These poisonous gases (1)/ will effect (2)/ our health. (3)/ No error (4)
344. The only Indian (1)/ to win the Nobel Prize for the Literature (2)/ was Rabindranath Tagore. (3)/ No error (4)
345. After his illness, (1)/ the patient was (2)/ sick with life. (3)/ No error (4)
346. I told him (1) / that I availed (2)/ the opportunity. (3)/ No error (4)
347. I think (1) / he owns an expensive (2) / painting by Hussain. (3) / No error (4)
348. It is time (1) / we should have done (2)/ something useful. (3)/ No error (4)
349. He will tell you (1) / about it when (2) / he will come back. (3) / No error (4)
350. A large sign near (1) / the entrance warns the visitors (2) / to beware about bears. (3) / No error (4)
351. I don't suppose (1)/ anyone will volunteer, (2)/ will they ? (3) / No error (4)
352. I am (1)/ looking forward for (2)/ the day of my wedding. (3)/ No error (4)
353. "Can you cope up (1)/ with all this (2)/ work ?" he asked. (3)/ No error (4)
354. He served as President (1)/ of the Lions Club (2)/ since fifteen years. (3)/ No error

(4)

355. That was (1)/the most unique opportunity (2)/he got in his life.(3)/ No error (4)

356. There is (1)/ no place of you (2)/ in this compartment. (3)/ No error (4)

357. Mother Teresa asked a building (1)/ where she and her workers (2)/could care for the poor people always. (3)/No error (4)

358. Shelley is (1)/ superior than Byron (2)/ in his vision of democracy. (3)/ No error (4)

359. When at last (1)/ we got to the theatre, (2)/the much publicized programme by the Bollywood stars was begun. (3)/No error (4)

360. Several prominent figures (1)/ involved in the scandal are required to (2)/appear to the investigation committee (3)/ No error (4)

361. According to the radio (1)/it can rain (2)/ this evening.(3) No error (4)

362. Due to heavy work (1)/ in the office (2)/ I was unable to catch the five thirty train. (3)/ No error (4)

363. Hari was appointed leader (1)/ of a group of young social workers (2)/that have accepted to help and develop the village in three months. (3)/ No error (4)

364. No sooner (1)/ they had received the guests (2)/ than they began entertaining them. (3)/ No error (4)

365. Why (1)/ on earth, (2)/ has he not come ? (3)/ No error (4)

366. Yesterday (1)/ it rained (2)/ like cats and dogs. (3)/ No error (4)

367. I would request to you (1)/ to consider my application (2)/ and grant me a job as early as possible. (3)/No error (4)

368. Each of these boys (1)/ play games (2)/ in the playground. (3)/ No error (4)

369. Not one of his lectures (1)/ have ever been (2)/ printed. (3)/ No error (4)

370. Either Sohan or his friends (1)/ is to be blamed (2)/ for this mischief. (3)/ No error (4)

371. The minister for Education (1)/ vehemently refused (2)/ the allegation that he had taken bribes. (3)/ No error. (4)

372. If I were Zubin (1) / I would not attend (2) / the wedding, come what may. (3) / No error. (4)

373. He says that (1) / he reads novels / (2) to pass away the time. (3) / No error. (4)

374. He left for Mumbai on Sunday (1)/ arriving there (2) / on Monday.(3)/ No error. (4)

375. No sooner did the teacher (1)/ enter the class room (2)/ the students got up. (3) / No error. (4)

376. It is (1) / nothing else (2) / than pride. (3) / No error. (4)

377. To the ordinary man, in fact, the pealing of bells (1)/ is a monotonous jangle and a nuisance (2) / tolerably only when mitigated by remote distance and sentimental association. (3) / No error. (4)

378. The increasing mechanisation of life (1)/ have led us farther away from daily contact with nature and (2) / the crafts of the farm.(3) / No error. (4)

379. If you have a way with words,(1)/ a good sense of design and administration ability (2) / you may enjoy working in the high pressure world of advertising. (3)/ No error. (4)

380. Last week's sharp hike in the wholesale price of beef (1) / is a strong indication for (2) / higher meat costs to come. (3) / No error. (4)

381. I had (1)/ a test in Mathematics (2)/ today morning. (3)/ No error. (4)

382. A girl must be gracious (1) / if she wishes (2)/ to be a ballerina. (3)/ No error. (4)

383. In a very harsh tone (1) / he shouted at his servants (2) / and told them that he does not need their services. (3)/ No error. (4)

384. The Committee is thinking (1) / not to bring around any change (2) / in the basic

structure.(3) / No error. (4)

385. The Chief Minister had no time (1)/ to pay attention (2)/ on such simple matters. (3) / No error. (4)

386. It was fortunate (1) / all of the inmates escaped (2) from the blazing fire. (3)/ No error. (4)

387. Drinking and driving (1) / are (2)/ a major cause of accidents. (3)/ No error. (4)

388. They are standing (1)/ at the gate of the auditorium (2) / as there is no place inside. (3) / No error. (4)

389. He is (1) / having many (2) / friends here. (3) / No error. (4)

390. Looking forward (1) / to meeting you (2) / in person. (3) / No error. (4)

391. Galileo proved that (1) / the earth revolves (2) / around the Sun. (3)/ No error. (4)

392. I want (1) / that you should (2) / perform well. (3) / No error. (4)

393. The servant (1) / hanged the lamp (2) / on the wall. (3) / No error.(4)

394. In the back side (1) /of our house (2) / we have a rock garden. (3)/ No error. (4)

395. Ask her to call me (1) / when she (2) / will come back. (3) / No error. (4)

396. The curator told us (1) / that the museum was not opened (2) to the public on Sunday. (3) / No error. (4)

397. Long car journeys (1) / are even less pleasant (2) / for it is quite impossible to read even.(3)/ No error. (4)

398. I declined the invitation (1) / not because I did not want to go,(2) / but because I have no time. (3) / No error. (4)

399. Kindly confirm by letter and telephone (1) / that you will be able (2) / to attend the interview. (3) / No error.(4)

400. I (1)/ came to school (2)/ at the same usual time. (3)/No error (4)

401. Rahul as well as (a)/ his sisters (b)/ was present in the party(c) /No error (d)

402. No sooner he reached home (a)/ than all the villagers gathered at (b)/ his home to listen to his story.(c)/ No error (d)

403. Up to the time the last vote was recorded it was (a)/ difficult to decide whether victory lay with (b)/ the ruling party or the opposition. (c)/ No error (d)

404. The members attending the meeting (a)/ were men on powerful positions, high in (b) the councils of their respective governments.(c)/ No error (d)

405. All the allegations (a)/levelled against him were found (b)/ to be baseless.(c)/ No error (d)

406. The brochure which is being enclosed (a)/ with the application form, will (b)/ give you information that you need. (c)/ No error (d)

407. I wish my bus did not arrive (a)/ so late; then I could have (b)/ reached home before breakfast. (c)/ No error(d)

408. As a gesture of goodwill India agreed (a)/ to write of a huge amount of loan (b)/ taken by some of her neighbours. (c)/ No error (d)

409. The intellectual interest which is the mainspring of George Eliot's inspiration (a)/ alters the angle from which she approaches (b)/ every aspects to her subject matter. (c)/ No error (d)

410. Little that I knew of the (a)/ English language, was not sufficient (b)/ to make me a teacher of English. (c)/ No error (d)

411. If you are living near a marketplace (a)/ you should be ready to bear (b)/ the disturbances caused by traffic. (c)/ No error (d)

412. The popularity of the novels of Prem Chand though (a)/ they are full of sad and painful incidents, (b)/ lies in the fact that they end with happiness.(c)/ No error (d)

413. The huge Negro would have been a comic figure if he had (a)/ not terrific, for he was dressed in a very loud grey (b)/ check suit with a flowing salmon colored tie. (c)/ No

error (d)

414. It is unreasonable to distort the statement (a)/ of a man simply because he does (b)/ not agree with your opinions. (c)/ No error (d)

415. The contractor did not keep his promise (a)/ that the work will be finished (b)/ before the end of the week.(c)/ No error (d)

416. Never has the inadequacy of police been in clear (a)/ focus than in the communal violence (b)/ that flared up recently. (c)/ No error (d)

417. Governments in developing countries are under increasing (a)/ pressure for recruiting and training teachers to meet the demands of (b)/ their rapidly expanding systems of education.(c)/ No error (d)

418. According to the planning commission estimates, (a)/ by the year 2000, India will become (b)/ self-sufficient in petroleum products.(c)/ No error (d)

419. He hesitated to accept the post as he (a)/ did not think that the salary was enough (b)/ for him to sustain his family.(c)/ No error (d)

420. To get one's name in the Rowland Ward's book (a)/ of hunting records was the hot (b)/ ambition of every serious hunter.(c)/ No error (d)

421. In India (1)/ working woman lead a life of dual responsibilities(2)/ if they are married and have a family.(3)/No error (4).

422. Greatly to our surprise (1)/ we find the ringleader (2)/was lame. (3)/ No error (4).

423. They have (1)/ played a game (2)/ last week. (3)/ No error (4).

424. The teacher made the boys (1)/ to do the sum (2)/ all over again. (3)/ No error (4).

425. Many overseas students (1)/ attend colleges (2)/ in the Great Britain. (3)/ No error (4).

426. My sister asked me/(1) that how long (2)/ I would stay there. (3)/ No error. (4)

427. The teacher, as well as the students, (1) have gone on an excursion (2)/ to Ooty during their summer vacation. (3)/ No error. (4)

428. The US (1)/ don't want (2)/India in the Security Council. (3)/ No error.(4)

429. The cruel lady made (1)/her step daughter to do (2)/ all the household chores. (3)/ No error. (4)

430. You can eat (1)/as much as you like (2)/at the newly launch bar. (3)/ No error. (4)

431. I whistled thrice (1)/ with full might and raise my arms (2)/ towards the sky. (3)/ No error. (4)

432. Both science and religion (1)/ are necessary for man and for their (2)/outer and inner self respectively. (3)/ No error (4)

433. At certain seasons (1), some areas on Mars (2)/ is subject to strong winds. (3)/ No error (4).

434. As an artist (1)/Raju is as good (2)/, if not better than, Ramesh. (3)/ No error (4).

435. The scientists (1)/could not hardly (2)/ complete all the experiments. (3)/ No error (4).

436. Could you please give me (1)/ a postal address (2)/ of the Indian Embassy in New York. (3)/. No error (4)

437. Short stories and poems (1)/of varying quality (2)/appears in dailies and periodicals (3)/. No error (4)

438. One of the (1)/most dangerous disease (2)/is AIDS (3)/. No error (4)

439. The director along with his assistants (1)/ have thoroughly examined (2)/ the new proposals. (3)/ No error. (4)

440. I bought (1)/ two (2)/ slippers. (3)/ No error. (4)

441. You are a very lovable person (1)/ but I (2)/ am not loving you. (3)/ No error. (4)

442. Being a holiday (1)/ we went out (2)/ for a picnic. (3)/ No error. (4)
443. If we have no definite aim before us (1)/ we would only wonder about in aimless pursuits (2)/ and achieve nothing. (3)/ No error. (4)
444. He is anxious not only (1)/ to acquire knowledge (2)/ but also eager to display it. (3)/ No error. (4)
445. I went to (1)/ see the Taj Mahal (2)/ in a moonlit night. (3)/ No error. (4)
446. Having found a piece of cheese, (1)/ two cats went to a dog (2)/ to divide it among them. (3)/No error. (4)
447. The new dish (1)/ that I ordered (2)/ is tasting good.(3)/ No error. (4)
448. Increasing racism and hate crimes (1)/ casted a shadow (2)/ over elections. (3)/ No error. (4)
449. I have got your letter yesterday (1)/ and felt happy to learn (2)/ of your recovery. (3)/ No error. (4)
450. Sam is working (1)/ in a bank in Chennai (2)/ for the past five years. (3)/ No error. (4)
451. People living in low-lying areas (1)/ find it difficult (2)/ to cope up with the floods. (3)/ No error. (4)
452. If I was he,(1)/ I wouldn't accept (2)/ this project. (3) / No error.(4)
453. The teacher advised to (1)/the student to borrow (2)/ a book from the library within three days.(3)/No error.(4)
454. I insisted (1)/ on his going (2)/ there immediately. (3)/ No error.(4)
455. We have been knowing (1)/ each other (2)/ since we were children. (3)/ No error.(4)
456. Neither of the teams (1)/ are sensible enough (2)/ to do this task. (3)/ No error. (4)
457. When one hears of the incident (1)/ about the plane crash (2)/ he feels very sorry. (3)/ No error (4)
458. I went there (1)/ with a view to survey (2)/ the entire procedure. (3)/ No error (4)
459. It had laid (1)/ in the closet (2)/ for a week before we found it. (3)/ No error (4)
460. He was present (1)/ in the court (2)/ to give witness. (3)/ No error (4)
461. He laughed (1)/ on her (2)/ as she fell off the tree. (3)/ No error (4)
462. The reporter (1)/ was unable (2)/ to illicit information from the police. (3)/ No error. (4)
463. Each of these boys (1)/ play (2)/ games. (3)/ No error. (4)
464. These all (1)/ mangoes (2)/ are ripe. (3)/ No error. (4)
465. The students were (1)/ awaiting for (2)/ the arrival of the chief guest. (3)/ No error. (4)
466. If you hear (1)/ engaged tone (2)/ replace the receiver and dial again. (3)/ No error. (4)
467. Henry asked his wife (1)/ what had she prepared (2)/ for dinner that night. (3)/ No error. (4)
468. The news (1)/ I have received (2)/ is not good.(3)/ No error. (4)
469. Who (1)/ arranged (2)/ the chairs ? (3)/ No error. (4)
470. People who live on (1)/ glass houses (2)/ should not throw stone at others. (3)/ No error. (4)
471. The library members were asked (1)/ to return back the books (2)/ to the library. (3)/ No error. (4)
472. Raghu came out of the bathroom (1)/with a towel (2)/in the hand. (3)/No error. (4)
473. Neither the girl nor her parents (1)/ was present (2)/ to receive the award. (3)/ No error. (4)
474. College girls seldom wear (1)/ sarees these days, (2)/ do they ? (3)/ No error. (4)
475. Scarcely had (1)/the function started (2)/

than it began to rain. (3) /No error. (4)

476. My friend (1)/has invited me (2)/ for tea this Sunday. (3)/No error. (4)

477. He discussed (1)/ the murder case (2)/ with his juniors. (3)/ No error. (4)

478. The paintings of natural sceneries (1)/ are selling (2)/ like hot cakes. (3)/ No error.(4)

479. I (1)/ go to school (2)/ by walk. (3)/ No error. (4)

480. It is a (1)/ desert (2)/ place. (3)/ No error. (4)

481. You shall get (1)/ all the informations (2)/ if you read this book carefully. (3)/ No error. (4)

482. My father gave me (1)/ a pair of binocular (2)/ on my birthday. (3)/ No error. (4)

483. Kalidas is (1)/ a Shakespeare (2)/ of India. (3)/ No error.(4)

484. The teacher as well as his students, (1)/ all left (2)/ for the trip. (3)/ No error.(4)

485. More you (1)/ think of it, (2)/ the worse it becomes. (3)/ No error.(4)

486. Hasan plays (1)/ both cricket and billiards (2)/ at the national level. (3)/ No error. (4)

487. When I fail (1)/ to solve the problem myself (2)/ I unhesitatingly called for his help (3)/ No error. (4)

488. I and Tina will (1)/ go to the market (2)/ in the evening. (3)/ No error.(4)

489. Krishnakali, an early riser and a nature-lover (1)/ goes to morning walk at Rabindra (2)/ Sarovar lake before dawn. (3)/ No error.(4)

490. As a boy Dhritiman is very obedient (1)/ polite and hardworking (2)/ but as a student, he is always inattentive in study. (3)/ No error.(4)

491. There would have been (1)/ a disaster (2)/ and for your prompt action. (3)/ No error. (4)

492. Eighty–five thousand rupees (1)/ is a large sum of money (2)/ to earn in a month. (3)/ No error (4)

493. His voice shook with emotion (1)/ and it was so funny to hear him (2)/ that all we longed to laugh and to cry. (3)/ No error (4)

494. It being a rainy day (1)/ I will decide to skip work (2)/ and stay at home. (3)/ No error (4)

495. Another baffling change (1)/ that I noticed in him now-a-days (2)/ is that he avoids speaking to me. (3)/ No error (4)

496. I had asked him (1)/ how he could go out (2)/ if it started raining. (3)/ No error (4)

497. She regards (1)/ negotiating prices with customers (2)/ as her special expertise. (3)/ No error (4)

498. The police is investigating (1)/ for the recent happening (2)/ in the area. (3)/ No error (4)

499. The redevelopment project is aimed (1)/ not just providing good houses to shanty dwellers, (2)/but also developing infrastructure around the major Mumbai localities. (3)/ No error (4)

500. Unless he apologizes (1)/ he should not be (2)/ allowed to stay with us. (3)/ No error (4)

501. I met the gentleman (1)/ today morning on my way (2)/ to the market. (3)/ No error (4)

502. Although we reached his house in time (1)/ he was left (2)/ for the airport. (3)/ No error. (4)

503. The two last (1)/ chapters of the book (1)/ are very interesting.(3)/ No error. (4)

504. I have seen (1)/ that film last year (2)/ but I do not remember its story.(3)/ No error. (4)

505. Mahatma Gandhi remained (1)/ a man of principles (2)/ all through his life. (3)/ No error. (4)

506. Rustam and (1)/ myself saw (2)/ the picture. (3)/ No error.(4)

507. A lot of money (1)/ were spent (2)/ on the common wealth games. (3)/ No error. (4)

508. You will come (1)/ to my party tomorrow (2)/ isn't it. (3)/ No error. (4)

509. The old man was (1)/ overwhelmed for joy at (2)/ the success of his only son. (3)/ No error. (4)

510. The hockey match (1)/ between India and Pakistan (2)/ was much exciting. (3)/ No error. (4)

511. His composition (1)/ is inferior (2)/ than mine. (3)/ No error. (4)

512. Mango, the most unique fruit (1)/ is available in India (2)/in plenty. (3)/ No error(4)

513. Our geography teacher told (1)/ to study the map of India (2)/ for a test. (3)/No error (4)

514. You are (1)/more beautiful (2)/ than her. (3)/ No error (4)

515. My brother-in-law(1)/who lives in Mumbai (2)/ have come to stay with us.(3)/ No error (4)

516. Have trust on(1)/God and everything (2)/ will be right. (3)/ No error (4)

517. Smoking is undoubtedly (1)/ very injurious (2)/ for health.(3)/ No error (4)

518. My friend Anu (1)/is one of the best tennis player (2)/ in the country. (3)/ No error (4)

519. The cattles (1)/ are grazing (2)/ in the fields. (3)/ No error (4)

520. When I was passing through the forest (1)/ I happened to see (2)/ a number of deers.(3)/ No error (4)

521. You can (1)/open the box (2)/ by a screwdriver.(3)/ No error (4)

522. There is no agreement (1)/ between you and I (2)/ so we are free to go our way. (3)/ No error (4)

523. His father would (1)/ rather die than (2)/ to beg from door to door. (3)/ No error (4)

524. He is guilty (1)/ for killing (2)/ an innocent bird. (3)/ No error (4)

525. I have just come (1)/ to know that Mr. Ray, one of my favourite (2)/ teachers, died with cancer recently. (3)/ No error (4)

526. Many persons must have read(1)/The Arabian Nights', (2)/ which is very interesting. (3)/ No error (4)

527. We should make green vegetables (1)/ an essential part of our daily diet,(2) / shouldn't we ? (3)/ No error (4)

528. He has promised (1)/ to pay me the whole amount (2)/ in cheque with the stipulated time. (3)/ No error (4)

529. We must have (1)/ sympathy for (2)/needy and the poor. (3)/ No error (4)

530. When I left (1)/ the house at 9 o'clock (2)/ my son was still at home. (3)/ No error (4)

531. I did not receive (1)/ any letter from my parents (2)/ for the last two months. (3)/ No error (4)

532. After tasting both (1)/ John prefers (2) / tea than coffee. (3)/ No error (4)

533. I loved (1)/ the drawings (2)/ they were so real. (3)/ No error (4)

534. Suddenly they saw a car coming (1)/ at a break neck speed. (2)/ An old man were crossing the road at the zebra crossing. (3)/ No error (4)

535. I sprained my ankle (1)/ when I was (2)/ playing basketball. (3)/ No error (4)

536. It is time (1)/ we should accept all our people as equals (2)/ and as partners in the task of building a strong and united nation. (3)/ No error (4)

537. Part of the research program (1)/ involved interviewing teenagers (2)/ in inner-city areas. (3)/ No error (4).

538. I could not put up at a hotel (1)/ because the board and lodging charges (2)/ were too expensive.(3)/No error (4).

539. Much harassed (1)/ he left hostel (2)/ bag and baggage. (3)/ No error (4).

540. The young man (1)/ was surprised (2)/ perhaps a shade scandalized. (3)/ No error (4).

541. Every boy and every girl (1)/ were given (2)/ a packet of sweets. (3)/ No error (4)

542. In 1906 a earthquake (1)/destroyed much (2)/of San Francisco.(3)/ No error (4)

543. His parents does not (1) / approve of (2)/ his business. (3)/ No error (4)

544. The college library is (1) / not only equipped with (2) / very good books but also with the latest journals. (3)/No error (4)

545. The lovers walked (1) / besides each other (2)/ in silence. (3)/ No error (4)

546. Men are wanted (1)/ for the army (2)/ and the navy, and the air force. (3)/ No error (4)

547. She had an (1) / miserable existence (2)/ living with him.(3)/ No error (4)

548. A weak-minded person is frighten away (1)/ by the initial difficulties and (2)/ gives up the attempt in despair. (3)/ No error (4)

549. The Beatles (1)/ will ever be my favourite (2)/ pop group. (3)/ No error (4)

550. She was shocked when (1)/ she heard the news (2)/that he has died. (3)/ No error (4)

551. The behaviour of young (1)/ boys are the subject of (2)/ comment the world over. (3)/ No error (4)

552. They dreamed of a society (1)/ where everyone (2)/ were equal. (3)/ No error (4)

553. On Senegal (1)/ it is considered impolite (2)/ if you do not share your food. (3)/ No error (4)

554. We discussed about the problem thoroughly (1)/on the eve of the examination (2)/ that I found it very easy to work it out. (3)/ No error (4)

555. The wise father told him (1)/ that the mangoes had gone bad as they were (2)/ in contact with the one rotten mango. (3)/ No error (4)

556. The box of eggs (1)/ are lying (2)/ on the table. (3)/ No error (4)

557. In his book (1)/ Churchi 1 l describes (2)/ that historical first meeting with Roosevelt. (3)/ No error (4)

558. The ant who was nearby (1)/ walked forward and bit the hunter (2)/ sharply in the ankle. (3)/ No error (4)

559. They can promise you (1)/ an experience (2)/ you won't never forget. (3)/ No error (4)

560. The dress that the (1)/ girl wore was (2)/ more attractive than the other girls. (3)/ No error (4)

561. Fifty years has passed (1)/ since man first ventured (2)/ into outer space. (3)/ No error (4)

562. A chill wind blew (1)/ and icy fingers of death (2)/ crept up my spine. (3)/ No error (4).

563. Such rules (1)/ do not apply to (2)/ you and I. (3)/ No error (4).

564. The river (1)/ has overflown (2)/ its banks. (3)/ No error (4).

565. IIM Calcatta's MBA programme (1)/ is regarded (2)/ as the finest in the country. (3)/ No error (4).

566. One of the most (1)/ widely spread (2)/ bad habit is the use of tobacco. (3)/ No error (4).

567. He feels his troubles (1)/ as much or (2)/ even more than they. (3)/ No error (4)

568. I like reading (1)/ more than (2)/ to play. (3)/ No error (4)

569. The old lady swooned (1)/ but was soon (2)/ restored at senses. (3)/ No error (4)

570. I shall have to (1)/ withdraw from my savings (2)/ to buy a new car. (3)/ No error. (4)

571. The whole block of flats (1)/ including two shops were (2)/ destroyed in fire. (3)/ No error (4)

572. The new device (1)/ aims at eliminating (2)/ the risk of short - circuiting. (3) / No

error (4)

573. I wish to heartily (1)/ congratulate you for (2)/ your astounding success. (3)/No error (4)

574. The visitor took the vacant seat (1)/ next from mine (2)/ one of the many huge sofas in the room. (3)/ No error (4)

575. He was (1)/ a learnt man among lords, (2)/ and a lord among learned men. (3)/ No error (4)

576. With our great annoyance (1)/ we found the ground (2)/ filled with broken glasses. (3)/ No error (4)

577. Paradise Lost (1)/ is (2)/a epic poem.(3)/ No error (4)

578. After toiling very hardly (1)/ over a long period of time (2)/he found that he had met no profit at all. (3)/ No error (4)

579. Excuse (1)/ me (2)/interrupting you. (3)/ No error (4)

580. At this time of the year (1)/ the mountains are (2)/usually covered with ice. (3)/ No error (4)

581. One of my friends (1)/ are (2)/an I.A.S officer. (3)/ No error (4)

582. The Arabian Nights' (1)/ are enjoyed (2)/ by all kinds of readers. (3)/ No error (4).

583. She has not completed (1)/ her course, (2)/ Isn't it ? (3)/ No error (4).

584. Every citizen is (1)/ entitled to (2)/ the voting. (3)/ No error (4).

585. The collector (1)/ visits the office regularly (2)/ Isn't it ? (3)/ No error (4).

586. No sooner did the rabbit (1)/come out of the bush (2)/ when the hunter killed it. (3)/ No error (4)

587. Shakespeare has written(1)/ many plays (2)/as well as some poetries. (3)/ No error (4)

588. Neither of the girls (1)/ were willing to (2) / accept the proposal. (3)/ No error (4)

589. A interesting book (1)/ 'A Tale of two cities' (2)/was written by Alexander Dumas. (3) / No error (4)

590. In India, (1)/ there are (2) / many poors. (3)/No error (4)

591. I worked (1)/ as medical representative (2)/ for eight months.(3)/No error (4)

592. One must learn (1)/ to distinguish (2)/ good from bad. (3)/ No error (4)

593. The children (1)/ laughed at (2)/ the clown. (3)/ No error (4)

594. Had the plane not been delayed, (1)/ I will reach here (2)/ in time for the function. (3)/ No error (4)

595. In India, hill stations (1)/ usually have (2)/ beautiful sceneries. (3)/ No error (4)

596. She was ill for five days (1)/ when the doctor (2)/ was sent for. (3)/ No error (4)

597. The United Nations (1)/ enquired for (2)/a cease fire. (3)/No error (4)

598. Ghana, Nigeria and Gambia (1)/ each have parts to play (2)/ in the development of Africa. (3)/ No error (4)

599. In these days of inflation (1)/a ten rupees note will not buy you (2)/ even an ordinary meal. (3)/ No error (4)

600. Most of my friends (1)/ heard the earthquake (2)/ but I was totally unaware of it. (3)/ No error (4)

601. He walks (1)/ as if the earth (2)/ belonged to him. (3)/ No error (4)

602. Many a man (1)/ have come to India from Bangladesh (2)/to live here permanently. (3)/ No error. (4)

603. Our football team(1)/comprises of (2)/ eleven skilled players. (3)/ No error. (4)

604. Knowledge and wisdom makes (1)/ an individual truly complete (2)/ and self-assured. (3)/ No error. (4)

605. One of the boys(1)/ who always give the correct answer (2)/ is Samuel. (3)/ No error. (4)

606. It is high time (1)/we renovate (2)/ our old house. (3)/ No error. (4)

607. Headmaster (1)/has instructed (2)/ the

teachers to follow the rules of the school. (3)/ No error. (4)

608. The first inning (1)/of the match (2)/ was very sensational. (3)/ No error. (4)

609. How long it takes (1)/to travel from Chennai to Trichy (2)/ by train? (3)/ No error. (4)

610. One should respect (1)/ the religions of others (2)/ as much as his own. (3)/ No error. (4)

611. On a holiday (1)/ I prefer reading story books (2)/ than visiting my friends. (3)/ No error. (4)

612. I was (1)/ laying down (2)/ when the door bell rang. (3)/ No error. (4)

613. I told the teacher (1)/ that the homework set for the day (2)/ was much too heavy for us to complete. (3)/ No error. (4)

614. Someone, they don't know (1)/ who, knocked at (2)/ their door in midnight. (3)/ No error (4)

615. Seldom if ever (1)/ nature does operate (2)/ in closed and separate compartments. (3)/ No error. (4)

616. Mohan leapt (1)/ on the opportunity (2)/ that came his way. (3)/ No error. (4)

617. Water contamination has become more serious (1)/ since chemists have begun to use (2)/ new substances. (3)/ No error. (4)

618. Due to inflation (1)/ the cost of living (2)/ escalated in the last one year. (3)/ No error. (4)

619. Just as (1)/ I was entering the room, (2)/ the family was going for a party. (3)/ No error. (4)

620. The arm was so badly injured (1)/ that he must have (2)/ it amputated (3)/ No error. (4)

621. You need not tell a lie (1)/ when the judge asked you where you were (2)/ When the crime was committed. (3) No error. (4)

622. The government (1)/ must provide facilities for the (2)/ upbringing of women. (3)/ No error (4)

623. You will not (1)/ succeed unless you (2)/ don't work hard. (3)/ No error (4)

624. He stated that (1)/ he prefers (2)/ tea than coffee. (3)/ No error (4)

625. She has been (1)/ complaining about headache (2)/ from morning. (3) No error (4)

626. The children left (1)/ the playground (2)/ one after one. (3)/ No error (4)

627. I knew the town well (1)/ so I was able (2)/ to advice him where to go. (3)/ No error (4)

628. He runs (1)/ more faster (2)/ than I. (3)/ No error (4)

629. The fight for liberation (1)/ brings out the best and (2)/ a noblest quality in mankind. (3)/ No error (4)

630. The baby was (1)/ clinging with her (2)/ mother in fear. (3)/ No error (4)

631. Not much (1)/ people realize (2)/ his sincerity. (3)/ No error (4)

632. The government (1)/ must provide facilities for the (2)/ upbringing of women. (3)/ No error (4)

633. He assured me that he will return in an hour.
   (1) No error
   (2) that he will return
   (3) in an hour.
   (4) He assured me

634. The car that he is using these days is belonging to his employer.
   (1) No error
   (2) these days is belonging
   (3) The car that he is using
   (4) to his employer.

635. Three years have elapsed since I had gone to visit my aunt in the city.
   (1) No error
   (2) visit my aunt in the city.
   (3) since I had gone to

(4) Three years have elapsed

636. I reached two hours before he had came.

(1) two hours before

(2) No error

(3) he had came.

(4) I reached

637. He needs not have shouted at me that way.

(1) No error

(2) not have shouted

(3) He needs

(4) at me that way.

638. Before we returned from swimming in the river near the camp, someone had stole our clothes, and we had to walk back with our towels around us.

(1) No error

(2) and we had to walk back with our towels around us.

(3) Before we returned from swimming in the river near the camp

(4) someone had stole our clothes

639. He went to the doctor because he had not been feeling well since several weeks.

(1) He went to the doctor

(2) since several weeks

(3) because he had not been feeling well

(4) No error

640. Had you participated in the drawing competition, you would have won the first prize.

(1) No error

(2) in the drawing competition

(3) Had you participated

(4) you would have won the first prize

641. Long life is good if one be happy and has friends.

(1) and has friends.

(2) if one be happy

(3) No error

(4) Long life is good

642. The thief did not know that there was a dog laying under the table.

(1) that there was a dog

(2) laying under the table

(3) No error

(4) The thief did not know

643. The scissors, which (1)/ are on the table, (2)/ belongs to Radha. (3)/ No error (4)

644. My brother, along with his friends, have gone to watch a movie at the nearest cinema hall.

(1) at the nearest cinema hall

(2) My brother, along with his friends

(3) have gone to watch a movie

(4) No error

645. The teachers, who I worked with, were very insensitive towards children's needs.

(1) The teachers, who I worked with

(2) were very insensitive

(3) towards children's needs

(4) No error

646. Bradbury, one of the most versatile writer ever lived, was a school dropout.

(1) Bradbury, one of the most

(2) versatile writer ever lived,

(3) was a school dropout

(4) No error

647. Each of the girls in my class sing well.

(1) Each of the girls

(2) sing well

(3) in my class

(4) No error

648. I shake his hand when he arrived and when he left.

(1) I shake his hand

(2) when he arrived

(3) and when he left

(4) No error

649. The old, grey horse that was standing beside the barn had a sad look in its eyes when it saw the shotgun that the farmer

was carrying.

(1) The old, grey horse that was standing
(2) No error
(3) had a sad look in its eyes when
(4) shotgun that the farmer was carrying

650. The young child singed a very sweet song for the audience.

(1) The young child
(2) singed
(3) a very sweet song
(4) for the audience

651. Nowhere is the resulting confusion more evident except in campaign speeches made by different campaigners of the same party.

(1) Nowhere is the resulting confusion
(2) more evident
(3) except in campaign speeches
(4) made by different campaigners of the same party.

652. As I prefer coffee than tea my friends always take the trouble to get me a cup of coffee.

(1) As I prefer
(2) coffee than tea
(3) my friends always take the trouble
(4) to get me a cup of coffee.

653. I always had a fancy towards big luxurious cars.

(1) had a
(2) fancy
(3) towards big
(4) No error

654. I'd like a bike in commuting to work.

(1) I'd like
(2) a bike
(3) in commuting to work
(4) No error

655. I prefer apples more than oranges.

(1) I prefer
(2) apples more than
(3) oranges
(4) No error

656. My husband was work, so I went shopping.

(1) My husband
(2) was work
(3) I went shopping
(4) No error

657. The moon are full and the stars are out.

(1) The moon are full
(2) and the stars
(3) are out
(4) No error

658. The fire in the apartment building effected over 20 families.

(1) The fire in
(2) the apartment building
(3) effected over 20 families.
(4) No error

659. She exercised discretion in investigating whether her husband eloped with his exgirlfriend.

(1) discretion in
(2) investigating whether
(3) eloped with
(4) No error

660. The lawyer deduced from the existing evidences that the accused was involved in the heinous crime.

(1) in the heinous crime
(2) deduced from the
(3) accused was involved
(4) No error

661. Neither the chips, which were cheaper, nor the pizza interested the kid.

(1) No error
(2) were cheaper
(3) nor the pizza
(4) the chips which

662. The travellers were pacified when to hear that the plane had landed on the runway much before the official announcement.

(1) landed on the runway
(2) much before the
(3) were pacified when
(4) No error

663. Since my mother was angry so I did not utter a word.
(1) was angry so
(2) utter a word
(3) since my mother
(4) No error

664. Wise men follow nobel (1)/ ideas whereas fools (2)/ disregard them. (3)/ No error (4)

665. The navel officers (1)/ successfully fought the pirates (2)/ who had looted and plundered for many years. (3)/ No error (4)

666. He acted not (1)/as per my advice (2)/ but somebody else. (3)/ No error (4)

667. The chairs in the (1)/room are in a (2)/ state disarray. (3)/ No error (4)

668. Ashoka the Great was (1)/ regarded one of the greatest emperors (2)/ the world has ever produced. (3)/ No error (4)

669. Will you please (1)/ give me little milk (2)/ for my cat ? (3)/ No error (4)

670. The light bulbs (1)/ on the hall (2)/ need to be changed. (3)/ No error (4)

671. A recent survey indicates (1)/ that the number of drug addicts (2)/ grew day by day. (3)/No error (4)

672. I want to exchange (1)/ my Maruti (2)/ from a Santro. (3)/ No error (4)

673. There were extensive (1)/ lawn in front (2)/ of the bungalow. (3)/ No error (4)

674. Each of the girls (1)/ have come (2)/ with her books. (3)/ No error (4)

675. Me and my wife (1)/ were at home (2)/ last night. (3)/ No error (4)

676. Essay writing is an art (1)/ that requires many planning (2)/ on the part of the writer. (3)/ No error (4)

677. Although they listen to me (a)/ but their actions (b) / prove otherwise (c) / No error (d)

678. He treats (a) / us as (b) / slaves (c) / No error (d)

679. Most of the girls are doing (a) / their post graduation because (b) / they may get good husbands (c) / No error (d)

680. Such was his pronunciation (a) / as (b) / I could not understand him (c) / No error (d)

681. He asked (a) / that who (b) / I was (c) / No error (d)

682. I am interested (a) / in such books (b) / that are interesting (c) / No error (d)

683. Each member of the alliance (a) / agree to take such action (b) / that it deems necessary (c) / No error (d)

684. She looked at him (a) / in such distress (b) / as he had to look away (c) / No error (d)

685. This films is interesting (a) / and the previous one (b) / was boring (c) / No error (d)

686. It is difficult to know (a) / whether (b) / you are selected or not (c) / No error (d)

687. He has no chance (a) / than to start (b) / his own business (c) / No error (d)

688. They had hardly finished (a) / their meals that at once (b) / they resumed their duty (c) / No error (d)

689. I don't know whether (a) / Raj is equally (b) / good as Vimal (c) / No error (d)

690. He (a) / will return (b) / on either Monday or Tuesday (c) / No error (d)

691. He is (a) / not honest and not (b) / truthful (c) / No error (d)

692. He has no other business (a) / but to play (b) / with computers (c) / No error (d)

693. Be smart (a) / not only in dress (b) / and also in action (c) / No error (d)

694. Hardly had I reached the airport (a) / where I learned about (b) / the powerful bomb explosion (c) / No error (d)

695. My book has been missing (a) / from my

room (b) / till yesterday (c) / No error (d)

696. The manager of the bank was busy (a) / so he asked them to come and see him (b) / between two to three in the afternoon (c) / No error (d)

697. No sooner did the sun rise (a) / when we took a hasty breakfast (b) / and resumed the journey (c) / No error (d)

698. Because he is physically strong (a) / therefore he was selected (b) / for the school boxing team (c) / No error (d)

699. The reason for his failure (a) / is because (b) / he did not work hard (c) / No error (d)

700. Arjun asked him (a) / that which was the way (b) / to the post office (c) / No error (d)

701. Unless you do not listen to his advice (a) / I am not going (b) / to help you (c) / No error (d)

702. How do you say (a) / that neither he or Raj has qualified (b) / in the examination ? (c) / No error (d)

703. We are not sure (a) / if he is coming (b) / to the party (c) / No error (d)

704. Sooner than he had arrived (a) / his friends arranged a reception in his honour (b) / in the best hotel in the town (c) / No error (d)

705. Mrs Dhaka went to Delhi (a) / because she might (b) / see Mrs Rai (c) / No error (d)

706. He gave him no money (a) / nor he did help him (b) / in any way (c) / No error (d)

707. The managing director well as (a)/ the Board members was in (b)/ favour of taking strict action (c)/ against the striking workers. (d)/ No error (e)

708. Unless he does not return (a)/ all the library books (b)/ he will not be relieved (c)/ from the service.(d)/ No error (e)

709. You must either tell me (a)/ the whole story or (b)/, at least, the (c)/ first half of it. (d)/ No error (e)

710. The old woman has had the (a)/ best medical facilities available (b)/ but she will not be cured unless she does not have (c)/ a strong desire to live.(d)/ No error (e)

711. Hardly had I reached (a)/ the airport where (b)/ I learnt about the powerful (c)/ bomb explosion.(d)/ No error (e)

712. The manager of the bank (a)/ was busy; so he asked them (b)/ to come and see him between two to (c)/ three in the afternoon. (d)/ No error (e)

713. Because he is physically (a)/ strong, therefore he was (b)/ selected for the school (c)/boxing team.(d)/ No error (e)

714. Being a strict (a)/ vegetarian he depended (b)/ on milk and fruit and (c)/ had to cook for himself.(d)/ No error (e)

715. Even though the shirt (a)/ is rather expensive but (b)/ I wish to purchase (c)/ it with my own money.(d)/ No error (e)

716. Unless Ashish does not (a)/ return all the library books, (b)/ he will not be awarded (c)/ the pass certificate. (d)/ No error (e)

717. I found(a)/ that he slow (b)/came near to me.(c)/No error(d)

718. The former(a)/ aim was noble (b)/but latter was attainable..(c)/No error(d)

719. Between major cities (a)/you can still find a train but (b)/their running status is becoming less frequent..(c)/No error(d)

720. In one of his(a)/ ideas, he suggested(b)/ the idea of evolution..(c)/No error(d)

721. He joined a group(a)/ of young sportsmen and gave(b)/ attention of the riches and marksmanship..(c)/No error(d)

722. A novel is (a)/only a abridge (b)/version of events..(c)/ No error(d)

723. It is clear that(a)/ the decline of a language must (b)/ultimately has political and economic causes..(c)/No error(d)

724. If one get(a)/ rid of bad habits, one(b)/ can think more clearly..(c)/No error(d)

725. He was so(a)/ tall because he could talk(b)/

to the stars in the sky..(c)/No error(d)

726. In the mountains(a)/ it is the weather (b)/ that ruled over everything. (c)/No error(d)

727. Ancient India and medieval (a)/Europe has seen (b)/the culture of busking.(c)/ No error(d)

728. After initiate exposure, they could (a)/ go to the guru's abode and (b)/learn for a longer duration. (c)/ No error(d)

729. National academies or even (a)/state ones ought to(b)/ have certificate standards. (c)/ No error(d)

730. Avvaiyar's poems describe (a)/the rich taste of meat, liquor (b)/and are full of script ions of warfare. (c)/ No error(d)

731. Some of them (a)/refused to marry (b)/ debauch feudal ruler. (c)/ No error(d)

732a. It is important to (a)/focus on storytelling to (b)/make museums around the country. (c)/ No error(d)

732b. There is no conscious(a)/ planning on (b)/ take our music forward. (c)/ No error(d)

733. I have been abroad(a)/ many times but I have neither (b)/tasted alcohol not had non-vegetarian food. (c)/ No error(d)

734. The strategy location(a)/ of the fort is further (b)/enhanced by the facts. (c)/ No error(d)

735. I have tried (a)/ to do a project in India for quite (b)/some time but nothing worked out. (c)/ No error(d)

736. Read not to contradict nor to believe but to weigh and consider.
(1) but to weigh and consider
(2) No error
(3) nor to believe
(4) Read not to contradict

737. The decapitated body of a young girl was discovered yesterday.
(1) No error
(2) The decapitated body
(3) of a young girl
(4) was discovered yesterday

738. We really wanted to go to the park but we were told not to go out if it rain.
(1) No error
(2) were told
(3) wanted to go
(4) if it rain

739. It has been said that history is the essence of innumerable biography.
(1) No error
(2) of innumerable biography
(3) that history is the essence
(4) It has been said

740. The International Day against Drug Abuse and Illicit Traffickings is observed on June 26th.
(1) Drug Abuse and Illicit Traffickings
(2) No error
(3) is observed on June 26th
(4) The International Day against

741. If man makes proper use of his time and opportunities and follow his aim in life with patience and perseverance, he is sure to succeed.
(1) and perseverance, he is sure to succeed.
(2) If man makes proper use of his time and opportunities
(3) and follow his aim in life with patience
(4) No error

742. Jewellery retailers across India decided to suspend sold of gold coins and bars for six months.
(1) to suspend sold
(2) of gold coins and bars for six months.
(3) No error
(4) Jewellery retailers across India decided

743. Who do you think will win the game ?
(1) Who do you

(2) No error
(3) win the game
(4) think will

744. My cousin cannot understand why his teacher says that the earth move round the sun.
(1) teacher says
(2) cannot understand
(3) No error
(4) move round the

745. Reading is no longer popular among the youthful of today. As the influence of the internet has taken over a very important and active hobby.
(1) among the youthful of today
(2) very important and active hobby
(3) influence of the internet
(4) No error

746. A person who sticks to one thing inspite of initial difficulties is sure to succeed in the end.
(1) A person who sticks to one thing
(2) is sure to succeed in the end
(3) inspite of initial difficulties
(4) No error

747. What make people angry or tense is actually a mystery which is difficult to explain.
(1) No error
(2) What make people angry
(3) or tense is actually a mystery
(4) which is difficult to explain

748. She gave me details of all the schools she had visited while she was on an official tour.
(1) all the schools she had visited
(2) No error
(3) She gave me details of
(4) while she was on a official tour

749. The doctor recommended that he should take a holiday.
(1) that he should
(2) take a holiday
(3) The doctor recommended
(4) No error

750. Education is the only effective tool to help eradicate the problem of violence against women.
(1) problem of violence
(2) help eradicate
(3) the only affective tool
(4) No error

751. Even a fool when he holdeth his peace is counted wise.
(1) when he holdeth his peace
(2) No error
(3) Even fools
(4) is counted wise

752. Henry is a capable boy of doing anything.
(1) a capable boy
(2) of doing anything
(3) Henry is
(4) No error

753. Africa is the second largest continent (1)/ and it contain about one fifth (2)/ of all the land in the world. (3)/ No error (4).

754. We had (1)/ hardly reached the (2)/ platform than the train came in. (3)/ No error (4).

755. When no individual is (1)/ responsible there are no (2)/ sense of responsibility. (3)/ No error (4).

756. I am not sure (1)/ if (2)/ he will come. (3)/ No error (4).

757. I felt privileged (1)/ to recite a poem in an honour of my teacher (2)/ at a recent school function (3)/ No error (4).

758. It is now (1)/ five years since (2)/ I visit the Delhi. (3)/ No error (4).

759. Prisoners, especially long term convict (1)/ have to suffer most (2)/ from emotional starvation. (3)/ No error (4).

760. This is not (1)/ a worth reading book (2)/ so don't read it. (3)/ No error (4).

761. The beautiful, young girl (1)/ jumped in the river (2)/ in a state of depression. (3)/ No error (4).

762. The tree (1)/ is losing (2)/ its leaves. (3)/ No error (4).

763. People have (1)/ different ideas about (2)/ what makes a good holiday. (3)/ No error (4).

764. They decided (1)/ to consult (2)/ a marriage guidance counsellor. (3)/ No error (4).

765. I saw (1)/ two deers (2)/ in the woods. (3)/ No error (4).

766. I enjoy jogging (1)/ and I enjoy (2)/ playing the piano. (3)/ No error (4).

767. For testing (1)/ the new microphone, (2)/ I tried to record my voice. (3)/ No error (4).

768. My friends said (1)/ me that he was (2)/ unable to come. (3)/ No error (4).

769. She has married (1)/ a young tall (2)/ Australian accountant. (3)/ No error (4).

770. The hurrying crowds (1)/ of people past (2)/ each other amazed him. (3)/ No error (4).

771. I have visited Mumbai two years ago (1)/ and I am planning to visit again (2)/ in the near future. (3)/ No error (4).

772. He neither talks too much (1)/ nor he causes any trouble (2)/ during the lesson. (3)/ No error (4).

773. If I would have realised (1)/ what a bad shape our library is in (2)/ I would have done something. (3)/ No error (4)

774. He has been (1)/ enhanced in position (2)/ as a result of his diligence and integrity. (3)/ No error (4)

775. It is I (1)/who is responsible (2)/ for the delay. (3)/ No error (4)

776. There is only one cure (1)/ to the evils which newly (2)/ acquired freedom produces and that cure is freedom. (3)/ No error (4)

777. He flew (1)/over extensively (2)/ the Pacific last winter. (3)/ No error (4)

778. A five–men (1)/ enquiry committee was appointed (2)/ to look into the matter. (3)/ No error (4)

779. The crime rate increases inspite (1)/ formal moral education (2)/ given in schools. (3)/No error (4)

780. As soon as they (1)/ entered the temple (2)/ they prayed to the gods on bent knees. (3)/ No error (4)

781. Three–fourths of the men (1)/has gone (2)/ to war. (3)/ No error (4)

782. The conversation (1)/ we are having is completely (2)/ out of the main topic. (3)/ No error (4)

783. On the arrival of the mail, (1)/ the car finally (2)/ made the start. (3)/ No error. (4)

784. Second hand (1)/ furnitures were(2)/ put to auction.(3)/ No error. (4)

785. If she had seen (1)/ the car coming, she (2)/ may not crossed the road. (3)/ No error.(4)

786. His father (1)/ bought these furnitures (2)/ the day before yesterday. (3)/ No error. (4)

787. Although Niratyay is very intelligent and sincere (1)/ to his dealing he (2)/ often tells lies. (3)/ No error.(4)

788. The other day my sister told me (1)/ that she will be moving (2)/ to her new apartment very soon.(3)/ No error (4)

789. Tony is giving me a lift. (1)/ He's coming to (2)/ call for me at ten.(3)/ No error (4)

790. Each of the students participating (1)/ in the drawing competition (2)/ have to bring his own materials.(3)/ No error (4)

791. Raj surprised everyone (1)/ when he created an unbreakable record (2)/ of one and a half centuries.(3)/ No error (4)

792. Do not write him of (1)/ as I feel he still has the fire (2)/ smouldering in him.(3)/

No error (4)

793. The poor man saves the money (1)/ but then he began to worry (2)/ that thieves might take it away.(3)/ No error (4)

794. He adviced me (1)/ to join (2)/ the computer course later in the year.(3)/ No error (4)

795. Some of our latest canon (1)/ that have come out of the production (2)/ line have a very long range.(3)/ No error (4)

796. Susan said that she shall (1)/ try to attempt the task (2)/ to the best of her ability.(3)/ No error (4)

797. He couldn't but help (1)/ shed tears at the plight of the villagers (2)/ rendered homeless by a devastating cyclone.(3)/ No error (4)

798. Most of the members at the meeting felt (1)/ that the group appointed to investigate the case (2)/ were not competent to do the job efficiently.(3)/ No error (4)

799. Neither the size (1)/ nor the colour of the gloves (2)/ were right.(3)/ No error (4)

800. It was only when they met that (1)/ they found he has a childish simplicity (2)/ in him.(3)/ No error (4)

801. I now realise that public speaking (1)/ requires as much courage (2)/ and confidence as to dance.(3)/ No error (4)

802. The children which are assembled (1)/ in the hall are the ones (2)/ chosen for the field trip.(3)/ No error (4)

803. It is to certify that he has won (1)/ the essay writing competition organised (2)/ by the Department of Arts and Culture.(3)/ No error (4)

804. Neither of the sisters (1)/ are sensible enough (2)/ to carry out the plan.(3)/ No error (4)

805. Give your answers (1)/ in your own words (2)/ as far as practical.(3)/ No error (4)

806. Tired I was I had to (1)/ keep on working till (2)/ the wee hours of the morning.(3)/ No error (4)

807. The suggestion given by him (1)/ is as bad, if not worst (2)/ than the one suggested by you.(3)/ No error (4)

808. Hearing these strange noise above, the thought at once occurred to me that thieves had entered the house.
(1) No error
(2) the thought at once occurred to me
(3) that thieves had entered the house
(4) Hearing these strange noise above

809. Everyone were happy to hear about his success.
(1) to hear
(2) about his sucess
(3) No error
(4) Everyone were happy

810. The lions kill the animals and eat his meat.
(1) The lions
(2) and eat his meat
(3) kill the animals
(4) No error

811. The team was now in the field and about to take their place.
(1) No error
(2) The team was
(3) about to take their
(4) now in the field and place

812. Our beloved Prime Minister is known to the prominent figures all over the world.
(1) the prominent figures all over the world
(2) is known to
(3) Our beloved Prime Minister
(4) No error

813. Professor Lal teaches both history as well as literature each semester.
(1) Professor Lal teaches
(2) No error
(3) each semester.
(4) both history as well as literature

814. The media play a vital role in popularising a brand.
(1) The media play
(2) in popularising a brand.
(3) No error
(4) a vital role

815. My friend will not come to attend this marriage unless he is not invited.
(1) No error
(2) My friend will not come
(3) to attend this marriage
(4) unless he is not invited.

816. This is the second communication we have sent and we are much surprised at receiving no answer.
(1) This is the second communication we have sent
(2) at receiving no answer.
(3) and we are much surprised
(4) No error

817. She is wealthy and can afford all the pleasures of life.
(1) and can afford
(2) all the pleasures of life.
(3) No error
(4) She is wealthy

818. By May next year I have been working in this college for twenty years.
(1) No error
(2) By May next year
(3) I have been working in this college
(4) For twenty years.

819. Everyone of us should realise that any act of negligence will cause a great harm to our country's security.
(1) No error
(2) Everyone of us should realise that
(3) any act of negligence will cause
(4) a great harm to our country's security.

820. I shall look forward to being with you sometime next month.
(1) No error
(2) I shall look forward
(3) to being with you
(4) sometime next month.

821. I really do regret not to learn to play the violin when I had so many opportunties to learn and practise in school.
(1) No error
(2) I really do regret not to learn to play the violin
(3) when I had so many opportunities
(4) to learn and practise in school.

822. The government granted relief payments of ₹ 5,000 each to those who injured in the fire accident.
(1) No error
(2) The government granted
(3) Relief payments of ₹ 5,000 each
(4) To those who injured in the fire accident.

823. You are required to give an explanation for your conduct within two days of the receipt of this letter.
(1) No error
(2) for your conduct
(3) within two days of the receipt of this letter.
(4) You are required to give an explanation

824. The ruins of the spillway are a vital clue to the epic struggle that unfold as generations of Khmer engineers coped with a water system that grew complex and unruly.
(1) coped with a water system that grew complex and unruly.
(2) to the epic struggle that unfold as generations of Khmer engineers
(3) The ruins of the spillway are a vital clue
(4) No error

825. Bobby learnt the alphabets at the age of

two.

(1) No error
(2) age of two
(3) Bobby learnt the
(4) alphabets at the

826. The sum and substance of this poem is as follows.
(1) of this poem
(2) No error
(3) The sum and substance
(4) is as follows

827. I watched how the pianoist used her left hand.
(1) I watched how
(2) the pianoist
(3) No error
(4) used her left hand

828. Who do you think I met ?
(1) Who
(2) No error
(3) do you think
(4) I met ?

829. Just outside my house are a playground for school boys and girls.
(1) Just outside my house
(2) are a playground
(3) No error
(4) for school boys and girls

830. He can be a basketball player since he is tall like a mule.
(1) He can be
(2) he is tall like a mule
(3) No error
(4) a basketball player since

831. It is not advisable to take heavy luggages while on a journey.
(1) to take heavy luggages
(2) while on a journey
(3) No error
(4) It is not advisable

832. A bird in the tree is worth two in the bush.
(1) A bird in the tree
(2) two in the bush.
(3) No error
(4) is worth

833. Several guests noticed Mr. Sharma falling back in his chair and gasping for breath.
(1) falling back in his chair
(2) Several guests noticed Mr. Sharma
(3) and gasping for breath
(4) No error

834. We have finished our work three hours ago and have been waiting for you since then.
(1) three hours ago and have been waiting
(2) We have finished our work
(3) for you since then
(4) No error

835. Many a man want to be rich quickly.
(1) rich quickly
(2) want to be
(3) Many a man
(4) No error

836. The Russian ambassador's whereabouts is not known to anyone.
(1) No error
(2) The Russian ambassador's
(3) not known to anyone
(4) where abouts is

837. A study is going underway to determine the exact concentration of lead in the water supply.
(1) to determine the exact concentration
(2) No error
(3) of lead in the water supply
(4) A study is going underway

838. The childrens were happy when the film started.
(1) The childrens

(2) when the film started
(3) No error
(4) were happy

839. His new job necessitated his getting up at six.
(1) No error
(2) His new job
(3) getting up at six
(4) necessitated his

840. This is Johns book on the table.
(1) No error
(2) John's book
(3) on the table
(4) This is

841. It is not advisable to take heavy luggages while travelling these days.
(1) No error
(2) to take heavy luggages
(3) It is not advisable
(4) while travelling these days

842. An ancients considered that knowledge had its limits.
(1) had its limits
(2) No error
(3) that knowledge
(4) An ancients considered

843. Despite the speed in which he was driving he couldn't reach on time.
(1) Despite the speed
(2) No error
(3) in which he was driving
(4) he couldn't reach on time

844. Being a very cold I could not go out for a morning walk.
(1) for a morning walk
(2) No error
(3) Being a very cold
(4) I could not go out

845. This is the girl whose brother is a doctor.
(1) is a doctor
(2) This is the girl
(3) No error
(4) whose brother

846. The children are driving me to distraction today.
(1) No error
(2) distraction today
(3) The children are
(4) driving me to

847. Thoughts about the slaughtered children is uppermost on my mind.
(1) is uppermost on my mind
(2) slaughtered children
(3) Thoughts about the
(4) No error

848. The luxuries of the riches are maintained by depriving the poor of their dues.
(1) The luxuries of the riches
(2) the poor of their dues
(3) are maintained by depriving
(4) No error

849. They brought to themself this disaster.
(1) No error
(2) to themself
(3) this disaster
(4) They brought

850. Everybody wants to enjoy habitual peace in mind.
(1) peace in mind
(2) No error
(3) Everybody wants to
(4) enjoy habitual

851. Orwell is one of those authors who do his best to irritate the reader.
(1) Orwell is one of those
(2) No error
(3) who do his best
(4) to irritate the reader

852. He was conferred to his bed by illness.
(1) by illness

(2) to his bed
(3) No error
(4) He was conferred

853. The full moon appearing in the sky and its silvery light spread across.
(1) The full moon appearing
(2) silvery light spread across
(3) No error
(4) in the sky and its

854. It began to rain as soon as we stepped out of the house.
(1) out of the house
(2) as soon as we stepped
(3) No error
(4) It began to rain

855. It is not good to breed over past failure.
(1) to breed over
(2) It is not good
(3) No error
(4) past failure

856. Things in Nature die a temporary deaths only to appear again.
(1) only to appear again
(2) die a temporary death
(3) Things in Nature
(4) No error

857. The Ph.D. degree was confide on him in the convocation.
(1) The Ph.D. degree
(2) him in the convocation
(3) was confide on
(4) No error

858. After he was caught cheating he was disqualified to appear at the examination.
(1) After he was caught cheating
(2) he was disqualified
(3) to appear at the examination
(4) No error

859. She stopped singing as soon as the telephone rings from across the hall.
(1) She stopped singing
(2) as soon as the telephone
(3) rings from across the hall
(4) No error

860. The old curtains were torn and they flapped in the light breeze.
(1) The old curtains were torn
(2) and they flapped
(3) in the light breeze
(4) No error

861. I do not know who you consider to be the best dancer.
(1) I do not know
(2) who you consider
(3) to be the best dancer
(4) No error

862. So hoarse he was that he could not make the speech.
(1) So hoarse he was
(2) that he could not make
(3) the speech
(4) No error

863. The kitchen need painting badly and I must get it done.
(1) need painting badly
(2) The kitchen
(3) No error
(4) and I must get it done

864. If I will play my best I can win any day against anybody.
(1) against anybody
(2) I can win any day
(3) No error
(4) If I will play my best

865. He finds fault at everything I do.
(1) No error
(2) at everything
(3) I do
(4) He finds fault

866. An idea was worth nothing if it has no

champion.

(1) No error

(2) if it has no champion

(3) An idea

(4) is worth nothing

867. The camp beside ours has been built in 1966 by John's brother.

(1) No error

(2) by John's brother

(3) The camp beside ours

(4) was built in 1966

868. I have been waiting for you since two hours.

(1) for you

(2) No error

(3) I have been waiting

(4) since two hours

869. There be a long queue for entry into the exhibition ground.

(1) for entry into

(2) No error

(3) There be a long queue

(4) the exhibition ground.

870. Until you are in the habit of putting off things you cannot ensure yourself of a good future.

(1) No error

(2) the habit of putting off things

(3) you cannot ensure yourself of a good future.

(4) Until you are in

871. Let us vie to one another in doing good.

(1) to one another

(2) Let us vie

(3) in doing good.

(4) No error

872. The article suggests that when a person is under unusual stress you should be especially careful to eat a well-balanced diet.

(1) The article suggests that when a person is under unusual stress

(2) you should be especially careful

(3) to eat a well-balanced diet.

(4) No error

873. The results of the survey were fairly disappointing.

(1) of the survey were

(2) The results

(3) fairly disappointing.

(4) No error

874. Some members of the committee were opposed to use the club members' money to redecorate the meeting hall.

(1) the club members' money to redecorate the meeting hall.

(2) No error

(3) Some members of the committee

(4) were opposed to use

875. I forbid you not to go there again.

(1) there again

(2) No error

(3) not to go

(4) I forbid you

876. We received much help from the neighbours.

(1) We received

(2) much help

(3) No error

(4) from the neighbours.

877. He looked upon me eye to eye for a few moments before he spoke.

(1) before he spoke.

(2) No error

(3) eye to eye for a few moments

(4) He looked upon me

878. As per the invitation card Rahim marries with Sayra on 13th December, Monday.

(1) As per the invitation card

(2) No error

(3) on 13th December, Monday.

(4) Rahim marries with Sayra

879. I was convinced that the only thing I wanted to do ever, is to write novels.
(1) I was convinced that
(2) No error
(3) the only thing I wanted to do
(4) ever, is to write novels.

880. This book is different than that.
(1) is different
(2) This book
(3) No error
(4) than that

881. Riches are uncertain things, and the fame that power give or is won by foul means is as shortlived as the dewdrop.
(1) is as shortlived as the dewdrop.
(2) that power give or is won by foul means
(3) Riches are uncertain things, and the fame
(4) No error

882. The doctor asked his patient to regularly take his medicine.
(1) asked his patient
(2) to regularly take his medicine.
(3) No error
(4) The doctor

883. Did you hear many news about the political situation while you were in that country ?
(1) about the political situation while you were in that country ?
(2) many news
(3) Did you hear
(4) No error

884. I meant to repair the radio but hadn't time to do it today.
(1) No error
(2) to do it today.
(3) I meant to repair the radio
(4) but hadn't time

885. The heavy-weight fighter was knocking out in one punch.
(1) The heavy-weight fighter
(2) in one punch.
(3) was knocking out
(4) No error

886. Thanks to an insight and persistence of the local doctor, hundreds of victims have been able to resume normal life.
(1) No error
(2) and persistence of the local doctor,
(3) hundreds of victims have been able to resume normal life.
(4) Thanks to an insight

887. In twenty wrecks five lives were fortunately lost.
(1) In twenty wrecks
(2) five lives were
(3) No error
(4) fortunately lost.

888. Do you think you could lend me good pair of gloves to wear to the wedding ?
(1) Do you think you could lend me
(2) to wear to the wedding ?
(3) good pair of gloves
(4) No error

889. When the workers threatened to go on a strike, the mill owner declared a lay off on his mill.
(1) declared a lay off on his mill.
(2) When the workers threatened to
(3) go on a strike, the mill owner
(4) No error

890. Iodine deficiency is an easy and inexpensive nutrient disorder to prevent.
(1) Iodine deficiency
(2) is an easy and inexpensive
(3) nutrient disorder to prevent
(4) No error

891. Whoever assumes his statement true is foolish
(1) his statement true

(2) No error
(3) Whoever assumes
(4) is foolish

892. The people gathered at the funeral to pay respect.
(1) No error
(2) The people gathered
(3) at the funeral
(4) to pay respect.

893. You must abide on (1)/ the terms of (2)/this government. (3)/ No error (4)

894. Electronic mail or E-mail (1)/ are a method of exchanging (2)/digital messages. (3)/ No error (4)

895. I will have (1)/ both the blue (2)/ or the black pen. (3)/ No error. (4)

896. My wife, having finish her work (1)/ rushed to meet me (2)/ at the event. (3)/ No error. (4)

897. She always fed (1)/ her childrens (2)/ before she fed her dog. (3)/ No error (4)

898. One must (1)/ obey one's (2)/ teachers. (3)/ No error (4)

899. Make what you write (1)/ and say more (2)/ absorbed and engrossing. (3)/ No error (4)

900. They came here in (1)/ the evening and begin making (2)/ further arrangements. (3)/ No error (4)

901. Reena was enough kind to help me with money and proper guidance.
(a) Kind enough
(b) Kindly enough
(c) enough kindly
(d) No improvement

902. The car flew off the road and fell into the valley because Amit was driving fastest.
(a) driving fastly
(b) driving fast
(c) drove fast
(d) No improvement

903. It is difficult to judge which is the older of the two brothers.
(a) old of
(b) older
(c) elder of
(d) No improvement

904. You should avail of every opportunity to practice your skill.
(a) avail yourself of
(b) avail overselves
(c) avail
(d) No improvement

905. A few word of gratitude are enough to express your feelings sincerely.
(a) Few word of
(b) a few words of
(c) the few word
(d) No improvement

906. Sunrise is a great phenomena.
(a) Phenomenon
(b) Phenomenons
(c) Phenomenas
(d) No improvement

907. You would better gone now or you'll be late.
(a) to go
(b) go
(c) going
(d) No improvement

908. We went there with a view to survey the entire procedure.
(a) have been surveyed the entire
(b) surveying the entire
(c) surveying a entire
(d) No improvement

909. One third of the students has passed.
(a) Have passed
(b) Kindly enough
(c) enough kindly
(d) No improvement

910. I made him to do the project against his

wishes.

(a) to be done

(b) to have done

(c) do

(d) No improvement

911. Being a cloudy I decided to go out for a walk.

(a) I Being cloudy

(b) It being a cloudy

(c) These being a cloudy

(d) No improvement

912. The fact that he can't be able to sing is known only to very few people.

(a) is not able to

(b) couldn't be able to

(c) can't be

(d) No improvement

913. The teacher asked them to stop write as soon as the peon long the bell.

(a) to have stopped writing

(b) to stop writing

(c) to stop written

(d) No improvement

914. Sonu would had got this offer if he had attended the interview.

(a) Would have had

(b) Would

(c) Would have

(d) No improvement

915. I have my own house, Don't I?

(a) Hasn't I

(b) Haven't I

(c) Didn't I

(d) No improvement

916. The toddler has a habit of throwing tantrums.

(A) Expressing emotions.

(B) Expressing frustrations.

(C) Expressing happiness.

(D) No improvement.

917. He had his breakfast, when we visited him.

(A) He had taken his breakfast

(B) He wished to have his breakfast

(C) He avoided his breakfast

(D) No improvement

918. Many workers were being held hostages.

(A) held to be hostages

(B) held as hostages

(C) held like hostages

(D) No improvement

919. On one occasion he persuaded me to accompany him on a shooting expedition he was planning.

(A) has planned

(B) had planned

(C) planned

(D) No improvement

920. My opinion of the play is that it will win the national award.

(A) opinion to

(B) opinion about

(C) opinion on

(D) No improvement

921. His powerful desire brought about his downfall.

(A) His intense desire

(B) His desire for power

(C) His fatal desire

(D) No improvement.

922. He speaks not only English but Hindi as well.

(A) as well as

(B) Hindi too

(C) also hind

(D) No improvement

923. The Portsmouth Summer art festival is the only place in New Hampshire where we are fortunately see such diverse tales all in one place.

(A) we are able to fortunately see.

(B) we are fortunate to see
(C) we are fortunate to seeing.
(D) No improvement

924. Anxiety and such other emotions are known to be unhealthy to the body.
(A) Dangerous.
(B) Detrimental
(C) Damaging
(D) No improvement.

925. He asked me if I can help him to lift the box.
(A) will
(B) could
(C) may
(D) No improvement

926. The greatest fear which is scaring of the world today is global warming.
(A) Which had scared of the world.
(B) That scared off the world.
(C) That scares the world
(D) No improvement

927. Every body was alarmed with the news of his murder.
(A) On
(B) after
(C) at
(D) No improvement.

928. His miserable condition made us wept.
(A) made us weep.
(B) Made us to weep.
(C) Made us to wept.
(D) No improvement.

929. The train rolls along the track.
(A) rumbles
(B) rattles
(C) ripples
(D) No improvement.

930. My uncle couldn't rise up from his bed no more.
(A) any farther
(B) any farthest
(C) any more
(D) no improvement

931. What she said is not correct at all.
(A) incorrect
(B) not incorrect
(C) correct
(D) No improvement

932. I don't understand why did you not call me last night.
(A) why had you not call
(B) why you did not call
(C) why not did you call
(D) No improvement

933. The thieves ran away in a black car.
(A) Fled
(B) escaped with
(C) Jumped away
(D) no improvement

934. Because that there were heavy rains the lake was flooded.
(A) Because of the
(B) As there were
(C) There was
(D) No improvement

935. The little boy fell from the roof.
(A) Fell below the roof
(B) Fell down the roof
(C) Fell off the roof
(D) No improvement

936. A thing of beauty is joy forever.
(A) is the joy
(B) Is joyous
(C) Is a joy
(D) No improvement

937. You must to do your homework, mustn't you?
(A) Shouldn't
(B) must
(C) ought

(D) No improvement

938. The air conditioner has made ceiling fans a little redundant in today's world
(A) Superfluous.
(B) Obsolete
(C) Extinct
(D) No improvement

939. The concert will start when the conductor comes.
(A) When the conductor arrives.
(B) When the curtain has been raising.
(C) When the audience will arrive.
(D) No improvement.

940. He absented from the meeting.
(A) was absent.
(B) absented himself.
(C) took absence.
(D) No improvement.

941. Either Kiran or Mala is sure to be chosen for the school debate team.
(1) Either Kiran or Mala are sure to
(2) Either Kiran nor Mala are sure to
(3) Either Kiran or Mala will
(4) No Improvement

942. Tom was standing besides the school-house poster, when the ball rolled towards him.
(1) standing beside the schoolhouse poster
(2) stand besides the school house poster
(3) stood beside the school-house poster
(4) No Improvement

943. No sane person or government can tolerate terrorists of any degree or kind.
(1) terrorism of any degree or kind
(2) terrorise of any degree or kind
(3) torture of any degree or kind
(4) No Improvement

944. Saibal has got an extensive to finish writing his thesis.
(1) an extended
(2) an extention
(3) an extension
(4) No Improvement

945. She stood by him under all conditions and undaunted by anything.
(1) without reserve
(2) without hesitation
(3) through thick and thin
(4) No Improvement

946. Sheela was reprimanded by the school Marshall for coming lately to school.
(1) to school lately
(2) late to school
(3) to school later
(4) No Improvement

947. Kunal looked very manliness in his police uniform.
(1) menliness
(2) man-like
(3) manly
(4) No Improvement

948. The school was very cooperation when we made a documentary film there.
(1) very co-operator
(2) very co-operative
(3) very co-operated
(4) No Improvement

949. "I would like to tell you about this my friend," said John.
(1) this friend of mine
(2) the friend of mine
(3) this friend
(4) No Improvement

950. The boat was drowned.
(1) was sunk
(2) was drown
(3) was sink
(4) No Improvement

951. I contradicted against him.
(1) contradicted over

(2) No improvement
(3) contradicted
(4) contradicted with

952. You must accustom yourself with new ideas.
(1) accustomed yourself with
(2) accustom yourself to
(3) No improvement
(4) get accustom to

953. You should cut off on the amount of cigarettes you smoke.
(1) No improvement
(2) cut up
(3) cut down
(4) cut out

954. No sooner than it stopped raining, the children went out.
(1) did it stopped raining than
(2) No improvement
(3) had it stopped raining than
(4) did it stop raining than

955. Try to lower the amount of fat in your diet.
(1) cut
(2) No improvement
(3) reduce
(4) lose

956. College students went at the rampage in the city yesterday.
(1) with the rampage
(2) No improvement
(3) on a rampage
(4) over the rampage

957. I met the two girls, which I believe, are identical twins.
(1) who I believe are
(2) No Improvement
(3) who to my belief, are
(4) whom I thought, are

958. Helen Kelller's efforts rehabilitate herself despite her triple handicap.
(1) managed
(2) No improvement
(3) readapt
(4) reinstate

959. I would gladly accompany your sister if you had asked me.
(1) will gladly accompany
(2) would have gladly accompanied
(3) would gladly accompanied
(4) No improvement

960. You cannot forbid him leaving.
(1) his leaving
(2) he leaving
(3) him to leave
(4) No improvement

961. It is a normal part of growth and development for a young child to be wary with strangers.
(1) of
(2) from
(3) at
(4) No improvement

962. She told me she has a headache.
(1) had
(2) is having
(3) will have
(4) No improvement

963. Finished my homework, I went out to play.
(1) The work was finished
(2) Homework completed
(3) Having completed my homework
(4) No improvement

964. We waited in six hours.
(1) within
(2) for
(3) during
(4) No improvement

965. It's time they went home.

(1) go
(2) had gone
(3) gone
(4) No improvement

966. Let's go for a walk, do we?
(1) aren't we
(2) shall we
(3) don't we
(4) No Improvement

967. A pair of slippers is cheap nowadays.
(1) slipper is
(2) slippers are
(3) No Improvement
(4) are cheap

968. Lot of water has overflowed the tank.
(1) Lot of waters
(2) A lot of water
(3) A lot of waters
(4) No Improvement

969. The speech he gave was highly informative.
(1) deliver
(2) made
(3) give
(4) No Improvement

970. She is tall as me.
(1) as tall as I am
(2) tall like
(3) tall like me
(4) tall as I am

971. Even though she was disliked by her in-laws at the beginning of her marriage, she did manage to win their hearts.
(1) win over their
(2) win over there
(3) win them over their
(4) No Improvement

972. Many a pilgrim were hurt during the festival
(1) have been
(2) was
(3) have
(4) No Improvement

973. My uncle and mentor are helping me.
(1) mentor is
(2) mentors have
(3) mentors were
(4) No Improvement

974. You can't avoid notifying the building while travelling.
(1) avoid to look
(2) avoid to noticing
(3) avoid noticing
(4) No Improvement

975. I am taking a book with me so that I'll have something to read on the train.
(1) I will be something to read
(2) I'll have something
(3) I have read
(4) No Improvement

976. Twenty kilometres are a good distance.
(1) were
(2) are
(3) is
(4) No Improvement

977. Rosa's hatred to work under the landlord resulted in animosity.
(1) disgust
(2) distaste
(3) resentment
(4) annoyance

978. The celebration was abandoned due to heavy rains.
(1) adjourned
(2) postponed
(3) inoperative
(4) No improvement

979. It is a myth that drinking within limits helps to improves the health.
(1) No improvement

(2) help improves
(3) helps improving
(4) helps improve

980. Her new shoes ensure her that she does not fall while running.
(1) ensures to her that
(2) ensures her that
(3) ensure that
(4) No improvement

981. As much as I tried to reduce my weight, I ended up nowhere.
(1) ended up to somewhere
(2) ended in less weight
(3) ended in lesser weight
(4) No improvement

982. Will you lend me few rupees in this hour of need ?
(1) lend me any rupees
(2) lend me a few rupees
(3) borrow me a few rupees
(4) No improvement

983. The car with a burst tyre halted swiftly.
(1) stopped fastly
(2) jolted to a halt
(3) stopped quick
(4) No improvement

984. Many incidents of the last month seem unimportant when viewed in perception.
(1) perceptive
(2) perspective
(3) prospective
(4) No improvement

985. The youths jostled their way in the crowd.
(1) through
(2) among
(3) over
(4) No improvement

986. What is wrong with the argument is that even if the two premises are true, then the conclusion isn't necessarily true.
(1) the conclusion is false
(2) the conclusions aren't necessarily true
(3) the conclusion will be true
(4) No improvement

987. He is entitled to a reward for honesty.
(1) entitle to
(2) entitled
(3) titled
(4) No improvement

988. The sight chosen for the school building is good.
(1) eye-sight
(2) side
(3) site
(4) No improvement

989. The matter must be considered in every point of view.
(1) at every
(2) on every
(3) from every
(4) No improvement

990. The poor villagers have waited in the bitter cold for more than two hours now.
(1) had waited
(2) have been waiting
(3) has been waiting
(4) No improvement

991. You must accustom yourself with new ideas.
(1) accustom to
(2) accustom yourself to
(3) accustomed with
(4) No improvement

992. Each self is unique, and therefore cannot be compared.
(1) incomparable
(2) non-comparable
(3) incomparably
(4) No improvement

993. Shall I sit between you at the concert?
(1) beside
(2) besides
(3) next
(4) No improvement

994. No one other reason than poverty is hampering India's progress.
(1) No other
(2) None other
(3) No another
(4) No improvement

995. The custom has took root in the society.
(1) taken root
(2) take root
(3) takes root
(4) No improvement

996. We will take care of your children when you are away at Mumbai.
(1) be looking for
(2) look after
(3) take care after
(4) No improvement

997. She cut a sad figure in her first performance on the stage.
(1) made a sorry figure
(2) cut a sorry face
(3) cut a sorry figure
(4) No improvement

998. You must complete this work up to Sunday.
(1) within Sunday
(2) by Sunday
(3) on to Sunday
(4) No improvement

999. Hole wheat bread is good for health.
(1) Whole
(2) Healthy
(3) Holed
(4) No improvement

1000. She has no pen to write.
(1) write with
(2) write at
(3) write in
(4) No improvement

SECTION–D
Mock Test

Mock Test 01

Direction (1–3). In the following questions, some part of the sentence may have errors. Find out which part of the sentence has an error and select the appropriate option. If a sentence is free from error, select 'No Error'.

Q1. Another change that (a) / I notice in her is that she (b) / avoids to speak to me. (c) / No error (d)

Q2. There is renewed sense (a) / of urgency in (b) / completing the project. (c) / No error (d)

Q3. Each boy was given (a) / a toy as a parting gift, (b) / which made them happy. (c) / No error (d)

Direction (4–5). In the following questions, the sentence given with a blank to be filled in with an appropriate word. Select the correct alternative out of the four and indicate it by selecting the appropriate option.

Q4. They wanted to know______ they should start the game.

(A) If
(B) that
(C) whether
(D) and

Q5. A Bad workman always __________with his tools.

(A) Quarrels
(B) fights
(C) works
(D) ignores

Direction (6–7). In the following questions, out of the given four alternatives, select the one which best expresses the meaning of the given word.

Q6. Stumpy

(a) rangy
(b) pudgy
(c) lanky
(d) lofty

Q7. Sheath

(a) weapon
(b) hide
(c) encourage
(d) coat

Direction (8–9). In the following questions, out of the given four alternatives, select the one which is opposite in meaning to the given word.

Q8. Ostentatious

a. Nescient
b. Awkward
c. Bankrupt
d. Reserved

Q9. Opprobrious

a. Respectful
b. Miscible
c. Inspiring
d. Imitable

Direction (10). Rearrange the parts of the sentence in correct order.

Q10. (1) The method used

(P) is no longer
(Q) to calculate RPI
(R) practice so it has had its national
(S) considered as best
(6) statistic status removed.

(a) QPSR
(b) RSPQ
(c) SPQR
(d) RPQS

Direction (11). A sentence has been given in Active/Passive Voice.

Out of the four given alternatives, select the one which best expresses the same sentence in Passive/Active

Q11. Why is time wasted by you?

(A) Why does you waste time

(B) Why did you waste time?

(C) Why do you waste time?

(D) Why have you wasted time?

Direction (12). A sentence has been given in Direct/Indirect Speech. Out of the of the four given alternatives, select the one which best expresses the same sentence in Indirect/Direct Speech.

Q12. They said to their teacher, "Shyam will leave for the show tomorrow."

(a) They told their teacher that Shyam would left for the show tomorrow.

(b) They told their teacher that Shyam will leave for the show the following day.

(c) They told their teacher that Shyam would leave for the show the following day.

(d) They told to their teacher that Shyam would leave for the show the following day.

Direction (13-14). In the following question, a word has been written in four different ways out of which only one is correctly spelt. Select the correctly spelt word.

Q13. a) CASTIGATEA

b) CASTIGATTE

c) CASTIGATE

d) CASTIGGATE

Q14. a) COERCE

b) COERRCE

c) COEERCE

d) COAERCE

Direction (15–16). In the following question, out of the four alternatives, select the alternative which best expresses the meaning of the idiom/ phrase.

Q15. I cannot understand why she did that, it really doesn't add up.

(a) doesn't calculate

(c) doesn't make sense

(b) isn't mathematics

(d) makes the wrong addition

Q16. All the students got high marks in the test but Mary stood out.

(a) got a lot of marks

(c) got very good marks

(b) got higher marks than someone

(d) got the most marks of all

Direction (17–18). In the following question, out of the four alternatives, select the alternative which is the best substitute of the words/sentences.

Q17. A person who talks in sleep is called as

a. Philatelist

b. Somnambulist

c. Somniloquist

d. Oneirocritic

Q18. The person who knows everything

a. Omnipresent

b. Omnipotent

c. Omniscient

d. Oblivious

Direction (19–20). In the following question, out of the four alternatives, select the alternative which will improve the bold part of the sentence. In case no improvement is needed, select "no improvement".

Q19. One should not tell lies to his friends.

(a) lie to one's friends

(b) lies to one's friends

(c) lie to his friends

(d) No improvement

Q20. Coins were made of an alloy half a gold and half a copper.

(a) half gold and half a copper

(b) half a gold and half copper

(c) half gold and half copper

(d) No improvement

Mock Test 02

Direction (1–3). In the following questions, some part of the sentence may have errors. Find out which part of the sentence has an error and select the appropriate option. If a sentence is free from error, select 'No Error'.

Q1. No sooner had the boss arrive (A)/ than their employees conducted a seminar (B)/in his honour in the middle of the working hours.(C)/ no error.(D)

Q2. The institutions for medical Science (A)/ are more expensive than the institutions (B)/ for engineering in India. (C)/ No error.(D)

Q3. You will not increase your (A)/ vocabulary unless you started (B)/reading newspaper regularly. (C)/No error.(D)

Direction (4–5). In the following questions, the sentence given with a blank to be filled in with an appropriate word. Select the correct alternative out of the four and indicate it by selecting the appropriate option.

Q4. The teacher fed up ______the behaviour of the students

(A) At

(B) on

(C) upon

(D) with

Q5. No sooner had the show begun______ the electricity started fluctuating.

(A) Then

(B) than

(C) when

(D) before

Direction (6–7). In the following questions, out of the given four alternatives, select the one which best expresses the meaning of the given word.

Q6. Paramount

(1) Superior

(2) Prevalent

(3) Influential

(4) Prime

Q7. Restrictive

(1) Alike

(2) Guarded

(3) Hostile

(4) Prohibitive

Direction (8–9). In the following questions, out of the given four alternatives, select the one which is opposite in meaning to the given word.

Q8. GUMPTION

A. Apathy

B. Nerve

C. Initiative

D. Sagacity

Q9. PIQUE

A. Hurt

B. Irk

C. Joy

D. Huff

Direction (10). Rearrange the parts of the sentence in correct order.

Q10. 1. One single bomb

P. had killed as many, wounded as many,

Q. laden to capacity with bombs,

R. striking at a city ten times

S. as a mass raid of 279 huge aircrafts

6. as populous.

(A) PRSQ

(B) PSRQ

(C) PSQR

(D) PQRS

Direction (11). A sentence has been given in Active/Passive Voice. Out of the four given alternatives, select the one which best expresses the same sentence in Passive/Active

Q11. These children are not being involved in this case.

(a) They are being involved in this case.

(b) These children are involving in this case.

(c) They are involving these children in this case.

(d) These children are involved in this case.

Direction (12). A sentence has been given in Direct/Indirect Speech. Out of the of the four given alternatives, select the one which best expresses the same sentence in Indirect/Direct Speech.

Q12. Has anyone from our team answered your question?

(a) Did someone from our team answer to your question?

(b) Is your question been answered by someone from our team?

(c) Has your question been answered by anyone from our team?

(d) have your question been answered by anyone from our team?

Direction (13-14). In the following question, a word has been written in four different ways out of which only one is correctly spelt. Select the correctly spelt word.

Q13. a) DETEROIRATE

b) DETERIORATA

c) DETERIORETE

d) DETERIORATE

Q14. a) UNFLAPPABLE

b) UNFLAPPABBLE

c) UNFLAPPABLLE

d) UNFLAPABLE

Direction (15–16). In the following question, out of the four alternatives, select the alternative which best expresses the meaning of the idiom/ phrase.

Q15. His voice is like a bear with a sore head for me.

a) very interesting

b) very irritable

c) very annoying

d) very pleasing

Q16. You should have given me a bell.

a) asked me

b) supported me

c) telephoned me

d) knocked me

Direction (17–18). In the following question, out of the four alternatives, select the alternative which is the best substitute of the words/sentences.

Q17. One who despises persons of lower social position.

(A) Prim

(B) Snob

(C) Prig

(D) Aristocrat

Q18. Something which is not tough or profound.

(A) Superficial

(B) Supernatural

(C) Superfluous

(D) Superstitious

Direction (19–20). In the following question, out of the four alternatives, select the alternative which will improve the bold part of the sentence. In case no improvement is needed, select "no improvement".

Q19. The principal asked Shivam and me where our teacher was.

(a) me and Shivam

(b) Shivam or I

(c) Shivam with I

(d) No improvement

Q20. The price of everything is raising fast.

(a) are raising fast

(b) is rising fast

(c) is raising fastly

(d) No improvement

Mock test 03

Direction (1–3). In the following questions, some part of the sentence may have errors. Find out which part of the sentence has an error and select the appropriate option. If a sentence is free from error, select 'No Error'.

Q1. They will (A)/ leave the office at six and (B)/ reach at home by seven. (C)/ No erro r (D)

Q2. The new lectu rer (A)/ seems to be very popular with (B)/ most of the class. (C)/ No erro r (D)

Q3. The museum's revolving doo rs (A)/ stopped the crooks (B)/ as they jam half way round. (C)/ No error (D)

Direction (4–5). In the following questions, the sentence given with a blank to be filled in with an appropriate word. Select the correct alternative out of the four and indicate it by selecting the appropriate option.

Q4. The gate _______ by the watchman on duty. Options.

A. opened

B. was opened

C. were opened

D. was Opening

Q5. The king was _______ while he was add ressing his subjects.

A. murdered

B. executed

C. assassinated

D. exterminated

Direction (6–7). In the following questions, out of the given four alternatives, select the one which best expresses the meaning of the given word.

Q6. Apposite

A. kind

B. favourable

C. eloquent

D. appropriate

Q7. Pragmatic

1) theoretical

2) realistic

3) perfect

4) simple

Direction (8–9). In the following questions, out of the given four alternatives, select the one which is opposite in meaning to the given word.

Q8. Generous

A. stoic

B. stingy

C. poor

D. specific

Q9. Barren

A. oily

B. polished

C. sorrowful

D. fertile

Direction (10). Rearrange the parts of the sentence in correct order.

Q10. 1. The king was distressed because his people were lazy.

P. All cursed the stone and blamed the Government.

Q. Then the king had the stone removed.

R. Next day people passed by and went round it.

S. He had a big stone put in the middle of the road one night.

6. Under the stone the king had placed a purse full of money.

1. PSRQ
2. SRPQ
3. QPRS
4. PQRS

Direction (11). A sentence has been given in Active/Passive Voice. Out of the four given alternatives, select the one which best expresses the same sentence in Passive/Active

Q11. Had she worked hard she would have won the gold medal.

A. The gold medal will have been won by her had she worked hard.

B. The gold medal would have been won by her had she worked hard.

C. The gold medal would have been won by her if she worked hard.

D. The gold medal will have been won by her if she worked hard.

Direction (12). A sentence has been given in Direct/Indirect Speech. Out of the of the four given alternatives, select the one which best expresses the same sentence in Indirect/Direct Speech.

Q12. The boss said to him," Please tell me what the old man said today."

A. The boss requested him to tell him what the old man had said that day.

B. The boss requested him to tell him what the old man had said today.

C. The boss requested him to tell him what the old man said that day.

D. The boss requested him to tell him what the old man said today.

Direction (13-14). In the following question, a word has been written in four different ways out of which only one is correctly spelt. Select the correctly spelt word.

Q13. 1) Liaison 2) Laiseon 3) Laision 4) Liesion

Q14. 1) Supernumarary 2) Supernumerary 3) Supernumarery 4) Supernumarey

Direction (15–16). In the following question, out of the four alternatives, select the alternative which best expresses the meaning of the idiom/ phrase.

Q15. From stem to stern

A. all the way from the front of a ship to the back.

B. from the beginning to the end.

C. top of a plant to its roots.

D. loose pleasantness to become strict

Q16. Over egg the pudding

A. add unnecessary details to make something seem better or worse.

B. fill the pudding excessively with egg.

C. add details in order to make something more exciting.

D. add important details to the content of a story.

Direction (17–18). In the following question, out of the four alternatives, select the alternative which is the best substitute of the words/sentences.

Q17. A state where there is no effective government.

1. Secular
2. Democracy
3. Governance
4. Anarchy

Q18. A person who opposes war or use of military force.

1. Narcissist
2. Fatalist
3. Pacifist
4. Fascist

Direction (19–20). In the following question, out of the four alternatives, select the alternative which will improve the bold part of the sentence. In case no improvement is needed, select "no improvement".

Q19. Twelve wo rkers were killed in the conflict between two trade unions.

1. quarrel
2. clash
3. confrontation
4. No improvement

Q20. The match was so very ordinary after all the hype generated by the fans.

1. very ordinary
2. nothing to write home about
3. so ordinary
4. No improvement

Mock Test 04

Direction (1–3). In the following questions, some part of the sentence may have errors. Find out which part of the sentence has an error and select the appropriate option. If a sentence is free from error, select 'No Error'.

Q1. The landlord made the boys (1)/ to do the garden (2)/ make over all over again. (3)/ No error (4).

Q2. My parents asked me (1)/ that how long (2)/ I would stay there. (3)/ No error (4).

Q3. As a chef (1)/ Kajal is as good (2)/, if not better than Mahender. (3)/ No error (4).

Direction (4–5). In the following questions, the sentence given with a blank to be filled in with an appropriate word. Select the correct alternative out of the four and indicate it by selecting the appropriate option.

Q4. I ______ the Andaman and Nicobar Islands yet. I have visited several places in India, but

Correction — **Q4.** I have visited several places in India, but I ______ the Andaman and Nicobar Islands yet.

A. haven't been visiting
B. didn't visit
C. haven't visited
D. don't visit

Q5. The rescue team dug out a soldier from the snow ______ how he could have survived for seven days buried under it.

A. wondering
B. wondered
C. to wonder
D. wonder

Direction (6–7). In the following questions, out of the given four alternatives, select the one which best expresses the meaning of the given word.

Q6. EVIDENCE

A. indication
B. refutation
C. denial
D. concealment

Q7. PERSIST

A. continue
B. cease
C. halt
D. forget

Direction (8–9). In the following questions, out of the given four alternatives, select the one which is opposite in meaning to the given word.

Q8. ALLURING

A. interesting
B. charming
C. repulsive
D. glamorous

Q9. TURBULENT

A. raging
B. peaceful
C. forceful
D. swirling

Direction (10). Rearrange the parts of the sentence in correct order.

Q10. A. She was a tall woman and she carried a large purse.

B. Suddenly a boy ran up behind her and tried to snatch her purse.

C. It was 11 o'clock at night and a woman was walking alone.

D. It had a long strap, and she carried it slung across her shoulder.

A. CADB
B. DCBA
C. ACDB
D. DBCA

Direction (11). A sentence has been given in Active/Passive Voice. Out of the four given alternatives, select the one which best expresses the same sentence in Passive/Active

Q11. The authorities are planning to lift restrictions on the movement of people in the Valley from the coming week.

A. It has been planned to lift restrictions on the movement of people in the Valley from the coming week.

B. Restrictions on the movement

of people in the Valley from the coming week are planning to lift the authorities in the Valley.

C. It is being planned by the authorities to lift restrictions on the movement of people in the Valley from the coming week.

D. Lifting restrictions on the movement of people in the Valley is planned from the coming week.

Direction (12). A sentence has been given in Direct/Indirect Speech. Out of the of the four given alternatives, select the one which best expresses the same sentence in Indirect/Direct Speech.

Q12. Mother said to Kavya, "Turn on the light."

A. Mother told Kavya to turn on the light.

B. Mother asked Kavya if the light was on.

C. Kavya told mother to turn on the light.

D. Mother requested Kavya to please on the light.

Direction (13-14). In the following question, a word has been written in four different ways out of which only one is correctly spelt. Select the correctly spelt word.

Q13. A. Adventitious

B. Adventitous

C. Adventitus

D. Adventituous

Q14. A. Adverisity

B. Advercety

C. Adversity

D. Advercity

Direction (15–16). In the following question, out of the four alternatives, select the alternative which best expresses the meaning of the idiom/ phrase.

Q15. When Anshul told everyone that he had resigned his job, all the members in the family were at their wits' end.

A. very serious

B. quite angry

C. quite perplexed

D. absolutely satisfied

Q16. full of beans

A. being upset

B. lively and energetic

C. full of crazy ideas

D. in good health

Direction (17–18). In the following question, out of the four alternatives, select the alternative which is the best substitute of the words/sentences.

Q17. A dome-shaped shelter built from blocks of solid snow used by Eskimos

A wigwam

B yurt

C tepee

D igloo

Q18. The Science which studies the crust of the earth

A zoology

B etymology

C biology

D geology

Direction (19–20). In the following question, out of the four alternatives, select the alternative which will improve the bold part of the sentence. In case no improvement is needed, select "no improvement".

Q19. He was surprised at me refusing to accept his offer.

A. No improvement

B. at me to refusing

C. at my refusing

D. on me refusing

Q20. For most people a six figure salary was unimaginable two decades ago.

A. For most of people

B. To much people

C. For a many people

D. No improvement

Mock Test 05

Direction (1–3). In the following questions, some part of the sentence may have errors. Find out which part of the sentence has an error and select the appropriate option. If a sentence is free from error, select 'No Error'.

Q1. Although he was late (1)/ but he stopped on the way(2)/ to have coffee with his friends. (3) / No error. (4)

Q2. She was taking care of her baby for two hours (1)/ before she (2)/ was called by her mother. (3)/ No error. (4)

Q3. No sooner did he see his teacher (1)/ when he (2)/ stopped copying. (3)/ No error(4).

Direction (4–5). In the following questions, the sentence given with a blank to be filled in with an appropriate word. Select the correct alternative out of the four and indicate it by selecting the appropriate option.

Q4. He ______ a heinous crime.

A. happened
B. committed
C. made
D. occurred

Q5. It is an ______ day to start your new business.

A. audacious
B. ominous
C. auspicious
D. occasional

Direction (6–7). In the following questions, out of the given four alternatives, select the one which best expresses the meaning of the given word.

Q6. PENITENCE

A. Patience
B. Repentance
C. Misery
D. Admiration

Q7. PATHETIC

A. Pitiful
B. Dull
C. Insignificant
D. Curious

Direction (8–9). In the following questions, out of the given four alternatives, select the one which is opposite in meaning to the given word.

Q8. VICIOUS

A. Baneful
B. Unfortunate
C. Virtuous
D. Sinful

Q9. HILARIOUS

A. Blithe
B. Merry
C. Sad
D. Happy

Direction (10). Rearrange the parts of the sentence in correct order.

Q10. A. Nevertheless, sound health, economic security and mental satisfaction are desired by all

B. A change that is conducive to happiness may be termed as progress.

C. But different people find happiness in different things.

D. So, If a change contributes to the growth of these factors, it is progress.

A. BDCA
B. ABCD
C. BCAD
D. DBCA

Direction (11). A sentence has been given in Active/Passive Voice. Out of the four given alternatives, select the one which best expresses the same sentence in Passive/Active

Q11. The thief was being arrested by the police.

A. The police has arrested the thief
B. The police arrested the thief.

C. The police had arrested the thief.

D. The police was arresting the thief.

Direction (12). A sentence has been given in Direct/Indirect Speech. Out of the of the four given alternatives, select the one which best expresses the same sentence in Indirect/Direct Speech.

Q12. He said to me, "What are you doing?"

A He said what I had been doing.

B He said that what I was doing

C He asked me what I was doing

D He asked me that what was I doing

Direction (13-14). In the following question, a word has been written in four different ways out of which only one is correctly spelt. Select the correctly spelt word.

Q13. A. Amatuer

B. Amature

C. Amateur

D. Ameteur

Q14. A. Benefited

B. Benefitted

C. Benifitted

D. Benifited

Direction (15–16). In the following question, out of the four alternatives, select the alternative which best expresses the meaning of the idiom/ phrase.

Q15. On shank's mare

A. On an elephant

B. On a lion

C. On a bicycle

D. On foot

Q16. A hard nut to crack

A. Not restrained

B. Easily encouraged

C. Easily disappointed

D. A difficult problem

Direction (17–18). In the following question, out of the four alternatives, select the alternative which is the best substitute of the words/sentences.

Q17. A period of ten years

A. Fortnight

B. Millennium

C. Decade

D. Century

Q18. One who leaves his own country to settle in another

A. Foreigner

B. Emigrant

C. Tourist

D. Native

Direction (19–20). In the following question, out of the four alternatives, select the alternative which will improve the bold part of the sentence. In case no improvement is needed, select "no improvement".

Q19. A man in need pleaded for help.

A. promised for help

B. commanded to help

C. No improvement

D. requested for helping

Q20. There is a great degrade in values in modern age.

A. degradation of values

B. deliberation for values

C. demonstration from values

D. No improvement

Mock Test 06

Direction (1–3). In the following questions, some part of the sentence may have errors. Find out which part of the sentence has an error and select the appropriate option. If a sentence is free from error, select 'No Error'.

Q1. He met me two days ago (1)/ but he never told me (2)/ about his grandmother's death. (3)/ No error (4).

Q2. She ran so fastly (1)/ that she was able to catch (2)/ the running bus (3)/ No error. (4)

Q3. Had you been to Mumbai, (1)/ I would also go (2)/ with you (3)/ No error(4).

Direction (4–5). In the following questions, the sentence given with a blank to be filled in with an appropriate word. Select the correct alternative out of the four and indicate it by selecting the appropriate option.

Q4. Drugs worth Rs 10 lakhs were_________ from the MP's apartment by the police.

A. manufactured
B. bought
C. confiscated
D. ruptured

Q5. The linguistic ___ of refugee children is reflected in their readiness to adopt.

A. conservatism
B. adaptability
C. inadequacy
D. structure

Direction (6–7). In the following questions, out of the given four alternatives, select the one which best expresses the meaning of the given word.

Q6. Windiness

A. Brevity
B. Proposition
C. Agreement
D. Prolixity

Q7. Despicable

A. Contemptible
B. Faithless
C. Desperate
D. Undesirable

Direction (8–9). In the following questions, out of the given four alternatives, select the one which is opposite in meaning to the given word.

Q8. Susceptible

A. Incredible
B. Predictable
C. Immune
D. Unpredictable

Q9. Luscious

A. Fickle
B. Insipid
C. Deteriorating
D. Languid

Direction (10). Rearrange the parts of the sentence in correct order.

Q10. This too, is a classic

P. "stock versus flow" problem, where
Q. focusing only on the latter
R. completely distorts the picture

(a) QRP
(b) RPQ
(c) PRQ
(d) PQR

Direction (11). A sentence has been given in Active/Passive Voice. Out of the four given alternatives, select the one which best expresses the same sentence in Passive/Active

Q11. He is writing the book.

(a) The book has been written by him.
(b) The book is being written by him.
(c) The book is written by him.
(d) The book was written by him.

Direction (12). A sentence has been given in Direct/Indirect Speech. Out of the of the four given alternatives, select the one which best expresses the same sentence in Indirect/Direct Speech.

Q12. Jyoti said to her sister, "The RBI is India's central bank".

(a) Jyoti told her sister the RBI was India's central bank.

(b) Jyoti told her sister that the RBI was India's central bank.

(c) Jyoti told her sister that the RBI is India's central bank.

(d) Jyoti told her sister the RBI is India's central bank.

Direction (13-14). In the following question, a word has been written in four different ways out of which only one is correctly spelt. Select the correctly spelt word.

Q13. A) Coersion

B) Coiercion

C) Coerssion

D) Coercion

Q14.

A. Affedevit

B. Afidevit

C. Affidevit

D. Affidavit

Direction (15–16). In the following question, out of the four alternatives, select the alternative which best expresses the meaning of the idiom/ phrase.

Q15. 'I take thee at thy word', said Romeo to Juliet.

A) listen to you carefully

B) do not believe you

C) feel angry with you

D) truly believe you

Q16. The village headman pretends to be a good Samaritan.

A) a religious person

B) a helpful person

C) a citizen of samaria

D) a law-abiding citizen

Direction (17–18). In the following question, out of the four alternatives, select the alternative which is the best substitute of the words/sentences.

Q17. One who abstains from alcoholic drink.

A) Drunkard

B) Idiot

C) Philosopher

D) Teetotaler

Q18. A specialist who tests eyesight.

A) Optician

B) Neurologist

C) Ophthalmologist

D) Psychiatrist

Direction (19–20). In the following question, out of the four alternatives, select the alternative which will improve the bold part of the sentence. In case no improvement is needed, select "no improvement".

Q19. Listen attention to what I say.

A) attentively

B) attend

C) attentive

D) No improvement

Q20. She has returned my jewellery box yesterday.

A) had returned

B) have had returned

C) has had returned

D) returned

Mock Test 07

Direction (1–3). In the following questions, some part of the sentence may have errors. Find out which part of the sentence has an error and select the appropriate option. If a sentence is free from error, select 'No Error'.

Q1. Our history can be seen as a long evolutionary dialectical development (a)/ in which there have been (b)/ a painstaking forging of rational and moral self (c)/. No error (d)

Q2. Our knowledge of history does not come to (a)/ our help and some times we even fail to (b)/ remember who invented America (c)/ No error (d)

Q3. Indian scientists are in no way (a)/ inferior than (b)/ any other scientist in the world (c)/. No error (d)

Direction (4–5). In the following questions, the sentence given with a blank to be filled in with an appropriate word. Select the correct alternative out of the four and indicate it by selecting the appropriate option.

Q4. We didn't _____the programme to be such a huge success.

A. except
B. expect
C. access
D. accept

Q5. We should_____ opportunities as they arise.

A. cease
B. size
C. sneeze
D. seize

Direction (6–7). In the following questions, out of the given four alternatives, select the one which best expresses the meaning of the given word.

Q6. Duplicity

A. artlessness
B. deceit
C. cleverness
D. repetition

Q7. Fidelity

A. resourcefulness
B. strength
C. weakness
D. faithfulness

Direction (8–9). In the following questions, out of the given four alternatives, select the one which is opposite in meaning to the given word.

Q8. Amicable

A friendly
B haughty
C unpleasant
D hostile

Q9. Aversion

A awareness
B hatred
C liking
D avoidance

Direction (10). Rearrange the parts of the sentence in correct order.

Q10. 1. Porcelain became popular at the beginning of the 19th century.

P. In a kin at more than 2372 degree Fahrenheit
Q. Refer to both China and Bisque dolls
R. porcelain is made by firing special clays.
S. porcelain is used generally, to
6. only a few type of clays can withstand such high temperatures

P SQR
Q RSP
P RQS
S QRP

Direction (11). A sentence has been given in Active/Passive Voice. Out of the four given alternatives, select the one which best expresses the same sentence in Passive/Active

Q11. They objected to my proposal.

(a) My proposal was objected by them.

(b) My proposal was objected to by them.

(c) My proposal was objected.

(d) My proposal was to be objected by them.

Direction (12). A sentence has been given in Direct/Indirect Speech. Out of the of the four given alternatives, select the one which best expresses the same sentence in Indirect/Direct Speech.

Q12. Sheela said to me, "Munni is dancing better than me."

A. Sheela told me that Munni have been dancing better than her.

B. Sheela told me that Munni was dancing better than her.

C. Sheela told me that Munni had been dancing better than her.

D. Sheela told me that Munni had dancing better than her.

Direction (13-14). In the following question, a word has been written in four different ways out of which only one is correctly spelt. Select the correctly spelt word.

Q13. A. internaly

B. coldly

C. fortunetely

D. uniquely

Q14. A. affectionately

B. afectionately

C. affectionnality

D. affectionately

Direction (15–16). In the following question, out of the four alternatives, select the alternative which best expresses the meaning of the idiom/ phrase.

Q15. He was out of spirits for a few days after his defeat.

A. gloomy

B. sober

C. lifeless

D. uninvolved

Q16. When the family in the next house packed off at midnight, I began to smell a rat.

A. to suspect a trick

B. to misunderstand

C. to see hidden meaning

D. to smell a bad smell

Direction (17–18). In the following question, out of the four alternatives, select the alternative which is the best substitute of the words/sentences.

Q17. Government by a small group of all powerful persons

A. monarchy

B. democracy

C. anarchy

D. oligarchy

Q18. Open to injury or criticism

A. vulnerable

B. naive

C. sensitive

D. invincible

Direction (19–20). In the following question, out of the four alternatives, select the alternative which will improve the bold part of the sentence. In case no improvement is needed, select "no improvement".

Q19. The prolific writer's work is published every year.

A. exquisite

B. didactic

C. great

D. No improvement

Q20. His lust for power brought about his downfall.

A. intense desire

B. desire for power

C. desire for sex

D. No improvement

Mock Test 08

Direction (1–3). In the following questions, some part of the sentence may have errors. Find out which part of the sentence has an error and select the appropriate option. If a sentence is free from error, select 'No Error'.

Q1. The new dish (a)/ that I ordered (b)/ is tasting good.(c)/ No error. (d)

Q2. I have got your letter yesterday (a)/ and felt happy to learn (b)/ of your recovery. (c)/ No error. (d)

Q3. Sam is working (a)/ in a bank in Chennai (b) / for the past five years. (c)/ No error. (d)

Direction (4–5). In the following questions, the sentence given with a blank to be filled in with an appropriate word. Select the correct alternative out of the four and indicate it by selecting the appropriate option.

Q4. His words were hardly .... with that screaming and shouting in the market.

A. legible
B. eligible
C. intelligible
D. None of these

Q5. He was............ angry to speak to me.

A. so
B. too
C. that
D. such

Direction (6–7). In the following questions, out of the given four alternatives, select the one which best expresses the meaning of the given word.

Q6. repeated

A. disputed
B. elaborated
C. explained
D. reiterated

Q7. revere

A. condemn
B. reverse
C. humiliate
D. respect

Direction (8–9). In the following questions, out of the given four alternatives, select the one which is opposite in meaning to the given word.

Q8. grating

A. musical
B. unmusical
C. hoarse
D. strident

Q9. capricious

A. fanciful
B. reasonable
C. intolerant
D. indifferent

Direction (10). Rearrange the parts of the sentence in correct order.

Q10.

P. requires a much
Q. bigger budget
R. of European forests

(a) PRQ
(b) QRP
(c) RPQ
(d) RQP

Direction (11). A sentence has been given in Active/Passive Voice. Out of the four given alternatives, select the one which best expresses the same sentence in Passive/Active

Q11. The dog killed the cat.

(a) The cat is killed by the dog.
(b) The cat got kill by the dog.
(c) The dog was responsible for killing the cat.
(d) The cat was killed by the dog.

Direction (12). A sentence has been given in Direct/Indirect Speech. Out of the of the four given alternatives, select the one which best expresses the same sentence in Indirect/Direct Speech.

Q12. Priyanka said to me, "I don't trust you".

(a) Priyanka said she don't trust me.

(b) Priyanka didn't trust me.

(c) Priyanka told me that she didn't trust me.

(d) Priyanka told me that she doesn't trust me.

Direction (13-14). In the following question, a word has been written in four different ways out of which only one is correctly spelt. Select the correctly spelt word.

Q13. A. campagnes

B. campaignes

C. campaines

D. campaigns

Q14. A. rhythim

B. rhithm

C. rhythm

D. rhithym

Direction (15–16). In the following question, out of the four alternatives, select the alternative which best expresses the meaning of the idiom/ phrase.

Q15. The issues were settled in court, but after a few days it was back to square one.

A. to return to the starting point

B. to run to the first square

C. to start and return

D. to come to a stop

Q16. Politicians enjoy blowing their own trumpets.

A. to boast about their achievements

B. to use one's own trumpet

C. to blow their trumpet loudly

D. to praise others trumpeting

Direction (17–18). In the following question, out of the four alternatives, select the alternative which is the best substitute of the words/sentences.

Q17. Science of human mind and behaviour

A. Physiology

B. Psychology

C. Sociology

D. Philology

Q18. A set of three related works by the same author

A. Topology

B. Trilogy

C. Trichology

D. Ecology

Direction (19–20). In the following question, out of the four alternatives, select the alternative which will improve the bold part of the sentence. In case no improvement is needed, select "no improvement".

Q19. When we bought the house, we could tell that it was a large, new, compact, tinted house.

A. it was a new, large and compact house

B. It was as new, large and as tinted

C. it was a new, large, compact and bright house

D. No improvement

Q20. Migrant workers can be seen working on many of the building places in New Delhi.

A. sites

B. premises

C. locations

D. No improvement

Mock Test 09

Direction (1–3). In the following questions, some part of the sentence may have errors. Find out which part of the sentence has an error and select the appropriate option. If a sentence is free from error, select 'No Error'.

Q1. The first portion 1)/ of the book was dull, 2)/ the later part 3)/ was interesting. 4)/ No error 5)

Q2. Several prominent celebrities (1) / involved in the scandal (2) / are required to appear (3) / to the investigation committee.(4) / No Error (5)

Q3. Although the pain (1) / was behind (2) / his capacity (3) / yet he didn't complain. (4) / No Error (5)

Direction (4–5). In the following questions, the sentence given with a blank to be filled in with an appropriate word. Select the correct alternative out of the four and indicate it by selecting the appropriate option.

Q4. He is very good .... writing quality content.

(A) in
(B) at
(C) on
(D) about

Q5. A large sign near the gate warns the visitors to beware .... Dogs.

(A) about
(B) from
(C) of
(D) with

Direction (6–7). In the following questions, out of the given four alternatives, select the one which best expresses the meaning of the given word.

Q6. CONTRIVE

(a) Demolish
(b) Dissent
(c) Devise
(d) Imprudent

Q7. HEED

(a) Conceal
(b) Attention
(c) Partial
(d) Credible

Direction (8–9). In the following questions, out of the given four alternatives, select the one which is opposite in meaning to the given word.

Q8. OSTRACISE

A. Amuse
B. Welcome
C. Entertain
D. Host

Q9. INTREPID

A. Ambitious
B. Determined
C. Talkative
D. Fearless

Direction (10). Rearrange the parts of the sentence in correct order.

Q10. As for the tasks

P. three important ones
Q. ahead, there appear
R. to be at least

(a) RQP
(b) QRP
(c) PRQ
(d) PQR

Direction (11). A sentence has been given in Active/Passive Voice. Out of the four given alternatives, select the one which best expresses the same sentence in Passive/Active

Q11. Someone has lit the candle.

(A) Someone was requested to light the candle.
(B) The candle had been lit by someone.
(C) The candle was lit by someone.
(D) The candle has been lit by someone

Direction (12). A sentence has been given

in Direct/Indirect Speech. Out of the of the four given alternatives, select the one which best expresses the same sentence in Indirect/Direct Speech.

Q12. Ram said, "I gave the book to Sachin, who kept it for a long time."

(A) Ram said that he had given the book to Sachin, who had kept it for a long time.

(B) Ram told Sachin that he had given the book to him to keep it for a long time.

(C) Ram said that he gave the book to Sachin, who kept it for a long time.

(D) Ram said that he has given the book to Sachin, who kept it for a long time.

Direction (13-14). In the following question, a word has been written in four different ways out of which only one is correctly spelt. Select the correctly spelt word.

Q13.

A. Abbreviate

B. Abreviate

C. Abrrviate

D. Abbreviat

Q14.

A. Aceelerate

B. Acelerate

C. Accelerate

D. Acellrate

Direction (15–16). In the following question, out of the four alternatives, select the alternative which best expresses the meaning of the idiom/ phrase.

Q15. Between Scylla and Charibdis

(A) Between two friends

(B) Between two enemies

(C) Between two dangers

(D) Between two rivers

Q16. To cool one's heels

(A) To be kept waiting for someone

(B) To talk rudely

(C) To give cold treatment to somebody

(D) To run away

Direction (17–18). In the following question, out of the four alternatives, select the alternative which is the best substitute of the words/sentences.

Q17. Unconcerned with the rightness or wrongness of something.

(A) Amoral

(B) Immoral

(C) Moral

(D) Psychopath

Q18. Symbol of peace

(A) Hammer and sickle

(B) Hammer and tongs

(C) An olive branch

(D) Judas kiss

Direction (19–20). In the following question, out of the four alternatives, select the alternative which will improve the bold part of the sentence. In case no improvement is needed, select "no improvement".

Q19. The seniors _______ (apology) for their rude behavior with juniors.

(a) apologetic

(b) apologising

(c) apologized

(d) apologetic

Q20. The woman to who I sold my house was a criminal.

(a) to whom I selled

(b) to whom I sell

(c) to whom I sold

(d) No correction required

Mock Test 10

Direction (1–3). In the following questions, some partof the sentence may have errors. Find out which part of the sentence has an error and select the appropriate option. If a sentence is free from error, select 'No Error'.

Q1. There is no conscious(a)/ planning on (b)/ take our music forward. (c)/ No error(d)

Q2. I have been abroad(a)/ many times but I have neither (b)/tasted alcohol not had non-vegetarian food. (c)/ No error(d)

Q3. The strategy location(a)/ of the fort is further (b)/enhanced by the facts. (c)/ No error(d)

Direction (4–5). In the following questions, the sentence given with a blank to be filled in with an appropriate word. Select the correct alternative out of the four and indicate it by selecting the appropriate option.

Q4. Government personnel on of ficial trips are ______ to claim reimbursement of their expenses.

A. entitled
B. incited
C. indicted
D. invited

Q5. The critics were ______ about his remarks on the efficiency of the government and gave many examples to prove they didn't agree with him.

A. optimistic
B. morose
C. rational
D. cynical

Direction (6–7). In the following questions, out of the given four alternatives, select the one which best expresses the meaning of the given word.

Q6. inscription

A. scrubbed
B. rivet
C. jaded
D. engrave

Q7. consolidate

A. centralize
B. variate
C. declare
D. announce

Direction (8–9). In the following questions, out of the given four alternatives, select the one which is opposite in meaning to the given word.

Q8. conjoined

A. sever
B. adjoin
C. meld
D. affix

Q9. adulterate

A. attenuated
B. purify
C. vitiated
D. dilute

Direction (10). Rearrange the parts of the sentence in correct order.

Q10. The twenty-four tributes

P-that could hold anything from a

Q-will be imprisoned in a vast outdoor arena

R-burning desert to a frozen wastelan

A. PQR
B. PRQ
C. QPR
D. RQP

Direction (11). A sentence has been given in Active/Passive Voice. Out of the four given alternatives, select the one which best expresses the same sentence in Passive/Active

Q11. They are going to open the shops at eleven o'clock.

A. The shops must be opened at eleven o'clock.

B. The shops were opened at eleven o'clock.

C. The shops are going to be opened at eleven o'clock.

D. The shops have been opened at eleven o'clock.

Direction (12). A sentence has been given in Direct/Indirect Speech. Out of the of the four given alternatives, select the one which best expresses the same sentence in Indirect/Direct Speech.

Q12. Uma asked me, "How's your brother?"

A Uma asked me how was my brother.

B Uma asked me how your brother was.

C Uma asked me how my brother was.

D Uma asked me how is my brother.

Direction (13-14). In the following question, a word has been written in four different ways out of which only one is correctly spelt. Select the correctly spelt word.

Q13. A. eraseable

B. probabble

C. secretes

D. esteemeed

Q14. A. missible

B. saosages

C. emullator

D. abdicate

Direction (15–16). In the following question, out of the four alternatives, select the alternative which best expresses the meaning of the idiom/ phrase.

Q15. dark horse

A someone who is fond of horse racing

B someone who has a wheatish complexion

C someone who breeds race horses

D someone who unexpectedly succeeds

Q16. hand in glove

A working together in the same office

B wearing gloves while working

C in partnership for something dishonest

D doing work in the garden

Direction (17–18). In the following question, out of the four alternatives, select the alternative which is the best substitute of the words/sentences.

Q17. Represent something as being less important than it really is.

A. discriminant

B. stride

C. underplay

D. imperious

Q18. an event or a group of events occurring as part of a sequence

A. stanza

B. episode

C. series

D. lesson

Direction (19–20). In the following question, out of the four alternatives, select the alternative which will improve the bold part of the sentence. In case no improvement is needed, select "no improvement".

Q19. Its always advisable put your car into neutral gear when you stop at a traffic signal.

A. Its always advisable putting

B. It's always advisable to put

C. No improvement

D. It is always advisable for putting

Q20. What a relief to sit down after walking in the park from a hour!

A. by an hour

B. No improvement

C. for an hour

D. in a hour

Mock Test 11

Direction (1–3). In the following questions, some part of the sentence may have errors. Find out which part of the sentence has an error and select the appropriate option. If a sentence is free from error, select 'No Error'.

Q1. The officer (a) / is angry, on the clerk (b) / for not attending to the work. (c) / No error (d)

Q2. No sooner (a) / She had spoken (b) than he left. (c) / No error (d)

Q3. What is your opinion? (a) /1 am sure the accused (b) / is not guilty of the offence. (c) / No error (d)

Direction (4–5). In the following questions, the sentence given with a blank to be filled in with an appropriate word. Select the correct alternative out of the four and indicate it by selecting the appropriate option.

Q4. Operant conditioning can be described as a learning.......... that is used to modify or change a person's behaviour through experiences and consequences.

A. method
B. object
C. goal
D. suspect

Q5. The priest called upon the families to .... their differences and agree to the wedding.

(a) sink
(b) abolish
(c) immerse
(d) lower

Direction (6–7). In the following questions, out of the given four alternatives, select the one which best expresses the meaning of the given word.

Q6. Nauseous

A. Loathsome
B. Benevolent
C. Worthy
D. Considerable

Q7. Protract

A. Delay
B. Advance
C. Unwise
D. Sharp

Direction (8–9). In the following questions, out of the given four alternatives, select the one which is opposite

in meaning to the given word.

Q8. Affable

A. rude
B. ruddy
C. needy
D. useless

Q9. Affluence

A. poverty
B. fear
C. persuasion
D. consideration

Direction (10). Rearrange the parts of the sentence in correct order.

Q10. P. Superstitions exist throughout the world despite scientific advances.

Q. One cannot heed anybody's sneezes if one has to be punctual on duty or 'cannot miss a flight.

R. But the spread of science and education among the masses has certainly given rise to a significant number of persons who do not believe in these superstitions.

S. The compulsions of modern life have also caused some of the superstitions to fade out.

A. RPSQ
B. SQRP
C. SRQP
D. PRSQ

Direction (11). A sentence has been given in Active/Passive Voice. Out of the four given alternatives, select the one which best expresses the same sentence in Passive/Active.

Q11. The manager gave her a negative feedback during her performance appraisal.

A. A negative feedback was given to her by the manager during her performance appraisal.

B. The manager will give her negative feedback during her performance appraisal.

C. A negative feedback is being given to her by the manager during appraising her performance.

D. Giving of a negative feedback to her during her performance appraisal has been done by the manager.

Direction (12). A sentence has been given in Direct/Indirect Speech. Out of the of the four given alternatives, select the one which best expresses the same sentence
in Indirect/Direct Speech.

Q12. The jeweller said to us, "These diamonds are polished here."

A. The jeweller informed us that these diamonds were polished there.

B. The jeweller informed us that those diamonds were polished there.

C. The jeweller informed us that those diamonds were polished here.

D. The jeweller informed us that these diamonds were polished here.

Direction (13-14). In the following question, a word has been written in four different ways out of which only one is correctly spelt. Select the correctly spelt word.

Q13. A. Committee

B. Commitee

C. Committtee

Q14. A. Amatuer

B. Amature

C. Amateur

Direction (15–16). In the following question, out of the four alternatives, select the alternative which best expresses the meaning of the idiom/ phrase.

Q15. In a flutter

A. Effective

B. Almost nothing

C. In a nervous state

D. Certain

Q16. All Greek to me

A. Out of danger

B. Incomprehensible

C. Very dear

D. Consulting seriously

Direction (17–18). In the following question, out of the four alternatives, select the alternative which is the best substitute of the words/sentences.

Q17. Any new participant in some activity.

A. Neophyte

B. Holophyte

C. Mesophyte

D. Epiphyte

Q18. A person who lives by himself.

A. Bemuse

B. Recluse

C. Applause

D. Abstruse

Direction (19–20). In the following question, out of the four alternatives, select the alternative which will improve the bold part of the sentence. In case no improvement is needed, select "no improvement".

Q19. In an industry where programmers search in (vain) for fresh ideas, it is no wonder that attention spans are short and cliche is king.

A. vein

B. wain

C. wane

D. No improvement

Q20. The famous Dr. Gupta (is only) physician in our village.

A. is a only

B. is an only

C. is the only

D. No improvement

Mock Test 12

Direction (1–3). In the following questions, some part of the sentence may have errors. Find out which part of the sentence has an error and select the appropriate option. If a sentence is free from error, select 'No Error'.

Q1. The economic disparity 1)/ has grown rapid 2)/ in the era of 3)/ globalization. 4)/ No error 5)

Q2. Either Ram 1)/ or Bhuvan forgot 2)/ to take 3)/ their pen. 4)/ No error 5)

Q3. Can you 1)/ repair my 2)/ digital-camera until 3)/ Wednesday? 4)/ No error 5)

Direction (4–5). In the following questions, the sentence given with a blank to be filled in with an appropriate word. Select the correct alternative out of the four and indicate it by selecting the appropriate option.

Q4. Galileo was the first scientist to recognize clearly that the only way to further our understanding of the physical world was to______ to experiment.

A. annihilate
B. resort
C. emerge
D. suspect

Q5. The criminal was __________ lest he should escape.

A. fetid
B. fettered
C. fettled
D. feted

Direction (6–7). In the following questions, out of the given four alternatives, select the one which best expresses the meaning of the given word.

Q6. CONTRABAND

A. BURGLED
B. SMUGGLED
C. BAFFLED
D. JUGGLED

Q7. DECIMATED

A. CAPTURED
B. DESTROYED
C. DAMAGED
D. WORRIED

Direction (8–9). In the following questions, out of the given four alternatives, select the one which is opposite in meaning to the given word.

Q8. INVINCIBLE

A. IMPREGNABLE
B. OMNIPRESENT
C. POWERLESS
D. POTENT

Q9. SCANTY

A. concise
B. small
C. precise
D. profuse

Direction (10). Rearrange the parts of the sentence in correct order.

Q10. 1. It is often said that lightning never strikes twice in the same place,

P Go ask the forest rangers.
Q But this isn't true.
R They will tell you that every thundershower brings several bolts of lightning to their lookout stations.
S Rangers spend their summers as fire-fighters.
6 So lightning does strike twice in the same place.

A. QSPR
B. SQPR
C. SPQR
D. QPSR

Direction (11). A sentence has been given in Active/Passive Voice. Out of the four given alternatives, select the one which best expresses the same sentence in Passive/Active

Q11. Please help me.
(a) You are requested to help me.
(b) You are being requested to help me.
(c) Let me be helped by you.
(d) None of the above.

Direction (12). A sentence has been given in Direct/Indirect Speech. Out of the of the four given alternatives, select the one which best expresses the same sentence in Indirect/Direct Speech.

Q12. He said to Akash, "Don't move".
(a) He told Akash not to move.
(b) He told Akash don't move.
(c) He said to Akash not to move.
(d) He told Akash to not to move.

Direction (13-14). In the following question, a word has been written in four different ways out of which only one is correctly spelt. Select the correctly spelt word.

Q13. A. campagnes
B. campaignes
C. campaines
D. campaigns

Q14. A. rhythim
B. rhithm
C. rhythm
D. rhithym

Direction (15–16). In the following question, out of the four alternatives, select the alternative which best expresses the meaning of the idiom/ phrase.

Q15. Drive home
A. Find one's roots
B. Emphasize
C. Refer
D. Draw

Q16. Drag one's feet
A. Make someting more complicated
B. Expedite
C. Be reluctant to act
D. Stop working

Direction (17–18). In the following question, out of the four alternatives, select the alternative which is the best substitute of the words/sentences.

Q17. Insatiable greed for riches
A. Avarice
B. Actuary
C. Antiquary
D. Apostate

Q18. Like a weak old woman
A. Amazon
B. Acetic
C. Anile
D. Archer

Direction (19–20). In the following question, out of the four alternatives, select the alternative which will improve the bold part of the sentence. In case no improvement is needed, select "no improvement".

Q19. Jane had told me that she hasn't done her homework.
A. told
B. tells
C. was telling
D. no improvement

Q20. This survey is concerning your health as well as that of your family.
A. concerns with
B. is concerned with
C. concerns to
D. no improvement

Mock Test 13

Direction (1–3). In the following questions, some part of the sentence may have errors. Find out which part of the sentence has an error and select the appropriate option. If a sentence is free from error, select 'No Error'.

Q1. When shall they (a) / arrive (b) to their destination? (c) / No error (d)

Q2. The teacher was happy (a) / when he entered the class (b) / which comprised of a hundred students. (c) / No error (d)

Q3. Females (a) / are not appointed (b) / in our college. (c) / No error (d)

Direction (4–5). In the following questions, the sentence given with a blank to be filled in with an appropriate word. Select the correct alternative out of the four and indicate it by selecting the appropriate option.

Q4. Vivekananda ______ the young to "arise" and "awake", to reject all doctrines and dogmas that were based on superstition and prejudice.

A. flattered
B. lauded
C. exhorted
D. commended

Q5. When negative attitudes toward religion, in the West or elsewhere, are motivated by a ______ for justice, they must be respected.

A. disinterest
B. concern
C. distraction
D. association

Direction (6–7). In the following questions, out of the given four alternatives, select the one which best expresses the meaning of the given word.

Q6. Profligate

A. Modest
B. Immoral
C. Upright
D. Virtuous

Q7. Oracular

A. Lucid
B. Distinct
C. Cryptic
D. Unambiguous

Direction (8–9). In the following questions, out of the given four alternatives, select the one which is opposite in meaning to the given word.

Q8. COMIC

A. awkward
B. amusing
C. tragic
D. absurd

Q9. GATHER

A. disperse
B. display
C. dispute
D. distract

Direction (10). Rearrange the parts of the sentence in correct order.

Q10. A. It is one of the highly developed countries of the world.

B. It stretches from the Atlantic Ocean in the east to the Pacific Ocean in the west.

C. The USA consists of 50 states including Alaska and Hawai.

D. The United States of America (USA) is the 4th largest country in the world.

A. ADCB
B. CBDA
C. DBCA
D. CBAD

Direction (11). A sentence has been given in Active/Passive Voice. Out of the four given alternatives, select the one which best expresses the same sentence in Passive/Active.

Q11. Show these visitors the butterfly farm.

A. These visitors should be showed the butterfly farm
B. Let these visitors be shown the butterfly farm

C. Let these visitors be showing the butterfly farm
D. You must show these visitors the butterfly farm

Direction (12). A sentence has been given in Direct/Indirect Speech. Out of the of the four given alternatives, select the one which best expresses the same sentence in Indirect/Direct Speech.

Q12. Reeta said Shivani, "You have to go to school".

Reeta told Shivani that she would have to go to school.

Reeta told Shivani that she has to go to school.

Reeta told Shivani that she have to go to school.

Reeta told Shivani that she had to go to school.

Direction (13-14). In the following question, a word has been written in four different ways out of which only one is correctly spelt. Select the correctly spelt word.

Q13. A. Benefited
B. Benefitted
C. Benifitted
D. Benifited

Q14.
A. Servent
B. Sarvent
C. Servant
D. Sarvant

Direction (15–16). In the following question, out of the four alternatives, select the alternative which best expresses the meaning of the idiom/ phrase.

Q15. Whoop it up
A. Be continually reminded of an unpleasant topic
B. Enjoying in a noisy way, usually in a group
C. Be totally ignorant or incompetent
D. Used as an exhortation to overcome or be rid of something

Q16. With a vengeance
A. A complete disaster
B. Having similar views or attitude to something
C. To look out for something without particular attention
D. Used to emphasize the degree to which somethings occurs

Direction (17–18). In the following question, out of the four alternatives, select the alternative which is the best substitute of the words/sentences.

Q17. Killer of prophet
A. Mariticide
B. Vaticide
C. patricide
D. Sororicide

Q18. A person who preserves skin of animals
A. Biloquist
B. Philologist
C. Taxidermist
D. Oculist

Direction (19–20). In the following question, out of the four alternatives, select the alternative which will improve the bold part of the sentence. In case no improvement is needed, select "no improvement".

Q19. Internet providers would not block content because it would (not to be make economic sense) and consumers would not stand for it.
A. not be making economical sense
B. not be make economical sense
C. not make economic sense
D. No improvement

Q20. "An interview after the campaign ends (is the normal) for every candidate and every campaigner in every election," he said.
A. is the norm
B. is the normally
C. is continuality
D. No improvement

Mock Test 14

Direction (1–3). In the following questions, some part of the sentence may have errors. Find out which part of the sentence has an error and select the appropriate option. If a sentence is free from error, select 'No Error'.

Q1. On a long bus ride with some (a)/ friends recently, I found one boy (b)/ was playing chess on his iPad. (c)/ No error (d)

Q2. In case of railway infrastructure, which (a)/ is in dire need of an upgrading, safety (b) is perhaps an even more critical consideration. (c)/No error (d)

Q3. The government also has asked (a)/ the SIT to investigate the role (b)/ of other companies.(c)/ No error (d)

Direction (4–5). In the following questions, the sentence given with a blank to be filled in with an appropriate word. Select the correct alternative out of the four and indicate it by selecting the appropriate option.

Q4. The actor wants to _____ his teenage son from media glare.

(a) renounce
(b) abandon
(c) promote
(d) avoid

Q5. He _____ himself a stiff drink before making his statement to the police offer.

(a) threw
(b) filled
(c) poured
(d) sipped

Direction (6–7). In the following questions, out of the given four alternatives, select the one which best expresses the meaning of the given word.

Q6. Laconic

A. Brief
B. Verbose
C. Lengthy
D. Unabridged

Q7. Propitious

A. Luxurious
B. Pitiful
C. Sad
D. Hopeful

Direction (8–9). In the following questions, out of the given four alternatives, select the one which is opposite in meaning to the given word.

Q8. Mellow

A. Ripe
B. Mature
C. Rich
D. Hard

Q9. Exhume

A. Dig
B. Reveal
C. Hide
D. Resurrect

Direction (10). Rearrange the parts of the sentence in correct order.

Q10. Although no convincing

P. arguments were made against
Q. was commotion in the House
R. the amendment, there

(a) RPQ
(b) QRP
(c) PRQ
(d) QPR

Direction (11). A sentence has been given in Active/Passive Voice. Out of the four given alternatives, select the one which best expresses the same sentence in Passive/Active

Q11. My cousin has written this essay.

A. This essay has been written by my cousin.
B. This essay was written by my cousin.
C. This essay has been wrote by my cousin.
D. My cousin wrote this essay.

Direction (12). A sentence has been given in Direct/Indirect Speech. Out of the of the four given alternatives, select the one which best expresses the same sentence in Indirect/Direct Speech.

Q12. "Don't you know the way to home?" asked the lady.

A. The lady asked why he didn't know the way to home.
B. The lady asked whether he didn't know the way to home.
C. The lady asked about the way to home.
D. The lady asked why he doesn't know the way to home.

Direction (13-14). In the following question, a word has been written in four different ways out of which only one is correctly spelt. Select the correctly spelt word.

Q13.

A. Foreign
B. Forien
C. Foriegn
D. Foreing

Q14.

A. monopoly
B. iliterrate
C. monnopoly
D. monnopolly

Direction (15–16). In the following question, out of the four alternatives, select the alternative which best expresses the meaning of the idiom/ phrase.

Q15. A tall order

(a) To exaggerate
(b) To be out fashioned
(c) To be disappointed
(d) A task difficult to perform

Q16. A green horn

(a) A nature lover
(b) A simple man
(c) A task with no risk
(d) An inexperienced man

Direction (17–18). In the following question, out of the four alternatives, select the alternative which is the best substitute of the words/sentences.

Q17. Of a man showing feminine attributes

(a) Spinster
(b) Celibate
(c) Bachelor
(d) Effeminate

Q18. A study of races

(a) Epitaph
(b) Gratis
(c) Ethnology
(d) Illicit

Direction (19–20). In the following question, out of the four alternatives, select the alternative which will improve the bold part of the sentence. In case no improvement is needed, select "no improvement".

Q19. He is too important for tolerating any delay.

(a) to tolerate
(b) to tolerating
(c) at tolerating
(d) No improvement

Q20. I need not offer any explanation regarding this incident - my behaviour is speaking itself.

(a) will speak to itself
(b) speaks for itself
(c) has been speaking
(d) No improvement

Mock Test 15

Direction (1–3). In the following questions, some part of the sentence may have errors. Find out which part of the sentence has an error and select the appropriate option. If a sentence is free from error, select 'No Error'.

Q1. Several great battles (a. / took place among (b. / the British and the Americans. (c. /No Error (d.

Q2. While flying over 1)/ India we had 2)/ glimpses of, 3)/ Ganges and Himalayas. 4)/ No error 5)

Q3. We cannot handle 1)/ this complicated case 2)/ unless full details 3)/ are not given to us. 4) No error 5)

Direction (4–5). In the following questions, the sentence given with a blank to be filled in with an appropriate word. Select the correct alternative out of the four and indicate it by selecting the appropriate option.

Q4. The criminal changed his name to an ___________ in order to elude the police.

A. alternative
B. alias
C. option
D. untrue

Q5. The ___________ my husband and I had was so loud it woke our children.

A. quarrel
B. coral
C. moral
D. laurel

Direction (6–7). In the following questions, out of the given four alternatives, select the one which best expresses the meaning of the given word.

Q6. Litter

A. Trash
B. Order
C. Possess
D. System

Q7. Obliterate

A. Construct
B. Annihilate
C. Revive
D. Initiate

Direction (8–9). In the following questions, out of the given four alternatives, select the one which is opposite in meaning to the given word.

Q8. Scrimp

A. Skimp
B. Conserve
C. Squander
D. Curtail

Q9. Guzzle

A. Carouse
B. Starve
C. Imbibe
D. Quaff

Direction (10). Rearrange the parts of the sentence in correct order.

Q10. As for ourselves, we
X-combing our hair
Y-a good wash and
Z-were contented with

A. ZXY
B. YZX
C. YXZ
D. ZYX

Direction (11). A sentence has been given in Active/Passive Voice. Out of the four given alternatives, select the one which best expresses the same sentence in Passive/Active

Q11. The fire destroyed the whole neighbourhood.

A. The whole neighbourhood is destroyed by the fire.
B. The whole neighbourhood was destroyed by the fire.
C. The whole neighbourhood was being destroyed by the fire.
D. The whole neighbourhood is being destroyed by the fire.

Direction (12). A sentence has been given in Direct/Indirect Speech. Out of the of the four given alternatives, select the one which best expresses the same sentence in Indirect/Direct Speech.

Q12. The accused said to the judge, "Let me meet my children before I die, sir."

A. The accused requests the judge to let him meet his children before he died.

B. The accused requested the judge to let him meet his children before he died.

C. The accused begs the judge to allow him to meet his children before he dies.

D. The accused begged the judge to let him meet his children before he dies

Direction (13-14). In the following question, a word has been written in four different ways out of which only one is correctly spelt. Select the correctly spelt word.

Q13. A. Threashing

B. Thrasheing

C. Threasheing

D. Thrashing

Q14. A. Conssensus

B. Consenssus

C. Consensus

D. Conssenssus

Direction (15–16). In the following question, out of the four alternatives, select the alternative which best expresses the meaning of the idiom/ phrase.

Q15. To heave a sigh of relief

A. To ecome very tired with routine or boring work

B. To suddenly feel very happy because something unpleasant has not happened or has ended

C. To Feel extremely sad over someone else's misfortune

D. To Feel silent anger over real or perceived injustice

Q16. To be on cloud nine

A. To extremely happy

B. To feely lucky

C. To experience the feeling of being intoxicated

D. To make one last attempt

Direction (17–18). In the following question, out of the four alternatives, select the alternative which is the best substitute of the words/sentences.

Q17. The upward force that a fluid exerts on a body floating in it

A. Upthrust

B. Plunge

C. Submerge

D. Capsize

Q18. The use of irony to mock or convey contempt

A. Sanction

B. Flatter

C. Compliment

D. Sarcasm

Direction (19–20). In the following question, out of the four alternatives, select the alternative which will improve the bold part of the sentence. In case no improvement is needed, select "no improvement".

Q19. She was uneasy because she (never be) on a plane before.

A. had never been

B. never been

C. is never been

D. no improvement

Q20. No one knows how he escaped (dash) to pieces.

A. being dash

B. being dashed

C. dashed

D. no improvement

Mock Test 16

Direction (1–3). In the following questions, some part of the sentence may have errors. Find out which part of the sentence has an error and select the appropriate option. If a sentence is free from error, select 'No Error'.

Q1. I, you and he (1) / must attend (2) / the seminar (3) / on career guidance. (4) / No Error (5)

Q2. You, he and I (1) / are to be (2) / blamed for (3) / the accident. (4) / No Error (5)

Q3. The Party Chief (1) / and the Chief Minister (2) / expressed his views (3) / on demonetization in India. (4) / No Error (5)

Direction (4–5). In the following questions, the sentence given with a blank to be filled in with an appropriate word. Select the correct alternative out of the four and indicate it by selecting the appropriate option.

Q4. A painting competition was held in the colony and Kavya was ______ winner in the age group 3-5 years.

A. described
B. supposed
C. declared
D. publicized

Q5. The National war memorial is ______ to our Armed Forces.

A. devoted
B. honoured
C. dedicated
D. inscribed

Direction (6–7). In the following questions, out of the given four alternatives, select the one which best expresses the meaning of the given word.

Q6. Boisterous

A. Clamorous
B. Ferocious
C. Fissiparous
D. Voluminous

Q7. Haggard

A. Emaciate
B. Insane
C. Rejected
D. Ridicule

Direction (8–9). In the following questions, out of the given four alternatives, select the one which is opposite in meaning to the given word.

Q8. COMIC

A. awkward
B. amusing
C. tragic
D. absurd

Q9. GATHER

A. disperse
B. display
C. dispute
D. distract

Direction (10). Rearrange the parts of the sentence in correct order.

Q10. P. And if I think about something which didn't happen I start thinking about all the other things which didn't happen.

Q. But there is only ever one thing which happened at a particular time and a particular place.

R. And there are an infinite number of things which didn't happen at that time and that place.

S. A lie is when you say something happened which didn't happen.

A. QSRP
B. SQPR
C. SRQP
D. SQRP

Direction (11). A sentence has been given in Active/Passive Voice. Out of the four given alternatives, select the one which best expresses the same sentence in Passive/Active.

Q11. Show these visitors the butterfly farm.

A. These visitors should be showed the butterfly farm

B. Let these visitors be shown the butterfly farm

C. Let these visitors be showing the butterfly farm

D. You must show these visitors the butterfly farm

Direction (12). A sentence has been given in Direct/Indirect Speech. Out of the of the four given alternatives, select the one which best expresses the same sentence in Indirect/Direct Speech.

Q12. Reeta said Shivani, "You have to go to school".

Reeta told Shivani that she would have to go to school.

Reeta told Shivani that she has to go to school.

Reeta told Shivani that she have to go to school.

Reeta told Shivani that she had to go to school.

Direction (13-14). In the following question, a word has been written in four different ways out of which only one is incorrectly spelt. Select the incorrectly spelt word.

Q13. A. reminascant

B. remnant

C. remittance

D. remembrance

Q14. A. hazy

B. hazard

C. hasty

D. hasitate

Direction (15–16). In the following question, out of the four alternatives, select the alternative which best expresses the meaning of the idiom/ phrase.

Q15. Pillar to post

A. Main support of an object

B. One place to another

C. To be reluctant

D. To incite others

Q16. Hobson's choice

A. To choose first in row

B. To make a careful choice

C. No real choice at all

D. To seek all favourable alternatives to choose from

Direction (17–18). In the following question, out of the four alternatives, select the alternative which is the best substitute of the words/sentences.

Q17. out of the woods

A. no longer in trouble

B. no longer young

C. no longer in sight

D. no longer famous

Q18. A person appointed by two parties to resolve a dispute

A. arbitrator

B. broker

C. valuer

D. auditor

Direction (19–20). In the following question, out of the four alternatives, select the alternative which will improve the bold part of the sentence. In case no improvement is needed, select "no improvement".

Q19. William Shakespeare is the greatest of (all other) writers.

A. all the

B. any other

C. the other

D. No improvement

Q20. She is not used (to sleep) for so long.

A. to be sleeping

B. to sleep

C. to sleeping

D. No improvement

Mock Test 17

Direction (1–3). In the following questions, some part of the sentence may have errors. Find out which part of the sentence has an error and select the appropriate option. If a sentence is free from error, select 'No Error'.

Q1. The lady said that she (A)/ should be away from home tomorrow as (B)/ Malti's friend had come to visit Mumbai.(C)/ No error (D)

Q2. Children who have a good (A)/ Pre-school education are most likely (B)/ to out-do other children at school. (C)/ No error (D)

Q3. Swati has such a fine (A)/ memory that she can recollect (B)/ anything what happened many years ago. (C)/ No error (D)

Direction (4–5). In the following questions, the sentence given with a blank to be filled in with an appropriate word. Select the correct alternative out of the four and indicate it by selecting the appropriate option.

Q4. It was his __________ that saved him from the coming danger.

A. prediction
B. presage
C. foresight
D. detection

Q5. Unhappy about the treatment meted out to her, Shanti.............demanded justice.

A. Sumptuously
B. Voraciously
C. Spasmodically
D. Vociferously

Direction (6–7). In the following questions, out of the given four alternatives, select the one which best expresses the meaning of the given word.

Q6. OBNOXIOUS

A. Depressing
B. Disgusting
C. Arrogant
D. Filthy

Q7. COVENANT

A. Case
B. Coupon
C. Contract
D. Settlement

Direction (8–9). In the following questions, out of the given four alternatives, select the one which is opposite in meaning to the given word.

Q8. SACROSANCT

(a) Irreligious
(b) Unethical
(c) Irreverent
(d) Unholy

Q9. HOSTILITY

(a) Courtesy
(b) Hospitality
(c) Relationship
(d) Friendliness

Direction (10). Rearrange the parts of the sentence in correct order.

Q10. As for the tasks

P. three important ones
Q. ahead, there appear
R. to be at least

(a) RQP
(b) QRP
(c) PRQ
(d) PQR

Direction (11). A sentence has been given in Active/Passive Voice. Out of the four given alternatives, select the one which best expresses the same sentence in Passive/Active.

Q11. I take exercise daily.

A. Exercise are taken daily by me.
B. Exercise is taken daily by me.
C. Exercise is being taken daily by me.

D. Exercise is been taken daily by me.

Direction (12). A sentence has been given in Direct/Indirect Speech. Out of the of the four given alternatives, select the one which best expresses the same sentence in Indirect/Direct Speech.

Q12. Robert will say to me, "I am your classmate".

A. Robert will tell me that he is my classmate.

B. Robert will tell me that he was my classmate.

C. Robert will tell me that he will be my classmate.

D. Robert said me that he is my classmate.

Direction (13-14). In the following question, a word has been written in four different ways out of which only one is correctly spelt. Select the correctly spelt word.

Q13.

A. Abbreviate

B. Abreviate

C. Abrrviate

D. Abbreviat

Q14.

A. Aceelerate

B. Acelerate

C. Accelerate

D. Acellrate

Direction (15–16). In the following question, out of the four alternatives, select the alternative which best expresses. The meaning of the idiom/ phrase.

Q15. To take umbrage

A. to feel depressed

B. to be offended

C. to be satisfied

D. to be pleased

Q16. To set the people by ears.

A. to box the people

B. to insult and disgrace the people

C. to excite people to a quarrel

D. to punish heavily

Direction (17–18). In the following question, out of the four alternatives, select the alternative which is the best substitute of the words/sentences.

Q17. To explain something mysterious or difficult.

A. Absolve

B. Antedate

C. Aggravate

D. Elucidate

Q18. A person who knows everything.

A. Soporific

B. Omniscient

C. Callous

D. Bourgeois

Direction (19–20). In the following question, out of the four alternatives, select the alternative which will improve the bold part of the sentence. In case no improvement is needed, select "no improvement".

Q19. But just how far he will manage to run with those shoes remains to be seen.

(a) But just how farther

(b) But just how much far

(c) But just how further

(d) No improvement

Q20. The valley lied quiet and peaceful in the sum.

(a) lied quietly and peacefully

(b) lay quiet and peacefully

(c) lay quietly

(d) No improvement

Mock Test 18

Direction (1–3). In the following questions, some part of the sentence may have errors. Find out which part of the sentence has an error and select the appropriate option. If a sentence is free from error, select 'No Error'.

Q1. Senior officers (a)/confirmation the contents(b)/ of the document. (c)/No error(d)

Q2. They succeeded(a)/ in play (b)/games of chess. (c)/No error(d)

Q3. Plastic containers(a)/ are cheap (b)/and lighting. (c)/No error(d)

Direction (4–5). In the following questions, the sentence given with a blank to be filled in with an appropriate word. Select the correct alternative out of the four and indicate it by selecting the appropriate option.

Q4. She __________ him angrily because he made the floor dirty with his muddy shoes.

A. scold
B. scolds
C. scolded
D. scolding

Q5. The criminal was __________ lest he should escape.

A. fetid
B. fettered
C. fettled
D. feted

Direction (6–7). In the following questions, out of the given four alternatives, select the one which best expresses the meaning of the given word.

Q6. CONTRABAND

A. BURGLED
B. SMUGGLED
C. BAFFLED
D. JUGGLED

Q7. DECIMATED

A. CAPTURED
B. DESTROYED
C. DAMAGED
D. WORRIED

Direction (8–9). In the following questions, out of the given four alternatives, select the one which is opposite in meaning to the given word.

Q8. INVINCIBLE

A. IMPREGNABLE
B. OMNIPRESENT
C. POWERLESS
D. POTENT

Q9. SCANTY

A. concise
B. small
C. precise
D. profuse

Direction (10). Rearrange the parts of the sentence in correct order.

Q10. A. The market which has remained clogged with vehicles was all clear for pedestrians.

B. The road has even been marked with stripes demarcating space for hawkers.

C. It is also lined with beautiful potted plants to give it a green look.

D. Visitors to the busy Karol Bagh market in Delhi were in for a surprise.

A. DABC
B. ADBC
C. BDAC
D. DCBA

Direction (11). A sentence has been given in Active/Passive Voice. Out of the four given alternatives, select the one which best expresses the same sentence in Passive/Active

Q11. They opened a new mall nearby last month.

A. A new mall was opened nearby last

month.

B. A new mall will be opened nearby last month.

C. Nearby a new mall is opened last month.

D. A new mall can be open nearby last month.

Direction (12). A sentence has been given in Direct/Indirect Speech. Out of the of the four given alternatives, select the one which best expresses the same sentence in Indirect/Direct Speech.

Q12. "I came home last night,"said he.

A. He told that he had come home last night.

B. He said that he came home last night.

C. He said that he had come home the previous night.

D. He says that he came home the previous night.

Direction (13-14). In the following question, a word has been written in four different ways out of which only one is correctly spelt. Select the correctly spelt word.

Q13. A. Scarety

B. Scarcity

C. Scarsity

D. Scarecity

Q14. A. Diarrhoea

B. Diarhea

C. Diarrhea

D. Diarrohea

Direction (15–16). In the following question, out of the four alternatives, select the alternative which best expresses the meaning of the idiom/ phrase.

Q15. Drive home

A. Find one's roots

B. Emphasize

C. Refer

D. Draw

Q16. Drag one's feet

A. Make someting more complicated

B. Expedite

C. Be reluctant to act

D. Stop working

Direction (17–18). In the following question, out of the four alternatives, select the alternative which is the best substitute of the words/sentences.

Q17. Experts who scientifically study insects

A. Gerontologists

B. Pathologists

C. Entomologists

D. Ornithologists

Q18. One who pretends to be what he is not

A. Hypocrite

B. Pessimist

C. Optimist

D. Infallible

Direction (19–20). In the following question, out of the four alternatives, select the alternative which will improve the bold part of the sentence. In case no improvement is needed, select "no improvement".

Q19. Jane had told me that she hasn't done her homework.

A. told

B. tells

C. was telling

D. no improvement

Q20. This survey is concerning your health as well as that of your family.

A. concerns with

B. is concerned with

C. concerns to

D. no improvement

Mock Test 19

Direction (1–3). In the following questions, some part of the sentence may have errors. Find out which part of the sentence has an error and select the appropriate option. If a sentence is free from error, select 'No Error'.

Q1. These conclusions(a)/ made the detectives (b)/to think that it was a fake theft. (c)/No error(d)

Q2. The role of precious(a)/ yellow metal is undergoing(b)/ dramatic change. (c)/No error(d)

Q3. When the investigators(a)/ tried to reconstruct the crime, (b)/ they come down against facts. (c)/No error(d)

Direction (4–5). In the following questions, the sentence given with a blank to be filled in with an appropriate word. Select the correct alternative out of the four and indicate it by selecting the appropriate option.

Q4. She kept her clothes neatly arranged in the ____.

A. warehouse
B. wardrobe
C. larder
D. godown

Q5. The old man has lost his memory. He is suffering from ______.

A. ambrosia
B. acacia
C. amnesia
D. anaesthesia

Direction (6–7). In the following questions, out of the given four alternatives, select the one which best expresses the meaning of the given word.

Q6. CANDID

A. sweet
B. frank
C. cruel
D. arrogant

Q7. SANE

A. crazy
B. foolish
C. sensible
D. sensitive

Direction (8–9). In the following questions, out of the given four alternatives, select the one which is opposite in meaning to the given word.

Q8. LENIENT

A. STRICT
B. SOLID
C. FORGIVING
D. STOIC

Q9. PROLONG

A. allow
B. shorten
C. increase
D. prevent

Direction (10). Rearrange the parts of the sentence in correct order.

Q10. A. When we can't laugh at the same joke again, why should we cry over the same problems?

B. One day he told them a joke and everyone roared with laughter.

C. People came to a wise man to complain about the same problems every time.

D. When he repeated the joke twice, nobody laughed anymore.

A. ADBC
B. DBCA
C. BACD
D. CBDA

Direction (11). A sentence has been given in Active/Passive Voice. Out of the four given alternatives, select the one which best expresses the same sentence in Passive/Active

Q11. How much monthly rent did you pay for the house?

A. How much monthly rent was paid for the house?
B. How much monthly rent is being paid for the house?
C. How much monthly rent is paid for the house?
D. How much monthly rent was being paid for the house?

Direction (12). A sentence has been given in Direct/Indirect Speech. Out of the of the four given alternatives, select the one which best expresses the same sentence in Indirect/Direct Speech.

Q12. She said, "Deepak slipped when he was trying to skate."
A. She said that Deepak was slipping when he was trying to skate.
B. She said that Deepak slipped when he was trying to skate.
C. She said that Deepak had slipped when he was trying to skate.
D. She said that Deepak has slipped when he was trying to skate.

Direction (13-14). In the following question, a word has been written in four different ways out of which only one is correctly spelt. Select the correctly spelt word.

Q13. A. genaral
B. genuine
C. guillty
D. generus

Q14.
A. Delineate
B. Deleneat
C. Dileneate
D. Deleneate

Direction (15–16). In the following question, out of the four alternatives, select the alternative which best expresses the meaning of the idiom/ phrase.

Q15. A left handed compliment
A. A subtle rebuke
B. Wholesome praise
C. An ambiguous compliment
D. A mild compliment

Q16. Beggar description
A. Cannot be described
B. Something described by a beggar
C. A poor account of something
D. A description of a beggar

Direction (17–18). In the following question, out of the four alternatives, select the alternative which is the best substitute of the words/sentences.

Q17. A remedy for all diseases
A. panacea
B. antidote
C. patent
D. antibiotic

Q18. That which cannot be heard
A. inaudible
B. invisible
C. incredible
D. incorrigible

Direction (19–20). In the following question, out of the four alternatives, select the alternative which will improve the bold part of the sentence. In case no improvement is needed, select "no improvement".

Q19. Those who have not received the invitation he should leave.
A. they should leave
B. he should be leaving.
C. should leave
D. No substitution

Q20. No other man in the city is as rich than he is.
A. so much rich as he
B. as rich as he
C. more richer than he
D. No substitution

Mock Test 20

Direction (1–3). In the following questions, some part of the sentence may have errors. Find out which part of the sentence has an error and select the appropriate option. If a sentence is free from error, select 'No Error'.

Q1. The economic disparity 1)/ has grown rapid 2)/ in the era of 3)/ globalization. 4)/ No error 5)

Q2. Either Ram 1)/ or Bhuvan forgot 2)/ to take 3)/ their pen. 4)/ No error 5)

Q3. Can you 1)/ repair my 2)/ digital-camera until 3)/ Wednesday? 4)/ No error 5)

Direction (4–5). In the following questions, the sentence given with a blank to be filled in with an appropriate word. Select the correct alternative out of the four and indicate it by selecting the appropriate option.

Q4. Galileo was the first scientist to recognize clearly that the only way to further our understanding of the physical world was to______ to experiment.

A. annihilate
B. resort
C. emerge
D. suspect

Q5. Private companies do not produce new varieties and inputs ______ as a result of their own research.

A. sincerely
B. purportedly
C. entirely
D. abjectly

Direction (6–7). In the following questions, out of the given four alternatives, select the one which best expresses the meaning of the given word.

Q6. Crescendo

A. Dominate
B. Escalation
C. Squander
D. Revere

Q7. Esoteric

A. Befitting
B. Germane
C. Abstruse
D. Relevant

Direction (8–9). In the following questions, out of the given four alternatives, select the one which is opposite in meaning to the given word.

Q8. Vaunted

A. unvanquished
B. fel
C. beittled
D. believed

Q9. Valor

A. admonition
B. injustice
C. cowardice
D. generosity

Direction (10). Rearrange the parts of the sentence in correct order.

Q10. P. The Mughal empire was extensive, but it was not integrated.

Q. It was rather an agglomeration of territories bound together by a common administration and common ties to the imperial authority.

R. The strong hand of the emperor held the country together, compelling obedience from the nobles who governed the provinces.

S. But these nobles felt no sense of national loyalty, for the simple reason that the empire was not a nation.

A. PRQS
B. SRQP
C. PRSQ
D. RSQP

Direction (11). A sentence has been given in Active/Passive Voice. Out of the four given alternatives, select the one which best expresses the same sentence in Passive/Active.

Q11. To pass, the candidate has to answer atleast 3 questions correctly.

A. If the candidate answers three

questions correctly then he will pass.

B. Atleast three questions will be answered correctly by the candidate to pass.

C. Atleast three questions have to be answered correctly by the candidate to pass.

D. Answering of three questions correctly by the candidate has to be done to pass.

Direction (12). A sentence has been given in Direct/Indirect Speech. Out of the of the four given alternatives, select the one which best expresses the same sentence in Indirect/Direct Speech.

Q12. The Principal said to us, "Today you will get your diplomas."

A. The Principal told us that on that day we would be getting our diplomas.

B. The Principal told us this on that day we would be getting our diplomas.

C. The Principal told us that on this day we would be getting our diplomas.

D. The Principal told us this on that day we will be getting our diplomas.

Direction (13-14). In the following question, a word has been written in four different ways out of which only one is incorrectly spelt. Select the incorrectly spelt word.

Q13. A. Adulterant

B. Antioxidant

C. Assailiant

D. Ascendant

Q14. A. Abhorrent

B. Abstinent

C. Achievement

D. Accruemant

Direction (15–16). In the following question, out of the four alternatives, select the alternative which best expresses the meaning of the idiom/phrase.

Q15. Jog someone's memory

A. Describing someone

B. Appreciating someone's humor

C. To be love with someone's intelligence

D. To cause someone to remember something

Q16. Be in the red

A. To be very angry

B. Close to death

C. To be in debt

D. Always energetic

Direction (17–18). In the following question, out of the four alternatives, select the alternative which is the best substitute of the words/sentences.

Q17. Insatiable greed for riches

A Avarice

B Actuary

C Antiquary

D Apostate

Q18. Like a weak old woman

A Amazon

B Acetic

C Anile

D Archer

Direction (19–20). In the following question, out of the four alternatives, select the alternative which will improve the bold part of the sentence. In case no improvement is needed, select "no improvement".

Q19. Even after 70 years of achieving independence, democracy, (in its true senses), was yet to come to India.

A. in its true sense

B. in its real sense

C. in its real senses

D. No improvement

Q20. The 'right to choice' of Aadhaar holders who do not want to link their accounts (may move up) for a decision.

A. may came up

B. may come up

C. may come ahead

D. No improvement

Answers

SECTION B

1. SPOT THE ERROR

1. (C) 'accident' should be 'an accident'
2. (C) 'who' in place of 'which'
3. (C) 'for' in place of 'from'
4. (D) no error
5. (B) 'in the morning' is grammatically correct
6. (A) 'can see' in place of 'can seen'
7. (A) 'A flock of birds' in place of 'A flock of bird'
8. (D) no error
9. (B) 'a rabble of butterflies' in place of 'rabble of butterflies'
10. (D) no error
11. (A) 'not only' should be used after 'eminent.'
12. (B) 'his parents would think' in place of 'his parents shall think'
13. (D) No error
14. (C) 'you are getting my schedule upset?' in place of 'my schedule is getting upset'
15. (A) 'As he can not do' in place of 'For he can not do'
16. (D) No error
17. (B) the first two will be used because ordinal followed by a cardinal.
18. (A) Remove 'the' before English Essay
19. (D) No error
20. (B)'stuffed' should be used
21. (B) use 'learn'(V.1) in place of (V.2.)
22. (C) use 'rising (gerund)' in place of 'rise (V.1)'
23. (A) use 'artists' in place of 'artist'
24. (A) 'a' is missing before 'young man'.
25. (B) use 'play' in place of 'plays' because subject is plural so verb should be plural.
26. (C) 'one of three chapters' in place of 'either of three chapters.'
27. (A) 'it is hoped' in place of 'it is hope' because here passive voice is required.
28. (D) No error
29. (B) use 'connect' because subject is plural.
30. (D) No error
31. (A) 'was' should replace 'is'
32. (A) 'drinks' should replace 'drink', as a singular verb is needed here.
33. (A) 'not only' will be placed after 'cheated'
34. (B) will have taken
35. (D)
36. (D)
37. (D)
38. (A) Replace 'laid' with 'lay'
39. (B) use 'angry with' (someone) because 'angry at' (something)
40. (B) use 'skill-building'
41. (D)
42. (A) 'She had offered' will be replaced by 'she had been offered'.
43. (A) 'neither' should be used before 'he' because in case of 'neither.........nor; either...........or; not only............but also etc. are followed by same part of speech.
44. (A) replace 'If Aruna would have' with 'If Aruna had'
45. (C) Use 'believe' instead of 'believes'
46. (B) Use 'their' instead of 'its'
47. (C) Efforts' should be replaced by 'an effort' because this is singularly related here.
48. (A) replace 'a little' with 'the little'
49. (B) replace 'and' with 'if'
50. (C) 'a quarter' should be used in place of

'quarter'.

Q.51. Option (c)

Explanation. arrive at should be used.

Q.52. Option (c)

Explanation. comprised=consisted of.

Q.53. Option (d)

Explanation. No error

Q.54. Option (b)

Explanation. angry with should be used.

Q.55. Option (b)

Explanation. had She spoken.

Q.56. Option (d)

Explanation. No error

Q.57. Option (a)

Explanation. prosecuted should be used.

prosecute(v)- institute or conduct legal proceedings against (a person or organization).

persecute(v)- oppress

Q.58. Option (a)

Explanation. you must tell me either

Q.59. Option (c)

Explanation. for twelve years.

Q.60. Option (c)

Explanation. waiting for her should be used.

Q.61. (A) use 'The rate of growth' in place of 'The rate off growth'.

Q.62. (B) use 'nearly one-third of' in place of 'near one-third of'.

Q.63. (A) use 'Thousands of aspirants' in place of 'Thousands of aspirant'.

Q.64. (C) use 'were studying' in place of 'was studying'.

Q.65. (B) use 'to the US for' in place of 'to US for'

Q.66. (C) use 'has reported' in place of 'have reported', because the subject is the flow.

Q.67. (B) use 'to turn' in place of 'to turned'.

Q.68. (A) use 'Overall, a cumulative' in place of 'Overall, an cumulative'.

Q.69. (D)

Q.70. (D)

Q71.(D) No error

Q72.(C) Use 'the new spacecraft' in place of 'the newly spacecraft'.

Q73.(B) Use 'its report' in place of 'their report'.

Q74.(A) Use 'The small adjustments are' in place of 'The small adjustments is', because the subject is plural.

Q75.(A) Use 'The committee has recommended' in place of 'The committee has recommend'.

Q76.(D) No error

Q77.(C) Use 'on alert' in place of 'in alert'

Q78.(C) Use 'in the examination' in place of 'on the examination'.

Q79.(A) Use 'were launched' in place of 'was launched'.

Q80.(D) No error

Q. 81. (B) replace 'criterions' with 'criteria' because 'criterion' is singular and its plural is 'criteria'.

Q.82. (C) use 'punishable offence' in place of 'punished offence'.

Q.83. (C) remove 'is' because it is unnecessary.

Q.84. (C) use 'into their hands' in place of 'out of their hands' because the idiom is 'take the law into your own hands'. It means to punish someone for an offence according to one's own ideas of justice, especially in an illegal or violent way.

Q.85. (D) 'avenge- inflict harm to other in return for an injury or wrong done not in relation.

Q.86. (B) use 'meeting' in place of 'meet' because here gerund is required.

Q.87. (B) remove 'that' because it is unnecessary.

Q.88. (A) use 'he has eaten' in place of 'he ate' because this sentence shows the sense of present perfect tense.

Q.89. (A) use 'has' in place of 'is having' because

'have' is not use in continuous tense.

Q.90. (B) 'has been working' in place of 'is working' the sentence shows the sense of present perfect continuous tense.

Q.91. (B) 'The first two' will be used because an ordinal number is followed by a cardinal number.

Q.92. (B) use 'the modern technological world'

Q.93. (D) No error

Q.94. (B) Use 'its' in place of 'her' because here the moon is used as an object whereas the moon personified 'her' is used for showing possession.

Q.95. (B) Use 'of' in place of 'from'

Q.96. (C) Use 'which were' in place of 'which was' because the subject is plural.

Q.97. (A) Use 'makes' in place of 'make' because when two subjects are joined by 'or', the verb should be according to the second subject.

Q.98. (B) Use 'a convenience for' in place of 'a convenience to'

Q.99. (A) Use 'The strength of a team' in place of 'strength of a team'. Definite article should be used here because 'strength' is specified.

Q.100. (D) No error

Q101. (B) Why did they want' will be replaced by why they wanted.

Q102. (A) She had offered will be replaced by she had been offered.

Q103. (B) What to make will be replaced by what makes/what has made/what made

Q104. (D) No error

Q105. (A) He could neither will be replaced by neither he could because nor is used before the subject he.

Q106. (C) 'a higher cost than' in place of 'a high cost than' because the use of 'than' shows comparative degree is required here.

Q107. (C) Use 'following' present participle in place of 'follow' V.1

Q108. (B) 'hers' possessive pronoun should be used in place of 'her' possessive adjective.

Q109. (D) No error

Q110. (C) 'in a new way' in place of 'in new way'

Q111. (C) 'a higher cost than' in place of 'a high cost than' because the use of 'than' shows comparative degree is required here.

Q112. (B) use 'following' present participle in place of 'follow' V.1

Q113. (B) 'hers' possessive pronoun should be used in place of 'her' possessive adjective.

Q114. (D) no error

Q115. (D) 'in a new way' in place of 'in new way'

Q116. (A) 'One of his elder brothers gives' in place of 'One of his elder brothers give' because the structures such as 'one of…., none of….., either of….., neither of……' are followed by singular verb.

Q117. (A) 'recently' in place of 'recent'

Q118. (B) 'seems to grow' in place of 'seems to grown' because infinitive [to+v.1] should be used.

Q119. (A) 'The educated unemployed' in place of 'The educated unemployment' because the educated unemployed means the educated people who are unemployed.

Q120. (C) use 'the poor or poor people' in place of 'the poor people' because 'the poor' itself means 'poor people.'

Q121. (D)

Q122. (C)

Q123. (D)

Q124. (C)

Q125. (D)

Q126. (B)

Q127. (A)

Q128. (B)

Q129. (D)

Q130. (D)

Q131. (B) 'with' will be replaced by 'from' because from is used after refrain, abstain, prohibit etc.

Q132. (A) "they" must be replaced by "those"

Q133. (C) 'Those of' must be added before Rampur, because there is comparison between hotels of Kanpur and hotels of Rampur.

Q134. (B) 'that of' will be used after to.

Q135. (A) 'was' must be replaced by 'had been', because this is a conditional sentence.

Q136. (B) 'has' must be replaced by 'have'

Q137. (C) 'on' must be removed, because after "attack" preposition must not be used.

Q138. (D) No error

Q139. (D) No error

Q140. (A) 'home' in place of 'homes' because 'at home' is a phrase.

Q141. (C)

Q142. (B)

Q143. (A)

Q144. (D)

Q145. (A)

Q146. (D)

Q147. (C)

Q148. (D)

Q149. (D)

Q150. (D)

Q151. (D) No error

Q152. (C) use 'are' after 'accidents' because of passive voice.

Q153. (C) were will replace was because the various consequences (Main Subject) is in plural.

Q154. (C) the helping verb 'do' will not be used

Q155. (C) the preposition 'of' will be used after search because 'in search of' (id.) means 'looking for'

Q156. (D) No error

Q157. (C) tried will replace tries because the principal clause is in past tense and the sentence expresses a past action.

Q158. (D) No error

Q159. (D) No error

Q160. (B) 'had I spoken' in place of 'I had spoken'

Q161. (4) No Error

Q162. (1) In this sentence there is an error of unattached participle because the subject of each part is different. Hence Adverbial clause (while) along.....will be a correct usage.

Q163. (1) Verb "tell" is always followed by an object. Hence, He says/ He is saying/ He is telling me.....should be used.

Q164. (2) Hence, great skill in keeping should be used. The word skill means. the ability to do something well, while the word talent means. a natural ability to do something.

Q165. (2) One of is followed by a Plural Noun/ Pronoun but a Singular verb. Hence, one of the volcanic eruptions takes place......... should be used.

Q166. (1) Here, Passive Voice should be used. Hence, tea is grown will be a correct usage.

Q167. (3) Article "the" is not used before the words- jail, prison, school, college etc. in general sense. Hence, he had in jail......is a correct usage.

Q168. (4) No error

Q169. (4) No Error

Q170. (3) Here 'much stronger than' should be used.

Q171. (B) Replace are with is

Q172. (D) No error

Q173. (B) Replace awaited with waited.

Q174. (A) Replace announcement with announcing.

Q175. (D) No error

Q176. (B) Replace took with taken

Q177. (B) Replace constitution with constitute.

Q178. (B) Replace sun with son

Q179. (C) Replace of with off

Q180. (D) No error

Q.181. (C) Wedness day's should replace wednessday because passive is needed here.

Q.182. (A) 'These' should replace 'there'

Q.183. (A) A national should replace 'nation' because we need an adjective here.

Q.184. (A) were should replace was because the subject is in plural number.

Q.185. (A) 'member' should replace member because 'a' makes the noun singular.

Q.186. (B) was should replace were because subject john was singular.

Q.187. (A) with should replace of because charged takes with not of.

Q.188. (B) 'from' should replace 'of'.

Q.189. (C) in should replace at.

Q.190. (B) 'thinks' should replace think because to subject one is singular.

Q.191. (b) use 'slowly' instead of 'slow'

Q.192. (c) use 'the' before 'latter'

Q.193. (a) use 'among' instead of 'between'

Q.194. (d) no error

Q.195. (c) c use 'to' instead of 'of'

Q.196. (b) use 'abridged' instead of 'abridge'

Q.197. (c) use 'have' instead of 'has'

Q.198. (a) use 'gets' instead of 'get'

Q.199. (b) use 'that' instead of 'because'

Q.200. (c) use 'rules' instead of 'ruled'

Q.201. (b) use 'confirmed' instead of 'confirmation'

Q.202. (b) use 'playing' instead of 'play'

Q.203. (c) use 'light' instead of 'lighting'

Q.204. (c) remove 'to'

Q.205. (c) use 'a dramatic change' instead of 'dramatic change'

Q.206. (c) use 'up' instead of 'down'

Q.207. (d) No improvement

Q.208. (b) use 'is' instead of 'are'

Q209. (b) use 'gifts' instead of 'gift'

Q210. (a) use 'leaving' instead of 'leave'

Q.211. (B) 'were' should replace was because 'hundred of sheep is plural and not the field.

Q.212. (B) 'is' should replace 'are' because more than takes a singular noun and a singular verb.

Q.213. (B) 'were' should replace was because the subject of the verb is issues which is plural.

Q.214. (D) No error

Q.215. (C) Remove most because unmatched does not take more or most before it.

Q.216. (B) 'better' should replace 'best' because here comparative degree is used.

Q.217. (C) 'luckier' should replace 'luckiest' because here two players are mentioned for which comparative degree is used.

Q.218. (C) 'was' should replace 'were' because besides (according to syntax rule) is main subject of the sentence which is singular here.

Q.219. (B) Add how much before milk as it is an uncountable noun so a countable adjective many can't apply for an uncountable noun.

Q.220. (A) 'A lot' should replace 'A lots' because lots is not used with article A.

Q221 (C) use 'based' instead of 'base'

Q222. (C) use 'seeks' instead of 'seek'

Q223. (B) use 'how to drive' instead of 'to drive'

Q224. (B) remove 'not'

Q225. (B) remove 'that'

Q226. (B) use 'with' instead of 'on'

Q227. use 'from' instead of 'for'

Q228. No error

Q229. remove 'will'

Q230. use 'has' instead of 'have'

Q.231. (C) Delete 'the' from the sentence because prepositions do not follow articles.

Q.232. (C) 'by' should be in place of with.

Q.233. (A) 'A' should be in place of 'an'.

Q.234. (C) 'Crises' should be in place of 'Crisis'.

Q.235. (C) 'To' should be in place of 'than'.

Q.236. (B) 'have' should be in place of 'has'.

Q.237. (D) No error

Q.238. (A) Delete 'the' from the part of the sentence.

Q.239. (B) 'When' should be in place of 'than'.

Q.240. (C) 'That' should be in place of 'due to'.

2. SENTENCE IMPROVEMENT

Q. 1. (C) Q.2. (B)
Q. 3. (A) Q.4. (B)
Q. 5. (C) Q.6. (A)
Q. 7. (A) Q.8. (D)
Q. 9. (B) Q.10. (B)
Q. 11. (B) Q.12. (D)
Q. 13. (B) Q.14. (D)
Q.15. (A) Q.16. (C)
Q.17. (D) Q.18. (C)
Q.19. (C) Q.20. (D)
Q.21. (C) Q.22. (B)
Q.23. (B) Q.24. (B)
Q.25. (C) Q.26. (D)
Q.27. (B) Q.28. (C)
Q.29. (B) Q.30. (A)
Q.31. (b) Q.32. (c)
Q.33. (b) Q.34. (d)
Q.35. (d) Q.36. (b)
Q.37. (c) Q.38. (d)
Q.39. (a) Q.40. (d)
Q.41. (b) Q.42. (c)
Q.43. (d) Q.44. (a)
Q.45. (c) Q.46. (a)
Q.47. (b) Q.48. (a)
Q.49. (c) Q.50. (d)
Q.51. (B) Q.52. (A)
Q.53. (B) Q.54. (C)
Q.55. (B) Q.56. (B)
Q.57. (D) Q.58. (A)
Q.59. (C) Q.60. (B)
Q.61. (B) Q.62. (A)
Q.63. (A) Q.64. (B)
Q.65. (C) Q.66. (B)
Q.67. (C) Q.68. (B)
Q.69. (C) Q.70. (D)

Q.71. (B) - Negative imperatives are made with do not + infinitive without to.

Q.72. (A) - Clauses with words like seldom, hardly, little, and few have a negative sense. Affirmative question tags are used after them.

Q.73. (B) - Clauses with words like seldom, hardly, little, and few have a negative sense. Affirmative question tags are used after them.

Q.74. (C) - Clauses with words like seldom, hardly, little, and few have a negative sense. Affirmative question tags are used after them.

Q.75. (B)- We use the structure 'needn't have' to mean that something was unnecessary.

Q.76. (A) - We use 'no more' with nouns to talk about quantity or degree.

Q.77. (C) - The two options are possible here.

Q.78. (C) - Suggest cannot be followed by object + infinitive.

Q.79. (B) - Some verbs are followed by object + infinitive.

Q.80. (A) - Finally suggests that we have been waiting a long time for something.

Q81. (A) Q82. (B)
Q83. (D) Q84. (B)
Q85. (D) Q86. (A)
Q87. (B) Q88. (B)
Q89. (B) Q90. (B)

Q91. (C) In a negative sentence, any should be used. Hence, any is the right usage.

Q92. (B) In such structures, would have + V3 should be used. Hence, would have surely assisted him is the right usage.

Q93. (4) No improvement

Q94. (1) none (Adv.). used with the and a Comparative to mean not at all. Hence, none is the right usage.

Q95. (1) It is a Preposition related error. Hence, in is the right usage.

Q96. (2) aptitude (N.). natural ability at doing something; talent. Hence, aptitude is the right usage.

Q97. (1) Here, Preposition-by is the right usage.

Q98. (2) Here, Preposition-to is the right usage.

Q99. (4) No improvement

Q100. (2) To show rate, a/an is used. Hence, an hour is the right usage.

Q101. (B) Q102. (A)
Q103. (A) Q104. (D)
Q105. (A) Q106. (A)
Q107. (B) Q108. (A)
Q109. (D) Q110. (A)
Q111. (C) Q112. (B)
Q113. (A) Q114. (A)
Q115. (C) Q116. (D)
Q117. (B) Q118. (A)
Q119. (B) Q120. (D)
Q121. (C) Q122. (A)
Q123. (D) Q124. (A)
Q125. (A) Q126. (C)
Q127. (D) Q128. (C)
Q129. (A) Q130. (D)
Q131. (C) Q132. (B)
Q133. (D) Q134. (C)
Q135. (C) Q136. (B)
Q137. (C) Q138. (C)
Q139. (D) Q140. (C)
Q141. (A) Q142. (C)
Q143. (D) Q144. (C)
Q145. (B) Q146. (C)
Q147. (D) Q148. (C)
Q149. (A) Q150. (C)
Q151.(2) Q152.(3)
Q153.(3) Q154.(2)
Q155.(2) Q156.(3)
Q157.(2) Q158.(3)
Q159.(1) Q160.(4)
Q161.(4) Q162.(4)
Q163.(3) Q164.(1)
Q165.(1) Q166.(4)
Q167.(3) Q168.(1)
Q169.(4) Q170.(1)
Q171.(1) Q172.(4)
Q173.(3) Q174.(1)
Q175.(2) Q176.(3)
Q177.(2) Q178.(4)
Q179.(1) Q180.(3)
Q181.(2) Q182.(3)
Q183.(2) Q184.(2)
Q185.(1) Q186.(2)
Q187.(4) Q188.(4)
Q189.(3) Q190.(2)
Q191.(1) Q192.(3)
Q193.(2) Q194.(3)
Q195.(3) Q196.(3)
Q197.(3) Q198.(4)
Q199.(1) Q200.(1)
Q201.(3) Q202.(2)
Q203.(4) Q204.(1)
Q205.(3) Q206.(1)
Q207.(3) Q208.(1)
Q209. (3) Q210. (1)
Q211. (1) Q212. (3)
Q213. (3) Q214. (4)
Q215. (2) Q216. (4)
Q217. (3) Q218. (1)
Q219. (2) Q220. (4)
Q221. (4) Q222. (2)
Q223. (3) Q224. (4)
Q225. (2) Q226. (1)
Q227. (2) Q228. (2)
Q229. (3) Q230. (2)
Q231. (3) Q232. (1)
Q233. (4) Q234. (2)
Q235. (1) Q236. (4)
Q237. (4) Q238. (4)
Q239. (4) Q240. (3)
Q241. (1) Q242. (1)
Q243. (2) Q244. (1)
Q245. (4) Q246. (2)
Q247. (3) Q248. (1)
Q249. (3) Q250. (2)
Q251. (3) Q252. (2)

Q253. (4)	Q254. (3)
Q255. (1)	Q256. (1)
Q257. (1)	Q258. (1)
Q259. (3)	Q260. (1)
Q261. (2)	Q262. (2)
Q263. (4)	Q264. (2)
Q265. (2)	Q266. (2)
Q267. (2)	Q268. (2)
Q269. (1)	Q270. (2)
Q271. (1)	Q272. (4)
Q273. (2)	Q274. (1)
Q275. (3)	Q276. (4)
Q277. (2)	Q278. (2)
Q279. (3)	Q280. (3)
Q281. (2)	Q282. (1)
Q283. (1)	Q284. (2)
Q285. (1)	Q286. (3)
Q287. (2)	Q288. (2)
Q289. (1)	Q290. (1)
Q291. (1)	Q292. (3)
Q293. (2)	Q294. (1)
Q295. (4)	Q296. (1)
Q297. (1)	Q298. (4)
Q299. (3)	Q300. (2)

3. FILL IN THE BLANKS

Q. 1. (B)	Q. 2. (A)
Q. 3. (C)	Q. 4. (C)
Q. 5. (B)	Q. 6. (D)
Q. 7. (C)	Q. 8. (C)
Q. 9. (A)	Q. 10. (B)
Q. 11. (B)	Q. 12. (D)
Q. 13. (B)	Q. 14. (C)
Q. 15. (B)	Q. 16. (B)
Q. 17. (D)	Q. 18. (C)
Q. 19. (B)	Q. 20. (C)
Q. 21. (C)	Q. 22. (C)
Q. 23. (A)	Q. 24. (B)
Q. 25. (B)	Q. 26. (B)
Q. 27. (B)	Q. 28. (A)
Q. 29. (A)	Q. 30. (C)
Q.31. (d)	Q.32. (b)
Q.33. (c)	Q.34. (a)
Q.35. (d)	Q.36. (a)
Q.37. (a)	Q.38. (b)
Q.39. (c)	Q.40. (d)
Q.41. (b)	Q.42. (a)
Q.43. (d)	Q.44. (d)
Q.45. (c)	Q.46. (b)
Q.47. (c)	Q.48. (a)
Q.49. (c)	Q.50. (a)
Q51. (C)	Q52. (D)
Q53. (B)	Q54. (B)
Q55. (B)	Q56. (B)
Q57. (A)	Q58. (B)
Q59. (B)	Q60. (A)
Q61. (A)	Q62. (A)
Q63. (C)	Q64. (B)
Q65. (B)	Q66. (C)
Q67. (C)	Q68. (A)
Q69. (D)	Q70. (C)
Q71. (A)	Q72. (C)
Q73. (B)	Q74. (B)
Q75. (C)	Q76. (D)
Q77. (B)	Q78. (D)
Q79. (C)	Q80. (C)
Q81. (4)	Q82. (2)
Q83. (3)	Q84. (1)
Q85. (2)	Q86. (3)
Q87. (1)	Q88. (2)
Q89. (3)	Q90. (4)
Q91. (B)	Q92. (C)
Q93. (C)	Q94. (D)
Q95. (D)	Q96. (A)
Q97. (D)	Q98. (C)
Q99. (B)	Q100. (A)
Q101. (B)	Q102. (D)

Q103. (C) Q104. (A)
Q105. (B) Q106. (A)
Q107. (C) Q108. (A)
Q109. (D) Q110. (B)
Q111. (D) Q112. (C)
Q113. (D) Q114. (A)
Q115. (A) Q116. (D)
Q117. (D) Q118. (C)
Q119. (B) Q120. (A)
Q121. (C) Q122. (B)
Q123. (C) Q124. (C)
Q125. (B) Q126. (B)
Q127. (B) Q128. (A)
Q129. (B) Q130. (B)
Q131. (a) Q132. (b)
Q133. (c) Q134. (a)
Q135. (d) Q136. (c)
Q137. (c) Q138. (d)
Q139. (d) Q140. (d)
Q151. (C) Q152. (C)
Q153. (D) Q154. (D)
Q155. (C) Q156. (D)
Q157. (C) Q158. (A)
Q159. (A) Q160. (A)

Q.161. c. Ravenous (adj.) means extremely hungry.

Q.162. a. Vulgarity (n.) means offensive speech or conduct.

Q.163. b. Magisterial (adj.) means overbearing or offensively self-assured.

Q.164. c. Punctual (adj.) means arriving exactly on time.

Q.165. b. To provoke (v.) is to incite anger or resentment; to call forth a feeling or action.

Q.166. c. To scintillate(v.) means to emit or send forth sparks or little flashes of light, creating a shimmering effect; to sparkle.

Q.167. d. To necessitate(v.) means to make necessary, especially as a result.

Q.168. c. To abet(v.) means to assist, encourage, urge, or aid, usually an act of wrongdoing.

Q.169. d. Prolific(adj.) means abundantly creative.

Q.170. c. galling(adj.) means irritating, annoying, or exasperating.

Q.171. c. To abdicate(v.) means to formally relinquish or surrender power, office, or responsibility.

Q.172. d. Volition(n.) means accord; an act or exercise of will.

Q.173. a. Malodorous(adj.) means having a foul-smelling odour.

Q.174. a.wired(adj.) means strange.

Q.175. d. Irreverent(adj.) means lacking respect or seriousness; not reverent.

Q.176. b. Keen(adj.) means being extremely sensitive or responsive; having strength of perception.

Q.177. b. Nefarious(adj.) means wicked, vicious, or evil.

Q.178. a. Excessive (adj) means too much.

Q.179. d. accomplice(adj.) means participating in or associated with a questionable act or a crime.

Q.180. a. Subversion(n.) means an overthrow, as from the foundation.

Q.181. (C) Q.182. (D)
Q.183. (B) Q.184. (B)
Q.185. (D) Q.186. (D)
Q.187. (D) Q.188. (C)
Q.189. (B) Q.190. (C)
Q191. (3) Q.192. (4)
Q193. (4) Q.194. (4)
Q195. (1) Q.196. (2)
Q197. (3) Q.198. (2)
Q199. (3) Q.200. (4)
Q.201. (3) Q.202. (3)
Q.203. (2) Q.204. (4)
Q.205. (3) Q. 206. (2)
Q.207. (3) Q. 208. (3)
Q.209. (1) Q. 210. (2)
Q.211. (1) Q. 212. (2)
Q.213. (2) Q. 214. (4)

215. (2) 216. (4)
217. (3) 218. (2)
219. (2) 220. (4)
221. (3) 222. (3)
223. (2) 224. (4)
225. (3) 226. (3)
227. (3) 228. (1)
229. (2) 230. (4)
231. (2) 232. (1)
233. (1) 234. (3)
235. (4) 236. (2)
237. (3) 238. (2)
239. (2) 240. (1)
241. (2) 242. (1)
243. (2) 244. (1)
245. (2) 246. (2)
247. (4) 248. (1)
249. (1) 250. (3)
251. (3) 252. (1)
253. (2) 254. (4)
255. (2) 256. (1)
257. (1) 258. (1)
259. (3) 260. (3)
261. (4) 262. (4)
263. (2) 264. (1)
265. (4) 266. (4)
267. (1) 268. (4)
269. (3) 270. (2)
271. (4) 272. (2)
273. (4) 274. (2)
275. (2) 276. (1)
277. (4) 278. (3)
279. (1) 280. (1)
281. (4) 282. (4)
283. (2) 284. (1)
285. (2) 286. (3)
287. (1) 288. (1)
289. (4) 290. (3)
291. (1) 292. (3)
293. (3) 294. (3)
295. (1) 296. (4)
297. (1) 298. (4)
299. (2) 300. (1)
301. (1) 302. (4)
303. (2) 304. (4)
305. (2) 306. (3)
307. (3) 308. (3)
309. (4) 310. (4)
311. (2) 312. (3)
313. (2) 314. (3)
315. (2) 316. (2)
317. (4) 318. (3)
319. (3) 320. (2)
321. (3) 322. (4)
323. (2) 324. (3)
325. (2) 326. (4)
327. (3) 328. (4)
329. (2) 330. (3)
331. (1) 332. (1)
333. (2) 334. (4)
335. (1) 336. (1)
337. (3) 338. (2)
339. (4) 340. (3)
341. (3) 342. (4)
343. (4) 344. (3)
345. (1) 346. (4)
347. (4) 348. (1)
349. (3) 350. (3)

4. ACTIVE/PASSIVE VOICE

1 (1) 2. (2)
3. (1) 4. (3)
5. (3) 6. (2)
7. (2) 8. (2)
9. (1) 10. (3)
11. (4) 12. (3)
13. (4) 14. (2)

15. (3)
16. (4)
17. (1)
18. (3)
19. (1)
20. (1)
21. (1)
22. (3)
23. (1)
24. (3)
25. (4)
26. (2)
27. (2)
28. (1)
29. (1)
30. (4)
31. (4)
32. (3)
33. (2)
34. (3)
35. (1)
36. (2)
37. (2)
38. (4)
39. (2)
40. (2)
41. (2)
42. (1)
43. (3)
44. (2)
45. (3)
46. (2)
47. (2)
48. (4)
49. (1)
50. (4)
51. (2)
52. (4)
53. (1)
54. (1)
55. (2)
56. (4)
57. (3)
58. (4)
59. (3)
60. (3)
61. (2)
62. (3)
63. (2)
64. (2)
65. (4)
66. (3)
67. (4)
68. (2)
69. (4)
70. (2)
71. (2)
72. (2)
73. (4)
74. (2)
75. (1)
76. (2)
77. (4)
78. (2)
79. (1)
80. (4)
81. (3)
82. (4)
83. (3)
84. (1)
85. (1)
86. (2)
87. (2)
88. (2)
89. (4)
90. (4)
91. (2)
92. (4)
93. (3)
94. (4)
95. (4)
96. (1)
97. (1)
98. (4)
99. (2)
100. (4)
101. (2)
102. (4)
103. (4)
104. (2)
105. (1)
106. (1)
107. (3)
108. (2)
109. (3)
110. (3)
111. (4)
112. (4)
113. (4)
114. (1)
115. (3)
116. (3)
117. (2)
118. (2)
119. (3)
120. (3)
121. (3)
122. (2)
123. (1)
124. (1)
125. (3)
126. (2)
127. (3)
128. (4)
129. (4)
130. (4)
131. (4)
132. (4)
133. (4)
134. (3)
135. (1)
136. (2)
137. (4)
138. (4)
139. (2)
140. (2)
141. (4)
142. (1)
143. (4)
144. (2)
145. (2)
146. (2)
147. (2)
148. (3)
149. (4)
150. (3)
151. (4)
152. (1)
153. (4)
154. (1)
155. (2)
156. (4)
157. (3)
158. (1)
159. (3)
160. (3)
161. (1)
162. (4)

163. (4)
164. (1)
165. (3)
166. (4)
167. (3)
168. (3)
169. (3)
170. (1)
171. (2)
172. (2)
173. (1)
174. (2)
175. (1)
176. (3)
177. (3)
178. (4)
179. (3)
180. (3)
181. (4)
182. (3)
183. (2)
184. (2)
185. (2)
186. (3)
187. (2)
188. (2)
189. (2)
190. (4)
191. (4)
192. (2)
193. (2)
194. (2)
195. (3)
196. (1)
197. (4)
198. (3)
199. (1)
200. (4)
201. (2)
202. (2)
203. (2)
204. (2)
205. (3)
206. (4)
207. (3)
208. (2)
209. (1)
210. (2)
211. (3)
212. (3)
213. (1)
214. (2)
215. (2)
216. (4)
217. (4)
218. (2)
219. (4)
220. (2)
221. (3)
222. (3)
223. (1)
224. (2)
225. (2)
226. (4)
227. (4)
228. (1)
229. (3)
230. (4)
231. (3)
232. (1)
233. (4)
234. (1)
235. (1)
236. (2)
237. (4)
238. (1)
239. (2)
240. (3)
241. (4)
242. (3)
243. (2)
244. (2)
245. (4)
246. (2)
247. (2)
248. (1)
249. (3)
250. (3)
251. (1)
252. (2)
253. (2)
254. (1)
255. (3)
256. (1)
257. (4)
258. (4)
259. (1)
260. (4)
261. (2)
262. (3)
263. (4)
264. (2)
265. (3)
266. (2)
267. (2)
268. (4)
269. (1)
270. (2)
271. (3)
272. (2)
273. (4)
274. (1)
275. (3)
276. (2)
277. (4)
278. (2)
279. (3)
280. (4)
281. (1)
282. (4)
283. (1)
284. (3)
285. (3)
286. (2)
287. (4)
288. (2)
289. (4)
290. (4)
291. (1)
292. (2)
293. (4)
294. (3)
295. (2)
296. (4)
297. (4)
298. (3)
299. (3)
300. (1)
301. (4)

5. DIRECT- INDIRECT NARRATION

1. 2	2. 3	3. 1	4. 1	5. 4
6. 2	7. 1	8. 3	9. 4	10. 2
11. 3	12. 4	13. 1	14. 2	15. 3
16. 1	17. 4	18.2	19.3	20. 4
21. 1	22. 2	23. 3	24. 1	25. 1
26. 1	27. 3	28.2	29. 1	30. 4
31. 1	32. 2	33. 2	34. 1	35. 3
36. 4	37. 3	38. 1	39. 4	40. 4
41. 3	42. 4	43. 1	44. 2	45. 4
46. 1	47. 3	48. 1	49. 4	50. 3
51. 3	52. 1	53. 3	54. 4	55. 2
56. 3	57. 2	58. 1	59. 4	60. 2
61. 1	62. 3	63. 1	64. 2	65. 2
66. 4	67. 1	68. 1	69. 2	70. 1
71. 3	72. 1	73. 2	74. 2	75. 2
76. 4	77. 2	78. 2	79. 1	80. 2
81. 1	82. 2	83. 1	84. 1	85. 4
86. 3	87. 4	88. 3	89. 4	90. 2
91. 4	92. 3	93. 3	94. 1	95. 1
96. 4	97. 3	98. 3	99. 2	100. 4
101. 3	102. 1	103. 3	104. 3	105. 4
106. 3	107. 2	108. 2	109. 1	110. 1
111. 1	112. 2	113. 1	114. 2	115. 4
116. 3	117. 3	118. 1	119. 3	120. 4
121. 3	122. 3	123. 1	124. 3	125. 2
126. 2	127. 1	128.3	129. 1	130.2
131. 4	132. 1	133. 1	134. 1	135. 3
136. 3	137. 1	138. 1	139. 3	140. 2
141. 1	142. 2	143. 2	144. 3	145. 1
146. 2	147. 3	148. 2	149. 4	150. 1
151. 1	152. 1	153. 3	154. 2	155. 1
156. 4	157. 4	158. 2	159. 3	160. 3
161. 2	162. 2	163. 3	164. 2	165. 1
166. 3	167. 3	168. 4	169. 3	170. 4
171. 4	172. 3	173. 4	174. 2	175. 1
176. 1	177. 3	178. 2	179. 4	180. 2
181. 3	182. 1	183. 4	184. 3	185. 1
186. 4	187. 4	188. 4	189. 3	190. 1
191. 2	192. 4	193. 4	194. 2	195. 1
196. 4	197. 2	198. 4	199. 1	200. 2
201. 4	202. 2	203. 2	204. 1	205. 1
206. 4	207. 2	208. 4	209. 1	210. 2
211. 4	212. 2	213. 2	214. 1	

215. (2)	216. (2)
217. (4)	218. (4)
219. (4)	220. (4)
221. (1)	222. (1)
223. (2)	224. (4)
225. (2)	226. (3)
227. (1)	228. (2)
229. (2)	230. (4)
231. (2)	232. (2)
233. (2)	234. (4)
235. (1)	236. (4)
237. (3)	238. (3)
239. (2)	240. (4)
241. (3)	242. (1)
243. (3)	244. (3)
245. (4)	246. (3)
247. (2)	248. (2)
249. (1)	250. (2)
251. (1)	252. (2)
253. (4)	254. (3)
255. (4)	256. (3)
257. (3)	258. (1)
259. (3)	260. (4)
261. (3)	262. (3)
263. (2)	264. (3)
265. (4)	266. (3)
267. (1)	268. (2)
269. (1)	270. (2)
271. (4)	272. (1)
273. (1)	274. (3)
275. (4)	276. (2)
277. (2)	278. (1)
279. (1)	280. (1)
281. (4)	282. (2)
283. (2)	284. (2)
285. (1)	286. (3)
287. (3)	288. (4)
289. (4)	290. (2)
291. (4)	292. (3)
293. (2)	294. (1)

295. (2) 296. (1)
297. (3) 298. (4)
299. (2) 300. (2)

SECTION C – 1000 PRACTICE QUESTIONS

1.	2	2.	1
3.	2	4.	2
5.	2	6.	3
7.	2	8.	3
9.	3	10.	2
11.	3	12.	3
13.	2	14.	2
15.	2	16.	3
17.	3	18.	2
19.	2	20.	2
21.	3	22.	1
23.	3	24.	3
25.	2	26.	2
27.	2	28.	2
29.	2	30.	1
31.	2	32.	2
33.	1	34.	2
35.	2	36.	2
37.	3	38.	3
39.	3	40.	2
41.	2	42.	2
43.	2	44.	3
45.	2	46.	2
47.	2	48.	2
49.	1	50.	1
51.	3	52.	2
53.	1	54.	2
55.	3	56.	3
57.	2	58.	2
59.	2	60.	2
61.	3	62.	2
63.	3	64.	3
65.	4	66.	1
67.	1	68.	4
69.	2	70.	3
71.	3	72.	1
73.	2	74.	2
75.	1	76.	2
77.	1	78.	4
79.	2	80.	2
81.	4	82.	2
83.	2	84.	2
85.	3	86.	2
87.	3	88.	2
89.	2	90.	1
91.	1	92.	1
93.	4	94.	2
95.	2	96.	2
97.	3	98.	1
99.	2	100.	3
101.	1	102.	2
103.	3	104.	2
105.	2	106.	4
107.	3	108.	1
109.	4	110.	2
111.	2	112.	2
113.	3	114.	2
115.	1	116.	3
117.	2	118.	2
119.	1	120.	1
121.	2	122.	1
123.	2	124.	2
125.	1	126.	2
127.	2	128.	3
129.	3	130.	3
131.	1	132.	2
133.	2	134.	2
135.	3	136.	2
137.	2	138.	1
139.	1	140.	1
141.	2	142.	4

143. 2
144. 2
145. 2
146. 3
147. 3
148. 3
149. 2
150. 4
151. 2
152. 2
153. 2
154. 3
155. 2
156. 2
157. 3
158. 2
159. 3
160. 3
161. 2
162. 2
163. 2
164. 2
165. 1
166. 2
167. 2
168. 1
169. 2
170. 2
171. 1
172. 1
173. 5
174. 3
175. 2
176. 3
177. 2
178. 3
179. 2
180. 1
181. 3
182. 4
183. 2
184. 3
185. 3
186. 2
187. 2
188. 2
189. 4
190. 1
191. 2
192. 1
193. 3
194. 3
195. 3
196. 3
197. 2
198. 4
199. 2
200. 1
201. 2
202. 3
203. 1
204. 1
205. 2
206. 2
207. 3
208. 2
209. 3
210. 2
211. 3
212. 3
213. 2
214. 3
215. 4
216. 3
217. 2
218. 3
219. 1
220. 2
221. 4
222. 3
223. 4
224. 2
225. 3
226. 5
227. 2
228. 3
229. 4
230. 3
231. 2
232. 2
233. 3
234. 3
235. 2
236. 2
237. 2
238. 1
239. 3
240. 3
241. 1
242. 2
243. 4
244. 3
245. 2
246. 2
247. 2
248. 2
249. 2
250. 3
251. 1
252. 2
253. 2
254. 3
255. 1
256. 3
257. 3
258. 3
259. 1
260. 1
261. 3
262. 1
263. 1
264. 2
265. 1
266. 1
267. 2
268. 2
269. 4
270. 1
271. 4
272. 1
273. 3
274. 1
275. 3
276. 1
277. 3
278. 4
279. 5
280. 2
281. 1
282. 2
283. 1
284. 5
285. 4
286. 4
287. 3
288. 2
289. 4
290. 3
291. 3
292. 1
293. 3
294. 1
295. 4
296. 1
297. 3
298. 2

299.	1	300.	4
301.	3	302.	2
303.	2	304.	1
305.	2	306.	2
307.	1	308.	2
309.	3	310.	2
311.	2	312.	3
313.	2	314.	3
315.	2	316.	2
317.	1	318.	2
319.	3	320.	1
321.	1	322.	2
323.	1	324.	2
325.	4	326.	3
327.	2	328.	4
329.	1	330.	2
331.	3	332.	2
333.	3	334.	2
335.	2	336.	2
337.	1	338.	3
339.	2	340.	3
341.	2	342.	3
343.	2	344.	2
345.	3	346.	2
347.	4	348.	2
349.	3	350.	3
351.	4	352.	2
353.	1	354.	3
355.	2	356.	2
357.	1	358.	2
359.	3	360.	3
361.	2	362.	2
363.	3	364.	2
365.	4	366.	3
367.	1	368.	2
369.	2	370.	2
371.	1	372.	2
373.	3	374.	2
375.	2	376.	3

377.	3	378.	2
379.	2	380.	2
381.	2	382.	4
383.	3	384.	2
385.	3	386.	4
387.	2	388.	3
389.	2	390.	1
391.	4	392.	1
393.	2	394.	1
395.	3	396.	2
397.	3	398.	3
399.	2	400.	3
401.	3	402.	1
403.	1	404.	2
405.	4	406.	3
407.	1	408.	2
409.	3	410.	1
411.	2	412.	3
413.	2	414.	1
415.	2	416.	1
417.	2	418.	2
419.	1	420.	2
421.	2	422.	2
423.	1	424.	2
425.	3	426.	2
427.	2	428.	2
429.	2	430.	3
431.	2	432.	2
433.	3	434.	2
435.	2	436.	2
437.	3	438.	2
439.	2	440.	2
441.	3	442.	1
443.	2	444.	1
445.	4	446.	3
447.	3	448.	2
449.	1	450.	1
451.	3	452.	1
453.	1	454.	4

455. 1	456. 2	533. 3	534. 3
457. 1	458. 2	535. 4	536. 2
459. 1	460. 3	537. 2	538. 4
461. 2	462. 2	539. 1	540. 4
463. 2	464. 1	541. 2	542. 1
465. 2	466. 2	543. 1	544. 2
467. 2	468. 4	545. 2	546. 1
469. 4	470. 1	547. 1	548. 1
471. 2	472. 3	549. 2	550. 3
473. 2	474. 3	551. 2	552. 3
475. 3	476. 3	553. 1	554. 1
477. 4	478. 1	555. 3	556. 2
479. 3	480. 2	557. 3	558. 1
481. 2	482. 2	559. 3	560. 3
483. 2	484. 2	561. 1	562. 3
485. 1	486. 4	563. 3	564. 2
487. 1	488. 1	565. 3	566. 3
489. 2	490. 3	567. 3	568. 3
491. 3	492. 4	569. 3	570. 2
493. 3	494. 2	571. 2	572. 3
495. 2	496. 1	573. 2	574. 2
497. 3	498. 1	575. 2	576. 1
499. 1	500. 2	577. 3	578. 1
501. 1	502. 2	579. 3	580. 1
503. 1	504. 1	581. 2	582. 2
505. 4	506. 2	583. 3	584. 3
507. 2	508. 3	585. 3	586. 3
509. 2	510. 3	587. 3	588. 2
511. 3	512. 1	589. 1	590. 3
513. 1	514. 4	591. 1	592. 4
515. 3	516. 1	593. 4	594. 2
517. 3	518. 2	595. 3	596. 1
519. 1	520. 3	597. 2	598. 2
521. 3	522. 2	599. 2	600. 2
523. 3	524. 2	601. 4	602. 2
525. 3	526. 4	603. 2	604. 1
527. 4	528. 3	605. 4	606. 2
529. 3	530. 4	607. 1	608. 1
531. 1	532. 3	609. 1	610. 3

611. 3
612. 2
613. 4
614. 3
615. 2
616. 2
617. 2
618. 3
619. 3
620. 2
621. 1
622. 3
623. 3
624. 3
625. 3
626. 3
627. 3
628. 2
629. 3
630. 2
631. 1
632. 3
633. 2
634. 2
635. 3
636. 3
637. 3
638. 4
639. 2
640. 1
641. 2
642. 2
643. 3
644. 3
645. 1
646. 2
647. 2
648. 1
649. 4
650. 2
651. 3
652. 2
653. 1
654. 3
655. 2
656. 2
657. 1
658. 3
659. 4
660. 4
661. 4
662. 3
663. 1
664. 1
665. 1
666. 3
667. 3
668. 2
669. 2
670. 2
671. 3
672. 3
673. 2
674. 2
675. 1
676. 2
677. 2
678. 4
679. 2
680. 2
681. 2
682. 3
683. 3
684. 3
685. 2
686. 4
687. 2
688. 2
689. 2
690. 3
691. 2
692. 2
693. 3
694. 2
695. 3
696. 3
697. 2
698. 2
699. 2
700. 2
701. 1
702. 2
703. 2
704. 1
705. 2
706. 2
707. 1
708. 1
709. 5
710. 3
711. 2
712. 3
713. 2
714. 3
715. 2
716. 1
717. 2
718. 3
719. 1
720. 4
721. 3
722. 2
723. 3
724. 1
725. 2
726. 3
727. 2
728. 1
729. 3
730. 4
731. 3
732a. 3
732b. 2
733. 3
734. 1
735. 2
736. 4
737. 4
738. 4
739. 2
740. 1
741. 3
742. 1
743. 2
744. 4
745. 1
746. 4
747. 2
748. 3
749. 4
750. 4
751. 2
752. 1
753. 2
754. 3
755. 2
756. 4
757. 2
758. 3
759. 1
760. 2
761. 2
762. 4
763. 4
764. 4
765. 2
766. 2

767.	1	768.	1
769.	2	770.	2
771.	1	772.	2
773.	1	774.	4
775.	2	776.	2
777.	2	778.	1
779.	3	780.	3
781.	2	782.	4
783.	3	784.	2
785.	3	786.	2
787.	4	788.	2
789.	2	790.	3
791.	3	792.	1
793.	1	794.	1
795.	1	796.	1
797.	1	798.	3
799.	3	800.	2
801.	3	802.	1
803.	1	804.	4
805.	3	806.	1
807.	2	808.	4
809.	4	810.	2
811.	3	812.	4
813.	4	814.	1
815.	4	816.	1
817.	3	818.	3
819.	1	820.	1
821.	2	822.	4
823.	3	824.	2
825.	4	826.	2
827.	2	828.	1
829.	2	830.	2
831.	1	832.	1
833.	4	834.	2
835.	2	836.	1
837.	4	838.	1
839.	1	840.	2
841.	2	842.	4
843.	3	844.	3

845.	3	846.	1
847.	1	848.	1
849.	2	850.	1
851.	3	852.	4
853.	1	854.	3
855.	1	856.	2
857.	3	858.	3
859.	3	860.	4
861.	3	862.	1
863.	1	864.	4
865.	2	866.	4
867.	4	868.	4
869.	3	870.	3
871.	1	872.	2
873.	3	874.	4
875.	3	876.	2
877.	4	878.	4
879.	4	880.	4
881.	2	882.	2
883.	2	884.	4
885.	3	886.	4
887.	4	888.	3
889.	3	890.	3
891.	4	892.	2
893.	1	894.	2
895.	2	896.	1
897.	2	898.	4
899.	3	900.	2
901.	1	902.	2
903.	3	904.	1
905.	2	906.	1
907.	2	908.	2
909.	1	910.	3
911.	2	912.	1
913.	2	914.	3
915.	2	916.	4
917.	1	918.	2
919.	2	920.	4
921.	2	922.	3
923.	2	924.	2

925.	2	926.	3
927.	3	928.	1
929.	2	930.	3
931.	4	932.	2
933.	1	934.	2
935.	3	936.	3
937.	4	938.	4
939.	3	940.	2
941.	3	942.	1
943.	1	944.	3
945.	3	946.	2
947.	3	948.	2
949.	1	950.	4
951.	3	952.	2
953.	3	954.	3
955.	3	956.	3
957.	4	958.	1
959.	2	960.	1
961.	1	962.	1
963.	3	964.	2
965.	4	966.	2
967.	3	968.	2
969.	2	970.	1
971.	4	972.	2
973.	1	974.	3
975.	4	976.	3
977.	3	978.	2
979.	4	980.	3
981.	4	982.	2
983.	2	984.	2
985.	4	986.	3
987.	4	988.	3
989.	3	990.	2
991.	2	992.	1
993.	1	994.	1
995.	1	996.	4
997.	2	998.	2
999.	1	1000.	1

MOCK TEST

MOCK TEST 01

Q1. ERROR	C	Q11. VOICE	C
Q2. ERROR	D	Q12. NARRATION	C
Q3. ERROR	D	Q13. SPELLING	C
Q4. BLANK	C	Q14. SPELLING	A
Q5. BLANK	A	Q15. IDIOM	C
Q6. SYNONYM	B	Q16. IDIOM	D
Q7. SYNONYM	D	Q17. ONE WORD	C
Q8. ANTONYM	D	Q18. ONE WORD	C
Q9. ANTONYM	A	Q19. IMPROVEMRNT	B
Q10. PARAJUMBLE	A	Q20. IMPROVEMENT	C

MOCK TEST 02

Q1. ERROR	A	Q11. VOICE	C
Q2. ERROR	B	Q12. NARRATION	C

Q3. ERROR	A	Q13. SPELLING	D
Q4. BLANK	D	Q14. SPELLING	A
Q5. BLANK	B	Q15. IDIOM	B
Q6. SYNONYM	D	Q16. IDIOM	C
Q7. SYNONYM	D	Q17. ONE WORD	B
Q8. ANTONYM	A	Q18. ONE WORD	A
Q9. ANTONYM	C	Q19. IMPROVEMRNT	D
Q10. PARAJUMBLE	C	Q20. IMPROVEMENT	B

MOCK TEST 03

Q1. ERROR	C	Q11. VOICE	B
Q2. ERROR	D	Q12. NARRATION	A
Q3. ERROR	C	Q13. SPELLING	A
Q4. BLANK	B	Q14. SPELLING	B
Q5. BLANK	C	Q15. IDIOM	A
Q6. SYNONYM	D	Q16. IDIOM	A
Q7. SYNONYM	B	Q17. ONE WORD	D
Q8. ANTONYM	B	Q18. ONE WORD	C
Q9. ANTONYM	D	Q19. IMPROVEMRNT	B
Q10. PARAJUMBLE	B	Q20. IMPROVEMENT	B

MCOK TEST 04

Q1. ERROR	B	Q11. VOICE	C
Q2. ERROR	B	Q12. NARRATION	A
Q3. ERROR	B	Q13. SPELLING	A
Q4. BLANK	C	Q14. SPELLING	C
Q5. BLANK	A	Q15. IDIOM	C
Q6. SYNONYM	A	Q16. IDIOM	B
Q7. SYNONYM	A	Q17. ONE WORD	D
Q8. ANTONYM	C	Q18. ONE WORD	D
Q9. ANTONYM	B	Q19. IMPROVEMRNT	C
Q10. PARAJUMBLE	A	Q20. IMPROVEMENT	D

MOCK TEST 05

Q1. ERROR	B	Q11. VOICE	D
Q2. ERROR	A	Q12. NARRATION	C
Q3. ERROR	B	Q13. SPELLING	C
Q4. BLANK	B	Q14. SPELLING	B
Q5. BLANK	C	Q15. IDIOM	D
Q6. SYNONYM	B	Q16. IDIOM	D
Q7. SYNONYM	A	Q17. ONE WORD	C
Q8. ANTONYM	C	Q18. ONE WORD	B
Q9. ANTONYM	C	Q19. IMPROVEMRNT	C
Q10. PARAJUMBLE	C	Q20. IMPROVEMENT	A

MOCK TEST 06

Q1. ERROR	B	Q11. VOICE	B
Q2. ERROR	A	Q12. NARRATION	C
Q3. ERROR	B	Q13. SPELLING	D
Q4. BLANK	C	Q14. SPELLING	D
Q5. BLANK	B	Q15. IDIOM	D
Q6. SYNONYM	D	Q16. IDIOM	B
Q7. SYNONYM	A	Q17. ONE WORD	D
Q8. ANTONYM	C	Q18. ONE WORD	C
Q9. ANTONYM	B	Q19. IMPROVEMRNT	A
Q10. PARAJUMBLE	D	Q20. IMPROVEMENT	D

MOCK TEST 07

Q1. ERROR	B	Q11. VOICE	B
Q2. ERROR	C	Q12. NARRATION	C
Q3. ERROR	B	Q13. SPELLING	D
Q4. BLANK	B	Q14. SPELLING	A
Q5. BLANK	D	Q15. IDIOM	A
Q6. SYNONYM	B	Q16. IDIOM	A
Q7. SYNONYM	D	Q17. ONE WORD	D
Q8. ANTONYM	D	Q18. ONE WORD	A

Q9. ANTONYM	C	Q19. IMPROVEMRNT	D
Q10. PARAJUMBLE	D	Q20. IMPROVEMENT	D

MOCK TEST 08

Q1. ERROR	C	Q11. VOICE	D
Q2. ERROR	A	Q12. NARRATION	C
Q3. ERROR	A	Q13. SPELLING	D
Q4. BLANK	D	Q14. SPELLING	C
Q5. BLANK	B	Q15. IDIOM	A
Q6. SYNONYM	D	Q16. IDIOM	A
Q7. SYNONYM	D	Q17. ONE WORD	B
Q8. ANTONYM	A	Q18. ONE WORD	B
Q9. ANTONYM	B	Q19. IMPROVEMRNT	C
Q10. PARAJUMBLE	C	Q20. IMPROVEMENT	A

MOCK TEST 09

Q1. ERROR	C	Q11. VOICE	D
Q2. ERROR	D	Q12. NARRATION	A
Q3. ERROR	B	Q13. SPELLING	A
Q4. BLANK	B	Q14. SPELLING	C
Q5. BLANK	C	Q15. IDIOM	C
Q6. SYNONYM	C	Q16. IDIOM	A
Q7. SYNONYM	B	Q17. ONE WORD	A
Q8. ANTONYM	B	Q18. ONE WORD	C
Q9. ANTONYM	D	Q19. IMPROVEMRNT	C
Q10. PARAJUMBLE	B	Q20. IMPROVEMENT	C

MOCK TEST 10

Q1. ERROR	B	Q11. VOICE	C
Q2. ERROR	C	Q12. NARRATION	C
Q3. ERROR	A	Q13. SPELLING	C
Q4. BLANK	A	Q14. SPELLING	D
Q5. BLANK	D	Q15. IDIOM	D

Q6. SYNONYM	D	Q16. IDIOM	C
Q7. SYNONYM	A	Q17. ONE WORD	C
Q8. ANTONYM	A	Q18. ONE WORD	B
Q9. ANTONYM	B	Q19. IMPROVEMRNT	B
Q10. PARAJUMBLE	C	Q20. IMPROVEMENT	C

MOCK TEST 11

Q1. ERROR	B	Q11. VOICE	A
Q2. ERROR	B	Q12. NARRATION	B
Q3. ERROR	D	Q13. SPELLING	C
Q4. BLANK	A	Q14. SPELLING	C
Q5. BLANK	A	Q15. IDIOM	C
Q6. SYNONYM	A	Q16. IDIOM	B
Q7. SYNONYM	B	Q17. ONE WORD	A
Q8. ANTONYM	A	Q18. ONE WORD	B
Q9. ANTONYM	A	Q19. IMPROVEMRNT	D
Q10. PARAJUMBLE	D	Q20. IMPROVEMENT	C

MOCK TEST 12

Q1. ERROR	B	Q11. VOICE	A
Q2. ERROR	D	Q12. NARRATION	A
Q3. ERROR	C	Q13. SPELLING	D
Q4. BLANK	B	Q14. SPELLING	C
Q5. BLANK	B	Q15. IDIOM	B
Q6. SYNONYM	B	Q16. IDIOM	C
Q7. SYNONYM	B	Q17. ONE WORD	A
Q8. ANTONYM	C	Q18. ONE WORD	C
Q9. ANTONYM	D	Q19. IMPROVEMRNT	B
Q10. PARAJUMBLE	D	Q20. IMPROVEMENT	B

MOCK TEST 13

Q1. ERROR	C	Q11. VOICE	B
Q2. ERROR	C	Q12. NARRATION	D

Q3. ERROR	D	Q13. SPELLING	B
Q4. BLANK	C	Q14. SPELLING	C
Q5. BLANK	B	Q15. IDIOM	B
Q6. SYNONYM	B	Q16. IDIOM	D
Q7. SYNONYM	C	Q17. ONE WORD	B
Q8. ANTONYM	C	Q18. ONE WORD	C
Q9. ANTONYM	A	Q19. IMPROVEMRNT	C
Q10. PARAJUMBLE	C	Q20. IMPROVEMENT	A

MOCK TEST 14

Q1. ERROR	C	Q11. VOICE	A
Q2. ERROR	B	Q12. NARRATION	B
Q3. ERROR	A	Q13. SPELLING	A
Q4. BLANK	D	Q14. SPELLING	A
Q5. BLANK	C	Q15. IDIOM	D
Q6. SYNONYM	A	Q16. IDIOM	D
Q7. SYNONYM	D	Q17. ONE WORD	D
Q8. ANTONYM	D	Q18. ONE WORD	C
Q9. ANTONYM	C	Q19. IMPROVEMRNT	A
Q10. PARAJUMBLE	C	Q20. IMPROVEMENT	B

MOCK TEST 15

Q1. ERROR	B	Q11. VOICE	B
Q2. ERROR	D	Q12. NARRATION	B
Q3. ERROR	D	Q13. SPELLING	D
Q4. BLANK	B	Q14. SPELLING	C
Q5. BLANK	A	Q15. IDIOM	B
Q6. SYNONYM	A	Q16. IDIOM	A
Q7. SYNONYM	B	Q17. ONE WORD	A
Q8. ANTONYM	C	Q18. ONE WORD	D
Q9. ANTONYM	B	Q19. IMPROVEMRNT	A
Q10. PARAJUMBLE	D	Q20. IMPROVEMENT	A

MOCK TEST 16

Q1. ERROR	A	Q11. VOICE	B
Q2. ERROR	A	Q12. NARRATION	D
Q3. ERROR	C	Q13. SPELLING	A
Q4. BLANK	C	Q14. SPELLING	D
Q5. BLANK	C	Q15. IDIOM	B
Q6. SYNONYM	A	Q16. IDIOM	C
Q7. SYNONYM	A	Q17. ONE WORD	A
Q8. ANTONYM	C	Q18. ONE WORD	A
Q9. ANTONYM	A	Q19. IMPROVEMRNT	A
Q10. PARAJUMBLE	D	Q20. IMPROVEMENT	C

MOCK TEST 17

Q1. ERROR	B	Q11. VOICE	B
Q2. ERROR	D	Q12. NARRATION	A
Q3. ERROR	C	Q13. SPELLING	A
Q4. BLANK	C	Q14. SPELLING	C
Q5. BLANK	D	Q15. IDIOM	B
Q6. SYNONYM	B	Q16. IDIOM	C
Q7. SYNONYM	C	Q17. ONE WORD	D
Q8. ANTONYM	D	Q18. ONE WORD	B
Q9. ANTONYM	D	Q19. IMPROVEMRNT	D
Q10. PARAJUMBLE	B	Q20. IMPROVEMENT	A

MOCK TEST 18

Q1. ERROR	B	Q11. VOICE	A
Q2. ERROR	B	Q12. NARRATION	C
Q3. ERROR	C	Q13. SPELLING	B
Q4. BLANK	C	Q14. SPELLING	A
Q5. BLANK	B	Q15. IDIOM	B
Q6. SYNONYM	B	Q16. IDIOM	C
Q7. SYNONYM	B	Q17. ONE WORD	C
Q8. ANTONYM	C	Q18. ONE WORD	A

Q9. ANTONYM	D	Q19. IMPROVEMRNT	B
Q10. PARAJUMBLE	A	Q20. IMPROVEMENT	B

MOCK TEST 19

Q1. ERROR	C	Q11. VOICE	A
Q2. ERROR	C	Q12. NARRATION	C
Q3. ERROR	C	Q13. SPELLING	B
Q4. BLANK	B	Q14. SPELLING	A
Q5. BLANK	C	Q15. IDIOM	C
Q6. SYNONYM	B	Q16. IDIOM	A
Q7. SYNONYM	C	Q17. ONE WORD	A
Q8. ANTONYM	A	Q18. ONE WORD	A
Q9. ANTONYM	B	Q19. IMPROVEMRNT	C

Q10. PARAJUMBLE		Q20. IMPROVEMENT	B

MOCK TEST 20

Q1. ERROR	B	Q11. VOICE	C
Q2. ERROR	D	Q12. NARRATION	A
Q3. ERROR	C	Q13. SPELLING	C
Q4. BLANK	B	Q14. SPELLING	D
Q5. BLANK	C	Q15. IDIOM	D
Q6. SYNONYM	B	Q16. IDIOM	C
Q7. SYNONYM	C	Q17. ONE WORD	A
Q8. ANTONYM	D	Q18. ONE WORD	C
Q9. ANTONYM	C	Q19. IMPROVEMRNT	A
Q10. PARAJUMBLE	C	Q20. IMPROVEMENT	B